LAND AND POWER

STUDIES IN POLITICAL HISTORY

Editor: Michael Hurst
Fellow of St. John's College, Oxford

CHIEF WHIP: The Political Life and Times of Aretas Akers-Douglas 1st Viscount Chilston by Eric Alexander 3rd Viscount Chilston.

GUIZOT: Aspects of French History 1787-1874 by Douglas Johnson.

MARGINAL PRYNNE: 1600-1669 by William M. Lamont.

LAND AND POWER: British and Allied Policy on Germany's Frontiers, 1916-19 by Harold I. Nelson.

THE LANGUAGE OF POLITICS IN THE AGE OF WILKES AND BURKE by James T. Boulton.

THE ENGLISH FACE OF MACHIAVELLI by Felix Raab.

LAND AND POWER

British and Allied Policy on Germany's Frontiers 1916-19

by
HAROLD I. NELSON

LONDON: Routledge & Kegan Paul
TORONTO: University of Toronto Press
1963

First published 1963
in Great Britain by
Routledge & Kegan Paul Ltd
and in Canada by
University of Toronto Press

Printed in Great Britain by
T. & A. Constable Ltd

Reprinted in 2018
ISBN 978-1-4875-7367-6 (paper)

TO THE MEMORY
OF MY MOTHER

EDITOR'S NOTE

UNLIKE so many history series this one will not attempt a complete coverage of a specific span of time, with a division of labour for the contributors based on a neat parcelling out of centuries. Nor will it, in the main, be a collection of political monographs. Rather, the aim is to bring out books based on new, or thoroughly reinterpreted material ranging over quite a wide field of chronology and geography. Some will be more general than others, as is to be expected when biography is included alongside of detailed treatment of some comparatively short period of crisis like the appeasement of the Axis Powers. Nevertheless, whatever mode of presentation may have been appropriate, each work should provide an exposition of its subject in context and thus enable the reader to acquire new knowledge amidst things he knows, or could have known.

MICHAEL HURST

St. John's College,
Oxford.

CONTENTS

MAPS

PREFACE

I SEEK in this book to contribute to a reappraisal of the peacemaking after the Great War of 1914-1918 by examining one major problem which confronted the Paris Peace Conference in 1919: the territorial settlement with Germany. Since the British role in the peacemaking has been relatively neglected, I have approached the German territorial question primarily, but not exclusively, from the standpoint of British official attitudes and policy. In this respect my purpose is threefold: to discover the pre-conference evolution of British governmental thinking on German boundary issues; to bring out the relationship between British attitudes and those of their allies, especially of the American and French governments; and to determine the British influence on the drafting of the territorial provisions of the ill-fated Treaty of Versailles. While the central theme is British policy, I have chosen to treat the British factor in a broad context, particularly by examining the attitudes and policies of the American, French, and lesser Allies and by attempting a more or less balanced analysis of the territorial negotiations at the Paris Peace Conference. This approach will facilitate, perhaps, a better understanding of both British policy and the general handling of the German territorial problem at that time.

Other aspects of the treatment of the subject probably call for brief comment here. The study concerns only territorial issues directly between the belligerents and not affecting neutrals. The question of Schleswig-Holstein is therefore reserved for separate treatment. In discussing wartime views, I have been concerned mainly with discussions of territorial terms of peace based upon the assumption of decisive Allied victory over Germany. Since the main issues of peacemaking were interdependent, other European territorial problems and other issues such as reparations, disarmament, and the League of Nations have been alluded to but not treated substantively. While, generally speaking, several main influences shaped British peace policy—domestic opinion, imperial and Dominion interests, European and American pressures—I have concentrated largely on the international or external influences and their bearing upon the conduct of the British government. Since the German territorial negotiations were marked by a high degree of Anglo-American co-operation, the American factor has been particularly stressed.

For all errors of fact and judgment, I am of course solely responsible. My interest in the diplomacy of the First World War and of the Peacemaking was first aroused by Professor Philip E. Mosely. I wish to express my appreciation to Professor W. T. R. Fox of Columbia University and Professor René Albrecht-Carrié of Barnard College for their patience in reading the original manuscript and for their invaluable advice. I gratefully acknowledge the assistance of Dr. W. Kaye Lamb, Dominion Archivist, and his staff in the Public Archives of Canada, especially Mr. W. G. Ormsby of the Manuscripts Division; of Dr. Carl L. Lokke and his associates on the staff of the National Archives, Washington, D.C.; of Miss Katherine E. Brand and other members of the Manuscripts Division of the Library of Congress; of Dr. Charles Seymour, President Emeritus of Yale University and curator of the House collection and of the staff of the manuscripts room of the Sterling Library; of M. Debyser, director of the Bibliothèque de documentation internationale contemporaine in Paris; of Miss Hamerton, Chief Librarian, and of her staff in Chatham House, London; of Mr. K. W. Humphreys, Librarian, and Mr. Butler of the Library of the University of Birmingham, England; and of Mr. Robert Kunz, of Gormley, Ontario, who drew the maps.

I am indebted to my wife for her help and understanding. My family, too, deserve many thanks for their forbearance and fortitude.

For financial assistance, I wish to thank the donor of the Gilder Fellowship at Columbia University, the Nuffield Foundation, and the Canadian Social Science Research Council for underwriting my researches in Washington. Indeed, I am twice indebted to the latter because this book is published with the aid of a grant from the Social Science Research Council of Canada, using funds provided by the Canada Council.

Toronto, Canada.

PRINCIPAL ABBREVIATIONS

A.C.N.P.	The Records of the American Delegation to Negotiate Peace (U.S. National Archives)
D.B.F.P.	*Documents on British Foreign Policy, 1919-1939*, H.M.S.O., London
Délibérations	*Les Délibérations du Conseil des Quatres: Notes de l'Officier Interprète*, Paul Mantoux
I.W.C.	Imperial War Cabinet
P.P.C.	*The Paris Peace Conference, 1919*, in *Papers Relating to the Foreign Relations of the United States*, Department of State, Washington, D.C.

PART ONE

The Wartime Background

I

INITIAL ATTITUDES ON BASIC PROBLEMS

THE British approach to peacemaking after the Great War of 1914-1918 has been variously portrayed. 'At the Peace Conference of Paris', according to a Chatham House study group, 'Great Britain in keeping with her political traditions and her geographical position of semi-detachment from Europe followed a course mid-way between the idealism represented by President Wilson and the "Carthaginian" policy desired by the French.'[1] Against this picture may be set the tableau in which the dominant English leaders of that era are grouped among the practitioners of Old Diplomacy dramatically confronting Woodrow Wilson and the lesser apostles of New Diplomacy. As Ray Stannard Baker wrote privately in August 1918: 'The men who are in control in both France and England to-day . . . have for the most part little or no sympathy for our war-aims as expressed by Mr. Wilson. In some cases they give these aims a kind of perfunctory lip service, but the spirit is not in them.'[2] In a more sophisticated form this image has held captive most American scholarship on the peacemaking of 1919.

Similar controversy surrounds the dynamic, puzzling personality and role of Prime Minister Lloyd George. Charles Loch Mowat has written: 'The foundation of Lloyd George's foreign policy was conciliation, as advocated in his Fontaine-

[1] Royal Institute of International Affairs, *The Political and Strategic Interests of the United Kingdom*, p. 24.

[2] Baker Papers, Baker to Polk, letter 16, London, August 10, 1918.

bleau memorandum. The war was over, and a lasting peace would follow not from the dominance of the victors, but from bringing back the defeated and the outcast into the comity of nations. . . .'[1] Thomas Jones has struck a different note in his comment about the Paris negotiations: 'At the meetings, Wilson was concerned primarily with self-determination . . . and the League of Nations; Clemenceau with French security and the disabling of Germany; Lloyd George with the balance of power in Europe and its restoration, and with the House of Commons which had resulted from the new election.'[2] By way of contrast, the phrase 'balance of power' does not appear in the index of Lloyd George's apologia for his and the British delegation's role at Paris. Lloyd George depicted his colleagues and himself as proponents of moderation, justice, and national self-determination. Indeed, the British negotiators were credited with being more liberal and conciliatory than Woodrow Wilson himself, who is cast with Clemenceau in such marginal titles as: 'Clemenceau and Wilson irritated at British moderation'.[3] Walking with dignity alongside Lloyd George, there was always the figure of Arthur James Balfour, England's unknown foreign secretary, who frankly acknowledged his belief in the balance of power and the limitations of the principle of nationality as a foundation for peacemaking.

Such varying views raise intriguing questions about the peace aims and diplomacy of Great Britain and its Allies during and after the First World War. Since much new evidence is available, a reassessment of the peacemaking of that era is timely and feasible, although the results cannot be regarded as final if only because important archives remain closed.

This study is centered on the problems involved in the making of the German territorial settlement. While dealing primarily with British policy, I propose to treat that policy within a broad framework in order to illuminate both the Allied approach generally and the English approach in particular to that central issue of the Paris Peace Conference in 1919.

The essential elements of the German territorial problem are well known. When measured by area alone, the claims advanced

[1] Charles Loch Mowat, *Britain between the Wars, 1918-1940*, p. 53.

[2] Thomas Jones, *Lloyd George*, p. 168.

[3] David Lloyd George, *The Truth about the Treaties*, I, p. 720.

against prewar German territory were formidable. In western Europe, Alsace-Lorraine, the Rhineland, and the Saar Valley were the major regions at stake. Besides the Belgian claim to Eupen and Malmedy, Belgium's demands for the left bank of the Scheldt indirectly affected Germany. If the Dutch lost land to Belgium, they could be compensated with German territory. In the north, Germany's defeat provided an opportunity for settling the Schleswig-Holstein question in Denmark's favour. In fact, the French government sought to award more German territory to Denmark than the Danes wished to receive. In the east, with the re-establishment of a Polish state, the fate of East and West Prussia, of parts of Pomerania, of Upper Silesia, and of Danzig had to be determined. To the south, while prewar Imperial German lands were not involved, the problem did arise of whether to extend Germany's frontiers to include German Austria and in whole or in part the Bohemian fringes inhabited by a German-speaking majority. Altogether, at issue was the fate of over 20,000,000 people, of some 80,000 square miles of territory, of vital raw materials such as coal and iron, of valuable heavy and light industries, of rich agricultural lands, and of important strategic positions.

In the settlement of these territorial questions, Great Britain occupied a singular position between the European continent and the United States. British governments had no European territorial claims. A rearrangement of the map of Europe would not directly bring revenue, military strength, and commercial opportunity to England; quite the contrary in some respects. The cession of Alsace-Lorraine to France, for instance, could be disadvantageous to the Lancashire textile trade. Yet, geographical proximity alone made the European continent of greater importance to Great Britain than to the United States. The status of the Low Countries vitally affected the security of the Home Islands themselves. The United States had no comparable security interest in a European territorial settlement. Moreover, the nature of the postwar European balance of power and consequently the extent of Britain's commitments in Europe would substantially affect the political, military, and naval strength of the United Kingdom throughout the non-European world. The European balance affected the United States more remotely, primarily through its effect upon the

Atlantic position of England. It is doubtful whether Balfour was entirely right when he advised his government, in January 1917, to tell Washington that 'the Government and people of the British Empire had no more direct and immediate interest than had the United States' in the territorial changes suggested in the Allied reply to President Wilson's peace note of December 18, 1916.[1] Yet by the very logic of its intermediate position and interests between Europe and the rest of the world, including the United States, the British government was obliged to balance between Wilson and the continental allies. Not until after the American entry into the war and the loss of Russia as an ally did the full significance and possibilities of this situation become apparent.

If British and imperial interests were the first consideration of the policymakers in London, the definition of these interests in a shifting European scene and the formulation of policies to protect them were no simple matter. By and large, Lloyd George and his ministers approached the continent within the general historic framework of Britain's European and world outlook. Their main aim was a stable European equilibrium to underpin peace, to foster trade, and to avoid British involvement in another war. As for Germany after a total allied victory, the general objective was containment, not elimination. British leaders accepted Germany's continued existence as a nation-state and in the long run as a European Great Power. The Reich was to lose its position as a world power and was to be denied ascendancy in western and central Europe. Some way was constantly sought to block Germany's overland route to imperial influence and domination through the Balkans to the Middle East and beyond. Through territorial adjustments, Germany's war potential was to be weakened; that of France strengthened. In the search for a workable German and continental policy by which to realize these ends, Lloyd George and his political associates made a constant, if ultimately futile, attempt to maintain a working Anglo-American-European triangular relationship involving the commitment of United States' power on the continent, without alienating any of the partners, without breaking British wartime obligations, and without endangering vital British interests throughout the world.

[1] David Lloyd George, *War Memoirs*, III, pp. 111-12.

Early in the war, Asquith defined the British government's general war aims to be the recovery of Belgium, the protection of France against aggression, the destruction of Prussian military domination, and the defense of small nationalities.[1] His deceptively simple statement raised perplexing questions which were to worry, plague, and divide the makers of British peace policy throughout the war and after. How could the rights of the small Polish nation be upheld without offending Russia or creating an unstable European equilibrium? Could Prussian hegemony be shattered without dismembering the German nation against its will and arousing an enduring Teutonic desire for revenge? These and related questions were on the minds of British statesmen during the initial stages of the conflict, as Colonel House discovered during his European mission in the winter of 1915-16.

According to President Wilson's emissary, Lloyd George, then British Minister of Supply, in considering peace terms, envisaged the evacuation of Belgium and France, the restoration of Alsace-Lorraine to France, and the establishment of an independent Poland hewed out of Russian, German, and Austrian territories. While insisting on guarantees against the recurrence of war, Lloyd George favoured '. . . a peace to make friends and not enemies, meaning that when the war is over, Germany and England should have no such differences such as were left after the Franco-Prussian War'.[2] Here was a constantly recurring motif in Lloyd George's subsequent statements on peace policy. He envisaged a possibility of reconciliation which Balfour, then First Lord of the Admiralty, viewed sceptically. House found Balfour 'unalterably distrustful of Germany, and . . . forever coming back to whether Germany could be counted upon to keep any bargain or play any game fairly'.[3] At the same time,

[1] Oxford and Asquith, *Speeches*, p. 224. For an excellent summary of the evolution of Allied policy on war aims see 'The War Aims of the Allies in the First World War', by A. J. P. Taylor, in *Essays Presented to Sir Lewis Namier*, ed. Richard Pares and A. J. P. Taylor, pp. 475-505.

[2] House, Diary, VIII, p. 21. See also Lloyd George, *War Memoirs*, II, pp. 686 *et seq.*, and House-Wilson Correspondence, 1916, January 15, 1916. For the broader aspects of this mission see E. H. Buehrig, *Woodrow Wilson and the Balance of Power*, especially chap. VIII.

[3] House, Diary, VII, pp. 24-5. House countered that if all states were leagued together and the majority followed the leadership of the United States and Great Britain, Germany could be controlled.

Balfour revealed his consistent concern for the balance of power and his fear that the re-establishment of a Polish state would weaken the European equilibrium. In his estimation, an independent Poland could leave France at the mercy of Germany because, if a new war broke out, Russia could not invade Germany without violating Polish neutrality. Since this situation could disrupt the Franco-Russian alliance, he doubted whether France and Russia for this reason alone would support such a solution of the Polish question. Although Balfour later swung round to supporting an independent Poland, his subsequent efforts to limit Polish gains at Germany's expense showed his constant misgivings about the revival of Poland as a power.[1]

Asquith moved towards a fuller definition of British peace policy in August 1916, when he invited members of the War Committee of the Cabinet to state their thoughts on the subject in writing. In reply, Balfour,[2] Sir William Robertson,[3] then Chief of the Imperial General Staff, and Sir Ralph Paget and Sir William Tyrrell[4] of the Foreign Office submitted memoranda. Based upon the assumption that the postwar political and military situation would favour the Allies, the three plans raised many of the basic problems involved from an English viewpoint in defining Britain's vital interests on the continent and consequently in redrafting the map of Europe as it affected Germany. They also foreshadowed later differences of opinion among British policymakers and among the Allied and Associated Powers.

Robertson took a highly conservative approach based upon

[1] While the House mission had no important immediate results, the general conviction had emerged that Anglo-American understanding was a prerequisite for a durable peace settlement. A measure of agreement on peace policy was reached which as far as Germany was concerned envisaged the restoration of Belgium, the transfer of Alsace-Lorraine to France, and extra European compensations for German territorial losses in Europe. *Ibid.*, p. 72.

[2] Balfour's memorandum was dated October 4, 1916. See Lloyd George, *War Memoirs*, II, pp. 877 *et seq.*, or Dugdale, *Arthur James Balfour*, II, pp. 435 *et seq.*

[3] The General Staff's memorandum, signed by Sir William Robertson, was dated August 31, 1916. See Lloyd George, *War Memoirs*, II, pp. 833-43.

[4] The Foreign Office memorandum was dated August 1916. See Lloyd George, *Truth*, I, pp. 31 *et seq.* The two authors are identified in *The History of the Times*, IV, part 1, pp. 319-20.

strategical concepts of British interests on the continent. Revealing an anti-French and anti-Slav bias, the General proposed a postwar balance of power system pivoting around a strong Germanic central Europe. Germany was, accordingly, to be left strong on land while reduced to impotency on the sea. This plan seemed to assume a return to Bismarckian Germany and Europe. On the contrary, Balfour and the Foreign Office advisors assumed that Germany would remain truculent and aggressive after the war. Their calculation by itself led to a different view of territorial revision which was reinforced by the weight they assigned to the principle of nationality. Paget and Tyrrell showed a concern for harmonizing national with general interests which was lacking in the military outlook. They also pointed to the economic aspects of territorial reconstruction, one of the few such instances encountered in this study.

Balfour contemplated weakening Germany by the amputation of Alsace-Lorraine and of eastern provinces; so too did the Foreign Office planners. They differed principally over the role of eastern Europe and the proper relationship between England and France in the postwar system. Balfour, distrusting the viability of the potential new Slav states, preferred to balance Germany and Russia against one another through direct territorial contact and to strengthen western Europe through French acquisition of Alsace-Lorraine and by maintenance of the Anglo-French entente. Paget and Tyrrell envisaged a radical departure from the prewar system of states through the reconstruction of Europe along nationalist lines. They would separate Germany and Russia by a zone of Slavic states and restrain Germany in western Europe by means of a permanent Anglo-French-Belgian alliance. Paradoxically, in terms of the situation in 1916, the success of their bold plan depended upon the defeat of both Germany and Russia.

Yet the Foreign Office planners did not advocate reconstruction solely upon the basis of the principle of nationality. Considerations of the balance of power should modify this principle. As they put it, '. . . we should not push the principle of nationality so far as unduly to strengthen any State which is likely to be a cause of danger to European peace in the future'.[1] Moreover, Britain had to observe its commitments such as the Treaty

[1] *Truth*, I, p. 32.

of London which conflicted with the principle of nationality. Similar claims by allies might arise in the future in which case they advised: '. . . our attitude should be guided by circumstances generally, and British interests in particular'.[1] Balfour shared this flexible, practical approach.

In eastern Europe, many issues arose out of the Polish Question: what should be Poland's status? What territories should Poland acquire? What role could an independent Poland play in a new European balance? While leaving the initiative in answering these questions to Russia, Robertson accepted the idea of a Polish state with some territory taken from the German Empire. For several reasons, he foresaw difficulties in giving Poland access to the seas. It would 'scarcely seem feasible in any circumstances to cut off East Prussia from Germany'.[2]

In contrast to this cautious, lukewarm attitude towards Polish aspirations, Paget and Tyrrell were enthusiastic about Poland. Germany would cede Posen to the new Polish state, which might also consist of Galicia, Bohemia, and the Polish provinces of Russia. Besides underestimating Czech and Ukrainian sentiment, their plan raised the difficult problem of the new Poland's relations with the Russian Empire. Their solution was an independent Polish state linked to Russia by personal ties.

Balfour's views differed. He envisaged a Polish polity, composed of former German, Austrian, and Russian territories, which would possess 'home rule' status within the Russian Empire. While he could have defended this solution on the realistic grounds that Russia would refuse to cede territory to an independent Poland, Balfour instead questioned the feasibility of creating a Polish state because he mistrusted the Poles and their political ability. Fearing that Poland would be a continual centre of unrest and intrigue between Germany and Russia, Balfour doubted Poland's effectiveness as a buffer between its two powerful neighbours. Moreover, in his opinion, the separation of Russia and Germany would tend to free each state for expansionism: Germany to the west; Russia to the east.

In the three projects, two main solutions to the problem of German-Austrian relations were considered: the union of Germany and of the German provinces of the Dual Monarchy; or the maintenance of a shrunken Austro-Hungarian state.

[1] *Ibid.* [2] Lloyd George, *War Memoirs*, II, p. 837.

Sir William Robertson made no definite choice between the two solutions, but Paget and Tyrrell, taking their stand on the principle of nationality, advocated the complete dismemberment of the Dual Monarchy among the Italians, the Rumanians, and the Slavs, leaving only the Austrian and the Hungarian portions to be disposed of. They advanced three reasons for rejecting the maintenance of an Austro-Hungarian state in one form or another: the existence of such a state could not be reconciled with the objectives for which the Allies went to war; the dependence of Austria-Hungary upon Prussia could not be avoided; and the intended purpose of a diminished and independent Austria-Hungary could not be realized. In advancing the latter reason, they may have had in mind the argument in Robertson's memorandum that the Dual Monarchy, in close union with Germany, could help to balance Russia, the other Slavs, Italy, and France.

In proposing the union of Austria with Germany, they viewed *Anschluss* as a means of counterbalancing Prussian influence within the Reich through the addition of Roman Catholic and traditionally non-Prussian elements from the south. This, they claimed, would 'naturally tend in the direction of a more permanent settlement in Europe, as it will diminish the aggressive tendencies of the Central European Empires through the weakening of Prussia'.[1]

Characteristically, Balfour was pessimistic about the consequences of either course of action. Although he recognized the possibility of limiting Prussian influence within Germany by adding anti-Prussian influences, he feared that union would unduly strengthen Germany and Pan-Germanism. Doubting that the historic tendency among the Germanic people had been centrifugal and separatist, Balfour gloomily concluded: '. . . nor do I believe that anything which we and our Allies can accomplish will prevent the Germanic Powers, either united by alliance, or fused into a single State, from remaining wealthy, populous, and potentially formidable'.[2] Balfour held to this sombre view throughout the war and at Paris.

In western Europe, the return of Alsace-Lorraine to France was supported in the three projects but, except indirectly in the Foreign Office plan, the questions of the Saar and the Rhine-

[1] Lloyd George, *Truth*, I, p. 42. [2] Dugdale, *Balfour*, p. 440.

land were not broached. Paget and Tyrrell referred to the possibility of further strategic modifications in the German-French frontier provided the wishes of the inhabitants were respected and no extensive German territory was incorporated into France for purely strategic reasons. In the light of the peace negotiations in 1919, the Saar might have fitted this exception but not the Rhineland.

Belgian independence was regarded as indispensable. To strengthen Belgium, the General Staff made the most sweeping proposals for modifications of the Belgian frontiers: the annexation of Luxemburg to Belgium; the transfer of part of the Dutch province of Zeeland to give Antwerp secure access to the sea. The latter shift involved, by way of compensation, Dutch acquisition from Germany of Eastern Friesland and the East Frisian islands. While Balfour's scheme contained no reference to such transactions, Paget and Tyrrell provided for the incorporation of Luxembourg into Belgium, a proposal which could lead to friction with France.

The outstanding feature of the Foreign Office memorandum regarding Belgium was the drastic suggestion that the prewar international regime be abandoned in favour of a permanent Anglo-French-Belgian alliance. Fully recognizing the revolutionary nature of this proposal, Paget and Tyrrell wrote:

> This proposal is open to the objection that it commits us to continental alliances and a probable increase of our military obligations. In our opinion, however, there is no alternative so long as it is a vital interest of this country to prevent the German invasion of Belgium, and so long as the latter is incapable of undertaking its own defence.[1]

Balfour also had in mind a possible departure from the traditional English relationship with the continent. His pessimistic estimate of Germany's probable postwar power led him to conclude that France alone, even with Alsace-Lorraine, could be no match for Germany and even less for Germany and Austria combined. He pointed out:

> If, therefore, Europe after the War is to be an armed camp, the peace of the world will depend, as heretofore, on defensive

[1] Lloyd George, *Truth*, I, p. 33.

> alliances formed by those who desire to retain their possessions against those who desire to increase them. In that event the Entente is likely to be maintained.[1]

Although Balfour's proposals were not as sweeping as those of Paget and Tyrrell, the three men agreed that a special relationship must exist between France and England if western Europe, including Great Britain, was to be secure. These views contrasted with the suspicious attitude of the General Staff towards France. Evidently, Sir William Robertson contemplated returning to the traditional policy of no fixed commitments towards major European powers.

On the whole, the General Staff's scheme appeared to be the weakest and the least imaginative of the three. The Foreign Office planners and Balfour showed a wiser concern for broader interests. The General Staff's project was unrealistic, probably, in basing its recommendations upon fear of a future Slav-Russian preponderance in Europe. In attempting to erase this fear by constructing a balance of power system pivoted around a strong Germanic central Europe, the General Staff did not consider, overtly at least, whether a strong Germany would play a moderate and restrained role in postwar Europe or would on the contrary remain in the foreseeable future a graver menace than Russia and the Slav world. In any case, the General Staff revealed no understanding of the divisions within the Slav world among the smaller Slav peoples themselves and between them and Russia. A strong Slav power in central Europe seemed improbable enough, but assuming that such a state existed—perhaps a combination of the Poles and the Czechs within, roughly, the boundaries of 1919—would such a state be strong? Would it naturally incline towards Russia? The Poles, though Slavs, had few reasons to be either pro-Russian or pro-German; the Czechs were torn between Kramář's advocacy of an eastwards, and Masaryk's support for a westward, orientation. They were not likely automatically to gravitate towards Tsarist Russia.

In their more subtle approaches, the Foreign Office advisors and Balfour showed a keener appreciation of these realities. Quite rightly, they were more concerned about how to contain

[1] Dugdale, *Balfour*, pp. 440-1.

Germany than Russia. But how feasible was the Foreign Office plan for a series of strong buffer states, primarily Slavic, in east-central Europe to strike a balance between Germany and Russia, to weaken Germany in the east, demographically and economically, and to block German expansion to the south-east? Balfour's doubts about the viability of the proposed states and the possibility of their restraining Great Powers were well founded, both in the short run because of Russian unwillingness to cede territory to an independent Poland and in the long run because of the weak strategic, economic, and socio-political bases upon which the new states would likely rest. On the other hand, Balfour's solution—maintain stability through direct contact between Russia and Germany—ran counter to the principle of nationality which he and the Foreign Office planners had accepted. A peace which failed to satisfy national aspirations was unlikely to be durable. Neither was a peace which underestimated considerations of the balance of power. Here was the basic difficulty which perplexed the makers of British policy on German territorial questions: how to reconcile the balance of power with national self-determination.

The authors of these projects had assumed that Russia would remain a Great Power and that the United States' role in world politics would not appreciably alter. Both assumptions had to be seriously modified as a result of the Russian Revolution and of the American entry into the war.

On the eve of these developments, the responsibility of framing British peace policy fell to a new British cabinet. On December 6, 1916, Lloyd George, who was to lead the British delegation at the Paris Peace Conference, became Prime Minister, heading a government in which his old political foes, the Conservatives, predominated. The Tory complexion of the ministry was accentuated in the small War Cabinet which Lloyd George created for the supreme direction of British war policy. A Conservative succeeded Grey as foreign secretary: Arthur Balfour, former Prime Minister, an urbane man with a keen, philosophically inclined intellect, with a sure, pragmatic grasp of European territorial and political questions, but lacking boldness and incisiveness in propounding solutions.

Altogether, Lloyd George assembled an able and politically

experienced body of men to direct British policy. They lacked, however, political unity. While prepared to serve under the dynamic leadership of Lloyd George, the ministers were frequently antagonized by and resentful of his arbitrary and domineering ways. Lloyd George himself was in a delicate political position both within his government and in relation to the country at large. A bearer of the Liberal, 'Little England' tradition, he headed a Cabinet whose majority leaned heavily in the direction of Tory views on foreign policy with an emphasis on traditional, maritime, and imperial interests. Its Labour minority represented, if it did not always speak for, the aspirations of British socialists: a world safe for democracy and self-determination; abandonment of every form of Imperialism and wars of conquest; suppression of secret diplomacy; and popular control of foreign policy. Conflicts of personality and of views had an inevitable influence upon the peace policy of Lloyd George's government.

The establishment of the Prime Minister's personal secretariat in January 1917 added another influence on British policy. On Milner's recommendation, Lloyd George appointed Philip Kerr, editor of the *Round Table*, to the 'Garden Suburb' staff as expert advisor on foreign affairs. During the war no serious friction with Balfour and the Foreign Office appears to have arisen out of this arrangement. It was at the Peace Conference and especially after Curzon became foreign secretary that the role of Kerr and the Garden Suburb in the determination of policy caused difficulty and finally provoked the severe crisis of 1921-22.[1]

The first problem in foreign affairs which faced the new British government was one of peace policy posed in December by the peace notes of the German government and of Woodrow Wilson. The Allied reply to Wilson on January 10, 1917, committed the British government to a general statement of conditions of peace which ended with an affirmation of intent to base a peace settlement upon the reconciliation of national

[1] See D. N. Chester (ed.), *The Organisation of British Central Government, 1914-1956*, pp. 289-91; Joseph Davies, *The Prime Minister's Secretariat, 1916-1920*, especially pp. 102-4; T. H. Jones, *Lloyd George*, p. 166; Lloyd George, *Truth*, I, pp. 263-5; F. A. Johnson, *Defence by Committee: The British Committee of Imperial Defence, 1885-1959*.

self-determination with considerations of the balance of power.[1] As for Germany, the contraction of German territory was implied, but any aim of destroying the Reich was denied. Germany would have to recognize the independence of Belgium and to return Alsace-Lorraine to France, although the latter objective was not boldly stated. In the east, the partial dismemberment of Germany was vaguely forecast, but the form of the proposed Polish restoration was undefined because of the Russian government's unwillingness to loosen its hold over Poland. While the Allied Note hinted at the dismemberment of the Dual Monarchy, no commitment was made regarding the future relationship of Germany and Austria.

Lloyd George and Balfour expounded their views on peace aims with more candour than open diplomacy made possible when the first Imperial War Cabinet convened in March 1917. One purpose of summoning the Prime Ministers of the British Dominions was to discuss the peace policy of the Empire as a whole. In his initial address, Lloyd George envisaged the reconstruction of Europe upon the basis of a nationalist, democratic, and punitive peace. According to him, European territorial reorganization should rest upon the recognition of national rights, with the twin objective of securing a durable peace and of bolstering democracy in Europe. Charging that the war had come because of the existence of autocratic power ('. . . if Germany had had a democracy like France, like ourselves, or like Italy, we should not have had this trouble') the Prime Minister urged the punishment of Germany because, 'The conviction must be planted in the minds of the civilized world . . . that all wars of aggression are impossible enterprises. Men must in future be taught to shun war as every civilized being shuns a murder; not merely because it is wrong in itself but because it leads to inevitable punishment. That is the only sure foundation for any league of peace. . . .' The Prime Minister did not describe the map of Europe after a nationalist, democratic, and punitive peace had been fashioned. His only specific reference was to Poland, which would be restored under conditions giving freedom to its oppressed population.[2]

[1] James Brown Scott, *Official Statements of War Aims and Peace Proposals, December 1916 to November 1918*, pp. 35-7.

[2] Lloyd George, *War Memoirs*, IV, pp. 1767 *et seq.*

Later, on March 22, Balfour made a sweeping review of foreign policy,[1] against the background of his belief that America was 'coming in' and of the 'rapidly moving cinematograph of Russian politics'. Underlying his statement was the conviction that probably the greatest danger facing them was Germany's being in a strategic position to establish 'an unbroken avenue of influence from the North Sea to the Persian Gulf . . .' Balfour thought that they had gone far to break German designs in the Middle East but doubted whether the Imperial War Cabinet could be equally confident about shattering German ambitions in Europe. About the basic issues of the war he said: 'If we are not successful in the war, there is no hope of solving them. If the war is a drawn battle, these great causes, I am afraid, will never be satisfactorily dealt with by us. If we win triumphantly, then we shall be able to deal with them.' His aim towards Germany was to destroy the artificial creation of modern Prussia, but not 'German' Germany. That was to say, partial, but not complete dismemberment.

This definition came in the midst of a long discussion of the Polish Question, which Balfour termed 'the greatest crux of European diplomacy'. In Polish claims to Posen, Danzig, and Upper Silesia, especially in the fervent spirit in which they were advanced, Balfour saw several difficulties. Foremost was the problem of adjusting German-Polish interests and ambitions. The award of Danzig to Poland would deprive Germany of a predominantly German town. A Polish corridor would cut Koenigsberg and East Prussia off from Germany 'a thing which would touch German emotions and German interests very quickly'. Posen formed an integral part of Germany and German fears would be aroused if a potential Great Power were brought close to Berlin through the cession of the province. Yet, unless the Poles were satisfied, the 'nucleus of a bitter discontent' would exist. More immediately, Balfour feared that the Poles would go over to the Central Powers, but he affirmed that, because of Russian policy, the Allies could not openly espouse the Polish cause. In any case, he showed no genuine enthusiasm for an

[1] 'Mr. Balfour's Statement on Foreign Policy to the Imperial War Council', no date, copy sent to Lansing on May 18, 1917. U.S. Dept. of State, *The Lansing Papers, 1914-1920*, pp. 19-32; also, the Austen Chamberlain Papers, University of Birmingham.

independent Poland: 'Personally, from the selfish Western point of view, I would rather that Poland was autonomous under the Russians, because if you make an absolutely independent Poland, you cut off Russia altogether from the West.'

As for the fate of the Dual Monarchy in case of an Allied victory, Balfour still thought of a separate peace with the Habsburgs and along the lines of his 1916 memorandum. He did not suggest, therefore, any alteration in the southern boundary of Germany.

As for the Reich's western frontiers, Balfour assumed the restoration of Belgium. He made no reference to other Belgian claims, or to the Saar and Rhineland questions. A striking feature of his address was the discussion of Alsace-Lorraine primarily in terms of the balance of power. He strongly desired the return of the provinces to France, partly because it was politically and diplomatically desirable, partly because it would weaken Germany's industrial power. Restoration would not only fulfill the wish of Alsatians and Lorrainers to live under French rule but also '. . . would further increase the population of France relative to the population of Germany, which undoubtedly must make for the equilibrium of Europe, and because it makes for the equilibrium of Europe, makes also for the peace of the world'.

Balfour's exposition provoked a rather desultory discussion. Picking up the Foreign Secretary's remarks on the Middle East, Austen Chamberlain pointed to two schools of expansionist thought in Germany. One was the colonial school; the other, the 'overland' school which sought to bring under German control through Austria and the Balkans the whole of the Middle East to the borders of Egypt, Persia, Afghanistan, and India. Stressing that the defeat of Germany's colonial ambitions would mean more intensive German concentration on 'overland expansion', Chamberlain declared it was 'of vital importance to us that we should permanently frustrate the efforts of Germany to secure hegemony in the Middle East, and that we should cut the communications between the Central European Powers and the East which they have sought to dominate'. Apart from favouring the expulsion of the Turk from Constantinople, he did not elaborate on the implications of his views for the treatment of European territorial issues. Obviously, one way of cutting Germany off from the East, apart from entrenching Russia at Constantinople and the Straits, would be to support Greater Serbia and Greater Rumania as a barrier across the central Balkans, backed by an independent Greece supported by British naval power in the Mediterranean. This is what the British government was committed to in March of 1917.

Such a strategy could affect the handling of German territorial questions in several ways. Germany's power to expand could be limited by the loss of resources, which the transfer of Alsace-Lorraine involved. The creation of a Balkan barrier against the German *Drang nach Osten* might precipitate the destruction of the Austro-Hungarian Empire which would raise the problem of German Austria and of Czechoslovakia. Either or both of these states, if independent, could aid in blocking the extension of German influence through the Balkans. Or, the territorial settlement in eastern Europe north of Serbia and Rumania could be treated as a secondary British interest compared with breaking German efforts to build a sphere of influence from the North Sea to Suez and the Persian Gulf.

Although the evidence remains fragmentary, it seems clear that British statesmen at this time were having difficulty in defining Britain's vital interests in Europe whether as a basis for a negotiated peace or for peacemaking after a triumph over the Central Powers. Milner clearly viewed 'the enlargement of Yugoslavia and an extended Poland' as secondary objects.[1] Neither Balfour nor Lloyd George believed they could form a definite opinion in view of the existing state of the war. On March 23, the Imperial War Cabinet returned to the subject of peace terms, but evidently without decisive results. Smuts, who later deplored the 'balkanization' of eastern Europe, did not expect total victory and apparently urged a negotiated peace based upon a modification of the publicly announced terms. Borden seems to have opposed this approach[2] while certainly Lloyd George and Balfour sought a decisive military victory.

For the more intensive study of territorial terms of peace, the Imperial War Cabinet on April 12 established a sub-committee

[1] For Milner's moderate views at this time, see *The History of the Times*, IV, part 1, pp. 327-30.

[2] Henry Borden (ed.), *Robert Laird Borden: his Memoirs*, II, pp. 689-90.

under Lord Curzon's chairmanship.[1] The members, who included Austen Chamberlain, General Smuts, Robert Cecil, Walter Long, and J. D. Hazen, the Canadian Minister of Marine and Fisheries, were mainly interested in imperial and colonial problems. Of their recommendations, L. S. Amery, who was secretary of the sub-committee and prepared its draft conclusions on Europe, wrote: '. . . under Curzon's able steering we secured a report, in effect endorsing in improved form the report of the inter-departmental Committee on overseas problems, and putting Europe into proper perspective'.

The meaning of the latter phrase may be gleaned from a memorandum on peace terms which Amery circulated to the Imperial War Cabinet at this time, with the approval of Milner, Curzon, and Smuts.[2] In this paper, Amery contended that British peace policy could have only one objective—security for Britain and its Empire. British security was seen to depend on three basic conditions: the elimination of the threat of enemy bases to imperial commerce and possessions; the independence of the smaller states across the narrow seas; and a reasonable equilibrium in Europe. Amery suggested that, since the collapse of Russia 'might well put the complete break up of Middle Europe beyond our power', they might have to seek a military outcome which would liberate France and Belgium and eliminate the German-Turkish menace to the British position overseas. If these results were accomplished, 'it might well be the right policy to make peace, even if it involved leaving Czechs, Poles, Rumanians, and possibly even Yugoslavs, in the Austro-German orbit, with such measure of independence as we might be able to secure for them'. Smuts, Milner, and perhaps Curzon shared this line of reasoning. Clearly the Imperial War Cabinet and its advisors were torn between two main poles of thought in their approach to peacemaking in eastern Europe.

Curzon's sub-committee advised a moderate European settlement even in case of a total victory over the Central Powers.

[1] Lloyd George, *War Memoirs*, IV, p. 1749; Borden, *Memoirs*, II, p. 690; Austen Chamberlain Papers.

[2] In retrospect, Amery wondered if a more limited settlement along these lines might not have produced greater stability for Europe and the world. L. S. Amery, *My Political Life*, II, pp. 103-5.

The members envisaged an intrinsically stable continental settlement which would avoid as far as possible discontents and rancours likely to produce a new arms race and war. Regarding the restoration of Belgium as a vital British interest, the Committee attached scarcely less importance to sustaining Rumanian, Serbian, Montenegrin, and Greek independence in the postwar world. In raising the Alsatian, Polish, and Austro-Hungarian problems, their concept of major British interests implied a settlement with Germany based upon the preservation of Germany's national existence, the desires of the populations involved, the effectual weakening of German strategic resources and military strength, and the blocking of Germany's road to power and influence through south-east Europe to the Middle East and beyond. No fine blueprint for the attainment of these objectives was provided. This would have been premature because of their own divergent outlook, and since the outcome of the war remained unknown and therefore the attainable, if not the desirable, terms could not be precisely defined. Moreover, there was a tendency to feel that this type of initiative should be left to the European Allies. The Committee thus largely confined itself to generalities about a European settlement, proving that Woodrow Wilson had no monopoly on resounding phrases which hid disagreements and incompatibilities. The Imperial War Cabinet accepted the Report, with Arthur Henderson dissenting, not as rigidly binding but as a general indication of worth-while objectives.[1] In retrospect, the Curzon Committee erected certain guide-posts which point towards the general course taken by Lloyd George and his colleagues at Paris in 1919.

Within a year, the Imperial ministers had to reconsider their tentative decisions of 1917 because of the new situation created by the Russian Revolution and by the United States entry into the war.

In general, events in Russia had the political effect of bolstering the movement in Great Britain and abroad for peace without annexations and without indemnities and for a settlement based upon national self-determination. In turn, this development enhanced Woodrow Wilson's leadership of liberal and moderate socialist forces and increased the influence of his ideas

[1] Lloyd George, *War Memoirs*, IV, p. 1749.

of peace policy.[1] Where these diverged from Balfour's and his associates', British statesmen had to bend their peace policy to meet these currents of opinion while trying to preserve their position on such questions as the German colonies. In Europe, ministerial tendencies to resist broader French claims could only be politically strengthened by the growing popular appeal of the slogan 'peace without annexations'. But the outright transfer of Alsace-Lorraine to France and minor strategic rectifications of the Franco-German border might be harder to accomplish in the new situation.

In eastern Europe, the Russian Revolution ultimately made easier a policy of supporting the independence of Poland. This change was not possible overnight, since Russian policy towards the subject nationalities of the Empire did not quickly change. If the Russian Provisional government could not contemplate an independent Poland, at least it adopted formally a more liberal attitude on the Polish Question than did its Tsarist predecessor. The British government, in its note to Petrograd on June 11, praised the new Russian 'intention of liberating Poland, not only the Poland ruled by the old Russian autocracy but equally that within the dominion of the Germanic Empires'.[2] With the Bolsheviks' seizure of power and their championing of national self-determination for all peoples including the former subjects of the Tsar, an open espousal of the Polish claim to independence was possible. In fact, it became politically necessary to outbid the Bolsheviks. With the rapid German advance eastwards, it also was expedient in order to thwart Berlin's Polish designs and to gain a *point d'appui* in the quickly moving eastern European situation.

By the autumn of 1917, pro-Polish elements in western Europe and North America were increasing their pressure for Allied recognition of the Polish national movement.[3] Finally, at the Inter-Allied Conference in Paris near the end of the year, the Allies and the United States agreed: 'The creation of a Poland, independent and indivisible, under such conditions as

[1] Arno J. Mayer analyses Wilson's influence in his *Political Origins of the New Diplomacy, 1917-1918*.

[2] *The Times*, June 12, 1917, p. 6.

[3] Louis L. Gerson, *Woodrow Wilson and the Rebirth of Poland, 1914-1920*, pp. 75 *et seq.*

will ensure her free political and economic development, constitutes one condition of a solid and just peace, and of a regime of right in Europe.' Balfour had drafted this formula,[1] which avoided committing the British government to any one form of Polish access to the sea.[2] Since the Poles refused to accept the formula,[3] it was not published, but it did express inter-Allied agreement on the establishment of an independent Polish state. Without the Russian Revolution, such agreement would have been most unlikely.

Although the Russian Revolution had the effect of improving the position of the British government on the Polish question, the October Revolution in particular scarcely simplified the problem of peacemaking in central and eastern Europe. It partly accentuated, partly created a dangerously fluid situation as far as German designs and the European equilibrium were concerned. Before October, Russian power was quickly dissolving. After Brest-Litovsk, Russia withdrew from the war and appeared almost a satellite of the Central Powers. The rich natural and industrial resources of southern Russia were open to Germany. Beyond lay the Caspian and a new strategic threat to England's Middle Eastern position. For the British government, eastern Europe had a new importance. The limiting of German expansion eastwards was more imperative than ever. At the same time, the new Soviet government was appealing for violent and immediate revolution in the British homeland and throughout the world. Two enemies existed where only one had been before. How did these circumstances affect the devising of long-term policies on the German territorial and other questions of peacemaking?

[1] House Papers, 2/10, Balfour to House.

[2] See Gerson, *Wilson*, pp. 78-80, for further discussion of British attitudes during 1917.

[3] The Polish National Committee in Paris had wanted the Inter-Allied Conference to make the following declaration: 'The reconstitution of an independent Polish state comprising Polish territories which before the war belonged to Russia, Germany and Austria. This Polish state to be in possession of the Polish part of Silesia and a part of the Baltic coast with the mouths of the Vistula and the Niemen; to have proper extension and a sufficiently large population to enable it to become an efficient factor of European equilibrium.' *Foreign Relations of the United States, 1917*, supplement 2, I, p. 789.

The Russian Revolution opened up gloomy, perplexing vistas for the policymakers in London. Developments in eastern Europe precipitated by the Russian Revolution meant a voyage into the unknown. At the Congress of Vienna, those aristocratic peacemakers, Metternich, Castlereagh, and Alexander, had practically full control, military and political, of Europe from the Urals to the English Channel. In seeking to reconstruct Europe after two decades of war and revolution, to arrange a durable equilibrium of power, they worked under conditions which were reasonably calculable. How different a situation faced the bourgeois peacemakers at the close of the First World War! Much of Europe lay beyond their direct control. Waves of social unrest, economic troubles, political passion, nationalist conflict and revolutionary turmoil surged across the continent. While Russia alone was not the sole area of turbulence out of which these storms arose, the Revolution and the Civil War not only surrounded with uncertainty the future place of that anarchic land in the postwar order but also had unstabilizing repercussions throughout Europe. Consequently an uncertain and virtually uncontrollable element was introduced by Russian events into the reckonings of the peacemakers.

Consider one problem, for example: how were the borderlands between Russia and Germany to be reconstructed? At first glance, the Russian Revolution could be seen as reinforcing the position of the authors of the Foreign Office memorandum of 1916. The October Revolution and its aftermath apparently created conditions in eastern Europe which made a reconstruction of the borderlands along nationalist lines both politically possible and necessary even from the most conservative point of view. After the October Revolution, the concept of a buffer zone had a new attraction. A strong, nationalist, Roman Catholic Poland could be envisaged not only as an anti-German counterweight in the European balance of power, replacing debilitated Russia, but also Poland could hold the European marchlands against Bolshevik revolutionaries pressing from the east. If the borderlands could be so treated as a consequence of the October Revolution, a single, clear-cut strategy of peacemaking in eastern Europe would have many attractions —the Foreign Office plan of 1916, which had the further political merit of coinciding closely with the programme of

President Wilson. As for Germany, the implication would seem to be a whole-hearted dismemberment in the east to help fashion a strong Poland. A further implication would be the denial of Pan-German aspirations in south-central Europe in order to establish a strong Czech state as another link in the Slavic chain separating Russia and Germany.

In reality, the picture was not that simple. The October Revolution introduced an element of profound uncertainty into any balance of power calculations. In 1916, Robertson, Balfour, and the Foreign Office had thought in terms of a postwar European system in which both Germany and Russia would be great powers. Robertson had expressed a fear of Russia and the Slavs; Balfour, of the Germans. Now, however, Russia was, temporarily at least, no longer a Great Power, but it represented a subversive political and moral force, which after the German Revolution threatened to overrun much of Europe. In terms of the Robertson outlook of 1916, the new situation might be met by keeping Germany strong after the war to contain Soviet Russia in eastern Europe where the Bolsheviks might seek to build a powerful red federation and from this base move against the rest of Europe. Such a strategy would dictate the minimum dismemberment of Germany in the east and would reinforce the project for the union of the Germans of the Reich and of Austria. German power should not be diminished by the loss of Silesia. Germany should not be antagonized and perhaps pushed into Soviet arms by subjecting Germans to Polish or other alien rule.

Yet, the assumption had been that Europe should be in balance, not that Germany be the master of central and eastern Europe. To restore the balance after 1917 could lead to an effort to re-establish Russia as a 'normal' Great Power in the European system. Several strategies of peacemaking could follow from this approach: reconstruction of the former Russian Empire in Europe perhaps along federalist lines or the creation of a Great Russian national state which would be closely allied with an independent Poland, etc.

Balfour had hoped that peace and stability in eastern Europe would rest upon an equipoise of power between Germany and Russia. He had no confidence in the buffer state concept. But, the October Revolution shattered most of this project. Germany would remain aggressive; Russian power was eliminated from the balance; Soviet Russia posed a new threat to the *status quo*. Perhaps a buffer state system might be about all that was possible.

This solution had obvious weaknesses. If the violent rip-tides of social and ideological conflicts were added to the other sources of discontent and weakness in eastern Europe, the prospects of Poland and of other buffer states in the region seemed dim. They would be precariously situated between expansionist Germany and revolutionary Russia, two powers which might link up. With unavoidable minorities, they would lack the internal cohesion of genuine national states.

It is questionable whether Lloyd George and his ministerial colleagues believed that the potential buffer states in eastern Europe could assume the type of role played in the prewar balance by Russia and Austria-Hungary. Curzon, Balfour, and Austen Chamberlain, among others, doubted seriously whether Poland could be a viable, dependable state in the European system. One alternative, of course, was to revive Russian power, as the General Staff under Sir Henry Wilson advised in 1918; the other was to look to American power to replace Russia in the European balance, while satisfying the reasonable national aspirations of the European peoples, friend and foe alike.

II

THE AMERICAN FACTOR AND BRITISH POLICY, 1917-18

THE bearing of United States' intervention in the war upon the British government's approach to European territorial questions is only one aspect of the First World War chapter in the history of Anglo-American relations. About this relationship, George W. Brown has written:

> Between Britain and the United States the pattern has been one of deep affinities in thought and action, which, in times of great international crisis, have had a tremendous recurrent influence, but which even more often have been so overlaid, obscured, and frustrated by suspicious misunderstandings, and particular conflicts of interest, that the two nations have been repeatedly at critical points brought to the verge of open conflict. . . .[1]

The substance of this statement can be applied to Anglo-American relations during the First World War on questions of peace policy. There was a fundamental similarity of approach which was continually warped and concealed by national rivalry, by conflict over matters of emphasis and detail, and by discord among individual personalities and outlooks. Always inherent in this relationship was the possibility, after April 1917, of a possible United States' withdrawal from the war or the peacemaking.

There were other factors in the Anglo-American relationship

[1] George W. Brown, 'The "Atlantic Alliance" in Perspective', *International Journal*, Spring 1957, pp. 79-82.

on peace policy. Because of Britain's unique position between Europe and North America, the British government was obliged to balance and to conciliate between its continental allies, France and Italy, to whom it was pledged to make peace jointly, and its associate, the United States, which was not committed to make war or peace in common with the Allies. The result was a constant quest on the part of British statesmen for some amalgam which would maintain the European-Anglo-American triangle.

Numerous difficulties beset this search, the foremost being how to concert the approaches of Paris, Washington, and London to the postwar treatment of Germany. Early in 1917, the French government formulated a policy of detaching the Rhineland and the Saar as well as Alsace-Lorraine from Germany to redress the balance between Gaul and Teuton.[1] French aspirations posed a twofold problem for British policymakers. In the first place, a major British interest in Europe was the maintenance and strengthening of France as a friendly Great Power. Thus Balfour at least favoured the restoration of Alsace-Lorraine to France to augment French demographic and economic resources and correspondingly to weaken Germany. But how far could and should the British government go in supporting the detachment of more and undisputed German territory and peoples without either tipping the balance too far in France's favour or defeating, by the creation of an uncontrollable German desire for revenge, the aim of political stabilization in western Europe? Secondly, to what extent could the British government uphold, for political and security reasons, French ambitions and strategic requirements in western Europe, without endangering relations with Woodrow Wilson? The President, purporting to speak for the American people, declaimed against the balance of power, strategic frontiers, territorial transfers without popular consent, etc. Wilsonian and French views seemed to represent opposite poles of thought. In which direction should London move to preserve the triangular relationship in war and peace?

The men in London after April 1917 became increasingly

[1] Georges Suarez, *Briand*, IV, pp. 128 *et seq.*, III, pp. 411-12; Paul Cambon, *Correspondance, 1879-1924*, III, p. 184; Lloyd George, *Truth*, I, pp. 384-5.

preoccupied with the American factor in British peace policy. As an associate in the war upon whose aid the Allies became ever more dependent for victory, the Wilson administration gained added weight in the determination of British policy. Generally, that influence strengthened the moderates in London. The task of the makers of British peace policy was not eased by America's new role in the war. When anticipating the situation at the end of the conflict, British policymakers faced the dilemma of whether to base peace policy upon the assumption of an isolationist or an internationalist America. If they preferred to see the United States positively involved in postwar world politics—and most British ministers came to accept, however grudgingly, the utility of this—British statesmen then confronted the problem of how consciously to shape their peace policy so as to facilitate America's abandonment of its traditional isolationism and to cultivate American friendship and support after the war. Yet, a friendly, internationalist America was not the sole desideratum of British policy. There were others: the protection of Britain's vital interests in Europe and the world; the maintenance of the unity of imperial foreign policy; the honouring of engagements towards allies and the preservation of friendly relations with them. On balance, America's entry into the war under Wilsonian leadership probably added to the difficulties of Lloyd George's government in reconciling these complex, frequently contradictory considerations.

To offer one illustration, Wilson's views and those of some of the Dominions differed over the future disposal of the German colonies. Ironically, at the very time in 1917 when the Imperial War Cabinet adopted the policy of seeking annexation by Britain, South Africa, New Zealand, and Australia, of conquered German colonies, America's entry into the war under Wilsonian leadership profoundly altered one basic assumption underlying that policy, namely that in case of decisive victory over Germany, none of Britain's major partners would resist the proposed annexations. Whether the British and Dominion governments should modify their German colonial policy in a Wilsonian direction depended partly on how high a price they were prepared to pay for a postwar alliance or entente with the United States.

Lastly, there was always the haunting thought among the

imperial ministers that regardless of how far British policy was bent towards the Wilsonian line, the concession might make no difference. America, whatever the pliability of its associates in the war, might still revert to isolationism. And if, in the futile search for the American entente, London had antagonized its Allies, weakened imperial unity, prepared for one postwar world only to find a radically different one, where then would Britain and its Empire stand? Perhaps in that condition of perilous isolation which Lansdowne, Balfour, Joseph Chamberlain, and so many other Englishmen feared around the turn of the century. Thus as the belligerents bled on, American participation in the war represented for London at once an augury of victory, a promise of postwar security, and a riddle whose solution involved the fate of the British Empire.

The difference between British and American official attitudes towards peace terms can be dramatically exaggerated, particularly if it is assumed that each side was monolithic and consistent in its approach to postwar peacemaking. A comparison of Wilson's public pronouncements with views expressed in British governmental circles before April 1917 reveals few sharp contrasts, although areas of disagreement and much unexplored ground existed.[1] The British government's call for victory over Germany did clash diametrically with Wilson's advocacy of peace without victory.[2] The President's utterance, which so disturbed the Allies, was made of course before his country became involved in war against Germany. It proved only a passing Wilsonian phrase.

On certain issues of principle there was much in common. Both Wilson and Lloyd George shared a similar outlook in their stress upon the right of national self-determination and upon the building of peace on a democratic foundation. The Prime Minister's call before the Imperial War Cabinet for a punitive peace did contrast with Wilson's original appeal for peace without victory, but the President's later advocacy of

[1] A general comparison and a full analysis of Wilson's views and pronouncements would be out of place here. For a more detailed discussion see Thomas A. Bailey, *Wilson and the Peacemakers*, pp. 22-33; Edward H. Buehrig (ed.), *Wilson's Foreign Policy in Perspective*; and Arthur P. Dudden (ed.), *Woodrow Wilson and the World of Today*; Mayer, *op. cit.*

[2] R. S. Baker and William E. Dodd (eds.), *The Public Papers of Woodrow Wilson*, II, *The New Democracy*, pp. 407 *et seq.*

peace based upon justice contained a punitive element. Then too, Wilson, Balfour, and the authors of the Foreign Office project of 1916 agreed that a durable peace settlement must rest on the principle of nationality and on a genuine reconciliation between general and national interests. On the other hand, Balfour, Tyrrell, and others in London thought also in terms of alliances and balance of power. Here they seemed to diverge most from Wilson, who appeared to reject alliances and balance of power as the underpinning of a postwar territorial settlement.

On many other issues affecting the European settlement, views on either side had yet to be defined. The nature of the peace with Germany would depend greatly on the peacemakers' estimation of Germany's probable postwar conduct. The British General Staff in 1916 apparently had little fear of Germany's maintaining an aggressive posture; Balfour believed that Germany would remain strong and potentially expansionist. Where did Wilson stand on this vital question? His earlier speeches had not revealed his attitude.[1]

How, moreover, did Wilson and British statesmen propose to apply their ideas pragmatically? Wilson had been vague on how the word would be made flesh; though scarcely less so than Allied leaders had been. The President's one specific reference had been to Poland which he envisaged as united, independent, and autonomous[2]; a solution which fitted into the contradictory plans advocated by the British General Staff, the Foreign Office, and Balfour! Because of such uncertainties and probable disagreements over certain European and colonial questions, the British government attached importance to an exchange of opinions on peace aims with its new war partner. Such a review was one objective of the Balfour mission to the United States in April 1917.

Balfour and House, in canvassing territorial questions, assumed the restoration of France and Belgium and the transfer of Alsace-Lorraine to France. The problems of the German-Polish settlement engrossed them. House noted in his diary, '... I warmly advocated a restored and rejuvenated Poland, a Poland big and powerful enough to serve as a buffer state between Germany and Russia'.[3] In thus taking a stand similar to that of Paget and Tyrrell in 1916, House encountered Balfour's con-

[1] *Ibid.*, p. 414. [2] *Ibid.*, p. 412. [3] House, Diary, X, pp. 123 *et seq.*

tinued opposition to this proposal. Balfour, depicting Germany as potentially an infinitely greater postwar menace than Russia, held that to interpose Poland between Germany and Russia would prevent Russia from aiding France in case of German aggression. House rejoined that in fifty years Russia and not Germany would be the major danger to Europe, unless Russia was democratic and ceased to be expansionist. If Germany were regarded as the permanent enemy, he thought mistakes would follow in the peacemaking. Balfour was unimpressed. According to House, Balfour was holding to a general English view: 'She (England) is interested in having German hopes for a Middle Europe under Prussian control forever shattered . . .'[1]

On the issue of Polish access to the sea, Balfour and House agreed that only Danzig could provide an adequate outlet for Poland, but both feared the danger of creating another Alsace-Lorraine in eastern Europe. Balfour suggested making Danzig a free port, but House opposed this solution.[2]

When Balfour conferred on peace terms with President Wilson, they arrived at similar conclusions.[3] No comprehensive formal agreement was, however, drawn up between them. Later, an informal understanding was drafted which contained no direct reference to territorial issues except a brief phrase denying the intention of dismembering Germany.[4] If House's

[1] Charles Seymour (arr.), *Intimate Papers of Colonel House*, III, 134.

[2] *Ibid.*, p. 43. Probably after this meeting, Balfour sent to House his memorandum of October 1916, on peace terms. In the covering letter, Sir Eric Drummond wrote: 'I believe that to some extent his views as regards Poland have altered slightly and that the constitution of the future state as outlined in the recent Russian proclamation governing the condition (conclusion) of a military alliance between Russia and Poland would probably meet his present view.' House Papers, 5/15, Drummond to House, April 28, 1917.

[3] House, Diary, X, p. 134. The Colonel attended this meeting.

[4] The memorandum read:

'*Draft Statement*: The United States and the Allies are determined to carry on the struggle till the aims set out by the President have been secured. To effect this purpose the people of America will spare neither treasure nor life, no matter how long the war continues. In 1918 there will be one and a half million American soldiers on the Western front.

'The Allies can never abandon the cause of democracy and civilisation. But they have already declared that they have no quarrel with the German people; they have no desire to dismember Germany. The war against democracy was inspired and caused by a small military autocracy in Prussia

account is reliable, the Balfour mission revealed German boundary issues as a likely area of Anglo-American co-operation in the peacemaking, with the Polish Question, however, constituting one likely cause of disagreement.

After Balfour's return the evident desire on both sides of the Atlantic was to maintain a united diplomatic front on peace policy as an essential condition of winning the war.[1] In public speeches on peace terms, principles were at a premium; details at a discount. While the policy of either government on German territorial questions, therefore, was not more sharply defined for some time, Lloyd George, Wilson, and Balfour made statements of principle which had important implications for a postwar German boundary settlement.

In several speeches, Lloyd George defined the best guarantees of peace with Germany as: a settlement so equitable that no nation would wish to disturb it; the destruction of Prussian military power; and the democratization of the German government. He denied any intention of dictating forms of government to the German people, but he added

> . . . we should say we could enter into negotiations with a free government in Germany with a different attitude of mind, a different temper, a different spirit, with less suspicion, with more confidence, than we could with a government . . . dominated by the aggressive and arrogant spirit of Prussian militarism and the Allied Governments would, in my judgement be acting wisely if they drew that distinction in their general attitude in the discussion of the terms of peace.[2]

His doctrine was that democracy in itself was a guarantee of peace, and if Germany did not become democratic, other guarantees of peace would be necessary.[3]

Lloyd George's position was gradually paralleled through 1917 by Woodrow Wilson. The President, blurring his previous

[1] This policy was based on the understanding embodied in the Drummond memorandum.

[2] *The Times*, June 30, 1917, p. 8.

[3] *Ibid.*, July 23, 1917, p. 4.

which imposed its wishes even on the German empire. With this autocracy the representatives of the democratic countries can never deal. People must treat with people, otherwise there can be no peace. Germany now can never hope for a favourable decision by force of arms.'

A note in House's writing reads: 'This is Drummond's draft of our understanding. Balfour approves. EMH. May 23/17.'

distinction between the German government and the German people, began to see the German people as having submitted 'with temporary zest' to the domination of their 'masters'.[1] Through 1917, Woodrow Wilson began to refer to alternative types of settlement with Germany, one based on the assumption that Germany remained 'unrepentant and unchanged', the other on the assumption that the Germans had been converted to peace and democracy.[2]

On December 4, 1917, the President spelled out his intentions.[3] German power must be crushed or if not crushed it must be shut out from intercourse with the peaceful nations. If crushed, the price of peace could be paid—full, impartial justice in the final settlement for 'our enemies as well as our friends'. Later in the address he repeated that when German power had been defeated, right could be established as arbiter and peacemaker and 'we . . . shall be free to base peace on generosity and justice, to the exclusion of all selfish claims to advantage even on the part of the victors'. When would this time come? Wilson's answer was: '. . . when the German people have spokesmen whose word we can believe and when those spokesmen are ready in the name of their people to accept the common judgment of the nations as to what shall henceforth be the bases of law and of covenant for the life of the world . . .'. If, however, no change of heart and rulers occurred, Germany could expect to be excluded from the partnership guaranteeing the peace and from economic intercourse with the pacific nations. Wilson pursued this dualistic approach to peacemaking with Germany for the remainder of the war and at the Paris Peace Conference.

Balfour's position was not radically different from Wilson's although, even publicly, the British Foreign Secretary defended the concept of balance of power and avowed his doubts about the likelihood of a 'new world' emerging after the war.[4] In dealing with the fundamentals of peace, Balfour called for an improved international morality, an international system for the punishment of the aggressor, and a territorial rearrangement in Europe which would promote an equilibrium of forces

[1] Baker and Dodd, *op. cit.*, I, *War and Peace*, pp. 93-6.

[2] *Ibid.*, pp. 60 *et seq.*

[3] *Ibid.*, pp. 128 *et seq.*

[4] *The Times*, July 31, 1917, p. 8.

even though it would not be a balance of power 'in precisely the old eighteenth century sense of the word . . .'. Since he thought that a stable peace was more likely if concluded with a community based upon the popular will, he favoured the replacement of autocracy in Germany by parliamentary institutions. On the other hand, he warned that externally imposed constitutions would fail.

In a private clarification of his views in a letter to Lord Lansdowne, while affirming his opposition to the dismemberment or destruction of Germany, he made clear that he meant 'German' Germany. The transfer of Alsace-Lorraine to France and 'the re-creation of so much of the historic Poland as is really Polish' would not, according to his definition, constitute the dismemberment of Germany. As he pointed out, the Germans thought differently. As for imposing governments, he did not desire to compel Germany to accept parliamentary institutions, but 'I do want to see a form of government established in, say (German) Poland, to which Germany would certainly object'. And, like Wilson, he was prepared to employ postwar economic action 'in case Germany shows herself to be utterly unreasonable', while not wishing to destroy Germany as a trading community.[1]

The mission of Colonel House to England and France near the end of 1917 underscored the obstacles to co-operation on peace policy between the British government and the Wilson administration.[2] The American representative attempted to secure a general declaration that the Allied and Associated Powers did not seek aggression or indemnities but the elimina-

[1] Lord Newton, *Lord Lansdowne*, p. 465.

[2] Apart from Poland, German territorial questions do not appear to have received specific attention. According to House, the British government was primarily concerned with war aims in the Middle East and Africa. Seymour, *Intimate Papers*, III, pp. 235-7; House, Diary, XII, pp. 368-71. House told Lloyd George and Balfour: 'I thought what we agreed upon today might be utterly impossible tomorrow, and it seemed more than useless to discuss territorial aims at this time. They caught the point and agreed to stop the discussions.'

Balfour commented after a War Cabinet session, on December 29, that there was no problem about defining war aims. 'The real difficulty is to find out how far we shall be able to attain them, and how far the Allies are prepared to fight until they are attained;—and no amount of defining will help us to solve either of these problems . . .' Dugdale, *Balfour*, p. 253.

tion of militarism and the establishment of the right of nations to live and to develop their welfare.[1] This formula could be interpreted to exclude the annexation of colonies, Italian claims in the Balkans, and French aspirations in western Europe. It posed obvious difficulties for the British government.

The British role in the negotiations over the resolution remains obscure. At first, House informed Wilson that the British delegation would support his draft resolution, but later he reported his failure to persuade Lloyd George and Reading to uphold it. The British spokesmen may have disliked the 'no aggression, no indemnity' formula or they may simply have been seeking a compromise between House and the European Allies.[2] In any event, these abortive negotiations and the friction which they had revealed among the Allied and Associated Powers influenced the British government and Wilson to make a public restatement of peace policy in a more specific and liberal vein.

When examining the evolution of British peace policy during the final months of the war, we must not forget the general political complexion of the British government and Lloyd George's own political position. Was the Prime Minister hampered in the pursuit of a liberal peace policy because he was 'surrounded by alien influences'? In[3] part he was, although the picture can be over-drawn. As Lloyd George appreciated, the Cabinet contained men, like Balfour and Milner, with

[1] House to Wilson, November 30, 1917, *Foreign Relations, 1917*, supplement 2, vol. I, p. 328. Wilson's reply approving the draft resolution asserted that the United States would not fight for the selfish aims of any belligerent 'with the possible exception of Alsace-Lorraine'. The latter indicated a reserve on Wilson's part about French claims similar to the reserve attributed to Lloyd George by Paul Cambon and others. It was not shared by Balfour and, perhaps, by Bonar Law. Wilson to House, December 1, 1917, *ibid.*, p. 331.

[2] Seymour, *Intimate Papers*, III, p. 233, quotes House's note in his Diary for November 16 that the British government could not accept a 'no indemnities, no aggression' formula because it would mean conflict with the Dominions (except Canada) who might stop fighting. France feared being committed to abandoning the claim to Alsace-Lorraine. On pp. 278-286 Seymour contends that Lloyd George was too much tied to the British Conservatives to support enthusiastically the proposed liberal statement of war aims. Lloyd George failed to obtain a compromise formula which would meet Italian and French fears.

[3] J. L. Hammond, *C. P. Scott of the Manchester Guardian*, p. 219.

moderate views on peace policy. In the Prime Minister's estimation, the domestic political difficulty in defining that policy was to find a *via media* between the Unionists and the Opposition. As he complained, '. . . the moment he made any advance towards meeting the Opposition he risked the loss of the Unionist support which was essential to him'.[1] When the *Manchester Guardian* criticized portions of his speech on war aims before the Trades Union Congress, Lloyd George wrote to the editor, Scott: 'It is very difficult to fight the battle of common-sense in this war when you have against you the extravagance of the Jingo and the catankerousness [*sic*] of the Pacificist.'[2] There was much truth in his complaint. It well illustrates his domestic and foreign political difficulties not only in 1918 but also at the Paris Peace Conference where, in many respects, he and the other British moderates were caught between the jingoism of the French, Poles, etc., the Germanophobia of the 'Chambre introuvable' thrown up by the Khaki election, and the cantankerousness of Wilson.

Lloyd George's address to the Trades Union Congress on January 5, 1918,[3] was moderate, ringing, and inspirational in tone. As a definition of policy, it was informative but scarcely candid. In dealing with Germany, the Prime Minister denied seeking the dismemberment of either German territory or the German people. The British government only sought a renunciation of the quest for military domination. The German people themselves should decide their constitution; if they adopted a democratic system, a broad, democratic peace would

[1] *Ibid.*, p. 222.

[2] *Ibid.*, p. 232. Scott's view of Lloyd George's position was given in a letter to Felix Frankfurter, February 4, 1918: '. . . Our Government is not a Liberal and democratic Government. Broadly speaking, it is an Imperialist and reactionary Government despite the personality of the Prime Minister, who cannot, unsupported as he is by any great party or party machinery, do more than influence without controlling it, and lacks besides some of the essential qualities for such leadership. If the ideals and true purposes of the war are to be made to prevail, it can only be by the direct and continuous assertion of American influence.'

[3] Lloyd George, *War Memoirs*, V, 2517-27. For fuller discussion of currents of English opinion on war aims see *The History of the Times*, IV, part I, chap. VIII, 'Peace Making'; and A. J. P. Taylor's revealing essay, 'The Great War: The Triumph of E. D. Morel', in *The Trouble Makers: Dissent over Foreign Policy, 1792-1939*, pp. 132-66.

be possible. Here Lloyd George was adhering to the promise made earlier by Wilson and himself and which they have been accused of forgetting at the Paris Peace Conference.

Compared with Lloyd George's address, Wilson's Fourteen Points speech,[1] nine days later, struck much the same note on German territorial and ancillary questions. For political reasons, both were vague over details. They agreed on the restoration of Belgium with no suggestion of any modification of the Kingdom's frontiers in 1914. They spoke favourably about the French claim to Alsace-Lorraine, although Wilson was more affirmative in insisting that a wrong must be righted. Neither statesman indicated any support for further French claims against Germany. Each called for an independent Poland based upon genuine or indisputable Polish elements. Here Wilson went beyond Lloyd George in specifying Poland's need for access to the seas and in promising to seek a guarantee of the political and economic independence as well as the territorial integrity of the new state. The President and the Prime Minister stated essentially the same policy towards the Dual Monarchy, with the implication that German-Austria would remain separate from the Reich, although the principle of determining sovereignty over territory by the consent of the governed could signify support for the absorption of Bohemian and Austrian Germans in Germany. (In that case would the Czechs 'live on equal terms of liberty and safety' with the Germans?) Wilson claimed that his programme was bound together by a single principle: 'the principle of justice to all peoples and nationalities, and their right to live on equal terms of liberty and safety with one another, whether they be strong or weak'. Lloyd George had stressed justice, too, and like Wilson espoused the cause of national self-determination. Their wide measure of agreement foreshadowed Anglo-American co-operation at the Paris Peace Conference in the German territorial negotiations.

Many of Wilson's critics, both hostile and friendly, have overstressed the element of self-determination in his doctrine and have ignored the implications of his insistence upon the principle of justice. In some respects he stressed justice more than self-determination as in the peroration of the Fourteen

[1] Baker and Dodd, *Wilson Papers*, I, pp. 155-62.

Points' speech. Behind this emphasis lay his conviction that the Germans had been unjust and that it was the rights of their enemies in south-central Europe which had to be defended against them.

The duality of his approach should not, however, be exaggerated. In his thoughts and actions, he envisaged territorial settlements resting upon some amalgam of the two. It was not, perhaps, his fault that others have taken out of his remarks whatever suited their beliefs and interests. None the less, his preoccupation with sweeping generalities and the striking phrase hid the conflicts and confusions, the dangerous deceptions and vagaries which became visible during the actual peacemaking and which contributed so much to the undermining of his moral position. By his political naïveté and astounding egoism, he was setting himself a difficult if not impossible task.

His burden was not eased by his final major address before the end of the war in New York on September 27,[1] when he fervently called for peace based, not upon mere arrangement, compromise, and adjustment of interests but upon 'full and unequivocal acceptance of the principle that the interest of the weakest is as sacred as the interest of the strongest'. To accomplish this end, the peacemakers must pay the price of peace. The price? 'That price is impartial justice in every item of the settlement, no matter whose interest is crossed; and not only impartial justice, but also the satisfaction of the several peoples whose fortunes are dealt with.' At the same time, they must be prepared to create the instrument to ensure the maintenance of the peace settlement. Why would the peace have to be guaranteed by a League of Nations? Wilson's answer was: 'The reason, to speak in plain terms again, why it must be guaranteed is that there will be parties to the peace whose promises have proved untrustworthy, and means must be found in connection with the peace settlement itself to remove that source of insecurity.' Without a League of Nations, peace would rest in part upon the word of outlaws. He added, '. . . Germany will have to redeem her character, not by what happens at the peace table, but by what follows'.

Wilson also envisaged in this address that within the League

[1] *Ibid.*, pp. 253-61.

of Nations, no subsidiary leagues, alliances, or special agreements were to exist, nor any special, selfish economic combinations. Relationships of this kind, in his view, had been among the causes of the war. Therefore, they must be excluded from the settlement. Was there room here for the Foreign Office's west European alliance or for Balfour's Anglo-French entente? For that matter, was there a place in Wilson's system for an American-French-British treaty of guarantee?

Balfour in 1918 frankly questioned certain aspects of the Wilsonian viewpoint. Both men now shared a common mistrust of Germany and the Germans. They differed over how to organize security against German postwar expansion. Balfour was sceptical about the likely efficacy of a universal collective security system. Granting that the balance of power was 'more or less an antiquated doctrine', he believed, as he told the Commons,

> . . . until German militarism is a thing of the past, until that ideal is reached for which we all long, in which there shall be an International Court, armed with executive power, so that the weak may be as safe as the strong—until that time comes, it will never be possible to ignore the principle of action which underlies the struggle for the balance of power in which our forefathers engaged.[1]

Balfour also shied away from handling territorial issues on the basis of abstract principles. He believed in settling each question on its merits, an attitude very evident in the Foreign Office memoranda prepared under his direction during the post-armistice preparations for the Peace Conference. In a letter to Wilson,[2] explaining his attitude towards the Treaty of London, he admitted that the agreement assigned Slavs to Italy for strategical reasons. His defense was that strategic arguments should not be ruled out with 'pedantic consistency', a phrase which may have grated upon the ears of the former President of Princeton. Balfour argued that strategic frontiers could make for peace and if a particular strategic frontier would contribute to international stability he would not reject it 'in deference to some *a priori* principle', if the populations

[1] *British Parliamentary Debates, Fifth Series, House of Commons*, vol. 103, pp. 1463 *et seq.*

[2] Seymour, *Intimate Papers*, III, pp. 50-1.

concerned should be numerically insignificant. If the number of Slavs to be transferred to Italy could be considered insignificant, so too could the population of the Saar and perhaps of Bohemia's mountain fringes.

Balfour thus criticized both Lloyd George's and Wilson's insistence upon the principle of national self-determination. Can we conclude that here we see Balfour, the conservative, and Wilson, the liberal, confronting one another as the symbols of an old and of a new diplomatic order? Such a picture would be a misrepresentation. Certainly, their approaches to peacemaking did not coincide. Balfour saw in Wilsonism the false promise that the international millennium was close at hand. He sought to warn against the dangers of underestimating the difficulties of peacemaking and doubted the immediate feasibility of some of the methods for securing peace which Wilson was advocating. On his part, the President struck out with increasing vigour against the assumptions and methods of traditional diplomacy. Balfour's ideas were made to seem things of the past, discredited, useless for the future.

Yet Wilson had made clear his conviction that the war was being fought to prevent the domination of Europe by a single power. Although his utterances on German militarism were ambivalent and more optimistic than Balfour's, he had reached the position of believing that aggressive designs had infected much of German society even on the popular levels and that the grand strategy of the peacemaking might have to rest on the assumption that Germany would remain a danger to international peace after the war. In this contingency, the German nation would have to be excluded from the family of nations and the peace settlement imposed when it could not be freely negotiated. Peace in this situation would have to rest upon a balance of power: a preponderant grouping of forces against the potential aggressor. In these respects, Wilson and Balfour were not basically apart: an old order was not confronting a new.

During the spring and summer of 1918, the British government clarified its attitude on several questions affecting the future boundaries of Germany. On May 16, the question of French claims was raised in the Commons.[1] On behalf of the

[1] *British Parliamentary Debates, Commons*, vol. 106, p. 579.

government, the Foreign Secretary said that an enlarged Alsace-Lorraine 'was altogether outside our whole modes of thought on this subject'.

East European policy changed. On June 4, the British government joined with the governments of France and Italy in public affirmation of support for a united and independent Poland, with free access to the sea. Simultaneously, they expressed their sympathy for the national aspirations of the Czechs, a declaration of principle bearing on the future southern boundaries of Germany. A few days before, the American government had issued a similar statement. Near the end of June, Lansing announced that his government supported the cause of Slavic freedom from German and Austrian rule. This decisive shift in policy towards the Dual Monarchy was followed by the French government, while on August 9 London recognized the Czechs as an allied nation. On October 15, the British government recognized the Polish Army as a co-belligerent. Thus, during 1918, Anglo-American-French policy towards the Poles and the Czechs altered in their favour, with obvious implications for the drafting of a German boundary settlement.[1]

During the summer, British and Dominion statesmen held a lengthy debate on peace policy. The Imperial War Cabinet had not had an opportunity earlier to assess the implications of developments since mid-1917 for the provisional decisions then made on imperial peace terms. In August 1918, the main problem was whether to adhere to the decisions of 1917 or to modify them to conform more closely to Wilson's views and in the light of the changed political and military situation in Eastern Europe and the Middle East.

The debate took place in a more hopeful military atmosphere than had hitherto prevailed—the blackest days of the German military offensives had seemingly passed—although decisive victory did not appear likely before 1919 or 1920. Concurrently, however, a grave manpower situation faced the imperial ministers. According to information before them, by December 1919 British divisions in France would fall to 36 compared to 59 in August 1918. French divisions would total 65; American

[1] The various declarations are given in *Foreign Relations, 1918*, supplement 1, vol. I, pp. 790-884.

112; and German 170.[1] This weakness in manpower foreshadowed a diminution of British military power and diplomatic influence on the continent[2] when United States' power in Europe would be rising to a point of ascendancy over that of the Allies.

Amid this gloomy prospect, Balfour opened the debate on war aims on August 13. He touched upon four main areas: western Europe, central Europe, the Middle East, and the German colonies.[3]

In dealing with western Europe, Balfour made no reference to the Saar, the Rhineland, Belgium, the Low Countries, and Luxembourg. He concentrated on France and Alsace-Lorraine. As he pointed out, the British government had no treaty obligation respecting Alsace-Lorraine, but it was bound by its declarations to support the French claim. If the war ended in victory, the British government could honour this commitment. If the war ended in a limited Allied success, the British government, so the foreign secretary advised, must leave the initiative to the French about moderating their claims to the provinces.

In turning to central Europe, Balfour commented that 'we can only, perhaps, now say that Austria's future status is more or less finally decided . . .'. Envisaging the dissolution of the Dual Monarchy into its constituent ethnographical parts, he predicted that the German-Austrian portion would be absorbed into the German Reich which represented a change from his earlier attitude.

Obviously, Balfour was reluctant to contemplate the destruction of Austria. He gave primary weight to considerations of the balance of power and not to the ideal of the right of self-determination in discussing his reasons for coming to this decision. In his opinion,

1 Borden Papers, OC 628, 'Report of the Committee of Prime Ministers: Preliminary Draft, August 14, 1918'.

2 In October 1917, Lloyd George had revealed his concern about this implication of the British manpower problem when he opposed another Passchendale offensive because it might leave Britain too weak at the end of the war 'to make her voice heard and her will prevail in the momentous decisions to be come to in the Council of Peace'. Quoted by Frank Owen in *Tempestuous Journey*, p. 447. See also Lloyd George to Reading, August 26, 1918, *ibid.*, p. 491.

3 Borden Papers. The quotations below are from this source unless otherwise noted.

> . . . if there was the slightest hope that a renovated Austria, or an Austria at all, would be a counterpoise to Germany in Central Europe, it really would be worthwhile seeing whether we could not keep her and alter her. I confess that the whole trend of events in the last three or four years shows that either Austria goes to pieces or that Austria remains a satellite of Germany.

After examining the probable course of relations between Germany and Austria, he concluded that it would be impossible to conceive conditions under which Austria-Hungary

> . . . would play the part which we should like to see her play, namely, that of an independent powerful counterpoise to the other great Central Power, Germany. Thus consequently [*sic*] the whole movement, almost unconsciously, but quite steadily, has been going or drifting in the direction of giving autonomy, real independence, if possible, to the Poles . . . , to the Czecho-Slovaks . . . , and to the Jugo-Slavs. . . .

Balfour advanced no specific suggestions about the future frontiers of Germany and Bohemia. Although Bohemia had well-defined frontiers, he saw a major issue: the disposition of the mountainous fringe area, with its German-populated regions. He used this question to illustrate the general difficulty which they would encounter in attempting to draw frontiers based upon ethnography alone in areas of mixed populations or where incongruities existed between ethnographic and natural lines. On this problem he commented: 'I think myself that in some cases we shall have have [*sic*] to throw ethnology to the winds, and take a well-defined mountain range or a big river as a boundary where purely ethnological divisions might suggest some modifications of the natural divisions.'

Balfour went on to contrast the Czechs favourably to the Poles: the former he regarded as political realists; the latter as romantics. He expected the Poles to put forward extreme claims, based upon historic Poland which would surpass their genuine claims upon the sympathy of the Allies. The greatest future difficulty of all, according to the Foreign Secretary, would be the conflict between Polish and German vital interests in the coalfields and manufacturing districts of Posen and Silesia. These regions were among the most Polish of Polish territories. The Poles were their rightful owners. Yet, the Germans prized their resources and industries and feared the strategic threat to

Berlin of a Polish-held Posen. Because of these considerations, Balfour advised his colleagues to make no plans for the Polish-German frontier 'until we know how much we are going to beat Germany'.

On the issue of Danzig and a Polish corridor to the sea, he informed the Cabinet: 'At Versailles we promised access to the sea: we were too wise, too cautious, to promise a bit of coast-line.' Opposed to giving Poland either Danzig or a portion of coast-line, Balfour saw freedom of navigation along the Vistula as the proper solution of the problem of Polish access to the sea.

Those aspects of Balfour's speech which went beyond questions concerning Germany's future frontiers remind us that British statesmen were concerned not only with German and other European questions; the scope of their interests was world wide. They also illustrate the British absence of territorial claims on the continent; if territory was to be added, it lay in Africa and the Far East.

The world settlement which Balfour envisaged rested upon a concern for the balance of power and for strategical factors such as maritime bases, oil supplies, and control of black armies. This position did not exclude a general acceptance of ethnographic frontiers, especially in Europe, but in some areas he would depart from them for geographic and strategical reasons, as he had frankly told Wilson earlier. At the same time, Balfour's concern for the balance of power and for British security did not lead him to seek unlimited imperial expansion. Instead he warned against excessive gains—'I am anxious to keep down the extension of the British Empire as much as possible.' He sought some compromise between security and expansion which could cause jealousy and hence insecurity. Above all, he was a firm proponent of close relations with the United States in questions of the war and of the future peace-making.

During the discussion, General Smuts challenged most directly Balfour's statement of policy. The South African gave a strikingly pessimistic analysis of the military situation which led him seriously to question Balfour's views about British peace policy on the continent. Claiming that Balfour's programme presupposed Germany's total defeat, Smuts contended that this assumption was false and that once the military tide began to run in favour of the Allies, they should not wait for absolute victory but should make peace once Germany conceded the 'essential terms' of the Allies. While he did not precisely define essential terms, he made clear his view of certain of the non-essentials. He would not continue the war to secure a free Poland. The dissolution of the Dual Monarchy would not necessarily benefit the world. He was 'almost inclined' to put the question of Austria-Hungary, the Tyrol, and Dalmatia on the doubtful list and advised his colleagues not to take the stand that the British Empire would support the French and Italian claims to the end. The Empire should be prepared to take the initiative in securing a revision of their claims. In proposing the hastening of peace through French and Italian concessions, Smuts made no suggestion as to what he and his colleagues should give up, but certainly German South-West Africa was not likely to be expendable.

None of his colleagues, openly at least, shared his pessimism about the military situation, but they did not necessarily adopt a diametrically opposed position on European questions.

While Curzon 'viewed with very great alarm' the proposal made by Balfour that Constantinople be assigned to Bulgaria, he otherwise questioned the practical value of discussing peace policy in Europe at that time. In his view, it was not for them to lay down European war aims. 'All we can do is to indicate a general view of the way we should like things to develop.' It was for France to decide whether to abandon its claims to Alsace-Lorraine. In backing Balfour on this issue and in showing a stronger feeling than Smuts for solidarity with Britain's allies, France and Italy, Curzon at the same time shared Smuts' attitude towards Poland. 'For my part,' he said, 'I happen to disagree with the pronouncement made at Paris about Poland. I think it will be found impossible to secure a single and undivided Poland with access to the sea, and I do not believe our people would go on fighting for that if that were definitely laid down as a war aim for which we must persist in fighting until we secure [it].'

Barnes agreed that Balfour's programme was too ambitious. The recovery for France of Alsace-Lorraine was an objective for which the British public would fight on, but he doubted that British opinion would support an undue prolongation of the war to secure an independent Poland with access to the sea, to free the Slavs from oppression, or to enforce the Treaty of London. He blamed Wilson and Asquith for having 'committed us up to the hilt about Poland . . .'. To gain stronger public support for allied war aims, Barnes suggested that an Inter-Allied Conference be held to revise war aims: that is, the war aims of Italy and possibly other allies; Barnes had no modifications to suggest in imperial war aims.

Austen Chamberlain thought they only needed to consider a reasonable peace from their point of view. As for aims in Europe, he agreed with Balfour and Curzon that they could do no more than to express certain aspirations about the postwar reconstruction of the map of Europe. He supported Balfour and Curzon against Smuts and Barnes as far as revision of French and Italian war aims was concerned. 'I think it would be fatal if we were to seek to revise their war aims at this stage.'

Lloyd George closed the debate with a resounding declaration of faith in the Allies' ability to defeat Germany severely enough to dictate the terms of peace. Like Curzon and Chamberlain, the Prime Minister opposed Barnes' suggestion for an Inter-Allied Conference to revise war aims.[1] In his estimation, such a conference would only serve to increase the Allies' price for peace, a prize which had already been moderately stated by him and Wilson in January 1918.

The striking aspect of Lloyd George's remarks was his appeal for a punitive peace. His argument was that Germany had committed a crime against humanity. A repetition of such an offense must be made impossible, first, by demonstrating that any aggressor would be faced by an overwhelming preponderance of power and secondly, by imposing a punitive peace upon the vanquished. About the latter, the Prime Minister declared with obvious passion:

> When you come to impose terms . . . they must be terms which will be tantamount to a penalty for the offence. You have . . . to deal with nations as with individuals in that respect. You must say to a nation which offends: Your punishment is assured; you will not succeed; and your punishment will be a severe one, and when any

[1] A cogent reason against the summoning of an Inter-Allied Conference to revise war aims was bluntly put by Hughes: such a conference involving Woodrow Wilson would seriously embarrass the Imperial War Cabinet!

> nation gets tempted in future to attempt an operation of the same kind, their statesmen will say: Well, see what happened to Germany when they attempted the same thing 20, or 50 or 100 years ago.

Later, Lloyd George voiced the conviction that a dictated, punitive peace for Germany could be 'the only basis of any League of Nations'.

Lloyd George's peace strategy contrasted impressively with that of General Smuts. The latter sought a compromise peace resting upon a relatively equal balance of military power between Germany and the Allies and depending upon an economic alliance to restrain Germany in the postwar world; the former advocated a punitive, imposed peace based upon Allied military supremacy over Germany and restraining Germany by an overwhelming preponderance of power which would give its opponents the strength to inflict dire punishment upon the aggressor.

There was a contrast also between Lloyd George's view and President Wilson's, although not as sharp an antithesis as might be imagined at first thought. Wilson had pronounced against a vindictive peace and against punitive indemnities. In his address to Congress, December 4, 1917, he had claimed to hear the voices of humanity insisting 'that the war shall not end in vindictive action of any kind; that no nation or people shall be robbed or punished because the irresponsible rulers of a single country have themselves done deep and abominable wrong. It is this thought that has been expressed in the Formula "No annexations, no contributions, no punitive indemnities".'[1] Yet the President's views, repeatedly stated, had much in common with Lloyd George's stern utterances in the Imperial War Cabinet. Both rejected a compromise peace and settlement; each wanted an undoubted victory. Both spoke of basing peace upon a preponderance of power in the hands of the peaceful states to uphold the rule of law against aggressors. Wilson spoke frequently of justice—justice, which can be stern and punitive as well as impartial and gentle—and Wilson's concept of justice seemed to comprise these varied elements. His concept could be close to Lloyd George's thought that criminals must sometimes be deterred from further trans-

[1] Baker and Dodd, *Wilson Papers*, I, p. 131.

gression through the just imposition of severe punishment. The genesis of the dictated peace can be found in both Wilson's and Lloyd George's thoughts before the Armistice.

Of critical importance was the nature of the punishment which Lloyd George had in mind. His remarks about the reconstruction of Europe threw only a dim light on what he envisaged. In reply to Hughes' anxious query about what could be done to prevent Russia and the smaller nations from becoming German vassals, Lloyd George foresaw the re-creation of Russia and the federation with Russia of the border states. Here he was expressing the hope that the European balance of power could be constructed in part upon a revived Russian power.

What role would Poland play? Lloyd George seemed vague, but his involved remarks appeared to constitute a warning to his colleagues who had shown little enthusiasm about the reconstruction of Poland. He thought that Balfour had been too sanguine about Polish possibilities, but he continued:

> I am very much afraid that, with regard to Poland, you could not draw the line between aspirations and war aims. I do not believe you can, because each of these nations thinks naturally about its own branch of the business, and they say: Here these Powers have given a particlar [*sic*] pledge; they regard it as a pledge, and yet Poland has been sold so often. She was sold by Napoleon, who talked very much the same as we are apt to talk about her. I am very much afraid of the same thing happening here. The U.S.A. has been keen about that. There are millions of Poles there, with consequently a very large number of votes, and I do not think this was in their point of view a great war aim so much as it was a great electioneering aim. I am afraid that if we cannot achieve that in the end, Poland will say: Here we have been sold again. If we defeat Germany completely, it is quite within the realms of possibility that you can achieve your aim, and in that case Poland, as a Buffer State, will be very useful.

What was the Prime Minister saying? He was blaming American internal politics for the Allied pledge to restore Poland, an objective which he feared might not be realizable short of a decisive military victory over Germany. In that contingency, it might be possible to re-establish Poland which would have strategic value as a buffer state, presumably between

Germany and Russia. In sum, he seemed to join with Smuts, Curzon, Barnes, and others who were not prepared to prolong the war to redeem Poland. On the other hand, in favouring the restoration of Poland for its strategic value in case of victory, he seemed to align himself against the complete sceptics like Smuts who had pictured the Poles as more incapable than the Irish of governing themselves and as likely to fall victim to any great military power.

To sum up, there was disagreement about the proper attitude to be adopted towards revision of French and Italian claims. In general, opinion seemed weighted on the side of Balfour's position. The Polish question entered into every speech. No member forthrightly opposed the restoration of an independent Poland, but not many around the council table warmly regarded Poland and the Poles. In terms of the war, this could mean that Poland was expendable; in terms of a peace conference, this could mean restraint in handling Polish claims against their neighbours. Balfour's colleagues had little to say on the other European issues affecting the German territorial settlement. Smuts stood alone in questioning the wisdom of supporting the dissolution of the Dual Monarchy.

The government's general policy as outlined by the Foreign Secretary reflected the traditions of modern British foreign policy; opposition to single-power domination of the continent; maintenance of European peace through promoting a stable equilibrium on the continent; consequent freedom as far as Europe was concerned to protect imperial interests overseas. In expressing his concern about the balance of power on the continent, Balfour gloomily emphasized, as he had before, the potential strength of Germany in his last, pessimistic contribution to the debate. 'If all my war aims were carried out Germany would still remain the biggest military power in Europe by far—she has over 60 millions and with an increasing population, in addition to the Austrians.'

How could a counterpoise be devised to keep this giant in check? The dissolution of the Dual Monarchy and of the Russian Empire faced advocates of a European settlement based upon an equilibrium of power with a virtually insoluble problem in the uncertain situation of 1918. Poland was envisaged as a stabilizer in eastern Europe, but the Cabinet had little faith in this solution. Another solution was to reconstitute Russian power. Balfour, specifically supported by Lloyd George, had suggested the re-establishment of Russia to which the border states would be linked federally. Probably the Cabinet were agreed on the desirability, if not the feasibility, of this objective. It was a solution favoured by the Chief of the Imperial General Staff, General Wilson, who during August submitted a paper to the Cabinet recommending:

> The re-constitution of Russia in some form as an armed and independent state, strong enough to withstand German infiltration and aggression is a vital British interest. If the war closes without this being accomplished the future of the British Empire will be seriously menaced, and we shall ultimately have to fight at the gravest disadvantage.[1]

The alternative was to depend upon American power to contribute towards the maintenance of a stable European equilibrium. In the circumstances, such a course appeared highly logical and obvious, but it was surrounded by difficulties. Woodrow Wilson did not appear to think in terms of the balance of power, strategic frontiers, and *realpolitik*. A price would have to be paid for his friendship and support. And the future course of America in world affairs was uncertain: over a century of isolationism had to be overcome.

As a basic objective of foreign policy, the Imperial War Cabinet on this occasion favoured the involvement of the United States in postwar world politics. As the discussion on colonial war aims demonstrated, the British and Dominion ministers were grappling with a threefold problem: (1) whether to limit imperial expansion, (2) relations with the United States and the future American role in world affairs, (3) the bearing of these questions upon the security of the British Empire. The Canadian Prime Minister, Sir Robert Borden, held that imperial security in the future would depend not on new strategic acquisitions so much as upon the 'co-operation and support of the U.S.A., with whom the closest and most intimate relations should be maintained'. He wanted a colonial policy which would aid in inducing the United States to abandon its traditional isolationism. Reading, Balfour, Austen

[1] Borden Papers, OC 628.

Chamberlain, Barnes, and Lloyd George, while not prepared to abandon vital and legitimate claims, gave strong support to this point of view. In their eyes, an active American role in world politics and economics could only be beneficial. But how to ensure this outcome? Some of the conquered Turkish or German territories could be used as pawns in negotiations with the United States; if America accepted responsibilities in the colonial areas, isolationism would be hard to maintain. Americans, too, would have a better appreciation of the imperial responsibilities of Great Britain. Also, if Wilson could be persuaded to take German East Africa, for example, it would be easier for the British Empire to acquire coveted areas.

Some members of the Cabinet found this prescription distasteful. Hughes was not prepared to cede New Guinea to win American friendship. Curzon hoped that Hughes would persist in his attitude, although he did not dispute the desirability of co-operation with the United States. Curzon was typical of those English statesmen who had a hard time accepting the thought of America's rising strength and of its potential importance to Great Britain. If they realized the need for good Anglo-American relations they found some American attitudes unpalatable and bridled at the idea of sharing the world with a newcomer. Britain's growing weakness since the 1890's and the rise of American power impelled co-operation but produced friction as well. The colonial side of the August debate revealed, from London's point of view, both of these elements.

If the discussion of continental affairs did not openly hinge upon the same problem, none the less the American factor in British foreign policy was not far below the surface of the debate. American participation in European affairs on balance was in Britain's interest if thereby the United States contributed to the stabilization of postwar Europe. European territorial questions provided one area of policy in which close relations with the United States could be fostered. It was true that Britain's commitments to allies like Italy caused embarrassment in London's relations with Washington. But by and large, especially on German territorial issues, close identity of outlook was both possible and desirable. British policy on these issues could play a constructive part in a strategy of inducing the United States to pursue an internationalist course in the postwar world.

III

THE ARMISTICE AND TERRITORIAL QUESTIONS

THE negotiations for a German Armistice posed several issues for the British government which bore upon the ultimate territorial settlement.[1] Should the terms of armistice provide for little more than a mere cessation of hostilities or should they instead place the Allied and Associated Powers in a position to enforce their will upon Germany? Should they go further, however, and write into the terms of armistice as far as possible final conditions of peace? The latter course of action was not unconnected with the difficulties created for the Allies by the German government's proposal for the political conditions of an armistice. Berlin's request confronted the British government with a third question—whether the armistice should depend upon the prior acceptance by the belligerents of the bases of the future peace negotiations. If so, as the German government proposed, were the general conditions of peace to be those set forth by Woodrow Wilson in his Fourteen Points' and subsequent addresses?

These and the other problems involved in arranging a German Armistice were first considered by the Allies at the Inter-Allied Conference in Paris of October 5 to 9, 1918.[2]

[1] Harry R. Rudin in *Armistice, 1918*, and Sir Frederick Maurice in *The Armistices of 1918* cover the negotiations as a whole.

[2] Lloyd George, *War Memoirs*, VI, p. 3274. It is possible that the Allied leaders had hastily gathered in Paris to discuss the German note itself because on October 4 the French Intelligence Service had deciphered the

Called ostensibly to deal with the Bulgarian and the Turkish armistices, the Allied statesmen, Lloyd George, Clemenceau, and Orlando, turned to consider the German government's message to Woodrow Wilson on October 6 announcing its acceptance of the President's programme as the basis for peace negotiations and requesting a general armistice at once. Although the President had not consulted them, the Allied Prime Ministers on October 7 asked their military representatives on the Supreme War Council at Versailles to examine terms of armistice embodying the following principles: the total evacuation by the enemy of France, Belgium, Luxembourg, and Italy; a German retirement behind the Rhine[1]; a retreat from the Caucasus; the abandonment of all prewar Russian and Rumanian territory; and the immediate cessation of submarine warfare.[2] In this programme, territory figured prominently. If Germany acceded to these demands, the Reich would have surrendered its wartime conquests in western Europe, left Alsace-Lorraine defenseless, accepted the Rhine at least temporarily as its military frontier in the west, and released its hold over *Mittel Europa*, thereby removing the German threat to Great Britain's position in the Middle East. Thus, before peace negotiations began, the Allied governments would secure a substantial portion of their war aims in Europe.

In reporting back to the politicians, the Military Representatives and Marshal Foch advanced different proposals.

[1] It was, perhaps, curious that they suggested no Allied occupation of Alsace-Lorraine. Probably this was a tactical move. The military situation seemed uncertain. They were anxious not to make it too difficult for Germany to accept an armistice. If the Allies refrained from occupying Alsace-Lorraine, Germany might accept more readily the principle of evacuation of the provinces.

[2] Lloyd George, *War Memoirs*, VI, p. 3275.

German text. If so, they could scarcely have revealed to Wilson and the world how they came to be in Paris on October 5. On this aspect of the conference see Rudin, *Armistice, 1918*, p. 89; Mordacq, *L'Armistice du 11 Novembre 1918*, p. 151; Mordacq, *La Vérité sur l'Armistice*, p. 68; Weygand 'Le Maréchal Foch et l'Armistice', *Revue des deux mondes*, novembre 1938, p. 8; Bliss, 'Report on the Supreme War Council,' U.S. Dept. of State, *Lansing Papers, 1914-1920*, II, p. 289. The American military representative on the Supreme War Council had his doubts about the origins of the Inter-Allied Conference in Paris when he wrote, whatever might have been the 'ostensible purpose of the meeting which so hastily assembled . . .'.

The Generalissimo recommended demanding a German withdrawal within two weeks from Belgium, France, Alsace-Lorraine, and Luxembourg. But he wanted more: a German evacuation of the left bank of the Rhine within thirty days, followed by an Allied occupation and administration in concert with the local authorities 'up to the time of the signature of peace'; and, the establishment of two or three Allied bridgeheads across the Rhine with a radius of thirty kilometres. Allied occupation of the left bank was justified as a security for the payment of reparations, and the bridgeheads as a necessary military base from which to destroy the enemy's forces if the peace talks broke down.[1] These and other armistice terms proposed by Foch were described by Bonar Law as a demand for virtually unconditional German surrender.[2]

While Foch went beyond the Military Representatives in demanding bridgeheads across the Rhine, the Military Representatives outdid Foch in pressing for disarmament of the German armies.[3] They agreed with the Generalissimo that the Germans should retire across the Rhine because a mere, unhurried evacuation of conquered territories would enable the Germans to shorten their lines and to reorganize their armies, thus placing themselves in a better position to renew hostilities. Instead, the armistice should render the German forces *hors de combat* and guarantee an Allied military superiority over them.

This advice had a direct bearing on Wilson's note of October 8 to the German government which stipulated that in addition to acceptance of his peace terms, the Central Powers must withdraw at once from all invaded territory in order to secure an armistice.[4] In making this demand, the President was asking for less than the minimum demands of the statesmen and military advisors at Paris. With Lloyd George taking the lead, the Allied Prime Ministers warned Wilson about the dangers of seeking only the evacuation of occupied territories and urged him to allow the military authorities to advise on armistice conditions. Simultaneously they asked the President to co-operate more

[1] Foch, *Mémoires*, II, pp. 270-2.
[2] Lloyd George, *War Memoirs*, VI, p. 3278.
[3] *Lansing Papers*, II, pp. 291-2.
[4] *Foreign Relations*, 1918, supplement 1, vol. I, p. 343.

closely politically with his co-belligerents in the armistice negotiations.[1]

The military authorities expected that, once an armistice took effect, hostilities were unlikely to be renewed. The Allies, therefore, should take advantage of this probability immediately by securing a close approximation between armistice and peace terms. Undoubtedly the politicians had this consideration in mind as well. Their insistence upon the evacuation of occupied territories and of Alsace-Lorraine foreshadowed a peace treaty under which Germany would renounce its political and territorial ambitions in Europe and cede territory to the victors. Likewise, the disarmament proposals of the Military and Naval Representatives were intimately linked with their concepts of the final military and naval terms of peace. In the sense that intentions were partially revealed, the armistice provisions considered at the Inter-Allied Conference approximated ultimate conditions of peace.

Of course, the Conference dealt with the questions involved in an armistice in a preliminary fashion only. The principles and the details of a cease-fire had still to be hammered out among the Allied and Associated Powers and between them and the enemy. In this process, two important difficulties stood in the way of a close approximation between armistice and peace terms. One was the question of what conditions the Germans could be induced to accept. To ask too much would be tragic; to ask too little, lamentable. A more fundamental obstacle, however, was the absence of agreement among the Allied and Associated Powers over the conditions of peace with Germany. They would run serious risks if the armistice negotiations were delayed until prior agreement had been reached over the conditions of peace. The opportunity to end the war on favourable terms might be let slip if they temporized. And the effort to reach a common understanding on peace policy could produce dissension within the anti-German coalition, leading perhaps to its break-up while hostilities continued.

Indeed, the German proposal that the peace programme of Woodrow Wilson constitute the bases of peace negotiations imposed a heavy strain upon the unity of the Allied and

[1] Lloyd George, *War Memoirs*, VI, pp. 3280-2.

Associated Powers. This was foreshadowed at the Inter-Allied Conference at Paris. While Clemenceau's initial reaction to the Fourteen Points' proposal was not unfavourable, Lloyd George was reserved, even hostile in one respect. The British Prime Minister emphasized the vagueness of the President's statements. Perhaps to alarm Clemenceau, he pointed out that Wilson had not clearly committed himself to support the return of Alsace-Lorraine to France. And already Lloyd George's attitude towards Point Two on the freedom of the seas was uncompromising.[1] No decision, however, was taken by the Allies at this time regarding the Fourteen Points.

During the tense period between October 9 and October 23 when Woodrow Wilson finally brought his co-belligerents into the armistice negotiations with Germany, the British government insisted that the armistice provisions should be delineated, not by Wilson but by the military and naval advisors of the principal Allied and Associated Powers and that the terms should enable the victors to enforce the ultimate peace. Various proposals for writing final British terms of peace into the armistice were also advanced. As for the Fourteen Points, whether or not the British government sought to avoid their acceptance as the political precondition of an armistice, at least London sought clarifications and modifications which would give to British negotiators at the Peace Conference the fullest possible freedom of manœuvre.

On October 11, the Imperial War Cabinet heard the Prime Minister's report that the military authorities at Versailles sought stiff military and naval terms and a close approximation of armistice to peace terms. No objections were raised. Indeed the latter proposition was strongly supported by Hughes of Australia.[2] Later that day, after the Prime Minister had conferred with his military and naval advisors, the government decided to warn Woodrow Wilson about the necessity of rendering Germany unable to renew the struggle.

This advice reached the President about the same time as a clever response from the German government which assumed or pretended to assume that the sole conditions for an armistice were the Fourteen Points and the principle of evacuation with-

[1] *Ibid.*, pp. 3280-3.

[2] Imperial War Cabinet No. 35, October 11, 1918, Borden Papers.

out commitment to detail.[1] In London, in the other Allied capitals, and in the United States itself, there was fear that if Woodrow Wilson was not firm and cautious the Allied and Associated Powers might be committed to a weak and unsatisfactory armistice with Germany.

Woodrow Wilson's peace programme also aroused anxiety in London. The Policy Committee of Northcliffe's War Mission in America pointed out that Wilson's pronouncements were not a full definition of peace conditions since they had been outrun by events. The Committee also urged that Germany should accept certain principles as indisputable, reserving for negotiation only such details as the Allied and Associated Powers considered open for discussion.[2] On October 12, the incomplete and uncertain character of Wilson's programme was also underlined by the Political Intelligence Department of the Foreign Office.[3] Alsace-Lorraine was given as an example of apparent contradictions in Wilson's pronouncements. The Fourteen Points called for unconditional surrender; a later speech declared that 'peoples and provinces are not to be bartered about from sovereignty to sovereignty'. The P.I.D. interpreted this to mean that the peoples of Alsace-Lorraine must be consulted about their future status. Thus, both memoranda raised the question of the meaning of the President's programme and of its adequacy as a basis for diplomatic negotiation.

But more than issues of definition were involved in the reaction in London as Henry Wilson revealed to Haig:

> The question of peace terms is, of course, another and separate matter, and will be considered by the Prime Ministers if and after an armistice is agreed to. A certain amount of complication and difficulty exists at this moment because we do not agree to several of President Wilson's 14 points, and because, owing to the irregular way in which he is conducting conversations with the enemy, there is a real danger of the Germans claiming that the 14 points are the definition of an armistice. . . .[4]

[1] *Foreign Relations*, 1918, supplement 1, vol. I, pp. 357-8.

[2] Lloyd George, *War Memoirs*, VI, p. 3285.

[3] Political Intelligence Department, Foreign Office General/002, October 12, 1918, 'Memorandum on President Wilson's Speeches as a basis of Negotiations', Wiseman Papers, 90/86.

[4] Robert Blake (ed.), *The Private Papers of Douglas Haig, 1914-1919*, pp. 331-2.

In his diary, on October 13, Sir Henry Wilson noted that the British War Cabinet had agreed '. . . we would wire (Woodrow Wilson) to say that he must make it clear to the Boche that his fourteen points (with which we do not agree) were not a basis for an armistice, which is what the Boche pretend they are'.[1]

Several points emerge clearly from Henry Wilson's observations. British officialdom feared that the Allies might be manœuvred into accepting the Fourteen Points as the terms of an armistice, which could be highly dangerous and unsatisfactory from both a naval and military point of view. Secondly, there was opposition in London to some items of the President's peace programme. Henry Wilson himself believed that the whole subject of peace terms was a matter for consideration after an armistice had been arranged. In the latter respect, he may have been reflecting the preference of the civil authorities who, however, decided not to meet Woodrow Wilson head on over the issue of political conditions for an armistice. Instead they would ask the President simply to 'make it clear to the Boche that his fourteen points (with which we do not agree) were not a basis for an armistice . . .'.

Following the British War Cabinet's decisions of October 13, Balfour sent telegrams to Wilson urging him clearly to inform the German government that an armistice could be accepted only on terms rendering 'any resumption of hostilities by the Central Powers impossible'.[2] As for the Fourteen Points, Balfour's message did not constitute a rejection of them but did indicate firmly the British government's unwillingness to accept the President's programme without amendment. Balfour also frankly declared his government's wish to have as free a hand as possible at the Peace Conference. This may have been the way chosen to hint that the War Cabinet preferred to arrange an armistice without prior agreement among the belligerents on the bases of peace negotiations. If this was the point, it may have been left purposely vague in order to test Wilson's reaction. No doubt could exist, however, that the British government wished an exchange of views on peace terms if the Fourteen Points were to constitute the political preconditions for an armistice.

[1] Callwell, *Sir Henry Wilson*, II, p. 136.

[2] Baker, *Woodrow Wilson, Life and Letters*, VIII, pp. 478-9.

Wilson, heeding the advice from London, told the German government on October 14 that the terms of an armistice, including the provisions for the evacuation of territory, must be left to the judgment of the Allied military advisors and affirmed that his government repudiated any arrangement which did not provide absolutely satisfactory safeguards and guarantees for the maintenance of the existing military supremacy of the Allied and American armies.[1] In associating the Allied governments with these views, the stipulations were worded less strongly than in Balfour's message of October 13.

The President's views on these issues were clarified in conversations between him and Sir Eric Geddes on October 14[2] and Sir William Wiseman around October 16.[3] Geddes reported to Lloyd George that the President was becoming more cautious in his attitude towards the Germans. Yet, while Woodrow Wilson agreed that the armistice terms should be drafted by the military and naval officers, and that the enemy must be kept from exploiting the armistice, he felt it would be inexcusable unduly to humiliate the Germans. In his talk with Sir William Wiseman, the President made substantially the same points and stressed that if the German people were humiliated, 'we shall destroy all form of government, and Bolshevism will take its place. We ought not to ground [*sic*] them to powder or there will be nothing to build up from.' Wilson expected that the statesmen would have to modify the terms proposed by the naval and military experts. In this respect, he was beset by the same doubts and hesitations as those which were plaguing Lloyd George, Balfour and other civilian leaders.

Both Geddes and Wiseman probed the President's thoughts on the meaning of the Fourteen Points. Geddes concluded that Woodrow Wilson had no settled views on freedom of seas but that he recognized the inadequacy of the Twelfth Point since Allied commitments to the subject nationalities made the dissolution of the Dual Monarchy inevitable. In his talk with Wiseman, Wilson, referring to the necessary modifications of

[1] *Foreign Relations*, 1918, supplement 1, vol. I, pp. 358-9.

[2] Lloyd George, *War Memoirs*, VI, p. 3290.

[3] Sir William Wiseman, 'Notes of an Interview with the President at the White House, Wednesday, October 16, 1918', House Papers, 35/90. I am assuming that this report or its substance reached London.

Point Ten, pledged his 'support to the full' for the just claims of the Czechs and others. Speaking of Alsace-Lorraine, he said that Germany must return the provinces, *neither more nor less*, to France. This statement made clear his interpretation of the Fourteen Points on this issue while implying at the same time opposition to broader French aspirations in western Europe. Obviously, the two men did not thoroughly canvass the problems of a German territorial settlement. They dwelled on subjects which loomed larger in their thoughts at that time: the meaning of Point One, Freedom of the Seas, the German Colonial question, etc. But generally on territorial issues Wilson was optimistic about the chances of basing boundary adjustments upon the principle of national self-determination. As he told Wiseman: 'He had, however, seen the maps and the arguments prepared by his advisors, and thought that it was quite possible to arrive at a fair and lasting settlement on the basis of self-determination.'

While Wilson voiced his optimism about the possibility of reconstructing Europe upon the foundation of national self-determination, Balfour in London was preparing several papers stressing the difficulties involved in applying the principle.

The first paper was a general commentary on European readjustments. Balfour's argument ran as follows. Assuming the complete defeat of the enemy, the problem of territorial reconstruction upon the basis of the principle of nationality or the principle of self-determination seemed simple enough.

> Unfortunately it is not so, partly because these principles do not completely harmonize with each other; partly because outside Europe they have at the best but a qualified application; partly because in practice they are traversed by other considerations, historical, political, and strategic which cannot be wholly ignored. We cannot therefore follow out either of these with logical exactness to its extremest conclusion.

The frontiers in central and eastern Europe could not be redrawn without amendment or qualification simply upon the basis of the latest ethnographical data.

> The sentiment of nationality depends on many things besides race; and self-determination in its full and enduring significance cannot be safely measured by the results of a single plebiscite. The vote of

> a community, or of a selected fraction of a community, will show (if it be fairly taken) which of a small number of simple alternatives it prefers. But such a vote, considered by itself, supplies no sufficient evidence of those leading sentiments on which alone stable States are founded.

Balfour concluded that the principle of nationality and the principle of self-determination would have to be applied cautiously. But they would be the principal guide: 'They may not be complete or infallible, but cause must be shown why in any particular case they should be ignored.'[1]

Balfour offered Alsace-Lorraine as an example of the difficulties surrounding the simple application of the principles of nationality and of self-determination. He would not risk a vote to secure the return of the provinces to France! In his opinion it was doubtful whether 'Self-determination in the shape of a plebiscite would give a clear majority for re-union with France; the appeal to history can be made, and is made, by both parties; no argument can be founded on race, and the argument from language is double-edged.' How then, Balfour asked, can we justify our policy of returning Alsace-Lorraine to France? His reply was:

> Only, I suppose on the grounds that the arrangement of 1871 constituted a violent interruption of a beneficent process of development, that it was made avowedly in the interests of militarism and had no reference whatever to the wishes or traditions of the populations concerned. In such circumstances it is not only legitimate but necessary to restore continuity with a still living past, and thus re-knit the severed threads of history. We have to remember that the voters, in a given plebiscite, are

[1] 'Introductory Note on European Re-adjustments', A.J.B., October 1918, Foster Papers.

Balfour did not explain his idea of the difference between the two principles. The difference appears clear enough although they are not necessarily incompatible. By the principle of nationality, boundaries would be drawn according to the ethnographic character of the peoples involved. By the principle of self-determination, a people in any given territory should have the right to decide for themselves to which state they should belong. The possible conflict between the two can be seen in the case of Switzerland, where a strict application of the principle of nationality would destroy its unity. Instead, the different ethnic groups in Switzerland have chosen to live together in a single state.

> not infallible judges of the essential spirit of a people, or the character of their enduring ideals. Some good judges tell me that I am wrong to doubt the results of a plebiscite—that if a brief period (say, six months) were given before a vote was taken, so that the ancient dwellers in those Provinces could return—the verdict of the voters would be overwhelmingly French. This may be so. But I would not risk it.[1]

Unlike Wilson, Balfour showed a distrust of the principle of self-determination and saw little help in the principle of nationality. In supporting the return of Alsace-Lorraine to France, he believed that the justification would have to rest upon historical and moral grounds and on the contention that the *demos* are sometimes incapable of determining their best interests and their national identity. It will be recalled that Balfour supported the return of the two provinces to France to improve the equilibrium of Europe.[2]

The second case discussed by the Foreign Secretary was the German-Polish frontier.[3] In his view, the simplest plan would be to create a Polish state out of the areas where a Polish majority existed but this would exclude areas which the Poles desired for historic and social reasons and include areas which would be extremely hard to wrest from Germany.

He gave Galicia as an example of the difficulty of excluding non-Polish areas from Poland. Over the last six hundred years, Poland had embraced a large area in which the Poles formed a small minority. If these historic connections had left only memories, it would matter little. But in eastern Galicia (and in parts of Lithuania) the Poles comprised the wealthiest and the most educated classes. Balfour took the stand: '. . . This fact ought not to modify our policy at the Peace Conference . . .', but he warned that to divide Galicia would greatly pain many Polish nationalists.

He thought that the problem of including within Poland genuinely Polish areas was far greater.

> If this last operation were completely effected, East Prussia would be divided by a tongue of Polish land from Prussian Pomerania.

1 'Alsace-Lorraine', A.J.B., October 18, 1918, Foster Papers.

2 See p. 18 above.

3 'Poland', A.J.B., October 18, 1918; 'The Baltic Provinces', Foster Papers.

> Germany would be deprived of the Silesian coal-fields—a district of the utmost value to Germany, though ethnographically Polish from time immemorial—and the eastern frontier of Germany would be drawn fifty miles west of its present position, and not more than, I suppose, seventy miles from Berlin. Evidently, nothing but a crushing defeat can tear these territories. . . from Germany's grasp.

Turning to the problem of honouring the British government's promise to support Polish access to the sea, he defined the problem thus: 'Are we, then, to give Poland access to the sea through a city which is predominantly German, and which, as I have already explained, cannot be transferred to Poland without cutting off the German districts of East Prussia from direct access to the rest of Germany? I am myself inclined to answer this question in the negative. . . .' As in August 1918, the British Foreign Secretary favoured redeeming the pledge by giving Poland free transit rights along the Vistula. He now added the further suggestion that Danzig might be made a free port, thus foreshadowing part of the ultimate solution at the Paris Peace Conference.

His final conclusion was that at the Peace Conference the British government should 'try for' a strictly ethnical boundary between Germany and Poland 'except that, in addition to the city of Danzig a strip of territory should be reserved to Germany, giving a land connection between East and West Prussia'.

Balfour's memorandum on Poland is so clear that it requires no extended comment. The British Foreign Secretary still adhered to his 'Little Poland' policy, as his attitude towards Lithuania further emphasized. In Russia's former Baltic Provinces, Balfour preferred the establishment of three small national states along strictly ethnical lines. Instead of a Polish-Lithuanian union, he favoured encouraging Lithuania to federate in the future with Latvia, Esthonia, Finland, and some or all of the Scandinavian states. Balfour's views on Poland placed him in opposition to the claims of the Polish National Committee and its supporters. While Balfour was giving his advice, Dmowski was in Washington advancing Polish claims to Danzig, to a Polish land corridor to the sea, and to Upper Silesia.[1] It is equally apparent that Balfour was greatly worried

[1] Gerson, *Woodrow Wilson and the Rebirth of Poland*, p. 98.

about the conflict between Polish and German claims in the eastern borderlands and that he was seeking a solution which would reduce the friction to a minimum. While in the light of this concern he was prepared to recommend a strictly ethnographical frontier, he felt uneasy about the German attitude toward the economic and strategical losses involved in the cession of Posen and Upper Silesia, and recognized that only a weak and defeated Germany would accept such a retreat in eastern Europe. We can detect between the lines of his Polish memorandum his oft-repeated warning that Germany would remain strong after the war despite the worst its enemies were likely to do to it. Hence his search for a settlement which would be as freely acceptable to Germany as possible to hedge against the day when German power would revive in Europe.

The frontier of Bohemia was the third case discussed by Balfour.[1] After pointing out that along much of the northern and western frontiers of Bohemia nature and history joined in drawing a frontier which did not correspond with ethnic distribution, he wrote:

> It seems, and perhaps is, absurd to redraw the Bohemian frontier so as to leave in German hands the whole mountain chain which guards the country from invasion. Yet if this be not done there will be in the new Czecho-Slovak State a German element amounting to not less than one-quarter of the whole population, compactly situated, bitterly hostile to their Slav neighbours, and in sympathy with the Saxons, Bavarians, and German-Austrians dwelling beyond their border, and with the German capitalists and Germanized nobles within them.

Balfour's attitude towards Czech claims appeared distinctly reserved. While he made no firm recommendations regarding the frontiers of Bohemia, on balance he appeared to favour a frontier drawn closer to ethnological than to national and historical lines. In other words, he suggested that Czechoslovakia would be stronger and eastern Europe more stable if the Sudeten Germans were allowed to live within Germany and German Austria.[2]

[1] 'Czechoslovaks', A.J.B., October 18, 1918, Foster Papers.

[2] Balfour may have prepared other papers at this time on other aspects of the German territorial settlement. If so, they are not in the Borden or the Foster Papers.

Clearly Balfour did not regard the principle of nationality and the principle of self-determination as sacrosanct. Still, he did not reject them, but willingly or not, accorded each a certain priority: they should not be departed from without good reason. In two of the three cases which he discussed, Balfour favoured or inclined towards frontiers drawn primarily along ethnic lines.

On the practical question of where disputed frontiers should actually be drawn, Balfour was not far from Wilson's position at the time. They were agreed, for instance, on Alsace-Lorraine and were probably very close on the question of Polish frontiers, but they reached common positions on specific issues for different reasons. Wilson was an heir of Mazzini and other nineteenth-century liberal-democratic nationalists. He believed as they had that peace and stability could, in the last analysis, only rest upon international reconstruction along nationalist lines. To Balfour, peace and stability depended upon more than the principles of nationality and self-determination. His approach was pragmatic, not doctrinaire. Each case should be decided on its merits. If the stability of western Europe and French security depended on weakening German power by the loss of Alsace-Lorraine, this transfer should occur even though it might run contrary to sentiments of nationality. This is not to say that Balfour failed to recognize the threat to peace and stability inherent in nationalist rivalries. To reduce them and especially to satisfy the stronger, he would strictly apply the principle of nationality in the German-Polish settlement.[1]

Taking a different tack, General Smuts not only advised a moderate peace along the lines of the Fourteen Points, negotiated while the fighting continued, but he also warned that the proposed reconstruction of central Europe along nationalist lines was likely to lead to 'a wild war-dance of the so-called free nations in the future . . .' which no League of Nations could control. He feared the consequences of the disintegration of the Dual Monarchy. 'With the creation of an "independent" Poland, there will be a chain of these discordant fragments right across Europe from Finland in the north to Turkey in the south.' Smuts looked rather nostalgically back to the 'bad, but

[1] In October 1918, Woodrow Wilson was not prepared to accept the full Polish claims. Gerson, *Woodrow Wilson and the Rebirth of Poland*, pp. 98-9.

more or less orderly, political pre-War system of Europe . . .'.[1]

What reactions were to his dire prophecies and to Balfour's advice, remains uncertain. Little more than hearsay evidence exists about the proceedings of the British War Cabinet between October 10 and 25. Curzon indeed complained privately about a failure to hold proper War Cabinets over this period, leaving certain members in semi-darkness yet still responsible for decisions taken in their name.[2] Nor can much be said about the British ministers' reaction to the entire substance of the Wilsonian peace programme.[3] Over this fifteen-day period, the opinions of the moderates—Lloyd George, Balfour, Milner, Austen Chamberlain—generally prevailed. They neither accepted nor rejected the totality of Wilson's programme. There were important areas of agreement, particularly in principle, on such questions as the League of Nations, Poland, Alsace-Lorraine, the disintegration of Austria-Hungary, and the general principle of reconstructing Europe upon the basis of nationality and national self-determination. There was disagreement, particularly over the Colonial Question and over freedom of the seas. 'Freedom of the Seas'—'Go to Jericho!' Such was Austen Chamberlain's succinct statement of the British position on Point Two. The War Cabinet also sought a clarification of other aspects of the Fourteen Points. It wanted Germany to understand that the term 'restoration' included

[1] Lloyd George, *War Memoirs*, VI, pp. 3306-8.

[2] Curzon to Austen Chamberlain, 15 October 1918; 23 October 1918. Austen Chamberlain Papers.

[3] If Sir Henry Wilson was a reliable reporter, the War Cabinet agreed on October 25 to notify all capitals that it could not accept all of Wilson's Fourteen Points and speeches and wished to supplement them with other points. At the same meeting, ministerial opinions differed over the type of peace settlement desired: 'Austen wants a good peace, i.e. rather easy terms. Bonar Law the same. Curzon rather stiffer, Lloyd George undecided. Smuts has written a paper (which I have not seen) agreeing apparently to any terms. . . .' Callwell, *Sir Henry Wilson*, II, p. 143. Sir William Wiseman painted for House's edification a far more dramatic picture: the War Cabinet had been holding stormy sessions over the President's peace terms. The Colonel appropriately noted in his diary, 'they rebel against the "freedom of the seas" and wish to include reparations for losses at sea'. It would be a mistake to draw hasty or definite conclusions from such evidence about the efforts of the British ministers to determine their policy towards the Fourteen Points.

reparations for damages to civilians. Its members were sceptical about open diplomacy and wanted to know more exactly what the President meant in Point Three.

Meantime, the statesmen were receiving a variety of advice from the military and naval authorities. At the one extreme, there stood Generals Pershing and Bliss[1] who favoured the unconditional surrender of Germany and a dictated, not a negotiated peace. At the other extreme, there stood Sir Douglas Haig, the commander-in-chief of the British army on the Western Front. During mid-October Haig was advising minimum armistice terms for Germany. As he explained on October 19 in a meeting with Lloyd George, Bonar Law, Lord Milner, Balfour, Wemyss, and Henry Wilson,[2] it would be militarily adequate if the Germans were obliged to evacuate their forces to the German side of the frontier of 1870 and accept an Allied occupation of Alsace-Lorraine. He guessed that the Germans were not likely to accept the stronger terms being advanced by Henry Wilson and Foch. At this meeting, Henry Wilson, revealing clearly the divisions of opinion on armistice terms among British military leaders, criticized Haig's terms as insufficient. According to a note in his diary, he contended

> . . . the allies would have no real asset with which to enforce all the terms which they thought absolutely essential to peace, i.e. Poland, Yugoslavia, indemnities for Belgium, Rumania, Italy, etc. . . . unless we held real guarantees, i.e. occupation of Boche territory, we would never be able to enforce terms which would give us a durable peace.

[1] Pershing, *My Experiences in the World War*, pp. 673 *et seq.* He preferred unconditional surrender, but if the Allied governments decided on an armistice, he advised an armistice rigid enough to prevent a German renewal of hostilities. For Bliss's views, see his report in *Lansing Papers*, II, pp. 293 *et seq.*

[2] Callwell, *Sir Henry Wilson*, II, p. 138. Haig noted in his diary about this meeting: '. . . I therefore advise that we only ask in the armistice for what we intend to hold, and that we set our face firmly against the French entering Germany to pay off old scores. In my opinion, under the supposed conditions, the British Army would not fight keenly for what is really not its own affair. Mr. Balfour spoke about deserting the Poles and the people of Eastern Europe, but the Prime Minister gave the opinion that we cannot expect the British to go on sacrificing their lives for the Poles.' Duff Cooper, *Haig*, II, p. 397.

If the Chief of the Imperial General Staff was a reliable reporter, Balfour and Bonar Law tended to agree with him while Lloyd George and Milner inclined towards Haig's point of view. Unable to reach a decision, they agreed to postpone further discussions until October 21.[1]

On October 20, Balfour defended Henry Wilson's stand in a memorandum on additional provisions for the armistice. German territory, so he argued, should be occupied beyond the areas, like Alsace-Lorraine, which they intended to sever from the Reich, to provide pledges for the payment of reparations and for the settlement of the eastern frontier.[2] Next day the British War Cabinet accepted this advice.

During the meeting of the War Cabinet on October 21, the German reply[3] to Wilson's note of October 14 reached 10 Downing Street. The ministers generally felt that the German countermove was 'quite adroit' in taking advantage of one sentence in Wilson's first note to take for granted that only occupied territories would be evacuated, thus excluding Alsace-Lorraine. According to Austen Chamberlain, Woodrow Wilson had 'muddled things dreadfully' with the effect of 'weakening the "will to victory" among the Allied troops and peoples'.[4] Once again, the War Cabinet instructed Balfour to warn Woodrow Wilson[5] that the Germans plainly intended to obtain a conditional armistice. The German reply had said nothing about naval terms and assumed that an 'undisturbed retreat . . . to their own frontier' had been accepted in principle. British experts were convinced that such a policy would give the German army time to establish a much better line. Balfour urged that the armistice contain securities against any resump-

[1] *Ibid.*, II, p. 138.

[2] Lloyd George, *War Memoirs*, VI, p. 3305. Lloyd George does not say whether Balfour went into the details of his proposal. Lord Curzon, on October 15, had urged in a memorandum for the Cabinet that the armistice should contain a summary of the main items of British peace terms, including the surrender of the German war and mercantile fleet; provisions for compensations, reparations, and indemnities; and provisions for the trial of leading war criminals. Evidently, Curzon made no specific reference to German territorial questions, except to mention the necessity of securing the surrender of Heligoland. *Ibid.*, VI, p. 3291.

[3] *Foreign Relations*, 1918, supplement 1, vol. I, pp. 380-1.

[4] Austen Chamberlain to his wife, October 21, 1918.

[5] Callwell, *Sir Henry Wilson*, II, pp. 139-40.

tion of hostilities by the enemy in case peace negotiations should break down and against German violations of the final peace treaty. His note urgently requested Wilson to avoid committing himself on these vital questions without first consulting the Allies.[1]

The President may have been somewhat irked by the British government's unsolicited advice.[2] None the less, in his reply of October 23[3] to the latest German note, Wilson informed the German government that the only armistice which he would feel justified in submitting for the consideration of the Allied and Associated Powers would be one which would make impossible a renewal of hostilities on Germany's part and one which would 'fully protect the interests of the peoples involved and ensure to the Associated governments the unrestricted power to safeguard and enforce the details of the peace to which the German government had agreed'. Thus the substance of the British government's advice had been accepted by the President and communicated to the rulers of Germany.

Lloyd George, who around this time had described Woodrow Wilson as a 'mixture of old Bryce and Sir Arthur Yapp',[4] approved the tone of Wilson's note of October 23.[5] Cabinet opinion generally agreed, although General Smuts in papers circulated to the Cabinet on October 23 and 24 contended that the armistice proposals before them differed 'in no material respect from an unconditional surrender, which is not justified by the present relative military position of the belligerents . . . an armistice conference between the military leaders on these lines is, therefore, bound to prove abortive . . .'.[6] Accordingly, Smuts made the novel suggestion that there be no armistice at all but that instead they bargain on peace terms with Germany along the lines of the Fourteen Points and secure German acceptance while the war continued.

Smuts was one of the few, if not the only, member of the War Cabinet who believed in a negotiated peace with Germany. He

[1] Baker, *Woodrow Wilson, Life and Letters*, VIII, p. 501.
[2] *Ibid.*, VIII, p. 500.
[3] *Foreign Relations*, 1918, supplement 1, vol. I, p. 382.
[4] Austen Chamberlain to his wife, October 16, 1918.
[5] Lloyd George, *War Memoirs*, VI, p. 3305.
[6] *Ibid.*, pp. 3306-7.

saw clearly that prospects for a compromise and moderate peace settlement would be endangered by an armistice which gave the Allied and Associated Powers a position of overwhelming military strength. Woodrow Wilson was also aware of this hazard. Wise though Smuts and Wilson may have been, and Smuts was to be more consistent in this regard than Wilson, their type of moderation did not suit the occasion.

Perhaps Austen Chamberlain's reaction at this time was typical of the British ministers.[1] Resentful of Woodrow Wilson's failure to consult the Allies before October 23, he had little good to say about Wilson when the President did turn to them:

> . . . The President has at last consented to consult his Allies—none too soon—but characteristically he has made it very clear that he wishes the limelight man to keep the bullseye full on him and he wishes his Allies—I beg his pardon! 'the Associated Governments' to give him a testimonial of their unbounded admiration and gratitude which he may eye for electoral purposes. Meanwhile he has put us all in the cart and our first business is to get out and get him out. . . . He lays down fourteen points and two speeches as the basis of an armistice. The Germans accept and 'assume' the Entente Powers agree with him. How can we enter on negotiations without telling the Germans that 'they' assume too much. And how can we say that without putting the President's nose out of joint?

Although hopeful that Germany would accept their armistice terms, Austen Chamberlain feared that Woodrow Wilson's 'unskilful' correspondence with the German government had lessened the chances of peace at that time. And Chamberlain believed the moment was propitious for peace, especially from the British viewpoint. He had in mind the gloomy manpower prospects of the British Empire with which the Imperial War Cabinet had been confronted in August 1918, when he wrote:

> . . . I at least would not fight on for vengeance only or even to secure punishment beyond what is inherent in the circumstances of the case—loss of all colonies, loss of Alsace-Lorraine, some losses in the East of Europe, some surrender of battleships etc., a large indemnity. Vengeance is a luxury that few can afford in public or private life. If we fight on, Germany is ruined, but at what cost to ourselves. Our armies must dwindle; the French are no longer

[1] Austen Chamberlain to Ida Chamberlain, October 26, 1918.

> fighting; a year hence we shall have lost how many thousands more men? And American power will be dominant. Today *we* are topdog. *Our* fleets, *our* armies, have brought Germany to her knees and today (more than at any later time) the peace may be our peace. So I am for peace if we can get a *good* peace, i.e. a decisive peace and one that is as secure as human foresight can make it.

The time for final decisions had arrived. On October 23, Wilson turned over to the Allied governments his correspondence with Germany.[1] The Allies became direct participants in the armistice negotiations. At Senlis, the generals held a Council of War on October 25 to discuss final armistice terms.[2] Pétain wanted the German forces virtually disarmed, German evacuation of all invaded territory and of Alsace-Lorraine, an Allied occupation of the Rhineland and of a zone fifty kilometres deep on the right bank. Haig held to his moderate proposals. Pershing agreed that any armistice should provide guarantees against a renewal of hostilities. The terms which he favoured were closer to those of Pétain than to Haig's.

On the following day, Generalissimo Foch, in submitting his recommendations to Clemenceau, contended that his proposals would produce an armistice capable of protecting the interests of the peoples concerned and of assuring to the victors the power of imposing and of safeguarding the peace. His advice simply expanded upon his views of October 8.

To add to the wealth of military advice, General Bliss on October 28 formally submitted his views to the Supreme Council. His essential argument was that the German armies should be completely disarmed and demobilized. According to Bliss, even though the enemy might be heard on some issues of peacemaking, 'he must submit to whatever the Associated Powers finally agree upon as being proper to demand for the present and the future peace of the world'.[3] Pershing, to the confusion of Wilson and others, now favoured the continuation of the war to secure the unconditional surrender of Germany.[4]

Thus, Lloyd George, Clemenceau, House, and Orlando had a wide range of military advice from which to choose. Their

[1] *Foreign Relations*, 1918, supplement 1, vol. I, p. 383.

[2] Foch, *Mémoires*, II, pp. 280 *et seq.*; Baker, *Woodrow Wilson, Life and Letters*, VIII, pp. 515-16.

[3] *Lansing Papers*, II, pp. 293-6.

[4] Baker, *op. cit.*, pp. 532-3.

reaction is known to us largely through House's accounts. Shortly after his arrival in Paris on October 26, the Colonel formed the impression that Haig and Milner were moderate in their approach to armistice terms, that Lloyd George was immoderate, and that Clemenceau wanted to be moderate but was under the influence of Foch, who assumed Germany had been decisively beaten.[1] In a few days, House reported to Wilson that Lloyd George, along with Balfour, had privately criticized the military and naval proposals as too severe. Balfour's objections were directed particularly against the terms recommended by the Naval Council, while[2] Lloyd George strongly opposed Foch's insistence on the occupation of the east bank of the Rhine. Clemenceau argued that it was politically impossible for him to oppose the Foch proposals and, so House told Wilson, '. . . gave us his word of honour that France would withdraw after the peace conditions had been fulfilled'. House sympathized with Clemenceau's demand! Lloyd George continued to oppose.[3]

In the meantime, Woodrow Wilson had received Pershing's report on the Senlis Conference, including a full description of the American commander's position. In addition, the President had information on Foch's terms and on Bliss's attitude. Wilson's response was to urge moderate armistice terms. Particularly he disagreed with specific major proposals advanced by Pershing, Foch, and Pétain. He questioned whether it was necessary for the Allied or American forces to occupy Alsace-Lorraine. He doubted the advisability of occupation on the east side of the Rhine! 'That is practically an invasion of German soil under armistice.' He veered away from occupation of German submarine bases: 'That would mean Allied or American occupation of German soil not now in their possession.' And, 'In general, the President [felt] that the terms of the armistice should be rigid enough to secure against renewal of hostilities by Germany but not humiliating beyond that necessity, as such terms would throw the advantage to the military party in Germany.'[4]

[1] *Ibid.*, pp. 519-20; Seymour, *Intimate Papers*, IV, pp. 92-3.

[2] Seymour, *Intimate Papers*, IV, pp. 117-18.

[3] *Ibid.*, p. 118. Both prime ministers agreed that the naval and military terms required modification.

[4] Baker, *Woodrow Wilson, Life and Letters*, VIII, pp. 520-2.

A more impressive expression of Wilson's opposition to immoderate armistice terms was contained in a message to House on Monday, October 28. The text ran:

> My deliberate judgment is that our whole weight should be thrown for an armistice which will prevent the renewal of hostilities by Germany but which will be as moderate and reasonable as possible within those limits, because it is certain that too much success or security on the part of the Allies will make a genuine peace settlement exceedingly difficult, if not impossible. The position of Haig and Milner and Pétain as reported by our commander-in-chief is therefore safer than Foch's. See Baker's despatch of today to commander-in-chief. Foresight is better than immediate advantage.[1]

In retrospect, Wilson was right: the proposed armistice would make the Allies too bold in their attitude towards Germany in the peacemaking, making a genuine reconciliation between victor and vanquished, and a stable peace settlement, more difficult to accomplish. As events turned out, Wilson himself was not immune from the influence of the victor's military and strategic superiority over Germany.

In matters of detail, Wilson stood closer to Lloyd George than to Clemenceau on the issue of Allied occupation of strong points on the east side of the Rhine. It is surprising that Colonel House evidently made no attempt to secure a modification of the military terms in accordance with the spirit and the substance of Wilson's criticisms. As we have seen, he did not support Lloyd George's objections to Foch's proposals regarding the east bank of the Rhine. On November 1 he let slip by a similar opportunity.[2]

It is questionable whether a message like that of October 28 left Colonel House with an entirely free hand. There were other indications of Wilson's desires, namely the specific objections to

[1] *Ibid.*, VIII, p. 523.

[2] Charles Seymour in *Intimate Papers*, VI, p. 110, wrote: '. . . The legend that pictures the United States as pleading for softer terms has no historic foundation. President Wilson sent Colonel House to the Supreme War Council with a free hand, entirely without instruction; and House from first to last made it clear that in all military matters the United States Government was inclined to accept the recommendations of Foch.

"The only indication of Wilson's desires was contained in a cable which the president sent to House on October 29 and which was entirely in line with his public statements.'

the proposed armistice terms which he raised in Baker's wire of October 27. Perhaps the Americans were so disorganized in Paris that Pershing never communicated these views, with which he was unsympathetic, to Colonel House. Clearly Wilson was urging House and Pershing to seek more moderate terms than those being proposed by Foch. House, however, did not do battle on these grounds. He missed opportunities to support more temperate conditions which British statesmen like Lloyd George evidently desired. Perhaps the Colonel was too much inclined to 'leave it to Marshal Foch'. It was hard, of course, to ignore Foch's views. With the exception of Haig's, the weight of military opinion was against Wilson and Lloyd George. House probably felt also that Allied acceptance of the President's peace programme together with the economic and political influence which the United States could wield over the policies of the Allied governments would be sufficient to counteract the dangerous temptations created by an extreme imbalance of power as between the victors and vanquished.

The final phase of the negotiations over the Fourteen Points began in Paris on October 26. If the British representatives had ever planned to attempt to conclude an armistice without being committed to Wilson's programme, they must have been rapidly disillusioned. Colonel House had come to Europe, as the personal representative of Woodrow Wilson, for the primary purpose of imposing the President's version of peace terms upon the Allied governments. Wilson saw himself in a dominant and balancing position among the Allies and was determined to exploit this situation to the full.[1] Left virtually without instructions on details, the Colonel faithfully and vigorously sought to further the President's policy on the Fourteen Points, mainly by threatening Lloyd George, Clemenceau, and Orlando with the possibility of a separate peace between the United States and Germany if they persisted in seeking modifications and clarifications in the President's programme.[2] To what extent there was a general engagement between House and the British represen-

[1] Wilson to House, October 29, 1918, House Papers; Baker. *Woodrow Wilson, Life and Letters*, VIII, p. 529.

[2] The United States, it will be recalled, had not formally entered the Allied coalition and was not committed to make peace only in concert with France, England, and Italy.

tatives over acceptance of the President's programme is not easily determined. Despite the sound and fury of battle depicted in the Colonel's diary and in his despatches to Wilson, House to some extent appears like Don Quixote in Texan garb.

The high-water mark in the Paris negotiations over the Fourteen Points was probably reached on October 29. At lunch, Lloyd George, accompanied by Balfour and Reading, gave notice to Colonel House that the British government could not accept without qualification Point Two regarding freedom of the seas. By the end of the conversation, however, House had received the impression that they were close to agreement along the lines suggested in the Cobb-Lippmann memorandum.[1]

In part, the Cobb-Lippmann memorandum satisfied the demand of the British government for a clarification of the more obscure or objectionable portions of the Fourteen Points. 'Open covenants, openly arrived at' was interpreted to mean 'open covenants, secretly arrived at!' This assurance, while it may not have satisfied Wilson, did leave the most polished practitioners of the 'old diplomacy' content. As for the future boundaries of Germany, the commentary by no means entirely resolved doubts about the substantial meaning of the President's programme.[2]

[1] House to Wilson, October 29, 1918, *Foreign Relations*, 1918, supplement 1, vol. I, pp. 421-3; House Diary, XIV, pp. 12-13. For the text of the Cobb-Lippmann memorandum see *Foreign Relations*, *op. cit.*, pp. 405-13. This memorandum helped to provide grounds for agreement in the negotiations. House had been well aware of the vagaries in Wilson's peace programme. In an effort to counter criticism, the Colonel had two United States journalists, Frank S. Cobb, the editor of the *New York World*, and Walter Lippmann, the secretary of The Inquiry, who were in Paris, to prepare an interpretative memorandum on the Fourteen Points. Wilson's approval of the principles outlined in the commentary was secured. House then used this document as an official basis for discussions with Lloyd George, Clemenceau, and Orlando.

[2] On January 21, 1920, Colonel House wrote: 'It has been stated that many of the fourteen points were so vague and so general that they were practically meaningless, and the Entente could very well refuse to interpret them in the way they were meant. This is not true, for each point was interpreted before the Armistice was made and the interpretations filled many typewritten pages. They were cabled in advance to the President for his approval; therefore Clemenceau, Orlando, Lloyd George and the others were barred from pleading they did not understand what each meant. These interpretations were on the table day after day when we sat in conference in Paris while the Armistice was in the making. Many times they

Point Eight was clarified—Alsace-Lorraine was to be restored completely to French sovereignty. In drawing attention to the demands being voiced in France for the Saar Valley, the authors declared: 'No claim on grounds of nationality can be established, but the argument leans on the possibility of taking this territory in lieu of indemnity; it would seem to be a clear violation of the President's proposal.' About Czechoslovakia, they sagely advised that some provision must be made for the Germans within its territories. By implication perhaps Bohemia was to retain its historic frontiers. As for German-Austria, they commented that it should by right be permitted to join Germany but they saw strong objections against this solution because *Anschluss* would increase the Reich's population.[1] The two authors scarcely added to the substantial meaning of the Thirteenth Point in merely pointing out the problems involved but not offering solutions apart from saying that *if* Posen and Silesia were to go to Poland provision must be made to protect the German and Jewish minorities there, as elsewhere, in the new Polish state. Referring to the President's words 'indisputably Polish territory', they advised that this phrasing might imply the taking of an impartial census before the frontiers were drawn. While helpful, the Cobb-Lippmann memorandum was less precise than House later pretended.

On the afternoon of October 29, Lloyd George and Balfour conferred at the Quai d'Orsay with House, Clemenceau, Pichon, and Sonnino.[2] The British Prime Minister took the initiative, bluntly asking whether Wilson's programme was acceptable as

[1] Regarding Point Ten, they said: '. . . the United States is clearly committed to the program of national unity and independence. It must stipulate, however, for the protection of national minorities, for freedom of access to the Adriatic and the Black Sea, and it supports a program aiming at a confederation of South Eastern Europe.'

[2] There are three main sources of information about this meeting: Seymour, *Intimate Papers*, VI, pp. 161 *et seq.*; Lloyd George, *Truth*, I, pp. 74 *et seq.*; House to Wilson, *Foreign Relations*, 1918, supplement 1, vol. I, p. 422.

asked the meaning of this or that point and I would read from the accepted interpretation.' Seymour, *Intimate Papers*, VI, p. 153. It is rather amusing to compare this letter with the minutes of the meeting of the Supreme War Council of November 1, 1918, when House kept evading questions about the meaning of certain of the Fourteen Points with the explanation, 'Je n'ai pas mes notes avec moi . . . ,' Mermeix, *Les Négociations secrètes et les quatre armistices*, pp. 227-8.

the basis of peace negotiations.[1] Thereupon they proceeded to a reading of the Fourteen Points. Pichon read the First Point. Lloyd George supported Clemenceau's objections to open diplomacy. House read reassuringly from the Cobb-Lippmann script. With a helping hand from Balfour, the First Point was generally accepted as interpreted. After the Second Point was read, Lloyd George stated the British government's refusal to accept this term on the grounds that it implied the abolition of the right of Blockade. The effort of Colonel House to put a more favourable construction upon the meaning of the Second Point failed to convince Lloyd George. Sonnino, who supported Lloyd George's general position, suggested that agreement upon a peace programme seemed impossible to reach at the same time they were undertaking to draft an armistice. He called for settling the military and naval terms of an armistice first and leaving the bases of peace until later.

House reacted strongly against Sonnino's proposal. He rightly claimed that it would clean the President's programme off the armistice slate. He threatened a separate peace between the United States and Germany which would leave the French, British, and Italians alone to face the Central Powers. According to the Colonel's report to Wilson that evening, his statement had an exciting effect upon those present. But Lloyd George refused to give in completely under this pressure. He defied the Colonel's threat: '. . . so far as item II was concerned, it was impossible for the British Government to agree. If the United States of America were to make a separate peace, we should deeply regret it, but, nevertheless, should be prepared to go on fighting. (M. Clemenceau here interjected: 'Yes.') . . .'[2]

[1] In Seymour's version of the discussion, Lloyd George is reported to have said: 'Do we or do we not accept the whole of Wilson's Fourteen Points? I am going to put quite clearly the points which I do not accept. Should we not make it clear to the German government that we are not going in on the Fourteen Points of peace?' The minutes from which Lloyd George quotes give his remarks a different tone. According to them he simply asked whether the President's terms were acceptable and commented that before they agreed to an armistice, they must make it clear what their attitude towards these terms was. Did Lloyd George at the beginning of this meeting attempt to secure the postponement, if not rejection, of the Fourteen Points as the basis of peace negotiations and as a condition for an armistice?

[2] Lloyd George, *Truth*, I, p. 78; see also Seymour, *Intimate Papers*, IV, pp. 165-6.

At the same time, the British Prime Minister defined carefully the limitations which he wished to place upon acceptance of the Fourteen Points. He did not raise a blanket objection against them but restricted himself to freedom of the seas and reparations. Balfour too struck a conciliatory note by stressing the urgency of maintaining unity among the Allied and Associated Powers.[1]

The remainder of the discussion touched upon the meaning of the Third Point and upon Italian claims in relation to the Fourteen Points. In the latter connection, House after asserting that Wilson's conditions of peace had been put in very broad terms, explained:

> In the case of Alsace Lorraine, for example, he did not say specifically that it should go back to France, but he intended it positively.
>
> M. Clemenceau said that the Germans certainly did not place that interpretation on it.
>
> Colonel House said that the President had said so much on other occasions. He had insisted on Germany's accepting all his speeches, and from these you could establish almost any point that anyone wished against Germany. Reparation for Belgium and France, which had been alluded to, was certainly implied in Clauses Seven and Eight, where it had been stated that these invaded countries must be evacuated and 'restored'. The same principle applied to illegal sinkings at sea and to the sinking of neutrals.[2]

The Colonel's assertion, if correctly reported, that the meaning of the Fourteen Points and subsequent speeches by Wilson was so broad that almost any claim against Germany could be supported by reference to one of the President's statements was astonishing. It was an admission that the President's programme was loose and vague. To facilitate agreement, House was promising the Allied Prime Ministers a substantial measure of freedom of manœuvre at the peace conference. Undoubtedly it impressed the British representatives who were seeking to leave themselves with as free a hand as possible in the peace negotiations.

[1] The British Foreign Secretary also spoke of the necessity of informing the German government beforehand of their modifications in the political conditions of the armistice. Unfortunately, his advice was not thoroughly carried out.

[2] Lloyd George, *Truth*, I, p. 80.

In this debate German territorial questions played almost no role. For its part, the British government had no cause to dispute the general principles of territorial settlement laid down in Wilson's programme. In broad terms they were in agreement. In western Europe, for example, the British representatives on October 29 had as much interest in binding France to limited territorial claims as had House and Wilson. It is therefore rather misleading to comment that Lloyd George, apart from freedom of the seas and reparations 'was willing to support Wilson's principles' because in fact the President had no monopoly on many of the principles involved. Lloyd George's position on October 29 reflected his country's mixed and complex position *vis-à-vis* the continent and the United States.

On November 1, when the statesmen met with Foch and Weygand to prepare for the Supreme War Council that afternoon, Lloyd George continued his opposition to Foch's proposals for the east bank of the Rhine, which he described as 'a very stiff demand'. The discussion turned to Haig's proposals. According to Foch, the English commander's recommendations could only lead to improving the defensive position of the German army which he could never accept. Lloyd George replied that Field-Marshal Haig had argued somewhat as follows: 'Why do you wish to take more than the territories he had proposed? If you had these you would have in hand everything you desired in the west at the peace conference, and if the armistice broke down it would not be necessary for you to attack, but for the enemy to do so.'[1]

Wittingly or not, Lloyd George had raised the vital political issue beneath this vigorous debate which was conducted primarily in military terms. Almost bluntly, Foch was being asked—why do you wish to occupy more than northern France, Belgium, Luxembourg, and Alsace-Lorraine? 'If you had these, you would have in hand everything you desired in the west at the peace conference.'[2] Was this all that Foch wanted in the west? Charles Seymour suggests[3] that during these negotiations

[1] Seymour, *Intimate Papers*, IV, p. 20. Evidently the author is reproducing here the official minutes of the meeting.

[2] Rudin, in his excellent and sometimes exciting history of the making of the armistice, completely overlooks these significant words.

[3] Seymour, *Intimate Papers*, IV, p. 119.

the British were chiefly troubled, as far as Foch's proposals were concerned, by the prospect of an Allied occupation of German territory because they feared that by asking for more than was absolutely essential the opportunity for gaining an armistice might be lost. Were the British representatives at Paris chiefly troubled by this concern? Or, more correctly perhaps, was this their only concern about the implications of Foch's proposals for the Rhineland and the bridgeheads? Lloyd George hinted very broadly that Foch's armistice proposals were politically as well as militarily inspired, thus revealing the British concern about French territorial designs against Germany in western Europe.[1]

While we cannot be dogmatic in drawing this inference, we can recall the attitude of French statesmen in 1916 and early 1917 towards the future of the Rhineland and towards the acquisition of the 1814 frontier of Alsace-Lorraine. That Foch had these schemes in mind during the armistice negotiations is incontestable. Foch, on October 17, in a letter to Clemenceau raised the question of the future of the left bank of the Rhine. Foch asked Clemenceau if the occupation of the Rhineland would be a sufficient guarantee to secure reparations for France and her Allies. He went on: 'If the answer is "yes", what is to be the fate of this territory when reparation has been made? Will our occupation be continued or modified? Shall we annex all or a part of this territory, or shall we endeavour to create autonomous, independent, neutral states, forming a buffer? Ought the armistice to reserve the question of the future of this territory now?'[2]

Clemenceau did not apparently reveal his position. Certainly, such a reservation did not appear in the French memorandum of October 26 which became the basis for the armistice discussions. Insistence upon reserving the future of the Rhineland in the armistice agreement might have produced a disastrous rebuff. Almost certainly, a bitter fight would have been precipitated with Wilson and Lloyd George. The German will to resist could have been strengthened and French hopes imperilled before peace negotiations began. The best tactic was

[1] Haig took the view that 'On the whole, Foch's reasons were political not military.' Duff Cooper, *Haig*, II, p. 400.

[2] Foch, *Mémoires*, II, pp. 278-9; Foch, *L'Armistice et la paix*, pp. 26 *et seq.*

to avoid controversy and to safeguard French claims by securing military and administrative control of the area which could be a long and perhaps essential step toward the French annexation of all or part of the region or the establishment of a buffer state system. Even if the occupation and administration were Inter-Allied, French military and civilian personnel would be stationed in the Rhineland to exert a pro-French influence. Then too, if at the Peace Conference the Allied and Associated Powers agreed upon a new regime for the Rhineland, and the Germans disagreed, they would have to fight to reverse the decision. The occupation would also be a guarantee of the enforcement of the peace treaty.

If Lloyd George did battle in the name of Haig's proposals both because he had these political considerations in mind and because he feared endangering the prospects of an armistice, he had little success. In a preparatory meeting on November 1, Colonel House offered him no support or encouragement, 'being disposed to leave the matter in Marshal Foch's hands'. Lloyd George, completely isolated, except for Orlando's weak attempt at compromise, finally capitulated to Foch and Clemenceau.[1] Their political interest in the Rhineland had been protected. For his part, Lloyd George, who had finally turned down the advice of the British field commander, had safeguarded his position in case the Foch armistice strategy failed.

The Supreme War Council gave a first reading that afternoon to the proposed armistice conditions. During the discussion, Lloyd George noted the omission of armistice conditions for eastern Europe. Foch was asked to draft relevant provisions. At the next meeting the Marshal recommended the evacuation by German troops of the territories of Poland before the first partition, including Danzig. According to Pichon, the French Foreign Minister, a reference to these territorial limits in the German armistice would avoid debate on the issue at the Peace Conference.

Outspoken opposition came from Balfour, who asserted they

[1] Seymour, *Intimate Papers*, IV, pp. 119 *et seq.* In supporting the Foch terms he said that he 'would like it to be known that this [Haig's] view had been most carefully considered, and that a contrary decision had only been taken after all the generals had been consulted and on the unanimous decision of the Supreme War Council'.

were obligated not to restore the Polish boundaries of 1772 but only to reconstitute a Polish state composed of Poles. The Poland of 1772 did not meet this objective:

> . . . elle n'était pas composée uniquement de Polonais. On y voyait englobés des territoires non polonais, alors que des territoires polonais n'en faisaient pas partie. Cette formule pécherait donc pas insuffisance autant, que par excès. La délimitation exacte des frontières de cette nouvelle Pologne est un sujet si compliqué que je vous conjure de ne pas l'introduire dans des clauses d'armistice. . . .

Balfour proposed that Germany simply be requested to withdraw its forces in the east to the frontiers of 1914. House supported him. Pichon gave in. The Council accepted Balfour's formula.[1]

The final terms agreed upon by the Supreme War Council, as they affected German territory, provided in western Europe for German evacuation within fifteen days of Belgium, France, Luxembourg, and Alsace-Lorraine, to be followed by an Inter-Allied occupation. The German armies were to withdraw from the left bank of the Rhine, which would also be subject to an Inter-Allied occupation. Garrisons of the victors would hold the principal Rhine crossings at Mainz, Coblentz, and Cologne, including bridgeheads on the right bank with a radius of thirty kilometres. Along the right bank from the Dutch border to the Swiss frontier, there was to run a neutral zone, ten kilometres wide. The Rhineland provisions were to be executed within thirty days. In eastern and southern Europe, German forces within the prewar territory of Austria-Hungary, Rumania, and Turkey were to pull back within the German frontiers of August 1, 1914. German troops on former Imperial Russian soil were likewise to withdraw to Germany's prewar boundaries, but only when the Allies deemed that the internal situation of these regions permitted a German retreat. (The object was to employ the German army to maintain order in this part of Europe as against the Bolsheviks until a substitute force existed.) These provisions meant that German troops might remain in Russian

[1] Mermeix, *Les Négociations secrètes et les quatre armistices*, pp. 246-8. Subsequently, the Council adopted a more precise wording which appeared in the final text.

Poland and would certainly remain in Prussian Poland after the armistice. The Allies were to have freedom of access to the territories evacuated by the Germans in eastern Europe to supply the populations or to maintain order. Danzig or the Vistula were specifically mentioned as the routes of access.[1]

These and other clauses of the proposed armistice conditions, including Clause XXVI providing for the maintenance of the blockade, embodied impressive securities against the contingency of a German refusal to accept final peace terms. This was in line with British policy, although Haig and Lloyd George had doubted whether such guarantees were obtainable or necessary.

The territorial clauses approximated final terms of peace, although the parallel was not complete. If the British representatives had sought to moderate the Rhineland provisions partly to guard against laying a basis for French efforts to erect a special regime on the left bank, they had failed. On the other hand, Balfour had successfully parried a French effort to underwrite in the armistice the historic frontiers of Poland and the award of Danzig to the Poles. The German evacuation of south-eastern Europe and of France, Belgium, Luxembourg, and Alsace-Lorraine also approximated British objectives.

Flatterers told the Colonel on November 4, after the Supreme War Council had accepted the President's peace programme with the two public reservations, that he had scored one of the greatest diplomatic triumphs in history.[2] Echoing this sentiment, House told Wilson on November 5 that they had won a great victory. In perspective, the claim seems greatly exaggerated, especially when viewed in the light of German territorial questions.

[1] Maurice, *The Armistices of 1918*, pp. 93-100; *Conditions of an Armistice with Germany signed November 11, 1918*, Cmd. 9212, Miscellaneous No. 25 (1918).

[2] House Diary, XIV, pp. 23-4. As far as Lloyd George and his colleagues were concerned, the main battle was over Point Two. Here Lloyd George, perhaps not with the whole-hearted approval of some of his associates, braved House's threat of a naval armaments race with the United States and risked compromising the 'Anglo-American alliance' to fight House and Wilson to a complete standstill. The two Americans had to be satisfied with Lloyd George's promise to discuss the principle of the freedom of the seas sometime in the future. Wilson had wanted Allied acceptance of the principle followed only by the discussion of definitions and limitations. House suffered a severe defeat in this phase of the negotiations.

Did the British negotiators at Paris, conversely, suffer a diplomatic defeat? This question can only be fully answered when we know more about what they intended to secure in the armistice negotiations between October 26 and November 4. Whether Lloyd George and Balfour came to Paris to sidetrack the Fourteen Points and to secure an armistice without any commitments by the Allied and Associated Powers on the basis of peace negotiations[1] is not clear. But it is unlikely. They were anxious to secure an honourable and advantageous end to the war. Complete rejection of political preconditions for an armistice, as the situation looked in October 1918, might have led to the prolongation of the war, have made Wilson resentful and unco-operative, or have produced a separate U.S.-German peace. If Lloyd George began to run this risk early in the Conference on October 29, certainly, after House's threats, both the British Prime Minister and the Foreign Secretary made very plain their acceptance of Wilson's programme as the basis of peace negotiations with Germany.

Lloyd George and Balfour came to Paris—so the available evidence suggests—prepared to accept political preconditions for an armistice along the lines of Wilson's programme. Why not? There was a wide area of agreement between the peace policy of the moderate majority in the British War Cabinet and Imperial War Cabinet and Wilson's programme. If they could secure certain clarifications and reservations and leave British negotiators at the Peace Conference with as free a hand as possible to protect British interests and to advance British claims, the Paris talks would be a success, not a defeat, for British diplomacy. When considered in these terms, Lloyd George and Balfour secured at Paris a substantial victory.

If we consider the Fourteen Points as they applied to Germany, the elements in this success were impressive. Lloyd George received satisfaction and Wilson suffered partial defeat on the issue of open diplomacy. Lloyd George successfully parried the effort to commit the British government to Point Two. Point Five was broad enough to permit various solutions of the colonial question and the British government was not committed at Paris to trusteeship although the Cobb-Lippmann memorandum made plain the American intention of seeking

[1] Baker, *Woodrow Wilson, Life and Letters*, VIII, p. 554.

this solution. There was no dispute over territorial restoration as implied in Points Six and Seven. As for Point Eight, a basic war aim of the British government had been to break the German hold over northern France and to end German territorial ambitions in western Europe. There was no hostility here toward the Fourteen Points nor toward House's interpretation of the reference to Alsace-Lorraine as meaning the return of the provinces to France. At the same time, the British government came from Paris with the satisfaction that no encouragement had been given to possible broader French claims against Germany. Also, as far as Points Seven and Eight were concerned the British negotiators had secured a major clarification of the Fourteen Points in the form of the reservation regarding reparations, although they had blundered in proposing a formula which could seriously endanger British claims for an equitable share of German payments. The obsolete character of Point Ten had been recognized by all. As for Point Thirteen, the British government had no quarrel with the principle involved and was uncommitted in future negotiations over details. In general, the British negotiators had obtained satisfactory interpretations and reservations. Above all, the policy of the free hand in peace negotiations had not been seriously compromised. On this point they had been expressly assured by Colonel House.

From a British vantage point, Austen Chamberlain on November 2 dramatically summed up the significance of the proposed armistice conditions for the ultimate terms of peace with Germany.[1] Believing 'we have them at our mercy and that they must accept our terms', he wrote:

> . . . But what a smash it must be! Surrender of Alsace-Lorraine, surrender of arms, of battleships and merchant ships, of Prussian Poland including part at least of East Prussia and the birthplace of the Hohenzollerns, surrender of their colonies and of all their dreams of the 'drang nach osten', and a huge indemnity, and then for what is left a crushing load of taxation, a starving people and starved industries. If the guilt was immense, the punishment will be overwhelming. So be it! But I should like to see Berlin bombed and Essen systematically destroyed. However I think I mentioned that if we can get a *good* peace, I am ready to forgo vengeance.

[1] Austen Chamberlain to Hilda Chamberlain, November 6, 1918.

This concept of an onerous, smashing peace did not embrace the Rhineland and the Saar or other proposals for the extreme dismemberment of Germany. The width of the English Channel clearly was one measure of extremism or moderation in the treatment of the Reich.

The Imperial War Cabinet discussed the proposed terms of an armistice on November 5. Apparently only Prime Minister Hughes of Australia raised objections to acceptance of the Fourteen Points as the terms of peace. In reply

> The Prime Minister pointed out that the Peace Terms were not limited by the Fourteen Points, but by all the addresses that President Wilson had delivered since January, 1918, inclusive, and, having been carefully through them, he could not find a single point which we wanted that was not amply covered, with the exception of the points regarding the freedom of the seas and indemnities, and of our position in regard to these matters notice has been duly given.[1]

The Ministers formally approved the decisions reached in Paris.

Within six days the cries and clatter of battle ceased along the Western Front. Death's reign over the trenches ended. Yet, in the eerie silence only the dead knew peace and repose. Among the living, there was no peace; only a partial cease fire. Men remained discordant, spiteful, insecure. Now the war leaders were to turn into peacemakers, but Poincaré was wrong when he told them later at Paris: 'You hold in your hands the future of the world.' Outsiders like Lenin and Lodge held some keys to the future. The Big Four exercised no divine authority with which to refertilize the shell-ploughed fields and to transform the rubbish piles into factories and homes again. They could not exorcise the evil spirits of ambition and hate which impassioned the souls of men. And they and their company moved in an atmosphere of apprehension and uncertainty which Sir Robert Borden, the Canadian Prime Minister, sensed when he wrote on Armistice Day as the *Mauretania* carried him to Europe: 'Revolt has spread all over Germany. The question is whether it will stop there. The world has drifted far from its old anchorage and no man can with certainty prophesy what the outcome will be.'

[1] I.W.C., No. 36, November 5, 1918, Borden Papers.

PART TWO

Pre-Conference Preparations

IV

ADVICE OF THE EXPERTS

ONLY a brief fourteen weeks separated the initial German plea for an armistice from the opening in Paris of the Preliminary Peace Conference. During this crowded period, while the British Isles rang with the exciting electoral cries of 'Hang the Kaiser', 'Make Them Pay', and 'Britain for the British', in the quiet recesses along Whitehall, civilian and military officials busied themselves with intensive preparations for the peace negotiations.[1] Printed papers piled up in the great departments of state. Their authors sought to define British interests in areas as great as China and as small as Zips. They recommended policy to the Cabinet on such diverse issues as the Rhineland and Yap. A similar outpouring of data and advice came from the expert advisors of the French and the American governments. The result was that the statesmen had an unprecedented wealth of information and expert counsel available to them on almost every subject involved in the peacemaking.

But how effective was all of this? What influence were the experts to exert upon the fashioning of the settlement? A partial

[1] For an account of British preparations since 1916 see Lord Hardinge, *Old Diplomacy*, pp. 215-17; L. S. Amery, *My Political Life*, I, pp. 103-4; F. S. Marston, *The Peace Conference of 1919: Organization and Procedure*, pp. 228-9. The utility of these preparations is discussed in H. W. V. Temperley (ed.), *A History of the Peace Conference of Paris*, I, pp. 240-1; Lloyd George, *Truth*, I, pp. 211-12.

answer to these questions will emerge from the subsequent chapters. Here certain general comments and considerations should be borne in mind.

The preparatory work of the English, French, and American officials has been criticized as poorly directed politically, uncoordinated, often too late to be of use, and frequently unheeded. As for the role of the experts at Paris, differing pictures have been drawn. Lloyd George, who praised highly the work of British departmental officials, testified that at the Peace Conference British statesmen constantly turned to them for guidance.[1] H. W. V. Temperley, who felt that the pre-conference efforts of the civil servants had suffered from a lack of inter-departmental co-ordination and from the failure of the Cabinet to issue clear-cut instructions, granted that as the Conference wore on the preparatory work of the bureaucracy proved of increasing value.[2] On the other hand, some, like Lord Hardinge, then Permanent Under Secretary of State for Foreign Affairs, have complained of being unconsulted. The Prime Minister was said to have pursued a purely personal diplomacy and to have leaned upon his private secretariat and a small coterie of advisors, ignoring the Foreign Secretary and his staff.[3] Harold Nicolson has commented that Foreign Office personnel, like himself, who were used in negotiations, were often left to fend for themselves without definite instructions from either the Prime Minister or the Foreign Secretary.[4] From such accounts, a confused, rather contradictory picture emerges of the role of the British experts and of their French and American counterparts.

The relationships between the professional advisors and the statesmen and the consequent influence of the former upon policy and the settlement are elusive, perplexing matters. The experts could reach the political leaders through their memoranda, assuming these were read, and verbally through formal consultations or informal, frequently hurried, conversations. Communications were facilitated where more personal relationships existed, such as Henry Wilson seemed to enjoy with Lloyd

[1] Lloyd George, *Truth*, p. 212.
[2] Temperley, *History*, p. 241.
[3] Hardinge, *Old Diplomacy*, p. 241.
[4] Nicolson, *The Peacemaking*, 1919, p. 91.

George. Technical advisors were often directly involved in the negotiations at Paris as members of the territorial and other committees, as go-betweens for the Big Three, etc. Woodrow Wilson's use of the pro-French Charles Homer Haskins in the Saar negotiations undoubtedly resulted in Haskin's affecting the settlement of that question. These were the major channels through which the expert advisors could bring personal, factional, and departmental points of view to bear upon the statesmen and the settlement. While this influence was neither consistent nor uniform, it existed. The experts were part of the cast. Their role and views cannot be ignored.

What counsel, then, did British civil and military servants give their government on German and related territorial issues? How did their attitudes compare with those of their French and American counterparts?

From the Foreign Office there came a series of memoranda which were distinguished by their caution, moderation, and foresight. None were attributed to individuals. It can be surmised that, for instance, Sir Esme Howard contributed to the paper on Poland and Harold Nicolson to the one on south-eastern Europe. But in the absence of direct confirmation of authorship and although individual opinions within the ministry undoubtedly varied, these memoranda must be treated in terms of 'the Foreign Office point of view'.

The overall approach of the Foreign Office to the peace-making was set forth in a paper simply entitled 'The Settlement'.[1] Its anonymous author saw two guides for the British government in arranging a general settlement; Wilson's statements to which the British government was bound except for the two reservations concerning freedom of the seas and reparations; and the general interests of Great Britain and the British Empire. After observing that both guides were capable of various interpretations, the author commented that the interests of Great Britain as of other states would vary according to post-war conditions. 'Matters would have a very different complexion if the conception summed up in the ideal of a League of Nations were in fact realized from that which they would have were the old system to continue.' Assuming that some form of League was attainable and desirable, the author went on to say:

[1] Foster Papers.

'. . . It is, however, only realizable if it is deliberately made a guide to the settlement . . . this means that every point in the settlement must be considered in its bearing on the constitution of a League of Nations, and the solution adopted should be one which will harmonize with the general idea which we must keep before our minds.'

Obviously the attitude to be adopted towards a League of Nations was linked with the question of British relations with the United States, about which the author of the memorandum wrote: 'It is in our interest to work vigorously and honestly in co-operation with America on the general lines of the programme which President Wilson has put forward, and to which we have given our adhesion.' British support for a settlement based upon the League of Nations and for Wilson's programme, however, would have to be conditioned by the uncertainties surrounding the future effectiveness of the proposed League:

> But, on the other hand, so long as the League of Nations has not in fact been established, and even after it has been established, until it has been shown that it can maintain itself in practice, it will be necessary to guard ourselves against the possibility that it may fail. This means that we cannot at present afford to neglect the guarantees for national security and the maintenance of British interests which would be necessary if international relations were to revert to their former conditions.

In sum, the British negotiators should work for a League of Nations and co-operate intimately with the American delegation, while keeping in mind the novel and uncertain character of the proposed League. Therefore they should not sacrifice the traditional means for protecting British security and interests.

British interests in Europe were defined in a separate paper which stressed the balance of power and its compatibility with the reconstruction of the continent upon the basis of nationality and national self-determination.[1] The important introduction to the memorandum ran:

> 1. As regards the Continent of Europe, as contrasted with Asia and Africa, this country has no direct territorial interests or ambitions, nor has it special and peculiar commercial interests; our general object must be the establishment of a stable condition;

[1] 'Europe', *ibid.*

> the great danger to be guarded against is anything which would again threaten to entangle us in a great Continental War; it is also in our interest that civil disturbances should, as far as possible, be avoided. What we want is peace and order with open facilities for trade.
>
> 2. There have been, however, always been, and there still will remain, two special points which we cannot afford to neglect. These are:—(1). The Balance of Power. (2). The security of the coast-line opposite our shores.

The balance of power, it was contended, '. . . is, and will remain, a fundamental point just as much after the establishment of a League of Nations as it has before'. In this context, the concept meant a policy of preventing the rise of a single power or group of powers so strong that they could dominate the continent and form a coalition of the Continent of Europe in active opposition to the interests of this country. To avert such a situation 'our interest now is, as it always has been, to maintain the full and complete independence, political, military, and economic, of the different States between which the Continent is divided'.

A necessary change was seen in the methods by which this principle should be maintained. Historically, British governments had supported the independence of existing states. Now

> . . . our object is to establish national States. This is a great gain, for there is every reason to hope that States based on the conscious existence of a common nationality will be more durable, and afford a firmer support against aggression than the older form of State which was often a merely accidental congeries of territories without internal cohesion, necessary economic unity, or clearly defined geographical frontiers. In this matter our interest entirely coincides with the principle of nationality and the doctrine of self-determination, though there must be very great difficulties in applying it.

If Europe was divided into national states, only two were envisaged as a danger to the independence of the others because of their great population and internal strength—Germany and Russia.

The security of the coast-line opposite the British Isles involved the continued independence of Holland and Belgium, an aim closely associated with the balance of power. The paper read:

> The essential point is that the territory of these States should not fall into the hands of any Great Power, whether it be France or Germany. The establishment of some system by which under some form of international guarantee the existing boundaries of States shall be made permanent is therefore entirely in our interests, and we shall have nothing to lose, but everything to gain, by placing the security of the frontiers under the control of a League of Nations. . . .

It was argued that the other general European questions of concern to the British government were: the territorial redistribution; and provision for free commercial intercourse under international guarantee.

Territorial problems were seen as almost entirely limited to eastern Europe. The settlement of the Alsace-Lorraine question, it was hoped, would satisfactorily conclude the territorial settlement of western Europe, which would consist of states whose limits coincided with those of a self-conscious national community (France, Spain) or of states whose population, though of diverse national origins, accepted political unity (Belgium, Switzerland). The cessation of the territorial struggle in western Europe was viewed as essential for the attainment of permanent security in the region: 'the indispensable condition without which a League of Nations cannot be established. When this condition has been reached, it will for the first time be possible for the different States mutually to guarantee to one another their present frontiers. The establishment of such a guarantee should be the first point to be secured in a League of Nations.'

A far less optimistic view was taken of territorial problems in eastern Europe, which had been among the chief causes of the war, and whose satisfactory solution would vitally affect the League's success or failure in avoiding future wars. Upon what basis should this part of the settlement rest?

> No settlement can be stable and permanent unless it is just. It is of the highest importance that no well-founded sense of injustice should be allowed to remain and to use President Wilson's words, 'We must be just towards those to whom we should wish not to be

just.' The Germans in Bohemia and the Magyars must be treated on exactly the same principle as the Czechs and the Roumanians.

Arguing that Great Britain had no direct or immediate interests which were antagonistic to the new states or to old states 'the boundaries of which will be enlarged', the memorandum commented: 'The British Government can therefore assume the position of a disinterested and impartial mediator, and in this we may hope to be able to have the cordial co-operation of the United States.' Highly desirable advantages for Great Britain were anticipated in this utopian vision:

> 12. It is needless to say that the position is one which will give an unprecedented opportunity for the legitimate extension of British influence: a good political understanding will afford the best basis for commercial and financial openings. Our object should be that when the whole transaction is concluded, all these nations, Czecho-Slovaks, Jugo-Slavs, Poles—we may perhaps add even Hungarians, Magyars, and Germans—will feel that on the part of the British nation there has been an honest attempt to carry through a disinterested policy which has sought the best interests of all, for, in the long run, the interests of each nation are not antagonistic to those of the other nations. If we succeed in this, we shall begin the new era with a large fund of goodwill which will be of great advantage to us.

The paper did not recommend that the British government take the initiative in proposing solutions; a mediator was held to be most effective if the parties to disputes were responsible for proposing settlements in the first place. If they failed, then the arbitrator should step in. This reasoning suggested a procedure different from the one actually employed at the Peace Conference for the settlement of territorial questions in eastern Europe: first, negotiations between the parties concerned; if they reached agreement, the Peace Conference would need to do little more than to ratify the agreement; if they failed to reach agreement, the Peace Conference should determine the solution and enforce it by arms, if necessary. It was suggested that each state should be admitted to the League of Nations only after its frontiers had been settled.

Lastly the government was advised to resist committing itself at that time to solutions of territorial questions for which the Poles, Czechs, and Italians, in particular, were pressing. An echo of this warning may be heard in Balfour's remarks to the War Cabinet about log-rolling.[1]

To turn to specific regional issues, the memorandum on Poland[2] sought the creation of a Polish state including all indisputably Polish territory and excluding large alien minorities as far as possible since they would only weaken the position of Poland. The argument stressed Poland's vulnerability:

> . . . If, at the Peace Congress, any large stretches of genuinely Russian or German land, or any territory whose inhabitants desire union with Russia or Germany, were conceded to Poland, we should run the risk of recreating the conditions which in the 18th century led to the partition of Poland. Both Germany and Russia are bound in the end to recover, and in view of their numbers are bound to be the two strongest powers in East Europe. Should their national unity be broken up and their most vital interests be injured, they would undoubtedly combine with a view to redressing what they would look upon as wrongs inflicted on them in the hour of defeat, and Poland would then be likely to suffer even in her legitimate interests.

Therefore, 'For the sake of Poland's own future we must firmly oppose exaggerated Polish claims.'

How then should the Polish frontiers, especially those with Germany, be determined? Russian Poland, though not necessarily all, was seen as the core of the new Polish state. To this, areas formerly under the sovereignty of the other two eastern Empires would be added, but not on *a priori* grounds. The ultimate decision would have to rest upon the wishes of the inhabitants and upon geographical practicality. Since the latter was difficult to determine because of the absence of natural frontiers and the former was not easy to assess because of the intermingling of national groups, it might, therefore, be necessary to conduct investigations on the spot. Neutral zones might have to be established whose fate would later be decided by commissions or by plebiscites.

The minimum solution suggested for the western frontier

[1] See chap. V, note 1, p. 137, below.

[2] 'Poland', December 9, 1918; also 'The Baltic Provinces and Lithuania', no date, Foster Papers.

of Poland is outlined on Map 2.[1] The area east of this line was considered indisputably Polish and could be awarded forthwith to Poland. Questionable areas would then be decided according to the principles described above.[2] It was stipulated that the minimum line should be drawn so as to give the Poles control of the Breslau-Teschen railway from Oppeln onwards. Although Bromberg on the Vistula was less than half Polish, it created an awkward German salient, and its transfer to Poland could be held 'to compensate for' the Polish districts which, according to this plan, the Poles would lose in the north. It was assumed that on a 'give and take' basis approximately the same number of Germans and Poles would be so transferred. Significantly for the Paris negotiations, the award of all of Upper Silesia was not contemplated in this Foreign Office memorandum.

The most difficult German-Polish frontier problem was in the north. Here, the Foreign Office differed sharply with the French and American experts. Polish claims to the valley of the Vistula and to Danzig could not be met without driving a Polish wedge between East Prussia and Pomerania and without giving the German city of Danzig (its population was less than 10 per cent. Polish) to Poland. In the memorandum on Poland, the solemn warning was made: 'Either of these measures would create an unstable position which would probably render the Polish position untenable if, and when, Germany recovers.'

The other horn of the northern dilemma was the promise to give Poland access to the sea. Effective access was obtainable only along the Vistula. According to the paper, only one solution of this problem existed. Danzig should remain German. The small port of Neufahrwasser, lying about five miles from Danzig and close to genuinely Polish territory, should be given to Poland together with the districts of Putzig and Neustadt, both of which were predominantly Polish. It was hoped that this would satisfy the Polish demand for a port at the mouth of the Vistula on Polish territory. The paper continued

> At the same time it is essential to preserve the connection between East Prussia and Pomerania and to leave to Prussia the corridor through which the connecting railway passes. To give this the Polish districts of Karthaus, Bevant, Konitz, and Stargard must

[1] See p. 195.

[2] Lodz, parts of Suvalki and of Eastern Cholm were given as examples.

be sacrificed. The result of this arrangement would be to create a small Polish enclave west and northwest of Danzig in which Neufahrwasser would lie, and full guarantees would be required for Polish trade down the Vistula, or down the railway.

As for Mazuria, that borderline area between East Prussia and the Polish interior, whose population spoke Polish but was Protestant rather than Roman Catholic in religion, a plebiscite was recommended to determine the wishes of the inhabitants.

Farther to the east, the advisors contemplated an independent Lithuania which should acquire Memel from Germany as an indispensable port. The Germans, it was argued, had 'no vital interest' in retaining Memel. In separate advice, the establishment of the Baltic Provinces, Lithuania and Poland as a line of buffer states was favoured as a means of hindering commercial co-operation between Germany and Bolshevik Russia.

All in all, the experts envisaged a Polish state of some 20,000,000 people, of whom 16,000,000 would be Polish, 2,000,000 Jewish, and more than 1,000,000 German.

The outstanding feature of this treatment of the German-Polish frontier question was the concern with Poland's future between Germany and Russia once they had recovered their power and influence. The author of the paper was searching for a solution which would minimize Polish-German friction. To this end, a moderate settlement of the Corridor-Danzig problem was recommended. The British government was advised to oppose Polish claims for a land corridor to the Baltic and for Danzig while supporting a settlement which would give a port to the Poles and guarantee them transit privileges. These recommendations contrast with the ultimate solution adopted at the Paris Peace Conference particularly as far as the Polish corridor was concerned. Undoubtedly, the point of view expressed in the memorandum lay behind Lloyd George's stand on these questions during the debate at Paris on the report of the Commission on Polish Affairs, a stand which was sometimes attributed to his capricious character rather than to the results of long considered views in British official circles.

The problems of the German-Czech frontier and of the post-war relationship between Germany and Austria were analysed in a paper on south-eastern Europe and the Balkans.[1] In summarizing British desiderata in this part of Europe, the memorandum defined the purposes of British policy to be: a just and permanent settlement based on the principles of nationality, self-determination, security, and free economic opportunity; a settlement which would leave no avoidable cause for future friction in south-eastern Europe, thus preventing if possible a combination between Italy, Bulgaria, and Rumania against Greece and Yugoslavia; the liberation of the main economic routes and outlets so as to draw the trade of central Europe to the Mediterranean while at the same time laying the foundation for a future customs union; full provision for the rights of national minorities in the new states; the inclusion of the settlement in the final act of the peace conference thereby giving it the sanction, if not the actual guarantee, of the League of Nations; the prohibition of secret understandings and agreements between the countries of south-eastern Europe; and the securing of a public realization in these countries that the settlement was imposed by the League of Nations and would be permanent. No statement of general purposes could show more clearly the common ground upon which American and British negotiators could meet in attempting to solve European territorial problems. Woodrow Wilson himself could scarcely have improved upon this declaraction of basic principles. Nor did he have a monopoly upon policies which sought to square circles.

In dealing with Czechoslovakia, a Czechoslovak state of 12,000,000 people was envisaged, of whom 8,300,000 would be Czechs and Slovaks, 3,500,000 Germans, and about 150,000 Hungarians. British support for the establishment of a Czechoslovak state was defended on the grounds that the Czechs throughout the war had been Britain's most devoted and most efficient allies in eastern and central Europe. They were said to have shown energy, self-control, and statesmanship, and to have been the real destroyers of the Dual Monarchy. It was further contended they had

> proved magnificent organizers, and in the very act of taking over the administration of their country, in the order which they had

[1] 'South-Eastern Europe and the Balkans', Foster Papers. Excerpts are given in Lloyd George, *Truth*, II, pp. 904 *et seq.*

> hitherto managed to maintain in it, they have fully proved their ability to carry on good government even in most difficult circumstances. They are likely to prove to us the greatest asset in Central and Eastern Europe. It would be most deplorable should they leave the Peace Conference disappointed and with a feeling of having been abandoned to the Germans or Magyars.

The problem of the future frontiers of the new state with Germany and Austria was intensively examined. The main argument was that the frontier between the Czechs and the Germans could not be drawn upon a purely ethnical basis, although a more or less clear-cut ethnical boundary existed, because Bohemia was a unit which for geographical, strategical, and economic reasons must not be broken up. 'The Bohemian mountain bastion is one of the most striking gestures on the map of Europe; its unity is almost as clearly marked as that of an island.' Another difficulty was seen. The German minority in Bohemia did not inhabit a compact part of the country but held almost the entire mountain fringe from the Danube to the Oder. Thus, 'Should all the German districts of Bohemia and northern Moravia be separated from the Czecho-Slovak state its position would be practically untenable.' A third reason advanced for deviating from the ethnical principle was the economic argument. The German-inhabited fringe contained the most important industrial and mining districts of Bohemia. Without these raw materials the industries located in the Czech cities would be almost crippled. For these reasons, the two areas should remain united. Either the German parts of Bohemia must remain part of the Czech state or Bohemia must be included in German land.

But why prefer the right of the Czechs to national self-determination to that of the Germans in Bohemia? It was argued that the latter solution would mean that the Czech nation would not exist among the nations of Europe, 'whereas the inclusion of the German fringe of Bohemia in the Czech state does not inflict any serious injury on the German nation'. Besides, there were more Czechs than Germans in Bohemia and the majority should prevail.

Since the inclusion within Czechoslovakia of a large German minority would be both extremely inconvenient and downright dangerous to the Czechs, it was obvious that the numbers of

Germans in Czechoslovakia should be reduced if at all possible. In the paper the prospects of such a reduction were viewed pessimistically: the three western and purely German districts of Austrian Silesia might be detached without hurting the Czech state, which could be more readily done because it was not proposed to award the adjacent German districts of Prussian Silesia (Ratibor and Leobschutz) to Poland. Otherwise only minor frontier rectifications in southern Bohemia and southern Moravia seemed feasible. It was granted that rectifications of this kind would not appreciably diminish the German minority in Czechoslovakia. The reduction would be only about 500,000.

Basically, the only solution to the German problem in Bohemia was seen to lie in agreement between the two nationalities. While the economic interests of the Bohemian Germans might incline them towards accepting union with the Czechs, it was impossible to say how those interests would be affected contrarily by nationalist tendencies. On this, the memorandum read

> The Bohemian and Moravian Germans are speaking in rather softer accents than they are wont to do, but this may be due to temporary helplessness; they have been beaten, and are on the brink of starvation, whilst it is within the power of the Czechs to supply them with the much-needed food. But will they continue sufficiently long in that comparatively humble mood, and will the Czechs succeed in using the opportunity with a view to establishing some possible *modus vivendi*? Should it prove impossible to reach it, German Bohemia will remain a storm-centre in Europe as long as politics are discussed in terms of nationality, and it will probably be found beyond the reach of statesmanship to devise any solution for the problem.

Having made this extremely pessimistic prediction, the memorandum then considered what the Allied Powers might do to help solve the German-Czech problem. It was felt that the Allies could do nothing more than mediate between the two nationalities and work to discourage the extreme Czech nationalists, some of whom were seen to believe that any policy as long as it was anti-German would prove pleasing to the victor powers.

> Yet it is not for us to work out any detailed schemes of frontier rectifications to be allowed to the Germans, as this would require

> a minute knowledge of local conditions such as only the parties directly concerned possess. The two nationalities will have to put forward their claims, and we must stand by the Czechs whenever they can prove paramount interests, and must not allow these interests to be overridden by an absolute claim to national self-determination. On the other hand, we must make it clear to the Czechs that the right of nationality acknowledged by the Allied Powers is not meant to be exclusively a means for anti-German map-making.

Wise policy could thus check schemes of a clearly aggressive anti-German (or for that matter of an anti-Magyar) nature.

The dangerously exposed strategic position of Czechoslovakia was seen as a potential brake upon Czech anti-German activities as well. Since the Czech state would contain a large German minority and would be more than half surrounded by German territory it could not safely embark on an anti-German policy, at least not until Russia had recovered. According to the memorandum, 'Russia has always been, and must remain, the pivot of Czech policy. The Czechs are determined to work for Russia's recovery and seem admirably suited for that task. Both politically and economically they are likely to prove a valuable link between the Anglo-Saxon Powers and Russia.' Ruling out the feasibility of Czech federation with German Austria or with the Magyars, the memorandum termed 'desirable' an alliance between the Czech and the Polish states. But it was not thought that this could be secured unless 'the Poles abandoned their aggressive imperialist schemes against Russia and gave up their anti-Russian attitude'. The possibility of a direct Polish-Czech clash was not seriously considered.

The memorandum also revealed a concern with the land-locked position of the new Czech state. The British government was advised that the economic interests of the new Czechoslovakia should be guaranteed by means of international provision for Czech commercial access to rail and water routes.

Apart from the enthusiastic pro-Czech attitude of the author or authors of this memorandum, its salient feature was the effort to reconcile overlapping national interests. To give the Czech nation frontiers embracing a viable economic and strategic area, a serious deviation was proposed from the principle of national self-determination and of boundaries drawn according to ethnic lines. It was frankly recognized that the political consequences of such a territorial settlement between Czechoslovakia and Germany might endanger the internal unity of the Czech state and threaten its international existence. In realistically calculating that the problem of Czech-German conflict would remain as long as men's minds and ambitions were dominated by nationalist considerations, the report could only hope that the Bohemian Germans' economic interests might counterbalance somewhat their nationalist tendencies, that Allied policy might moderate extreme Czech nationalist sentiments, and that the Czechs themselves would have the good sense to pursue a conciliatory policy towards the German minority and Germany.

The problem of German-Austrian relations was also considered in the memorandum on south-eastern Europe. The Czech demand that the Allied Powers prevent the Austrian Germans from joining Germany was termed unreasonable and contrary 'to our principles'. Any attempt to intervene between Austria and Germany was thought likely to be futile. Prophetically as events turned out the warning was made: '... if Germany and the Austrian Germans are not allowed to settle the question now according to their own wishes, on the day when this happens the problem of German Bohemia is likely to be unrolled once more'.

The idea of preventing the Austrian Germans from joining Germany was dismissed on grounds of principle and of expediency. It was held that the Austrian Germans had abandoned any hope of reconstituting Austria along the lines of a Danubian federation with Vienna as the centre. On November 12, 1918, the National Assembly of German Austria had unanimously adopted a new constitution which declared that German Austria was an integral part of the German Republic. Although this unanimity was described as somewhat artificial, it was argued that opposition to Austro-German Union was hopeless when no alternative existed:

> Unless some kind of Austria is reconstituted, which is contrary to our interests, as well as to the interests of the Czecho-Slovaks and the Jugo-Slavs, the Austrian Germans are bound to join Germany.
>
> We cannot exterminate the Austrian Germans; we cannot make them cease to feel German. They are bound to be somewhere. Nothing would be gained by compelling them to lead a separate

> existence from that of Germany. Such enforced separation would merely stimulate German nationalism, but could not prevent co-operation between the two branches, nor their final reunion. Lastly [a reflection of earlier Foreign Office views], the inclusion of German Austria in Germany is not altogether disadvantageous from our point of view; it would restore the balance between the Catholic south and the Protestant north, and help to check Prussianism in Germany.

It was also contended that *Anschluss* would prevent the German 'Ostmark' on the Danube from ever reconstituting a Danubian federation under German leadership.

Turning to territorial questions in western Europe, the French claim to the Lorraine-Saar coalfield was examined in an informational type of memorandum prepared by the Political Intelligence Department of the Foreign Office.[1] In general, the value of the coalfield to Germany was minimized and its potential value to France played up. The conclusion was that the Saar Basin offered a convenient supply of coal for Alsace-Lorraine and eastern France, coal which Germany did not need. The disadvantage of French acquisition of the Saar was pointed out: France would face 'a serious race problem'. While a definite policy was not recommended, the tone of the paper indicated sympathy for the French claim to the Saar Basin.

The Foreign Office paper on Belgium,[2] in dealing with territorial questions, supported rectifications in the Limbourg region, but warned that the Belgians would be wise not to press their claims if they received Luxembourg and a satisfactory arrangement for the navigation of the Scheldt. A minor frontier rectification in the Malmedy region was supported.

On the other hand, Belgian annexation of the south bank of of the mouth of the Scheldt was opposed although it was granted that the existing frontier was inconvenient from a geographical point of view and that the situation at the mouth of the Scheldt

[1] 'French Claims to Lorraine-Saar Coal Field', December 21, 1918, Foster Papers. If papers on the Rhineland Question were prepared, they do not appear in the Foster and the Borden collections.

[2] 'Belgium', December 11, 1918, Foster Papers. Curzon reported that the King of the Belgians had pressed a claim to the Dutch territories on the left bank of the Scheldt. The Belgian minister in London, however, had told Balfour that the Belgians were only seeking freedom of navigation along the Scheldt for warships.

would be much simpler if such an annexation occurred. The proposed transfer was resisted, however, partly on historic grounds, partly on the basis of the right of national self-determination. Instead, it was recommended that Belgium be given the right, by treaty, in case of unprovoked attack, to call for aid.

Admiralty policy on the question of the Scheldt was laid down in a memorandum of January 1919[1]: Belgium should not be granted the right to navigate the Scheldt with men-of-war and any Belgian claim to annex the Dutch provinces south of the Scheldt should not be supported. The reasons were briefly stated:

> Should Holland have the sole power to permit the use of the Scheldt by men-of-war or should this power be shared by Belgium? Possession of this power permits the establishment of a naval base close to the British coast which could menace British trade and naval power in wartime. Therefore, it is 'obvious' that the fewer nations that have this power the better. In years to come Belgium may be allied with powers hostile to Great Britain. . . .

Therefore, from the naval point of view the Belgian claims should be opposed.[2] By implication, neither the Foreign Office nor the Admiralty advisors recommended German territorial cessions to Holland in return for Dutch transfers to Belgium.

In defining its desiderata, the General Staff recommended[3] that Dutch Limbourg remain under Dutch sovereignty, while granting that if it were annexed to Belgium, the length of the Belgian frontier would not thereby be increased and that Belgians could be expected to defend it more energetically than would the Dutch. On the other hand, it was thought that any

[1] 'Summary of Admiralty Policy in relation to the Peace Settlement', Admiralty, January 1919, Foster Papers.

[2] Although the Admiralty's statement on policy was comprehensive and world-wide in its scope, as far as German territorial questions were concerned the only important issue to the Admiralty, apparently, was the question of the Scheldt. Of course, the removal of the menace of Heligoland was advocated.

[3] 'General Staff Desiderata regarding Territorial Adjustments', Paris, February 19, 1919 (Henry Wilson, General, Chief of the Imperial General Staff, Chief of the Military Section, British Delegation), Foster Papers. This was not a 'pre-conference' plan.

resistance which the Belgians could mount would not likely be as effective a deterrent to a German invasion as would the infringement of Dutch neutrality 'the maintenance of which has been proved by the experience of this war to be an important German interest'.

In dealing with other issues, Sir Henry Wilson, who was a member of Lloyd George's intimate circle at Paris and Chief of the Imperial General Staff, argued that French and Belgian demands 'for territorial aggrandisement on their eastern frontiers' while not strengthening their offensive power, would improve their defensive ability. Therefore, the Saar Valley should be given to France, which strategically would not lengthen the French frontier and would give the French more room for manœuvre and another east-west railway. France would also acquire coal for exploiting the Briey ironfield.

Sir Henry showed grave concern for the growing preponderance of German manpower over that of France and Belgium. To reduce the deficit, he advised detaching the Rhineland from the German military system, but opposed any French claim to the Rhineland. In his opinion, Malmedy and Moresnet should be annexed to Belgium.

In eastern Europe, the General Staff recommended that the frontiers of Poland be settled on ethnical grounds, while taking into consideration the necessities of transportation, particularly of the best possible communications between Poland and Czechoslovakia. Poland could gain access to the sea if a Polish enclave was created between the Vistula and the eighteenth degree of longitude as far south as Bromberg, where a narrow strip of German territory should exist to permit direct communications between east and west Prussia. 'Across this strip of territory communication between the Polish *enclave* on the coast and Poland would be provided by a national "corridor".' It is not quite clear what the General Staff had in mind, but probably Polish transit rights across the German strip were envisaged. The proposed Polish 'corridor' was not considered militarily defensible, but neither was 'a narrow tongue of Polish territory projecting from Poland proper to the sea'.

Regarding the Czecho-German frontier, the General Staff advised that the military security of the Czechoslovaks should override any violation of the principle of national self-determination. Nothing was said about German-Austrian relations.[1]

In December 1918, the British Board of Trade circulated a memorandum on economic considerations affecting the terms of peace.[2] Although the Board of Trade had no recommendations to make regarding specific territorial adjustments, it did deal at length with economic considerations affecting territorial changes in Europe and elsewhere. An analysis of this memorandum as a whole would take us beyond the immediate scope of this study. The general statement, however, dealing with economic considerations affecting territorial changes is worth noting in full.

> It is fully realized that in the determination of territorial changes made possible by the successful issue of the war, whether such changes take the form of the distribution among the successful belligerents of conquered territories, or are made in pursuance of the recognition of the national rights of hitherto subject races, military and political desiderata must, generally speaking, outweigh commercial considerations. Nevertheless, these last are of great importance; there is good reason to believe that some at least of the Governments associated with the British Government will attach much weight to them; and, as will be shown later, they must seriously influence the course to be taken in respect of any new States to be established by the victorious Governments. In these circumstances it is absolutely necessary for the British Government to determine its own economic desiderata as clearly as possible, especially as our own commercial interests are not always identical in these matters with those of some of our Allies, while in other cases in which there may be no actual divergence of interest, the relative importance attached to particular points by different Allied countries would differ very widely. There is

[1] Like the Admiralty statement of policy and the General Staff's paper, the memorandum by the Chief of the Air Staff on the peace settlement, dated January 22, 1919, was world-wide in scope. In making his recommendations from the standpoint of air power and the future of both service and civil aviation, the Chief of the Air Staff had little to say about German territorial questions in Europe. It is remarkable that frontier questions in western Europe were not deemed of sufficient interest from the standpoint of air power and of Britain's position in the new air age to warrant discussion.

[2] 'Memorandum by the Board of Trade on Economic Considerations affecting the terms of Peace', Board of Trade, November 1918, revised December 1918, Foster Papers.

obviously a danger in such cases that particular British interests may be sacrificed unduly in comparison with interests which affect equally the Allies as a whole.

The economic considerations involved in the questions of Alsace-Lorraine and of Poland were given as specific examples of what the Board of Trade had in mind. The Lancashire trade was deeply interested in maintaining in Alsace the customs regime known as 'admission temporaire' for textile goods exported to be printed near Mulhouse and then re-exported. French practice in this regard had been much less liberal than the German. Measures, therefore, should be taken to ensure that British trade would not suffer differential treatment or be subject to treatment more onerous than that which prevailed when the territory was under the sovereignty of the previous regime. Similarly, British iron-masters might be interested in utilizing the iron-ore deposits of Lorraine. They were, therefore, interested in the absence of obstacles, such as export duties imposed by the French government. Alsace also was a major source of potash and its transfer to France would make the Allied countries more independent of Germany. Some agreement should be reached with France to secure a reasonable share of the potash for other countries. A transfer of Lorraine would decrease by half German production of iron ore and double French production besides transferring a large pig-iron industry to France. One result of the incorporation into France of such an important mineral producing and manufacturing area as Alsace-Lorraine might be to intensify domestic competition in the French market. This might lead to an increase in French tariffs with serious consequences for British trade. These considerations were not advanced as reasons for opposing the transfer but as a warning to the British government about the consequences of the territorial changes envisaged.[1]

The Board of Trade was also insistent that the principle of freedom of transit should be applied to all transferred territories. It argued that the question of direct access to the sea for the new

[1] In general, the British Board of Trade advocated, as a policy most favourable to British interests, the principle of the open door for the trade and shipping of all Allied countries in transferred territories. It pointed out that if Great Britain was protected against discrimination, actual tariff levels were of secondary importance.

states of eastern and middle-eastern Europe was 'of far greater importance to Great Britain as the premier shipping and export country than to many of her allies'. One specific example given was Poland. The Board of Trade pointed out that unless Danzig was ceded to Poland, the free navigation of the Vistula would be a question of vital importance to the new state. It urged that the traditional British doctrine regarding international rivers be upheld, namely that they be open to the ships of all nations at least for the purpose of through traffic. It warned that the domination of Poland by Germany would be certain if Poland could only communicate with overseas countries either by its own ships or by the ships of other riparian states and if no non-riparian states had the right to send their ships into its territory. The Board of Trade took no definite stand on Danzig; its major recommendation was that freedom of transit should be ensured.

In general, the position of the Board of Trade was that, whatever territorial changes took place on the continent, the British government should make sure that existing states which gained territory from the enemy and new states carved out of former regimes should, as a *quid pro quo* for British support and that of other Allied and Associated Powers, not subject the trade of Allied countries to differential treatment, to prohibitive or excessive duties—especially to duties heavier than those to which their trade was subjected under the former regime. To realize this end, the Board of Trade recommended that British economic interests involved in territorial transfers should be advanced by the following lines of policy: the principle of the open door (with exceptions); recognition of all valid concessions held by subjects of citizens of Allied countries and transferred territories; provision for compensation in case of expropriation; and the application of the principle of freedom of transit to all transferred territory.

What were the trends of French bureaucratic thought on German and allied territorial questions?[1] It will be recalled that in late 1916 the Briand government defined French war aims as

[1] The organization of French studies on the departmental level and in the *Comité d'Etudes* under the direction of Ernest Lavisse are discussed in Jules Laroche's *Au Quai d'Orsay avec Briand et Poincaré, 1913-1926*, pp. 58-9; see also Marston, *Peace Conference*, p. 112.

including not only the recovery of Alsace-Lorraine but also the acquisition of the Saar Valley and the detachment of the left bank of the Rhine from Germany for both strategic and economic reasons. As the more extreme provisions of the Petrograd Agreement of February 1917 showed, French political leaders were by no means of one mind about how to deal with the Franco-German borderlands. Similarly, the civilian and military advisors of French governments were divided over the settlement to strive for in both western and eastern Europe, although opinion in Paris appears to have been monolithic on Alsace-Lorraine and the Saar, and on the desirability of weakening the political and economic foundations of the Bismarckian Reich.

A basic strategic blueprint for French postwar security policy was drafted in the Ministry of Foreign Affairs in the autumn of 1917.[1] Three key ideas were advanced: (1) the permanent demilitarization of the Rhineland to strengthen the defense of Paris, of the vital mining regions of France and of Belgium (the latter consideration, it was thought, would especially appeal to England and America); provision for additional security through perpetual Inter-Allied control of the German railway system on the left bank of the Rhine; (2) the promotion of German political and economic disunity; and (3) a Franco-British defensive military alliance supplemented by a permanent Franco-British-American economic entente.

The core of the scheme were the proposals to secure German political and economic disunity by offering economic inducements to Bavaria, Wurtemburg, Saxony, and former German states annexed by Prussia to declare their independence. The exact form of the new German order was not made entirely clear. A federated Germany was envisaged in which each state would have equal rights with truncated Prussia and would possess privileges '. . . analogues à ceux dont jouissent les Etats qui se sont groupés dans la fédération des Etats-Unis d'Amérique'. A major deviation from the American system was however proposed, namely, the dissolution of the Zollverein, which would be replaced by three economic regions, each of which would stand in a different relationship toward the Allies: Prussia, in

[1] 'Note préliminaire sur la réorganisation de l'Allemagne', October 27, 1917, Klotz Archives.

an unfavourable position; the Rhineland in a highly favourable one; and the other German states associated with Prussia, in a mixed one.

To prevent union between the reorganized Germanic federation and Austria, the plan proposed offering special economic advantages to the Austrian Germans, including the same favourable customs regime to be applied to the Rhineland.

The postwar defensive military alliance between France and Great Britain together with the economic entente linking France, Great Britain, and the United States were intended to uphold the proposed new German order and to provide 'la principale garantie de la France contre des aggressions futures ou contre une pénétration économique de la part de l'Allemagne'.[1]

The significance of the *Note préliminaire* of October 27, 1917, is hard to assess. At least, the *Note* represented a current of thought which anticipated Clemenceau's post-Armistice grand policy. The view that close relations with Great Britain and the United States would constitute the most effective guarantee of French security lay at the heart of Clemenceau's course in the peace negotiations of 1919.

The general aim underlying the varying views of French civilian and military advisors in late 1918 was defined thus: 'Pour assurer à l'Europe une paix durable, il faut détruire l'œuvre de Bismarck, qui a créé une Allemagne militarisé, bureaucratisée, méthodique, sans scrupules, une formidablement machine de guerre, épanouissement de l'histoire de cette Prusse qui a été définie: une armée qui a une nation.'[2] How to attain this end was a subject of some disagreement among French bureaucratic planners.

In *L'Allemagne de demain et les allemands d'Autriche*, the idea of rendering Germany harmless by a return to the pre-1866 regime was dismissed as puerile and chimeric. The existence and force of German nationalism could not be ignored. To attempt to

[1] The Note referred to the Inter-Allied Economic Committees as preparing the way for the economic entente and urged therefore that the role of the Committees be further developed. French diplomacy at the Paris Peace Conference sought, without success, to win American approval for the continuation of the wartime inter-Allied economic organization.

[2] 'L'Allemagne de demain et les allemands d'Autriche', Ministère des Affairs étrangères, October 25, 1918, Klotz Archives.

re-create German disunity as it existed before Bismarck would simply lead to endless conflict. Instead, 'Il faut mieux laisser aux Allemands le moins possible d'aspirations non satisfait, mais justifiables, c'est à dire basées sur un désir d'unité nationale, non sur un désir de conquête.'

Germany, however, should be weakened in various ways. Non-German areas like Alsace-Lorraine and the Polish provinces should be removed from the Reich. Prussian territorial supremacy in Germany should be eliminated by forcing the restoration of Hanover and by dispossessing Prussia of its Rhineland provinces. Constitutionally Prussia should lose its commanding position. Politically and culturally Prussian influence in Germany should be counter-balanced by the addition of German Austria. This solution for German reorganization did not call for the destruction of Germany as a Great Power in terms of area, population, or internal unity.

In many respects, these moderate French views were similar in spirit and in detail to those held in the British Foreign Office since 1916 on territorial dismemberment and Austria. The proposed interference in internal German constitutional and political affairs, however, was not paralleled on the British side. They were close to Balfour's insistence on preserving German Germany, although they were more sanguine on the Austrian Question than the British Foreign Secretary had been.

A far more extreme position was taken by Gabriel Hanotaux.[1] Convinced that the leaders of the German revolution had entered into a conspiracy with Germany's former rulers to preserve German unity as the indispensable foundation for the revival of German power, Hanotaux's target was the destruction of the Bismarckian Reich. Seeking to turn the clock back to the early nineteenth century, Hanotaux urged the reduction of Prussia to its pre-1866 boundaries and the restoration of Germany 'à sa vie conféderative naturelle', through the establishment of a system of German states linked by a common Diet with severely limited powers. Also, he supported extreme territorial dismemberment, including the severance from Germany of Alsace-Lorraine, the left bank of the Rhine,

[1] 'Après la signature de l'armistice: du sort de l'Allemagne unifiée', November 11, 1918, Ministère des Affaires étrangères, Klotz Archives.

Hanover, Schleswig, and the Polish provinces, among others. To secure German acceptance of such a draconian anachronistic settlement, he advised a prolonged occupation of the west, south, and centre; a vigorous propaganda campaign throughout Germany on behalf of liberty; and separate peace treaties with the German states to give international sanction to the break-up of the Bismarckian Reich. In addition, Hanotaux advocated using the lever of food supply in the following spirit, as he put it, 'Ainsi que l'a dit M. Clemenceau, nous nourrions l'Allemagne "dans la limite où cela ne nous nuira pas".'

If the advisors of the Clemenceau government differed in their approach to the problem of the overall political and territorial treatment of Germany, they differed also over more specific questions like that of Austro-German relations. By implication, Hanotaux opposed union between Vienna and Berlin. On the other hand, there were strong advocates of *Anschluss*. The author of *l'Allemagne de demain et les allemands d'Autriche* opposed the maintenance of the Habsburg Empire in whole or part, under new or old political forms, for fear the German Austrians would remain German satellites and their subjects, mere tools of Pan-Germanism. In his view, which seems typical of French hopes in general, if the non-German peoples of Danubian Europe were separated politically from Austria, they would be in a better position in the future to unite and to obtain support against Germanism.

He supported union between German Austria and Germany on several grounds. *Anschluss*, secret or public, would be difficult to prevent, in which case '. . . ne vaut-il pas mieux regarder en face le danger, l'avoir toujours présent sous les yeux pour se rappeler la nécessité de s'armer contre lui?' Moreover, union was seen to offer certain positive advantages. The addition of Roman Catholic Austria to the Reich would alter the political, religious, and cultural balance of Germany to the disadvantage of Prussia. At the same time, a source of German irredentism would be eliminated. 'Serai-t-il logique et raisonnable de semer à côté d'elle un levain de nationalisme, en maintenant les Allemands d'Autriche séparés de leurs frères de race, ou en ne les réunissant à eux que pour diviser à nouveau l'Allemagne?' The objection that union would bring territory and resources to Germany was countered with the argument that these accretions would be more than counterbalanced by German territorial losses elsewhere.

This line of argument was reiterated and strengthened in *La Physionomie de l'Allemagne de demain au point de vue de la configuration et de la superficie en cas de réincorporation des allemands d'Autriche.*[1] After reviewing the probable effects of union, the author concluded: '. . . cette annexion ne comporterait pas pour nous un danger de nature à nous amener à faire n'importe quel sacrifice pour l'éviter'. In any event, in his opinion, '. . . cette annexion est inévitable'. Instead of opposing the movement for Austro-German union, the French government should use it as a pretext for demanding compensation for the advantages being gained by Germany. But, this should be done at once. Otherwise, '. . . il pourrait arriver que, le jour òu elle se réaliserait, nous ne nous trouvions plus en situation de poser nos conditions'. This prophesy was to be realized in March 1938.

Contrary advice came from the General Staff which favoured an independent Austria as a buffer state between Germany and Italy. Italy, it was assumed, was likely to gravitate towards Germany after the war in a search for military support against the Slavs in the Adriatic and under the impulse of colonial and Mediterranean rivalries with France. In these circumstances, the General Staff feared that a common Italo-German frontier would facilitate an alliance between Rome and Berlin. Thus the curt military injunction: 'Empêcher la création de cette frontière.'[2]

The spirit of the French approach to the problems of the Franco-German borderlands was cogently expressed in one Foreign Ministry paper: 'Nous avons le droit de vouloir vivre. Prenons nos sûretés.'[3] One guarantee of French and European security was unquestioned: the return of Alsace-Lorraine to France. But the Rhineland Question evoked differences of opinion. Hanotaux sought the detachment of the left bank from Germany. The author of *La Physionomie de l'Allemagne* simply envisaged preventing Germany from using the left bank as a

[1] Ministère des Affaires étrangères (no date, but probably after October 25, 1918), Klotz Archives.

[2] 'Propositions de l'état-major de l'armie, Qème. Bureau A', November 23, 1918, Klotz Archives.

[3] 'L'Allemagne de demain . . .', *op. cit.*

military base, an objective which could be attained short of separating the area from the Reich. In view of Clemenceau's ultimate acceptance of a compromise Rhineland settlement which included demilitarization, it is significant to note that within the French Ministry of Foreign Affairs in both 1917 and 1918 there was a current of opinion on the Rhineland Question which appears restrained and moderate when compared with the Briand position in 1916 or Foch's and Hanotaux's at the end of the war.

Unanimity evidently prevailed in the Quai d'Orsay on the Saar Question: France should annex the entire Saar Basin to compensate for wartime mining losses and to acquire a defensive glacis which would provide a sounder strategic frontier than the line of either 1814 or 1815. From the Ministry of War came additional arguments designed to show that the French postwar coal position would be weaker compared to the prewar situation because the coal requirements of Alsace-Lorraine would increase the chronic French coal deficit.[1] Acquisition of the coal resources of the Saar would partially solve this problem.

The link between the problem of French security in western Europe and the settlement in eastern Europe was incisively brought out in a Ministry of Foreign Affairs' project of December 20, 1918, for the handling of the Polish Question.[2] This candid exposition gives a striking insight into the Quai d'Orsay's approach to peacemaking generally and in the vital eastern European area particularly.

The basic strategic aim of the recommendations were embodied in a single sentence: 'Or nous avons un besoin vital d'une Pologne forte, anti-allemande et anti-bolchevique.' The thought behind this objective was thus explained:

> MOTIFS:
>
> (1) L'Allemagne ne sera définitivement vaincue que si elle perd les provinces polonaises.
>
> (2) La France a besoin pour assurer sa sécurité sur le Rhin qu'il existe par dela 'les Allemaignes' une puissance forte. La Russie étant affaiblie, probablement pour longtemps et d'ailleurs

[1] November 30, 1918, Klotz Archives.

[2] 'Une méthode d'action in Pologne', December 20, 1918, Klotz Archives.

ne devant plus avoir de frontière commune avec l'Allemagne, cette puissance forte ne peut être que la Pologne alliée à la Bohème et à la Roumanie. Plus tard nous aurons à menager une entente russo-polonaise. Plus nous agrandirons la Pologne aux dépens de l'Allemagne, plus nous serons certains qu'elle restera son ennemie.[1]

(3) La Pologne est actuellement l'écran necessaire entre le bolchevisme russe et la révolution allemande. Elle est l'un des segments solides du cordon sanitaire que nous avons besoin de tendre autour de la Russie malade et contagieuse. Nous ne viendrons à bout du bolchevisme que quand nous pourrons nous appuyer sur la Pologne et nous servir de ses armées.

In dealing with problems of frontier delimitation some compromise was sought between strategy and the principle of self-determination: 'Le problème de la délimitation consiste à faire une Pologne aussi grande et forte que possible en respectant le Droit des peuples.' How were these aims worked out in the specific recommendations covering the German-Polish borderlands?

The general principle was laid down that Poland should take over from Germany all territory whose population was more than 30 to 35 per cent. Polish. If this rule seemed to depart from the principle of self-determination by majority rule, 30 to 35 per cent. was justified because Prussian population statistics were alleged to be not only biased but also swollen artificially by the presence of Prussian officials, military garrisons, and colonists implanted under the anti-Polish settlement laws. To achieve a fair settlement under this rule, the report recommended local adjustments by a frontier delimitation commission and population exchanges to eliminate enclaves. Map 2 shows the approximate recommended frontier.[2]

In view of the ultimate settlement of the Danzig problem, the suggestions advanced were significant. The preferred solution was to award the city to Poland under provisions safeguarding the rights of the German inhabitants and leaving to Germany the area east of the western mouth of the Vistula. To

[1] Ironically, this advocacy of stimulating tensions between states was in a memorandum whose pages, like other papers in the dossiers of the French plenipotentiaries, were bound together with thin metal tabs upon which was imprinted the word PAX.

[2] See p. 195.

assure proper transit facilities, Germany should have unrestricted use of the Berlin-Koenigsberg railway and all nations should enjoy freedom of navigation for their ships and goods along the Vistula. However, it was contemplated that during the peace negotiations, '. . . on pourrait être amené à une transaction faisant de Dantzig une sorte de ville libre rattachée à l'Allemagne òu les Polonais auraient en toute propriété un port, des docks, des gares, etc.'. This proposal anticipated the actual final settlement.

The discussion of Polish-Lithuanian relations is also noteworthy. In the first place, it was asserted that the policy of the Entente was now to guarantee the independence of Lithuania provided that the Lithuanians united with Poland economically and militarily, leading perhaps to a federal union between the two countries. Several advantages were seen in this course of action. Poland would be strengthened. Russia would be cut off from direct territorial access to Germany. The French interest in the diminution of Prussia would be served by the transfer of East Prussian districts to Lithuania. Lastly, East Prussia, isolated from Germany, weakened by losses to Poland and Lithuania, would in time likely be fully absorbed by its neighbours. 'Memel deviendra le port de la Lithuanie, qui, par suite de cette annexion, restera l'ennemie de l'Allemagne.' Thus, in another area, hostility between Germany and its eastern neighbours would be encouraged in an effort to ensure that new east European states like Poland and Lithuania would be French clients in an anti-German security system.

How had the views of American specialists developed while their English and French counterparts had been shaping their recommendations on German territorial questions? In 1917, on instructions from President Wilson, Colonel House had organized 'The Inquiry', a research body whose specific function was to examine and to report to the President upon the issues which would arise at the Peace Conference after the war.[1] Staffed primarily by university professors leavened with journalists, 'The Inquiry' gained a unique and independent position in relation to the state and other governmental departments, particularly in giving advice to the President on terri-

[1] *P.P.C.*, I, pp. 9 *et seq.*, contains useful materials on the development and work of 'The Inquiry'.

torial and political questions. Also, leading members of the staff of 'The Inquiry' were frequently employed at Paris as American negotiators on such issues. A summary of the results of the American studies is found in the Black Book or 'Outline of Tentative Report and Recommendations' of January 21, 1919.[1] Prepared for the American plenipotentiaries to the Paris Peace Conference, the Black Book contained the recommendations of the American technical advisors on European and extra-European territorial problems, thus providing a convenient capsule picture of their pre-conference approach to German boundary issues.

In western Europe they recommended the return to France of Alsace-Lorraine within the boundaries of 1870. They further recommended the annexation by France of that part of the Saar Valley which had been French in 1814, provided that equitable compensation was paid those Germans who wished to sell their property and return to Germany. They justified this transfer of territory on historic grounds and as an indemnity to France for the damage done by Germany to the French coal-mines. They granted that the proposed annexation would involve the transfer of some 355,000 people who did not wish union with France. But they felt that the French need for the coal supplies of the Saar overrode the present desires of the Saarlanders.

As for the Rhineland, they advised that, while it should remain under German sovereignty, the left bank of the Rhine should be completely demilitarized for strategic reasons. If demilitarization of the left bank proved unacceptable, however, the French frontier should be extended to include most of the

[1] A.C.N.P., vol. 297, 185.112/1, 'Outline of Tentative Report and Recommendations', prepared by the Intelligence Section of the American Delegation, in accordance with instructions, for the President and the Plenipotentiaries, January 21, 1919. Copies also in the *Miller Diary*, Wilson Papers, House Papers, Bliss Papers. This report contained recommendations for the territorial settlement in Europe and Asia Minor, as well as on economic and labour questions. It had been prepared on orders given to Mezes by Wilson on or around January 1. It did not constitute a set of instructions. The copies in the archives of the plenipotentiaries do not make clear whether it was actually read—marginal notes are non-existent. See J. T. Shotwell, *At the Paris Peace Conference*, pp. 133-4, for a short discussion of the 'Black Book'.

basin of the Saar and the territory between the Lauter and the Queich should be annexed to Alsace. This proposal was upheld on strategic and historic grounds.

Turning to Belgium, the American technical advisors recommended revision of the treaty of 1839 and the abolition of neutral status. As for the Scheldt, the south bank of some 275 square miles with its 'only' 79,000 inhabitants should be ceded to Belgium to give that country a natural defensive frontier and commercial freedom. They also advised rectification of the Belgian frontier in the regions of Malmedy and Maastricht. Once again, the principle of vital strategic necessity was invoked to justify the recommendation and to override the factor of national self-determination.

In the east, they proposed that an independent Poland should include all areas with Polish majorities who lived adjacent to the main Polish group, thus avoiding Polish irredentism as far as possible. They submitted a German-Polish line which included only unmistakably Polish territory 'insofar as the sinuosities of the linguistic frontier permit'.

In discussing the problem of Polish access to the sea the American specialists employed arguments which were to become very familiar during the negotiations. They reminded the Commissioners of the difficulties: if access were given to Poland, 1,600,000 Germans in East Prussia would be cut off from the rest of Germany; if Poland were denied such an access, 600,000 Poles would come under German rule and 20,000,000 Poles would have a hampered and precarious outlet to the world. German transit rights across the corridor could be assured more easily than port facilities on German territory. In the judgment of the American specialists, Poland had vital interests involved, while Germany, apart from the force of Prussian sentiment, had only secondary interests at stake. For these reasons, the Commissioners were advised that Poland should acquire a corridor and Danzig. The Report also claimed that a sharply defined linguistic line separated Poland from East Prussia. It recommended a boundary in this region which left only small Polish and German groups under the sovereignty of the other state. An alternative line was shown which left to Germany all but the south-eastern corner of West Prussia.

The American advisors did not pronounce on the German-

Lithuanian frontier. Since they preferred a political union between Poland and Lithuania, it might be inferred that the fate of Memel was a foregone conclusion.

In the south, they recommended the historic frontier between Bohemia and Germany, thus including the district of Eger in Czechoslovakia. Granting that this proposed frontier would place 2,500,000 Germans in the new Czechoslovakian state, the American specialists argued that the economic interests of the Sudeten Germans bound them to Czechoslovakia. They also claimed that the Sudeten Germans, according to reports, mainly favoured the proposed union if their minority rights and economic equality were guaranteed. As for German-Austria, they suggested its establishment as a sovereign state.

On the eve of the Paris Peace Conference, where then did the bureaucrats and special advisors stand on the issues associated with the German territorial settlement? It would be folly to pretend to answer this question fully. The evidence is inadequate. Some of the men and the departments involved had not made up their minds. But the British, French, and American proposals examined above had obvious similarities and ominous differences. If they did not necessarily represent fixed governmental policies, they did embody the ideas of men who were to play an important part in the Paris negotiations. In the case of the British delegation, a close parallel will be found to exist between the Foreign Office plans in particular and the attitude taken by Lloyd George and Balfour, if not by all of their advisors, in drafting the German territorial settlement.

To sum up, the British Foreign Office sought to pour old wine into new bottles. Its basic approach to the European settlement started with British interests and it attempted to reconcile particular with general interests. The settlement should harmonize with the idea of the League of Nations while safeguarding national security in case the League of Nations proved still-born or ineffective. British interests on the continent were given a traditional definition with a new twist. According to the Foreign Office view, Britain had no direct territorial and no special commercial interests in Europe. It sought peace, order, trade, and non-entanglement in continental wars. England should seek these ends through the balance of power, through security along the coast-line opposite Britain's shore, and through upholding the principles of nationality and of national self-determination. In the attempt to apply these principles in practice, a striking pattern emerged. In western Europe, France should be strengthened, but not to the extent of antagonizing Germany. If old sources of friction in the west could be removed and no new ones created, western Europe would probably enjoy a natural stability. France was not to be unduly strengthened, for instance, through the acquisition of Luxembourg. The Duchy should be employed to bolster Belgium economically and politically if its people desired union with the Belgians. The security of the coast opposite England should be further enhanced through a short-term alliance with Belgium. If Belgium was to be strengthened, it was not to be at the price of antagonizing the Dutch. In eastern Europe, the Foreign Office envisaged Great Britain playing the role of mediator. The erection of a Polish state would be supported, but not the establishment of a Greater Poland which could place the Poles in an impossible position between Germany and Russia. The aim was to minimize, not to maximize, friction between the Poles and their neighbours, especially the Germans. The Foreign Office was prepared to counter-balance German territorial losses by the union of German Austria to the Reich, which, it was hoped, would have a stabilizing influence. Great confidence was placed in the new Czech state as a constructive force in eastern Europe and as an intermediary between Britain and Russia. Therefore, the Czechs must have defensible frontiers and economic viability. Over all, the plan rested more on the principle of nationality than upon the principle of self-determination, although alone of the major proposals made before the Conference, the Foreign Office schemes made specific provision for plebiscites in certain areas as the means of determining the wishes of the inhabitants.

Any comparison between the views of the Foreign Office and those of the French and of the American advisors must be incomplete and rather misleading. From the various French proposals examined above, a certain general pattern emerged. Germany should be severely weakened in both western and eastern Europe, while centrifugal forces within the remainder of the Reich should be encouraged. France should be greatly strengthened. Poland and Czechoslovakia should be given strong frontiers as a further restraint upon Germany.

In many, if not all, respects, the pattern which emerged from the recommendations of the American advisors was closer to the French than to the English 'grand strategy'. The tone of the American experts' report, with its stress on strategic, historic, and economic factors, fitted imperfectly into the President's pronouncements on principles of peacemaking. These, in turn, both coincided and conflicted with the approach of the British Foreign Office. The latter's stress on nationality, fairness, plebiscites, moderation, the League of Nations struck a Wilsonian note; its idea of British interest and the balance of power sounded themes which Wilson had condemned. Yet, on balance, the Foreign Office proposals came closer to the spirit of his approach than did those of some of his advisors.

As for details, the British, French, and American advisors supported the return of Alsace-Lorraine to France with the frontiers of 1871, although the latter favoured the addition of the area between the Lauter and the Queich if the Rhineland was not demilitarized. French advice was unanimously in favour of securing the Saar. The American advisors were prepared to accept the 1814 line, and more if the Rhineland remained militarized; the Foreign Office seemed to sympathize with the French demand, while the General Staff favoured annexation of the Saar by France. A strong current of opinion in the French Foreign Office sought the military neutralization of the Rhineland, while advisors like Foch and Hanotaux demanded its full separation from Germany. Among the British, Sir Henry Wilson favoured demilitarization but opposed political separation. Probably this was the attitude of most governmental officials in London. The American advisors accepted demilitarization under German sovereignty. All agreed that Belgium should acquire Malmedy and should not return to its former neutralized status, but the Foreign Office and the Admiralty rejected the transfer of the left bank of the Scheldt to Belgium; the Americans advised it. With respect to Poland, the Foreign Office and the American experts insisted that ethnical lines must be followed with suitable geographic and other modifications; the French proposals sought maximum Polish gains at Germany's expense primarily for strategic reasons.

On the vital issues of Danzig and Polish access to the sea, both the British Foreign Office and General Staff opposed the idea of awarding Danzig to Poland and of establishing a Polish-owned land corridor to the Baltic. In opposition to this position, both the American and French specialists favoured a Polish corridor and Polish sovereignty over Danzig although in the latter case, the Quai d'Orsay memorandum suggested the ultimate acceptability of establishing Danzig as a Free City in which Poland would possess port and commercial privileges. There was agreement about maintaining the historic German-Bohemian frontier, but significant differences existed over German-Austrian relations. The diplomatic advisors of the Foreign Office and the Quai d'Orsay supported the unification of Germany and German-Austria, while the American specialists sided with French military opinion in upholding the maintenance of an independent Austrian state.

These plans had much in common but their divergences foreshadowed difficulties for the victors in their attempt to devise a united front among themselves before they encountered the vanquished across the conference table.

V

GOVERNMENTAL ATTITUDES BEFORE PARIS

To turn from the realm of the civil servants to that of the politicians, although British ministers during the hectic pre-conference period faced a wide range of domestic and imperial issues, they were largely preoccupied with threshing out British policy on the settlement of the war. This process also involved preliminary exchanges of views with England's principal European allies and with the United States. The intergovernmental negotiations were highlighted by two major conferences in London: the Inter-Allied Conference of November 30 to December 3 among British, French, and Italian representatives, and the conversations between British statesmen and Woodrow Wilson during his trip to England at Christmas time. In these governmental preparations for the Peace Conference, German territorial questions occupied a rather modest place.

The shaping of British policy at the Cabinet level towards German territorial questions remains hidden in relative obscurity. Although the Imperial War Cabinet held twelve sessions between November 20 and December 31, the Imperial statesmen were not primarily concerned with European territorial issues. To them the vital problems of the peacemaking were the Italian claims, the future of Russia and Turkey, the Colonial question, reparations, freedom of the seas, and the League of Nations. They seldom discussed the great territorial issues involving Germany and its neighbours in western, eastern, and south-central Europe. In retrospect it seems quite logical that the Prime Ministers of the Dominions should concern themselves chiefly with the issues of greatest direct concern to their countries and to the Empire as a whole. After all, what was Upper Silesia compared to New Guinea from an Antipodean point of view! Perhaps, too, the English ministers tended to reserve European territorial questions for discussion in their more limited circle, apart from Italian claims in the Adriatic which were linked with Imperial questions. Since the British War Cabinet's records are not available and in view of the paucity of information in the existing memoirs and biographies, not much therefore can be said about the views of individual ministers and the evolution of British policy on the ministerial level before Paris on most European territorial questions.

Was the Government's approach to German boundary questions influenced by the Khaki election? The electoral campaign of late 1918 has been blamed for driving the British government in the direction of immoderate and vindictive treatment of Germany at the Peace Conference.[1] Undoubtedly, as the campaign developed, the leading issues and the tone of governmental pronouncements altered. In his opening address, Lloyd George defined his ideal as a peace settlement based upon the best of Gladstonian traditions—respect for the rights and liberties of all nations.[2] In the Lloyd George-Bonar Law manifesto of November 21, the Coalition pledged itself to seek a League of Nations, disarmament, and the abolition of conscription.[3] For the first week to ten days of the campaign, the government appeared to be going to fight the election primarily on domestic questions and on a restrained, liberal, Wilsonian peace policy.

Then, near the end of November, different subjects began to be emphasized by most governmental spokesmen, as evidenced by Lloyd George's appeal on questions of peace policy at Newcastle-on-Tyne on November 29.[4] Enemy aliens, war costs, the prosecution of the Kaiser and other alleged war criminals

[1] J. M. Keynes, *The Economic Consequences of the Peace*; Lloyd George, *The Truth about Reparations and War Debts*; *Truth*, I, 157-9; R. B. McCallum, *Public Opinion and the Last Peace*, chap. I.

[2] *The Times*, November 18, 1918, p. 4.

[3] *Liberal Magazine*, 1918.

[4] *The Times*, November 30, 1918, p. 6.

overshadowed the League of Nations, disarmament, and the abolition of conscription. Lloyd George's new electoral appeal clearly appeared in the political manifesto issued from 10 Downing Street on December 5.[1] While the contrast must not be overdrawn, in substance and tone the Manifesto of December 5 differed from the one issued on November 21. The latter was calm, moderate, reasoned. The former, largely negative, punitive, and emotional in character, recalling the Prime Minister's earlier calls in the Cabinet for stern treatment of the enemy. Lloyd George had sensed the mood of the electorate and dramatized a few, simple issues in his almost over successful effort to outbid the Labourites and the Asquithian Liberals. Asquith's speeches showed greater breadth and moderation, but the Coalition won the election. Thus Lloyd George went to Paris burdened with unwise promises, with false popular expectations and with the ultra blue House of Commons thrown up by the Khaki election.

If the result was disastrous for British policy on such subjects as reparations, the British attitude on German territorial questions seems largely unaffected by the campaign. The latter were scarcely mentioned in electoral speeches. At Queen's Hall on December 10, Lloyd George raised territorial problems in a general way before a crowd of newly enfranchised women.[2] While advocating a stern, just, and equitable peace, the Prime Minister cautioned: 'You must have no Alsace-Lorraining in our case.' When this statement provoked heckling, Lloyd George contended that the peacemakers must avoid settlements which would inevitably foster persistent national antagonisms as had the question of Alsace-Lorraine between Germany and France. Here Lloyd George reflected the considered views of the Foreign Office and anticipated similar assertions which he made in the Council of Four. It is doubtful whether the election and its political aftermath had much, if any, influence on the British course in territorial negotiations at Paris.

In intergovernmental negotiations, the British government

[1] *Liberal Magazine*, 1918; another manifesto issued on December 10 as Lloyd George's election programme stressed trial of Kaiser, punishment of those responsible for atrocities, fullest indemnities, Britain for the British, rehabilitation, and a happier country for all. *The Times*, December 11, 1918, p. 6.

[2] *The Times*, December 10, 1918, p. 4.

had to contend in the first place with its French partner. Shortly after the signing of the German armistice, the French Foreign Office, in communications with foreign governments, took the general position that frontiers should be based upon the principle of the right of peoples to decide their destinies by a free and secret vote. This principle was modified by two others: the principle that boundaries in part should depend upon 'a certain homogeneousness of the states . . .' and the principle that existing administrative borders should be followed when convenient. Bohemia was given as an example of the former; the Polish-German frontier of the latter. By the homogeneity of states, the Quai d'Orsay evidently had in mind geographical and strategical factors of the type existing in Bohemia where nature seemed to have created a natural geographical unity which did not correspond with ethnical lines.[1] Besides urging the abrogation of all secret treaties, the French Foreign Office also regarded the Allied War Aims Declaration of January 10, 1917, as the basis of peace talks, rather than the Fourteen Points. Recognizing that this declaration did not constitute a working agenda for the Peace Conference, the French recommended that the Conference should first settle the questions arising out of the war and then proceed to organize a League of Nations.[2] From the Wilsonian point of view, various objections to these proposals arose: the Fourteen Points had just been accepted as the basis of peace negotiations; and the League must come first.

The French Foreign Office successively amended its draft programme for the Peace Conference. Its statement on the principles of boundary-making was clarified.[3] The suggestion was dropped that the Allied Declaration of January 10, 1917, provided the basis for negotiations. The Fourteen Points enjoyed a formal Gallic bow, as 'principles of public law', but they were still dismissed, because of their indefinite character, as the point of departure for the peace negotiations.[4]

[1] On December 19, the French government informed Vienna that it supported the historic borders of Bohemia, Moravia, and Austrian Silesia as the proper line for Czechoslovakia. *P.P.C.*, II, p. 383.

[2] For the entire memorandum see *P.P.C.*, I, pp. 344 *et seq.*

[3] *P.P.C.*, I, pp. 352-4.

[4] *P.P.C.*, I, pp. 365 *et seq.* The British Foreign Office received the text of this French memorandum on December 3, through the Italian ambassador in London. Foster Papers.

At long last—January 5, 1919—the Quai d'Orsay expressly recognized that the Peace Conference should negotiate on the basis of the general principles enunciated by President Wilson. At the same time, a revised statement on the principles of boundary-making was made. Frontiers should be determined on the basis of the right of popular self-determination; the right of nations, whether weak or strong, to be, in principle, on an equal footing; the right of ethnic and religious minorities to protection; and the right of all to guarantees against aggression. Such guarantees were seen to include rectification of frontiers, neutralization of certain areas, internationalization of transport routes, freedom of the seas, and so on. In the opinion of the French Ministry, the territorial settlement with Germany was the paramount problem and would affect the entire peace settlement.[1] This contention contrasted with the Wilsonian point of view that the League of Nations was the key to the peace-making.

In the meantime, the British government obtained a deeper insight into French views in proposals submitted by the French ambassador on November 26.[2] According to this statement, if the strategic guarantees necessary for peace and security were to be reconciled with the rights of peoples, three main problems had to be solved: '(1) guarantees regarding the left bank of the Rhine (military neutralization without political interference); (2) *complete* restoration of Poland (which will deal a final blow to Prussian hegemony); (3) the future government of Germany (in conformity with the right of nations to the free choice of their own system of government).'

Changes in the frontiers of Germany were proposed. France should regain Alsace and Lorraine which had been seized in *1815* and 1871. Marshal Foch, it was said, would indicate slight modifications in these lines in the valley of the Queich, and in the valley of the Rhine at Landau extending along the watershed which formed the northern boundary of the Saar Basin. The Belgian frontier should be rectified in the area of Malmedy.

[1] 'Plan of the Preliminary Conversations between the Allied Ministers', *P.P.C.*, I, pp. 386 *et seq.*

[2] 'French Proposals for the Preliminaries of Peace with Germany, communicated by the French ambassador, November 26th, 1918', Foster Papers.

In the east, the Polish districts of Prussia and of Posnania, as well as access to the Baltic Sea, should be ceded to Poland. Upper Silesia should be assigned to Poland on the basis of the principle of nationality rather than on that of restitution. A similar approach was taken to the southern districts of East Prussia—Mazuria—which were alleged to be Polish by language and race although forming part of the historical Duchy of Prussia. Other provisions dealt with colonial and other questions not bearing directly upon the German frontiers in Europe. At the very end, after subjects like reparations had been treated, certain general guarantees were advocated: German territories should be occupied to guarantee the execution of the peace treaty; and a special military regime should be established in the Rhineland.

The rather cryptic allusion to the problem of the future government of Germany was elucidated in the memorandum of November 28. While the French government did not openly advocate the complete territorial dismemberment of Bismarck's creation, it did seek '. . . to promote . . . the disunion of the countries which compose [Germany]'. This was explained to mean opposing centralist tendencies in the Reich: 'We are interested in favouring Federalism and furnishing a basis for it by elections held under universal suffrage and by promoting the manifestation of differences through the clauses of the treaty.' The French government seemed to advocate a self-defeating policy. It advocated the partial dismemberment of Germany and an economic settlement which could only encourage a nationalist reaction against French policy and thus strengthen the forces making for German unity.

A rather different plan for the future of the Rhineland and for the postwar organization of a west European security system was advanced by Marshal Foch at the Anglo-French conference of November 30.[1] Foch stressed the demographic imbalance of power between the countries of western Europe and Germany. Since he assumed that Germany would remain aggressive, he argued that the West could only be secure if Germany were limited to the right bank of the Rhine since the river provided a natural barrier against a Teutonic invasion. The core of his proposal was that Great Britain, France, Belgium, Luxembourg,

[1] Lloyd George, *Truth*, I, pp. 131 *et seq.*

and the people of the Rhineland should be grouped in an alliance of self-defence against Germany. Britain, France, and Belgium should control this alliance. In reply to Lloyd George's question about the political future of the Rhineland, Foch envisaged its probable independence. One Rhineland state or several states might exist. His main demand was that they should be included in the economic and military system of the west European alliance. As he explained, 'His object was not to annex or to conquer, but merely to profit by our experience and provide proper defence against the 75,000,000 inhabitants on the right bank of the Rhine.'

When Lloyd George enquired how these proposals could be reconciled with the Fourteen Points, the Marshal replied: the German signature could not be trusted; material precautions for Western security had to be taken; the military barrier of the Rhine had to be established. Obviously he felt that these were considerations overriding, if not incompatible with, the Fourteen Points. When Lloyd George asked what would happen if the people of the Rhineland declared their preference for German rule, the Marshal replied that economic benefits should be employed to turn them westwards. Self-interest might also draw them to the West because it was better to be on the winning side of the war. Foch appeared to have no fear of creating a new Alsace-Lorraine in western Europe.

Lloyd George assumed that Clemenceau supported the Marshal's proposals and stayed away from this conference in the hope that Foch would prove more persuasive than he himself might prove to be.[1] Whether Clemenceau at this time formally approved the proposals of Marshal Foch is not clear. Inner French counsels were divided. The cautious French memorandum of November 26 had indicated that the Quai d'Orsay contemplated a special regime for the left bank of the Rhine which could fall short of Foch's objective. In any case, by his absence, Clemenceau was avoiding committing the French government to a definite course. It was a better tactic to sound out the British attitude first, which initially was cool, if not hostile. While promising to consider the proposals carefully,

[1] *Ibid.*, p. 132. J. C. King in *Foch versus Clemenceau* deals at length with the political influences affecting French Rhineland policy and with the relations between Foch and Clemenceau on this issue.

Lloyd George warned 'we must be very careful not to create new problems in Europe'.[1] British opposition to the detachment of the Rhineland from Germany did not appear to have changed since Balfour's adoption of a negative attitude on French claims in the Commons in May.

If the inter-Allied conferences of November 30 to December 3 provided the occasion for a clearer definition of French views on the settlement, the formal conferences at least of the three Allies dealt with the questions other than those affecting the future frontiers of Germany. Still, the proceedings of the Inter-Allied Conference raised a question which had a direct bearing on the making of the territorial settlement. The Conference has sometimes been depicted as symbolic of the establishment of an Allied front against Wilson. Lord Esher for example voiced this suspicion in a letter to Haig on December 8, 1918, in which he said '. . . It is clear that we have entered into a cabal with France and Italy in order to counter the policy of the United States.'[2] A similar view was expressed by Robert Lansing in a letter to General Bliss on December 16: 'I am convinced that the two principal governments, with which we are to deal, have come to a working understanding and will endeavour to frustrate any plan which will defeat their ambitions.'[3] A very different opinion had been expressed a month earlier by House in a telegram to Wilson; according to the Texan Colonel, 'As far as I can see all the Powers are trying to work with us rather than with one another. Their disagreements are sharp and constant.'[4]

Probably, Esher and Lansing oversimplified the actual positions of the British, French, and Italian governments; the Colonel seems to have come closer to the truth. But, until more is known than at present about the relations of the three continental allies, dogmatic conclusions are best avoided.

Certainly both Lloyd George and Clemenceau made overt efforts to persuade House and Wilson that they earnestly desired to work closely with the United States in the peace-making. On November 19, for example, Lloyd George assured Wilson that the ideals of the two countries about international reconstruction were fundamentally the same. He felt sure that

[1] Lloyd George, *Truth*, I, p. 136.

[2] Esher, *Journal and Letters*, IV, pp. 219-20.

[3] *P.P.C.*, I, p. 396. [4] *Ibid.*, p. 135.

at the Peace Conference the British and the Americans would be able 'to co-operate fruitfully to promote the reign of peace and liberty and true democracy throughout the world'.[1]

Clemenceau through House gave similar assurances to Wilson. On November 9 Clemenceau declared that he intended to work in harmony with the United States in everything and promised never to bring up any question at the Peace Conference which he had not first discussed with the American Delegation. France wanted American moral approval far more than its financial and economic assistance. The United States had opened a new ethical era. France wished to stand with the United States in upholding it. Only their nations were willing to make an unselfish settlement. Not unnaturally perhaps he asked House to keep this conversation confidential.

In his report to the President, House omitted an important part of this outpouring. Clemenceau spoke of the possibility of asking for the return to France of the Saar coal-mines. He told House that England would likely not support this proposal 'because she desired to have France dependent upon her for coal'. If House advised against the claim, Clemenceau assured him it would not be advanced. House said he would treat it sympathetically.[2]

Later, Clemenceau renewed his effort to gain American support for the French claim to the Saar in return for French co-operation in the peacemaking. Just before his departure for London on the afternoon of November 30, the 'Tiger' called on the ailing colonel to give 'his solemn word of honour that he would discuss no question of any importance with George in London'. Charging that the English Prime Minister had called the conference merely for domestic political purposes, he sought to stir up House against Lloyd George by terming the conference in London 'inopportune' because it coincided with Wilson's pending departure for France. If Great Britain adopted a grasping attitude in London, Clemenceau assured House that France would oppose the British. In reporting this striking conversation to the President, House once again neglected to mention a substantial part of the episode.[3] Clemenceau accompanied his verbal protestations with a memorandum on the

[1] *Ibid.*, p. 5. [2] House, Diary, XIV, p. 31, November 9, 1918.

[3] House, Diary, XIV, pp. 36-47, November 30, 1918.

Saar Valley, with a map appended, outlining the French claims.

A very different spirit was manifested in the French proposals to the British government on November 26. The preamble read as follows:

> So soon as the clauses of the armistice have been executed, the Allies will have to draw up in common the conditions to be included in the preliminaries of peace. These conditions will determine the general lines on which the eventual Peace Treaty will be based.
>
> So far as the French Government are concerned the best procedure would seem to be for them to examine immediately the conditions which they have the right and the power to impose. When once the French Government have decided on the general principles which they themselves wish to assure, they will then come to an agreement upon them with His Majesty's Government.
>
> The arrangement thus reached between the two countries will enable them both to appear with complete safety at the Conference which, immediately after the arrival of President Wilson, will be held at Versailles for the purpose of exchanging views and agreements among the greater allies.
>
> In order to divide our enemies and to prevent any agreement among them, we wish to conclude peace with them separately and to compel them to accept without any discussion on their part the preliminaries of peace and the conditions already arrived at between us. These preliminaries and conditions will then have to be approved by the parliaments, or Constituent Assemblies, and the Governments of the interested states.
>
> The final settlement will be undertaken by a Congress which will ratify the whole body of definite treaties and subsidiary conventions concluded with the belligerents and, with the new States composed of the races forming part of the late Austro-Hungarian Empire, as well as with Poland, Roumania, and eventually the States of the former Russian Empire.[1]

The kernel of this proposal simply was that the French and British governments should reach agreement on conditions of peace with Germany prior to any conference with President Wilson and the leaders of the other Allied governments. Such an arrangement would enable them to enjoy a 'safe' position in

[1] 'French Proposals for the Preliminaries of Peace with Germany, communicated by the French Ambassador, November 26th, 1918', Foster Papers.

those vital negotiations. This scheme when taken in conjunction with Clemenceau's overtures to House indicates a French policy of trying to play Lloyd George and Wilson off against each other in an effort to overcome the closeness of Anglo-American relations and to secure greater liberty of action for French diplomacy in the forthcoming peace negotiations.[1]

While the British reaction to the French proposal cannot be fully documented, it appears unlikely that the British government entered into an anti-American cabal with France (and Italy) as regards the making of the territorial and other aspects of the peace settlement. The British government had common ground with France against the United States, in colonial matters for example. It had common ground with the United States against France, for instance respecting some French claims in western Europe. On issues like the German-Polish frontier, there was the possibility that the British government might face a Franco-American combination. In fact, at Paris, Lloyd George and Wilson initially joined against Clemenceau. Certainly the Imperial War Cabinet debates in December afford no support for the cabal theory. They do make clear that some ministers favoured the closest co-operation with the United States in the peacemaking while others were decidedly hostile in their attitude towards Woodrow Wilson. These differing, if not always sharply opposed, attitudes came out in connection with Woodrow Wilson's visit to London between December 26 and December 30.

The British government prepared carefully for the talks with the President. At the Imperial War Cabinet of December 18,[2] Lloyd George emphasized the importance of reaching a clear

[1] The implications of the French proposals for relations with the United States were clearly realized by the French ambassador and other members of his embassy in London. Through the counsellor of the French embassy, Monsieur de Fleuriau, the French project of November 26 was communicated to Gunther, the secretary of the American embassy in Great Britain. Beside claiming that the project had been drawn up by M. Cambon and himself and represented only their personal plan, the French diplomat handed to the Americans a memorandum which omitted the all-important preamble. In the text itself there were deviations from the wording in the British copy of the project. These may have been due to differences in translation or the French embassy may deliberately have toned down some of the passages.

[2] I.W.C., No. 43, December 18, 1918, Borden Papers.

understanding on the main issues of peacemaking before he and Balfour talked with Wilson. Both the Prime Minister and the Foreign Secretary stressed that they did not want to be bound by definite instructions but that they did seek to have the issues fully explored until the general view of the ministers emerged.[1] In the list of subjects which the Prime Minister wanted the Imperial War Cabinet to consider before the meeting with Wilson, German territorial questions had no place. Indeed, apart from the European claims of Italy and the fate of Turkey in Europe, European territorial questions in general were not singled out for special consideration by the Imperial War Cabinet.

On December 20, December 23, and December 24 the Imperial War Cabinet thoroughly examined the issues named by the Prime Minister.[2] During the discussion on December 23, when Italian desiderata were considered, a small insight was given into Lloyd George's and Balfour's current thinking on German territorial questions. Lloyd George, supported by Hughes, argued that the Fourteen Points did not apply to the settlement in the former territories of the Dual Monarchy. Bonar Law, as always the man of common sense, suggested that the President would not distinguish between the areas to which the Fourteen Points applied. To this the Prime Minister replied that Sonnino, whenever the Fourteen Points had been discussed in the Armistice negotiations, had always put in the proviso 'subject to the principle of security'. As he pointed out, that was the same principle which Hughes and Botha were applying to the German colonial question and that principle 'would have

[1] Balfour supported the request that their instructions be not too definite with the following argument: 'Difficulties would continually arise if they were so, and as an example of what he meant he said that we were continually being approached by the representatives of the different Allies (with the exception of America), asking us to back certain claims of theirs, and in view of questions like this arising it would be quite impossible for the Cabinet to tell the Prime Minister definitely what line he was to take in a discussion which might last for months. There was already a disagreeable tendency among some of our Allies to adopt a system of "log rolling" and he had little doubt that certain of our Allies were anxious to support our claims, on condition that we supported theirs.' Balfour gave several examples of what he had in mind but discreetly the minutes omit them.

[2] I.W.C., Nos. 44, 45, and 46, Borden Papers.

to be applied to some extent even as regards Germany itself. It would be impossible to give Poland her rights without taking over some German population.' Balfour remarked that an even more difficult problem existed in the case of the German population which lived within the natural strategic frontiers of Bohemia.

Although European territorial questions occupied an incidental place in these discussions, the problem of the attitude to take towards the United States was very much to the fore. While Hughes was outspokenly anti-Wilson, it was Winston Churchill and Admiral Wemyss who on December 20 provoked Milner, Borden, and Austen Chamberlain into making a strong statement on the need of working closely with the United States. They were discussing whether the United States should obtain a mandate over German East Africa or some area in the Middle East. Churchill asserted,

> If America were introduced into the heart of world politics, in Armenia, or anywhere else in the Mediterranean region, this would be an incentive to her to make herself the greatest Naval Power. An African colony used for purposes of investment would raise no strategic question. Wemyss agreed, saying that the admiralty would regard a large American fleet in the Mediterranean with greater apprehension than anywhere else.

Balfour and Borden demurred. Then Milner declared his opinion that world peace depended on a good understanding between the United States and Great Britain; bonds of union should be created to establish a better working relationship between the United States and Great Britain. The whole field should be surveyed from that point of view. Borden and Austen Chamberlain agreed. If an anti-American cabal existed on the part of certain members of the British government and the French government such a policy was opposed by a powerful group within the Imperial War Cabinet.

A post-mortem on the talks between Woodrow Wilson, Lloyd George, Balfour, and other British ministers was held in the Imperial War Cabinet on December 30 and 31.[1] Lloyd George's lengthy report on the President's views contained only a brief reference to German territorial questions. The Prime Minister

[1] I.W.C., Nos. 47 and 48, *ibid.*

had the impression that Wilson opposed the French scheme for the Rhineland although he might accept the French claim to the Saar Valley. The Labour representative, Barnes, was the only member of the Cabinet to comment on this. Describing the French claims to the Saar Valley as 'jingoistic', he regretted the President's apparent support of them.

The Imperial War Cabinet continued to grapple with the problem of Anglo-American relations at the Peace Conference and after. Hughes spoke almost violently against the President. Colonies, indemnities, League of Nations were his main themes. Curzon felt that many members of the Imperial War Cabinet shared Hughes' point of view. While agreeing that Anglo-American co-operation was vital for the postwar world, 'he did feel that if President Wilson persisted in the line reported it might be necessary, on some issues at any rate, for Mr. Lloyd George to work at the conference in alliance with M. Clemenceau'. Long agreed; Reading disagreed. To him the discussions had been friendly. The Imperial War Cabinet should not 'lightly abandon the position that, consistently with the maintenance of our rights, our main object was to bring about the closest co-operation hereafter between ourselves and the United States'. Curzon denied that he intended to reject such a policy. Sir Robert Borden deplored entering the Peace Conference with any feeling of antagonism towards Wilson or his country. Reaffirming the stand he took in 1917, the Canadian Prime Minister said that good postwar relations between the British Empire and the United States were the best asset they could get out of the war. While they should maintain their position on the colonial question and indemnities, he wished 'to make clear that if the future policy of the British Empire meant working in co-operation with some European nation as against the United States, that policy could not reckon on the approval or the support of Canada'. Indeed, he advocated a return or semi-return to the policy of splendid isolation: the Empire as far as possible should avoid European complications and alliances. Cecil agreed that good relationships with the United States would be the best guarantee for the maintenance of peace; the crucial point in securing a good relationship was to support the idea of a League of Nations.

On the following day, this theme continued to run through

the Imperial War Cabinet's deliberations. Barnes declared that if they had to choose at the Peace Conference between France or America 'he was entirely in favour of supporting America for all we were worth'. The Prime Minister wound up the discussion. Like Barnes, he agreed that Hughes had been too pessimistic in his assessment of the interviews with Wilson. He felt that only on one point were they encountering really hard resistance from President Wilson—on the question of indemnity. His view of the attitude to take towards President Wilson at the Peace Conference was so important that it must be quoted in full:

> Consequently he was not pessimistic about inducing President Wilson to agree ultimately, though possibly under protest, to the things to which we attached importance, providing he could secure his League of Nations, which, politically, was a matter of life and death to him. On the other hand, he entirely agreed with Mr. Hughes that if President Wilson should, in the last resort, prove obstinate, then the sacrifices of France and Great Britain were such that they were entitled to have a final say, and would say it. But they would not do that until every effort at agreement had first been made and exhausted. They would begin by assuming that, in the main, they were in agreement. The President had evidently been affected by his reception in this country . . . and the fact that the majority in the United States were more pro-British than he was, would also carry weight. Consequently, as long as he could go home saying that he had secured the League of Nations, for which he had fought, and had not had any too direct rebuffs on other questions, it would be all right. In any case, the British representatives were not going to leave the Peace Conference without securing the things which mattered most to us, though he was inclined to doubt whether Germany could actually pay all the indemnity we had a right to demand.[1]

Did this speech and the preceding discussions show that the British government entered into an arrangement with the French government to thwart the policies of President Wilson at the Paris Peace Conference? The answer would seem to be in the negative. The British position was more complex than that. Even the staunchest advocate of co-operation with Wilson did not interpret that policy to mean that the British delegation should give in on all points to the American point of view.

[1] I.W.C., No. 48, *ibid.*

Obviously, too, there were members of the War Cabinet who were very hostile in their attitude towards the President and who were jealous of the new position enjoyed by the United States in world politics. As the Prime Minister's concluding remarks also indicated, the Imperial War Cabinet was conscious of having a number of interests in common with France. But the Imperial War Cabinet was generally agreed that they should pursue a policy of working closely with the American delegation and to establish postwar Anglo-American relations upon a solid footing. Since the future role of the United States in world politics was surrounded with so many uncertainties, this policy at best had to be very carefully pursued and the Imperial position protected as far as possible against the dangers of its falling through.

The place of German territorial questions in this policy seems reasonably clear. It was not one of the fundamental divisive issues in Anglo-American relations. On the contrary it was one of the almost unpublicized grounds for effective co-operation between the American and the British negotiators.

PART THREE

The Making of the Settlement

VI

THE GERMAN-POLISH FRONTIER

When the preliminary Peace Conference first met on January 18, 1919, Clemenceau, the newly elected presiding officer, exhorted the delegates: 'Gentlemen, let us try to act quickly and well.' Numerous obstacles were to hinder the attainment of this goal. Not the least of these were the controversies over Germany's eastern boundaries.

The Polish claims against Germany were presented to the Council of Ten on January 29, by Roman Dmowski, President of the Polish National Committee in Paris and one of the Polish plenipotentiaries.[1] His remarks on the immediate situation in the Polish borderlands illustrated the intimate connection between short- and long-term considerations in the work of the Peace Conference. Dmowski vividly portrayed Poland as currently threatened by Bolshevik Russia, by Germany, and by the Ukrainians. To counter these dangers, he asked for arms and firm diplomatic support. Yet, according to Dmowski, Poland could not be effectively aided while the Germans controlled a hundred-mile-wide strip from the coast to the Polish frontier, including the Danzig-Thorn railway. His picture of Poland actually isolated from the sea underlined his arguments for a territorial settlement which would give the Poles free and secure access, via Polish-held territory, to the outside world.

Starting from the Polish boundaries before the first partition, Dmowski demanded the inclusion in Poland of Eastern Posen,

[1] *P.P.C.*, III, pp. 772-82.

DANZIG AND EAST PRUSSIA
Königsberg
Pröbernau
Danzig
Elbing
Dirschau
Marienburg
EAST PRUSSIA
OLEZKO
Allenstein
Marienwerder
Osterode
ALLENSTEIN
WEST PRUSSIA
Soldau
Mlawa
Thorn
POSEN
Warsaw
SCALE OF MILES
0
50
PREWAR INTERNATIONAL BOUNDARIES
PROVINCIAL BOUNDARIES
BRITISH LINE (APPROX.)
UNITED STATES LINE (APPROX.)
FRENCH LINE (APPROX.)
FINAL COMPROMISE OF MARCH 7
RAILWAY
THE BARTSCH AREA
Lissa
Fraustadt
PROVINCIAL BOUNDARY
BRITISH LINE
BARTSCH RIVER LINE
Guhrau
POSEN
Rawitsch
Adelnau
Oder River
Bartsch River
SILESIA
THE FILEHNE AREA
POMERANIA
WEST PRUSSIA
Schneidemühl
Wirsitz
Netze River
BRANDENBURG
Kolmar
Kreuz
Czarnikau
Filehne
Warthe River
PROVINCIAL BOUNDARY
BRITISH LINE
BOWMAN LINE
POSEN
Posen
LAUENBURG REGION
BALTIC SEA
Zarnowitz
Chottschow
Sauhn
Hohenfelde
Putzig
Lauenburg
Neustadt
PROVINCIAL BOUNDARY
BRITISH LINE
FRENCH RECTIFICATION
Danzig
SCHNEIDEMÜHL-FRIEDLAND REGION
Schlochau
Konitz
Friedland
PROVINCIAL BOUNDARY
BRITISH LINE
FRENCH RECTIFICATION
WEST PRUSSIA
Schneidemühl
POSEN

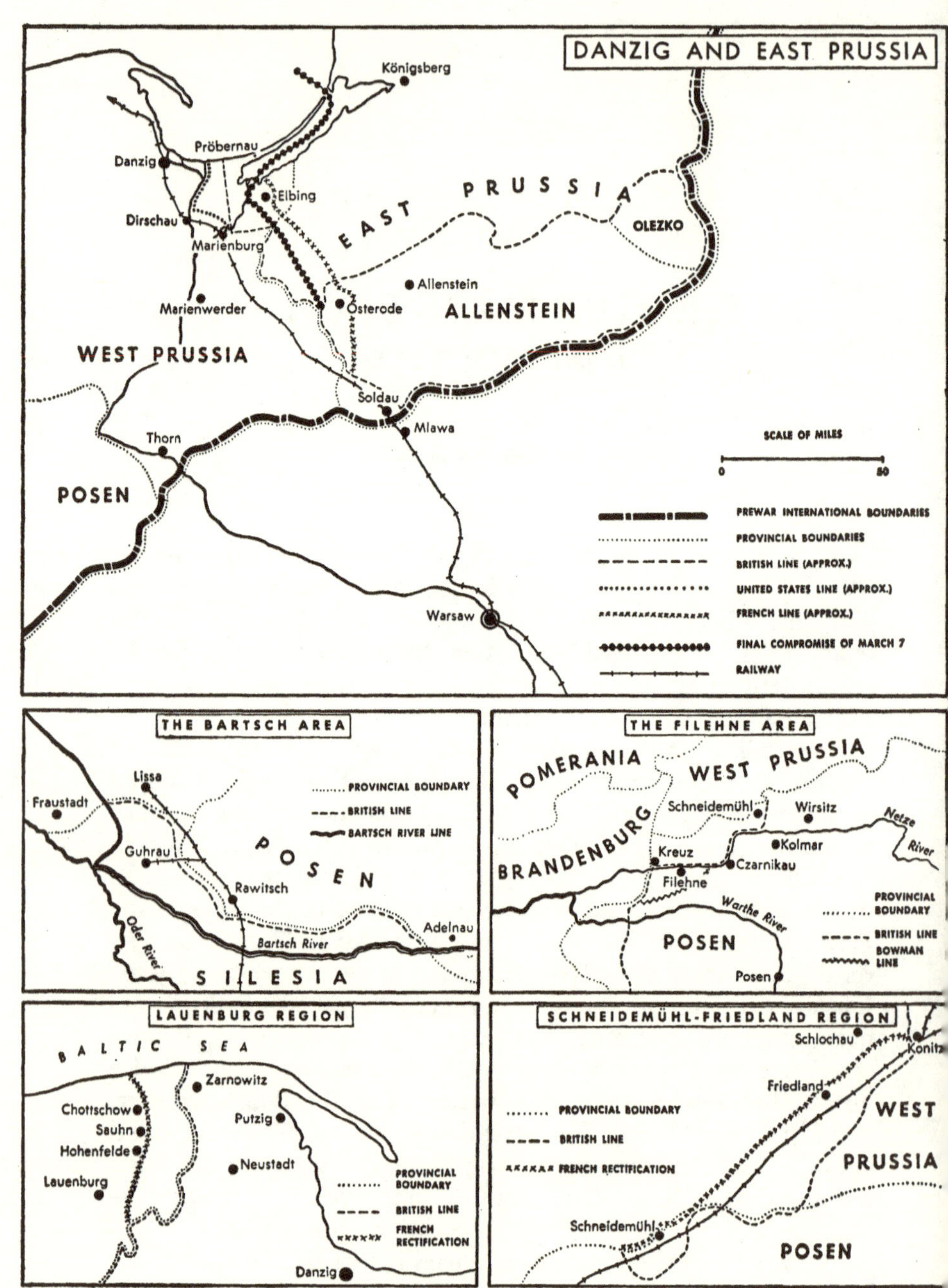

Map 1.

much of West Prussia and East Prussia, Danzig and Upper Silesia, and the establishment of a small, independent German republic carved out of the remainder of East Prussia, with Koenigsberg as its capital. On Balfour's motion, the Council of Ten postponed discussion of these territorial claims.

A long delay ensued, probably due to the multiplicity of issues and the general confusion which marked that stage of the Conference. Balfour believed that a committee had charge of the Polish boundary issues. When he found this to be an illusion he moved, on February 26, in the Council of Ten, that the problem be referred to the Commission on Polish Affairs which was instructed to report back not later than March 8. His step formed part of the effort, during Wilson's absence, under his and House's leadership to speed up the preparation of a preliminary treaty of peace with Germany.[1]

The Commission on Polish Affairs had been established by the Council of Ten, on Balfour's initiative, on February 12, to deal with reports and requests for instructions from the Inter-Allied Commission to Poland.[2] On matters of high policy, the Commission on Polish Affairs was to consult the Council of Ten. Its membership consisted of diplomatic and technical advisors from the delegations of the five Great Powers: Jules Cambon, who became Chairman (France); Isaiah Bowman (United States); Sir William Tyrrell (British Empire); Marquis P. della Torretta (Italy); and M. Otchiai (Japan).[3]

Before the Commission on Polish Affairs received this assignment,[4] the technical staffs of the British and the American delegations had met in a major attempt to co-ordinate their policy on territorial questions.[5] Although the pre-conference

[1] *P.P.C.*, IV, pp. 138-41.

[2] This Commission was established by the Council of Ten on January 29. Its instructions, which did not cover the drafting of a boundary settlement, are given in *P.P.C.*, III, p. 779.

[3] *P.P.C.*, III, pp. 82-3. Bowman retired on April 9. R. H. Lord took his place.

[4] When the Commission on Polish Affairs first met on February 20, the members, evidently going beyond their original instructions, decided to invite the Polish delegation to present its territorial case to them. A.C.N.P., 139, Minutes of Commission on Polish Affairs, February 20, 1919.

[5] Shotwell, *At the Paris Peace Conference*. On p. 153, Shotwell notes, under the date January 29, 1919: 'About six Beer drifted in with news of the afternoon's session over the Czechoslovaks. On the way out President Wilson

thinking of the two delegations had differed, particularly over the Polish Corridor-Danzig question, Sir Esme Howard and R. H. Lord (the chief advisors on Poland in their respective delegations) reached agreement on a provisional eastern frontier for Germany.[1] The understanding was summed up by Lord in the following five recommendations:

> (1) That on the north the Polish-German frontier should follow the linguistic frontier as closely as topography and some peculiarities of the railway permit. (2) That Poland should receive a secure access to the sea through ethnographically Polish territory. (3) That the city of Danzig be included in Poland. (4) That the portion of West Prussia which lies on the right bank of the River

[1] The text of the Howard-Lord agreement referred to in the minutes of the Anglo-American meeting of February 21 does not appear, as such, to be in the records of the American Delegation, although an undated memorandum entitled 'The German-Polish Frontier' and signed in typescript 'R. H. Lord' is in A.C.N.P., 299, 185.1127/11. This memorandum could be either one prepared by Lord for these negotiations or it could be the Lord-Howard agreement itself. Of course, it could be neither, but the text corresponds closely to the references to the Howard-Lord agreement in the minutes of the meeting of the 21st. I am assuming it is the agreement or Lord's version of it.

had a very encouraging conversation, the gist of which cannot go down here, but the result of which will be a very general co-operation between British and American specialists in the working out of problems before the Conference.' Writing in 1937, Shotwell comments that the President had suggested to Beer and Seymour that they co-operate with the British experts to present joint reports to expedite matters before the Conference. Shotwell claims that consultations first worked out over the mandate issue (p. 155).

An entry in Colonel House's diary for January 30 reveals that he and Wilson during the evening of the 29th reached an understanding on 'the united report which we desire the British and American technical advisers to make concerning boundary questions'. House on the 30th asked Sir William Tyrrell to contact Mezes to facilitate co-operation between the two sets of experts. Seymour, *Intimate Papers*, IV, p. 275.

On February 1, Shotwell records in his diary that he attended a meeting of the heads of the divisions of the Intelligence Section, held in Bowman's room, to devise means of co-operating with the British 'under Sir William Tyrrell who have invited us to study boundary lines together with them.' Shotwell, *op. cit.*, p. 161. This entry seems to confuse the question of who took the initiative in proposing co-operation.

Physical contact between the British and American delegations was facilitated by a private telephone system, set up by the United States Army Signal Corps, which linked the Crillon, Majestic, and Astoria. *Ibid.*, p. 167.

Vistula (except for a few Polish districts in the South-East), and the German parts of East Prussia should remain to Germany. (5) That in the Southern belt of East Prussia, commonly known as MAZURIA, a referendum should be held to determine whether the inhabitants prefer to remain to Germany or to be united to Poland.[1]

This understanding assigned to Poland most of Upper Silesia with its rich coal and iron deposits and the province of Posen except for border districts in the south-west, west, and north-west. According to the memorandum, the proposed line would include almost no districts without a Polish majority. Some German communities would be placed in Poland to ensure a straight frontier and to avoid the inconvenient cutting of railway lines. This would be counterbalanced by leaving some Polish communities in Germany. The proposed line was run through forests or thinly populated areas wherever possible. In West Prussia, the line followed the chain of lakes to provide 'an excellent natural barrier on that side of the Polish frontier nearest to Berlin'.

The Polish corridor to the sea was justified on the grounds that it would be a lesser evil to cut off 1,600,000 Germans in East Prussia from the rest of Germany than to leave 600,000 Poles in West Prussia and to expose 20,000,000 Poles to 'an awkward and precarious commercial outlet subject to the will of an alien and presumably hostile power'. This was the argument of the American Black Book. Moreover, it was added, the corridor was defensible on ethnical grounds: except for Danzig, each district in the proposed corridor had a Polish majority.

The memorandum did not ignore the German transit problem between East Prussia and the rest of Germany. Freedom of transit was to be assured by leaving management of the Schneidemuhl-Dirchau-Koenigsberg railway in German hands. In any case the Baltic would always provide a maritime connection.

The assignment of Danzig with its heavy German majority to Poland was defended as an economic and geographic necessity: once the corridor principle had been accepted, Danzig must be included because no room existed for another port, or if a new port was constructed, Danzig would stagnate. Any other

[1] A.C.N.P., 299, 185.1127/11.

solution was rightly described as a half measure which in the long run would be unsatisfactory to both parties.

As for West Prussia, ethnical considerations outweighed strategical ones in the memorandum. For the greater security of the corridor, the entire right bank of the Vistula should have been in Polish hands. Lord and Howard agreed that, to limit the number of Germans incorporated in Poland, German sovereignty should extend as far as Graudenz.

The Howard-Lord agreement constituted a substantial success for the Harvard professor over the career diplomat. Balfour, the Foreign Office, the General Staff had opposed a Polish Corridor and Poland's acquisition of Danzig. Howard, who was disposed to be sentimental about the Poles and yet was probably the author of the Foreign Office memorandum on Poland,[1] conceded much to Lord. In return, the American agreed to the British idea of a plebiscite in Mazuria. By and large, however, they were on common ground in their mutual acceptance of a frontier based primarily upon ethnical, rather than historical or strategical lines.

At the meeting of British and American advisors on February 21,[2] the Howard-Lord recommendations were accepted, although not without objections and reservations. Their line from Austrian Silesia to West Prussia was criticized for assigning at least one predominantly German district to Poland. Tentative approval was given on the understanding that this was the maximum Germany should cede. Over Danzig, differences of opinion developed. Critics of the assignment of Danzig to Poland held that 'the transference of a purely German town to Poland would undoubtedly arouse serious opposition in Germany and might have the result that even the more sensible Germans would refuse to accept the peace as a just and final settlement'. The proposal that Danzig remain German and Neufahrwasser be given to Poland, was rejected. Who took this stand is not recorded in the minutes of the meeting, but it coincided closely with the position of the earlier Foreign Office paper on Poland. The meeting accepted the proposed plebiscite in southern East Prussia, although some doubted whether the

[1] Howard, *Theatre of Life*, II, pp. 273 *et seq.*

[2] Minutes of Meeting of U.S.-G.B. Experts, February 21, 1919, House Papers, 30/165.

vote should be limited to the districts inhabited by Protestant Poles. The cession of East Prussian territory to Lithuania, including Memel and the town and railway junction of Tilsit, was also cautiously proposed.

The British and American advisors thus reached a broad agreement of some political importance. They established a common Anglo-American front which could dominate the territorial negotiations at the expense of the French, the Poles, and others who had more extensive aims in mind. Compared to the Howard-Lord agreement, Dmowski's claims were extreme and would likely be restrained by the cautious, moderate Anglo-American approach. Yet, in some respects, the measure of agreement was more apparent than real. Dissenting voices had been raised in criticism of the proposed German-Polish settlement. While the delegations were divided within themselves over Danzig and the Corridor, the objections reflected particularly pre-conference British viewpoints. The fact of Anglo-American co-operation on territorial questions should not be exaggerated.

House, on February 22, in a wire to Wilson, who had returned to the United States for a brief stay, summed up the existing situation as he saw it. Clemenceau supported the award of Danzig to Poland. The American experts agreed. He understood that the British experts did too, but that the British government disagreed.[1] Opinion within his delegation may not have been as unanimous as the Colonel believed. Shotwell and Young were not convinced that the Danzig corridor was wise or in Poland's best interests, but key figures like Bowman thought otherwise.[2]

On March 1, the Commission on Polish Affairs turned to the problem of Germany's eastern frontier.[3] The British representatives took the initiative. Colonel Kisch described a line which, he explained, rested primarily on ethnical distribution, modified by economic considerations, especially respecting lines

[1] Seymour, *Intimate Papers*, IV, pp. 334-5. The previous day House had noted the establishment of a committee consisting of Tyrrell and his experts, Mezes, Bowman, and Haskins as 'part of the plan to speed up things'. House Diary, XV, p. 62.

[2] Shotwell, *At the Paris Peace Conference*, pp. 189-90.

[3] Minutes of the Third Session of the Commission on Polish Affairs, March 1, 1919, A.C.N.P., 139, 181.213201/3.

of communication, and by local administrative boundaries. He believed that following the latter would simplify the problem of delimitation and probably involve the minimum of disturbance in local life. Bowman informed the Commission that the proposed American line embodied the same principles and followed the same course except in three instances in the Lissa and Birnbaum regions. Despite Bowman's emphasis upon differences between the British and American lines, he and Kisch were confronting the other representatives with a common stand in the negotiations. In substance, they proposed the transfer to Poland of Upper Silesia, most of Posen except for a small area in the west, and portions of West Prussia along a north-south line just west of Konitz. In the latter area, the limits remained undefined since they avoided suggesting a Polish-East Prussian line. (See Map 2.)

General Le Rond, the French spokesman simply remarked that the French experts had been working on the basis of the same principles. Toretta and Otchiai announced their readiness to accept conclusions based upon the principles of the Anglo-American studies.

The Commission struck a sub-committee of three—Le Rond, Bowman, and Kisch—to work out in detail a German-Polish boundary. They first met on March 3,[1] and started at the bottom of the map where the going promised to be easier.[2] The British line for Upper Silesia was accepted as the basis of discussion, although Bowman felt that it emphasized administrative boundaries too strongly. Le Rond suggested that obvious natural features, like rivers, lakes, etc., should be utilized to improve the British line. After broadening the negotiations to cover the proposed boundary from the Czech frontier to Bentschen, Le Rond made clear his delegation's preoccupation with strategic factors. According to him, the Allies had a natural interest in giving Poland defendable frontiers to bolster its doubly dangerous position between the German and the Russian menaces, which were accentuated by the necessarily extensive

[1] Minutes of the Sub-Commission for the Study of the Western and Northern Boundaries of Poland, A.C.N.P., 142. Unless otherwise noted, all references to its proceedings are drawn from this source.

[2] According to Mr. H. W. Paton, a British aide, in an interview with the author.

development of the Polish frontiers. Thus, along the south side of the Posen salient, which jutted into Germany, the Anglo-American line should be altered in the Adelnau-Guhrau region. Here, the English and American line followed the western frontier of Posen except for a deviation permitting the inclusion within Poland of the entire Lissa-Rawitsch railway. Instead, Le Rond pressed for a purely strategic line running along the Bartsch river from a point slightly west of Adelnau to west and north of Guhrau. Bowman and Kisch accepted this proposal. (See Map 1.)

Overnight there were second thoughts within the American and the British delegations. At the outset of the sub-committee's meeting on March 4, Bowman questioned whether the new Bartsch line really strengthened the Polish position. Kisch voiced the same doubts, but Le Rond vigorously talked him around to the French view again.

After clarifying the British intention of leaving in Polish hands the town of Bentschen, the railway station, and the first junction to the west, the sub-committee then turned to the frontier from Bentschen to the sea.

In the Filehne area, Bowman suggested an adjustment favourable to the Germans to compensate for the incorporation within Poland of additional Germans in the valley of the Warthe. (See Map 1.) Kisch agreed. Le Rond proceeded to link the Filehne and the Schneidemuhl questions together.

Upon principally military grounds, he urged the assignment of Schneidemuhl to Poland. The British line, in his opinion, created two dangerous salients in the Polish frontiers at Kreuz and Schneidemuhl. In each salient, the railways allowed the rapid, offensive concentration of troops against Poland. He added a moral argument: if a German majority inhabited Schneidemuhl, it was due to policies of forced colonization. To allow them to profit from their evil would be unjust.

Kisch suggested a horse-trade: Filehne for Schneidemuhl. Bowman and Le Rond agreed. (See Map 1.)

Now another problem arose. If Schneidemuhl were awarded to Poland, transit difficulties would arise along the Berlin-Koenigsberg railway because two border crossings would be created. Le Rond had a ready solution. Assign the entire Schneidemuhl-Konitz railway to Poland. (See Map 1.) Bowman assented, invoking the moral injustice of Prussian colonization policies in the region.

Before the session ended, Le Rond raised another objection to the British line near its northern terminus. To strengthen Polish control of the railway system west of Putzig, he suggested moving the line west of the provincial boundary from the salient south-east of Lauenberg and from thence to the sea. (See Map 1.) Agreed!

Thus in its first two meetings, the sub-committee had defined a German-Polish frontier from Czechoslovakia to the sea. Starting with the proposed British line, based upon ethnical considerations modified by economic factors and by existing administrative boundaries, they had accepted four alterations, one on Bowman's suggestion, three on Le Rond's. Bowman's amendment in the Filehne area sought to even up the number of Poles and Germans alloted to each state. Le Rond's changes had been designed mainly to serve the military end of strengthening the new Polish state *vis-à-vis* Germany. In reaching these conclusions the sub-committee met no serious difficulty, but ahead lay the contentious questions of the corridor, Danzig, and East Prussia.

Several memoranda circulated at this time which strongly backed the Polish claims to Danzig, a corridor, and Allenstein. One came from the Polish National Committee dated March 3, which brightly illuminated the illusions, hopes and plans of the Poles.[1] Poland was pictured as bearing the responsibility for peace and security in eastern Europe. If Poland were to replace Russia as a counterpoise against Germany and to check the expansion of Bolshevism, it must have proper frontiers. If the Baltic coast and Danzig remained German, Poland would be dependent upon Germany for communications with its western associates in the League of Nations. It would be virtually helpless between German armies based upon Breslau and upon the Koenigsberg-Mazurian lake region. Polish claims to Danzig and the Baltic coast were held to have special force because of these strategic considerations.

The Polish National Committee attempted to deal with the obvious objection that German majorities inhabited these areas.

[1] 'Le Probleme de Dantzig et de Koenigsberg', A.C.N.P., 307, 185.1142/24.

The problem of German irredentist movements in Danzig and East Prussia was solved by a generous dose of optimistic prophecy: if Danzig and an independent East Prussian state became part of the Polish tariff system, they would become prosperous, subject to Polish influence, and thus gradually Polonized. In the case of Allenstein, a German majority was conjured away. According to the memorandum, the majority of the population was really Polish and the Polish national movement there had recently become very active. These Poles, however, had held administrative and other posts under the Germans. They were afraid, during the Prussian census, to acknowledge their Polishness because they might lose their jobs. In part, therefore, the Prussian statistics showing a German majority were wrong, especially since the number of German soldiers, imported officials, etc., in the region, artificially swelled the German totals. These easy solutions of the problem of *Germania Irredenta* were endlessly repeated during the negotiations.

Another analysis of the Danzig-corridor-East Prussian problem came from British Naval Intelligence.[1] The authors sought first to deal with German claims.

One German contention was that ethnographically the Poles did not extend to the sea; instead, a German-populated 'bridge' joined Brandenburg-Pomerania to East Prussia, cutting off the Polish bloc from the Baltic. German sources also claimed Germans were in a majority along the Vistula. The authors of the Naval memorandum admitted German strength in the Vistula valley in the form of a belt five to ten miles in width. In their opinion, based upon a Prussian statistical map of 1910, this belt was not continuous and thus did not sever the corridor of Polish-populated territory stretching from Thorn to the sea.

They minimized the strategical disadvantage to Germany of the separation of East Prussia by a Polish corridor. Conceding that this was the most serious disadvantage involved, they pointed out that Germany no longer faced a powerful Russian military state but a weak and inexperienced neighbour which

[1] 'Memorandum Outlining Arguments for and against the Inclusion of Danzig in the New Polish State', Intelligence Department, Naval Staff, Section 32, March 1, 1919 (pencilled notation, 'from Mr. Balfour and submitted by Sir Wm. Tyrrell'), A.C.N.P., 307, 185.1142/23.

required the protection of a strategic frontier far more than did the Germans.

Economically, the Germans could claim that the separation of East Prussia would cut the arteries of land-borne commerce between it and the rest of Germany, with resulting economic hardships. After an elaborate statistical analysis, the Naval Intelligence study cogently concluded: '. . . East Prussia . . . is economically already largely an "island".' Prewar trade between it and the rest of Germany had been mainly sea-borne. Thus, the separation of East Prussia would not sufficiently disrupt German trade to justify denying to Poland Polish-populated areas and territorial access to the Baltic.

On the other hand, Poles claimed that an ethnically-based corridor would not ensure adequate access to the seas because it would include no serviceable port, and lacked rail and water transport facilities. Difficult terrain, moreover, would impede the construction of railways and waterways in the ethnical corridor. The further plea was made that since the Vistula ran for nine-tenths of its course through indisputably Polish territory, why not let it complete its run through Polish land, especially since Danzig depended upon the Polish hinterland. They viewed the Vistula as a 'national river'.

The authors of the report agreed with these contentions. Putzig could not easily become an alternative to Danzig. Neufahrwasser (which the Foreign Office had envisaged as Poland's port) could only be turned into a major port at the expense of Danzig. The study concluded: '. . . Danzig is, from its position and exceptional facilities, the nearest and only natural port for practically the whole of Poland'.

Why not leave the port in German hands with freedom of use assured to the Poles? The authors of the study rejoined that Danzig, if in German hands, would have only limited value to the Poles. Prussia would be unwilling to improve the port. Both the Poles and the Entente Powers would benefit if Danzig were a first-class port and Germany's geographical trading advantages were reduced to a minimum.[1]

[1] They also underwrote the Polish claim that Polish control of Danzig would enhance the economic independence of both Poland and Czechoslovakia besides enabling the Poles to negotiate favourable commercial agreements with Hungary, Rumania, and Ukraine.

The force of Polish and German national sentiment was not overlooked. The study concluded that a strictly ethnographical settlement would satisfy neither Poles nor Germans. Poles would object because the mouth of their national river would remain in German hands and they would have no port—only the village of Putzig. Germans would find permanent acquiescence difficult because they would lose much of their economic and strategic hold over Poland and lose their land connection with East Prussia. But the authors were optimistic. Polish acquisition of Danzig and of the left bank of the Vistula would be equitable if Germany were compensated with outlying areas of Polish-speaking territory on the western boundaries of Posen and along the left bank of the Oder in Silesia. While national sentiment 'on both sides will probably only become reconciled after a considerable lapse of time to any equitable settlement', they saw reconciliation as possible. On the Polish side, the moderate elements of Polish opinion, embracing the majority of Polish political groups, would probably in the long run prove stronger than the chauvinists who sought the frontiers of 1772. On the German side, they believed that, while German opinion would be shocked by the failure to establish domination over Poland, over the years moderate German opinion would not fail to realize the error of aggressive policy in West Prussia any less than in the cases of Alsace-Lorraine and in Northern Schleswig. Within Danzig itself, economic prosperity could have a moderating influence upon the German inhabitants who would likely in a few years be as 'contented with Polish suzerainty as their predecessors and as the German merchants of Riga under Russia'.

The Naval Intelligence memorandum contained a sound, convincing case, on the material side, for Polish acquisition of Danzig and a territorial corridor. On the psychological side, it did not ignore sentiment and realized the crucial nature of the conflict between German and Polish national feeling. Yet, the eighteenth and the twentieth centuries were worlds apart as far as nationalism in eastern Europe was concerned. The authors of the report tended to underestimate the strength of German feeling and the extent to which it could be 'bought off', assuming that the economic future would be as rosy as they forecast. They were right in inferring that German nationalists would be most severely wounded not so much by the loss of Danzig, the separation of East Prussia, etc., in themselves so much as by what they stood for: a severe defeat for their Middle European ambitions. For the prospects of peace and stability in eastern Europe, the important consideration was not German or Polish nationalism in themselves but that Germany was far stronger than Poland. In this respect, perhaps, the report's horizon was too limited. Whatever the intrinsic merits of the proposed German-Polish settlement, it failed to consider whether the additional affront to German sentiment involved by the loss of Danzig, for example, could be effectively counterbalanced by the prospect of Poland's receiving adequate external support to maintain its precarious position between Germany and Russia. This was the aspect of the problem which was to concern Lloyd George in his attempt to find a solution of the Danzig-corridor-East Prussian problem which would be more satisfying to German national sentiment while protecting the interests of the Poles.

The region of Allenstein, or Mazuria, posed an involved problem. (See Map 1.) The bulk of the people were Polish in origin and spoke a Polish dialect. At the same time, they were Protestant in religion and showed little sense of Polish national consciousness. A case could be made on religious or ethnical grounds for assigning them to Poland or to Germany.

Support for Polish claims to Allenstein came from H. W. Paton, one of the advisors to the British delegation, in a paper on religious considerations and the future frontiers of Poland.[1] According to his advice to the Commission on Polish Affairs, centuries of Prussian rule had thoroughly subdued the Mazurians. Their German Protestant pastors had exhorted them against the Poles as Roman Catholics. The Polish national movement had accordingly made little progress among the Mazurians, although Paton cautiously qualified this opinion with the remark that some saw the beginnings of a pro-Polish tendency among them. Paton appeared to be arguing that religious and Prussian influences had been warping the natural nationalist inclinations of these people. Why one influence was

[1] H. W. Paton, 'Memorandum on the Relation of Religious Considerations to the Future Frontiers of Poland, March 4, 1919', A.C.N.P., 388, 186.311/5.

less natural or more reprehensible than others was never explained in any of these memoranda and speeches.

Mr. Paton took the line that in Allenstein in the long run the ties of 'blood' and language would likely prove stronger than those of religion. He also advised the Commission that both Poland and the Mazurians would benefit if Allenstein were awarded to Poland. Prussian rule had only left the people in ignorance and in economic dependence; their permanent advantage lay in union with Poland. On the Polish side, the frontier would be disadvantageous to the Poles if Allenstein remained German.

The author's political realism made him sceptical of a pro-Polish outcome to an immediate plebiscite. If a vote were considered necessary, he advised that

> it ought to be done after the region has been assigned to Poland and the Poles have an opportunity of putting their case before the inhabitants and at the same time of improving their economic condition. Only so can a people politically so backward have a real chance of choosing between two alternatives—if indeed their opinion is of much value even then.

A splendid Balfourian touch!

Further support for Polish claims to Danzig, etc., came from a British Naval Intelligence memorandum on German colonization policies in the eastern provinces of Prussia.[1] The argument was typical of opinions expressed by members of the Commission on Polish Affairs and their advisors.

The case can be quickly described. German policy in the eastern provinces was formulated by men who anticipated war with Russia and a consequent reopening of the Polish Question. Intensive Germanization in the eastern provinces was promoted to prepare for such a contingency. Actual measures included: the encouragement of German settlers other than colonists; the exclusion of Russian and Austrian Poles; the attempt to convert German Poles into Germans; efforts to create a situation in which the claim could be made that the culture of the provinces was German in origin and nature; moves to increase the

[1] 'Memorandum on the Recent Policy of Germany in the Eastern Provinces (Prussian Poland)', Intelligence Department, Naval Staff, Section 32, March 9, 1919.

economic dependence of the provinces upon Germany; and representation of the numbers of Poles as less than they were in fact. These measures and the policy upon which they were based had as their objective the creation of a situation in which a German government could claim at a peace conference that Polish-populated territory did not stretch continuously between Pomerania and East Prussia or between Warsaw and Danzig.

Whether this interpretation was historically correct or not was beside the point. The vital fact was that this viewpoint represented the conviction of the negotiators—from advisors to the Council of Four—at Paris. Their conduct was conditioned by such opinions.

As the Naval Intelligence memorandum pointed out, the adoption of such a policy by German and Prussian governments had an important bearing upon all questions relating to the determination of the ethnical frontier between Poland and Germany. But the nature of this relationship was undefined. Presumably, if governmental measures of the previous twenty-five years had affected the territorial limits of the two nationalities, German claims based upon historic rights were to that extent modified. On the other hand, can it be claimed that the German colonization measures were unnatural—at least to the extent that any changes in society wrought by legislative and administrative action are unnatural? Of course, the intrinsic fairness and justice of the measures—were Poles dispossessed with or without adequate compensation—affected the relative justice and fairness of Polish and German claims to the disputed territory. Perhaps the strongest consideration of all, and to the German disadvantage, was simply this. If, in defining the frontier, ethnographic considerations had to be modified by economic, strategic, or other considerations—such as was implied in the thirteenth point—it was both pragmatically and psychologically easier to do so if the ethnographic character of the disputed territory had been moulded by recent German legislative and administrative measures which had been taken for political and strategic reasons. What had been sauce for the German goose could, with equal realism and moral justification, be sauce for the Polish gander.

Against this background of strong written arguments favouring the Polish claims, the sub-committee on March 6 turned to the question of Danzig and the East Prussian frontier.[1] Kisch, in opening the discussion, proposed a line placing the Danzig-Mlawa railway within Polish territory. As a result, the Soldau region would come under Polish rule. In the north, Elbing and most of the Nogat river should remain German, with the frontier running from a point east of Marienberg due north to the sea. Tiegenhof would fall to Poland. (See Map 1.) Kisch also proposed a plebiscite in Allenstein (excluding Soldau) and in Olezko.

Le Rond objected to the British line to the sea. It would cross the railway in several places in the Jungfer-Steegen region, and leave the Nogat mostly in German hands although it was the natural outlet for Marienberg. Elbing should be Polish because it was the natural rail and waterway terminal for the Lonza-Mlawa-Allenstein-Osterode area.

Bowman took a middle position between Kisch and Le Rond. The proposed American line left Danzig and the Vistula in Polish hands, while reducing the number of Germans assigned to Poland compared to the British line. (See Map 1.) Bowman, on the other hand, defended the transfer of the Germans in Danzig and along the Vistula on the grounds that their fate must be subordinated to a superior objective: Danzig would become a great port as the outlet of a great nation and river. Although he leaned more to the Polish side than did Kisch, Bowman opposed Le Rond's position. In Bowman's opinion, the use of the Nogat had only local significance, the water routes between Danzig and Elbing were unimportant, and Elbing itself was not indispensable to Poland.

At this point, Dmowski presented the Polish case directly to the sub-committee. Linking his specific demands to the broader strategic picture as outlined in the Polish memorandum of March 3, the Polish spokesman argued that the demand for Danzig and Elbing was not imperialistic. Poland's independence hinged upon its Baltic position. Danzig itself could not meet the future commercial and transport needs of Poland. Elbing and Koenigsberg were needed as well. In the past, all Polish trade had been carried on the Vistula, including its Nogat branch which therefore would once again become a great medium of communication with the seas. The Polish government could

[1] A.C.N.P., 142.

easily deepen the Nogat channel. In reply to a question by Le Rond, Dmowski agreed that Elbing was not currently important as an outlet for the Osterode and Mlawa regions, but it would become so with the suppression of customs barriers. Nor did he believe that the opinion of Germans living in Danzig and Elbing was hostile to the Poles: '. . . the commercial classes would even see without regret the incorporation of these cities into Poland because they believe that this settlement would greatly augment their economic rehabilitation'. No memorials were presented to support his claim.

Dmowski did not press for immediate Polish acquisition of Koenigsberg. Instead he proposed: '. . . the veritable solution of the problem consisted in organizing East Prussia as a republic entirely distinct from Germany and in imposing upon it a complete demilitarization. East Prussia would without doubt end by asking for a customs union with Poland upon which all its economic development would depend.'[1]

As for the Allenstein region, Dmowski looked to the future: 'There is reason to suppose that the national Polish movement will increase and that in ten years Mazuria will be just as Polish a country as Posnania for example.' In other words, Polish sentiment in Allenstein was currently weak. But Dmowski offered an intriguing argument for Polish possession of the region. It would help to bring Roman Catholicism and Protestantism in Poland closer together if a powerful Protestant Church could be organized in the new Poland. Therefore, 'the

[1] Another insight into Polish reasoning about the disposition of Mazuria and East Prussia is given in a report of an interview in mid-January with M. Jodko, Polish vice-minister of foreign affairs, and a leader of the P.P.S. party, forwarded by Coolidge on February 14. Jodko is reported as follows: '2. The general point of view in regard to East Prussia is that it should be made an independent republic or state and that in time it could become Polonized and become part of Poland. The Mazurian belt in East Prussia to be annexed to Poland for they are just as Polish as the Mazurs in Russian Poland and East Galicia who are of the Catholic faith. The only difference is that they are Protestants and speak a Polish dialect. The reasons for their inactivity with the Poles are, first because they are Protestants while most of Poland is Catholic and second that all their Protestant pastors are German and have spread Germanism among them. In recent years the elections in that district have shown a marked increase of Polish votes.' A.C.N.P., 180, 184.01102/97. The despatch was marked for circulation to Bowman, Seymour, Montgomery, and Dolbacres.

Poles attach so great an importance to the possession of the lake region'. Despite the ingenious effort to allay the apprehensions of those who opposed placing a Protestant minority in a strongly Roman Catholic state, it was an unconvincing appeal.

Dmowski neither opposed a vote in Allenstein nor showed enthusiasm for it. Believing that it would be difficult to organize a plebiscite among people who had been 'terrorized' by Prussia, he advised that the minimum condition should be the removal of all German officials and pastors from the region.

Dmowski's mixture of hard strategic fact, breezy optimism, and ready assurances failed to induce Kisch to recant. For the French delegation, Le Rond launched a vigorous offensive to secure better terms for Poland than those proposed by Kisch and Bowman. In the General's opinion, all the mouths of the Vistula should belong to Poland, together with Elbing. The minimum frontier should include Elbing, the Oberlandischer-Kanal, and Osterode. (See Map 1.) This line would realize three transit objectives: the outlying canal could be linked with the Narew; access to the sea would be improved; and the use of the Mlawa-Elbing railway would be enjoyed by Poland. Further, the French representative advanced a military argument. Poland's route to the seas must be defensible. The proposed British line offered no obstacle to a German attack from the east. Against this contingency, the only defensive protection was the Osterode-Elbing line.

Kisch offered a counter-suggestion: the demilitarization of East Prussia as Poland's strategic safeguard against German attack from the east—the same idea which the British delegation applied to the Rhineland.

Some disagreement existed over a plebiscite in Allenstein. Le Rond, while accepting the principle, was concerned about the conditions under which the plebiscite would be held. More importantly—although the minutes are not clear on this point—he seems to have hinted at the possibility of linking the settlement of the plebiscite question with that of the west frontier of East Prussia. Kisch did not rise to this bait. Nor did he accept conditions for the plebiscite which Bowman suggested and to which Le Rond agreed. The American member, in an effort to meet Le Rond's point of view, had proposed that Allenstein first be placed under Polish administration, after which the plebiscite would be held under Allied authority to secure an impartial expression of the wishes of the local inhabitants.

In the early evening of March 6, the Commission on Polish Affairs heard the report of the sub-committee on its agreements and disagreements.[1] As Le Rond summed up their discussions, they had reached agreement on the eastern frontier of Germany, on the eastern section of the East Prussian border, on a plebiscite in Allenstein and Olezko, on the northern boundaries of the plebiscite area, and on the inclusion of Danzig in Poland. Quite rightly, he minimized the differences between the lines proposed by Kisch and Bowman. The essential conflict had been between the French proposals which came close to the Polish claims (except on the status of East Prussia) in the Danzig area and the Anglo-American proposals which were more restrained. Le Rond criticized these proposals on several grounds. Especially after hearing Dmowski, he was convinced that all the mouths of the Vistula were natural commercial outlets for the state holding the upper reaches of the river. Also, the Anglo-American position, in his opinion, was strategically unsound since the Vistula and the Danzig-Mlawa railway would be left virtually without protection. Strategically, the most westerly line which he could accept for Poland was the Oberlandischer-Kanal. While Kisch, in accepting the idea of the demilitarization of East Prussia, had gone far to meet Dmowski's views, Le Rond considered the solution to be militarily inadequate. He might have added that it would set a bad example for the Rhineland negotiations.

None the less, on behalf of his delegation, the General suggested a compromise based upon two principles: Poland should receive all the mouths of the Vistula and the Danzig-Mlawa railway should be adequately protected. The Nogat could be divided between Poland and Germany if the boundary followed the *thalweg*. (See Map 1.) This would leave Elbing to Germany as Bowman and Kisch had insisted, while giving Poland the use of the Nogat. Le Rond emphasized that this was the minimum line which his delegation would accept.

[1] Dmowski, in an opening statement on Polish claims, added little to his earlier appeal except to make clear the desire to have a strategic frontier which would enable Poland to oppose German aggression, *unaided* if necessary. A.C.N.P., 139.

The British and the American representatives held their ground. Thus the fourth session of the Commission adjourned in deadlock over the western frontier of East Prussia.

During the session of March 7, the deadlock was resolved.[1] After some discussion, Kisch, Bowman, and Le Rond withdrew to trace an agreed line. The frontier would run along the median line of the lakes north of Raudnitz; then north-west to the Nogat; then the *thalweg* of the Nogat to its outlet into the Frische Hoff, and finally a line running south-east to north-west, east of Probernau. (See Map 1.) The French had retreated around Osterode[2]; the British and Americans had trudged eastwards to the Nogat.[3] A complex problem had been resolved satisfactorily in many respects. Elbing had been saved for Germany. Both Poland and Germany could use the Nogat. A screen of lakes would help to protect the Danzig-Mlawa railway. Against these substantial economic and strategic accomplishments, there stood only the ethnographical principles and factors involved: the compromise line added more Germans to Poland than Kisch and Bowman had desired. Most questionable, however, was the advisability of having awarded Danzig and a territorial corridor to Poland.[4]

While the Commission was finishing its report, the secret committee of Kerr, Tardieu, and Mezes on the frontiers of Germany first met on March 11.[5] Tardieu presented draft articles designed to give effect to the conclusions of the Commission on Polish Affairs. Germany was to renounce both sovereignty over and the right of customs union with the territories to be ceded to Poland. In addition, the clauses provided

[1] A.C.N.P., 139.

[2] The Commission accepted Le Rond's suggestion that if, as a result of the plebiscite, the Osterode region became Polish, a special covenant should assure to Poland the use of the waterway via the Oberlandischer-Kanal.

[3] Before the sub-committee had met, Le Rond had submitted German maps which showed that the Nogat was the administrative boundary between the Danzig and the Elbing regions—probably a weighty point with his British colleagues who earlier had stressed the importance of administrative lines.

[4] When the Commission met again on March 9, Sir William Tyrrell proposed that Germany be given full right of transit across the proposed Polish corridor. The Commission agreed.

[5] *Papers Respecting Negotiations for an Anglo-French Pact*, Cmd. 2169, 1924, pp. 59-66.

for a plebiscite conducted by an international commission in Mazuria, although the limits of the zone were undefined. German civil authorities and troops as well as members of Workers' and Soldiers' Councils were to withdraw from the area which would immediately come under the authority of the international commission (Article II). While Tardieu's draft had originally provided for the demilitarization of East Prussia, the committee altered this to allow Germany to maintain there a military force of no more than 10,000 men (Article III). This was intended to strengthen the local authorities in maintaining order and in guarding the frontier. Free passage between East Prussia and the rest of Germany would be guaranteed to the *civil* population by the regime established by the Commission on International Waterways and Railways (Article IV). The committee approved these provisions, although German-Polish boundary questions were not discussed at length. They were primarily concerned with the Rhine. Kerr, it should be noted in view of his close association with Lloyd George, did not oppose at this time the recommendations of the Commission on Polish Affairs.

The First Report of the Commission on Polish Affairs, dated March 19,[1] dealt with four topics: the procedure of the Commission; the principles underlying its recommendations; the applications of these principles to special cases; and a statistical summary. The four annexes contained verbal descriptions of the proposed frontiers, tables of statistics, and the draft articles for insertion in the preliminary peace treaty. A map illustrated the proposals.[2]

According to the report, the proposed frontier was based on an ethnical demarcation which had been made as equitable as possible for the two peoples concerned. Occasionally this

[1] By March 12, the Commission's report had been basically written and submitted to the Central Committee on Territorial Questions. The Committee accepted the report in principle, but since the draft articles had not been prepared and the details of the plebiscite arrangements remained obscure. Clemenceau, as chairman of the Peace Conference, was informed that no report on the western Polish frontier could be presented at that time. Not until March 18 did the Commission on Polish Affairs complete the drafting of the legal clauses giving effect to their recommendations.

[2] A.C.N.P., 140, contains the final copy and various drafts of the report. Copy also in House Papers, 23/121; Miller, *Diary*, VI, pp. 43-53.

principle had been departed from, in some places to German advantage, in others to Polish, when other factors or principles seemed to warrant a subordination of the ethnical principle. These other considerations were described as religious (in Mazuria), historical, economic, and strategic. In the latter case, the report claimed that military factors had been taken into account after the other factors had been weighed, and then only in terms of strengthening the defensive position of the new state, which was depicted as menaced from the east, west, and north on plains which lacked significant natural defenses.

The report went on to consider the application of these principles to special cases. In the south, the region of Leobschutz had been detached from Germany because it formed a peninsula connected with the main German body only by a narrow isthmus. No railways ran along this isthmus; thus access could only be had by crossing Polish or Czechoslovakian territory. For this reason, and because it would improve communications between Poland and Czechoslovakia, the boundary line was started five miles east of Neustadt.

The exceptional stress placed upon strategical factors in the Bartsch region was explained as follows: In this area the Polish frontier was very long. The Polish position was weakened further because this section of the frontier faced Breslau, whose railway complex permitted rapid and heavy troop concentrations against an uncovered Polish flank. Only the line of the river Bartsch could give some defensive strength to the Polish salient and provide protection for the Lissa-Rawitsch-Ostrowo-Oppeln railway.

In the Bentschen region, where the proposed boundary departed from the ethnographical frontier, the justification was offered that so clear a natural line as the lakes around Bentschen warranted a slight veering from ethnical lines. Where the recommended boundary followed the watershed between the Warthe and Netze rivers, thus including some Germans in Poland and some Poles in Germany, the explanation was advanced that the frontier would now cross a sparsely populated area and in addition would reduce the complications resulting from divided control of the Netze.

The assignment of a German majority in Schneidemuhl was explained on grounds of justice, strategy, and the presence of a numerous Polish population in the rural areas around the town. It was suggested that the German majority in the town itself was artificial in character: '. . . the town is largely composed of railway employees and their families, who are exclusively German owing to unfair discrimination against the Poles'. In these circumstances, '. . . it would be an act of simple justice to disregard the ethnographical boundary and include the district in Poland'. Strategically, German possession of the region would give to them a powerful springboard from which to attack the exposed northern Polish salient in Posen.

Regarding Danzig, the Commission offered six reasons for their unanimous decision that town and port should go to Poland. Firstly, unless Poland acquired Danzig, the legitimate Polish aspirations for secure access to the seas, endorsed by the victors, could not be realized. Secondly, if a Polish corridor were created, the interests of the 1,600,000 Germans in East Prussia could be adequately protected by guaranteeing their transit rights across the corridor. But it would be impossible to give some twenty-five million Poles adequate security of access to the seas across an outlet which, though guaranteed, was controlled by an alien and probably hostile power. Thirdly, the interests of the German merchants of Danzig would best be served by its development under Polish rule. Fourthly, every district in the Polish corridor was Polish except Danzig itself. Fifthly, the population of the city would probably grow and become more Polish in character because the removal of artificial Prussian restrictions upon the trade of Danzig would lead to population growth. This increase would be naturally Polish since Poles occupied most of the hinterland of Danzig. Finally, Danzig and the port of Neufahrwasser had to be treated together because the town and port formed an economic and physical entity.

The proposed settlement in West Prussia east of the Vistula was explained on the grounds of the importance to Poland of the Danzig-Dirschau-Mlawa-Warsaw railway. The result in ethnographic terms was justified by an allusion to the areas in this region where the Polish population held a majority, especially in part of Stuhm. It was noted that the railway question had led to the assignment of the Soldau district to Poland.

The final special case dealt with in the report was East Prussia. It was recognized that the proposed frontier constituted a source of Polish weakness if East Prussia could be used as a base for serious military operations. It was specifically pointed out that a proposal to extend the Polish frontier to the lakes north and west of Osterode had been turned down because the Commission had assumed that measures would be taken under guarantee of the League of Nations to secure the demilitarization of East Prussia. The report added: if demilitarization was not secured, this part of the boundary might have to be reconsidered.

The frontier recommended by the report assigned 58,632 square kilometres of German territory to the new Polish state, compared to the 85,644 square kilometres included in the Polish claims. It allotted to Poland 5,469,000 'souls', of whom 2,854,800 were Polish and 2,132,600, German. The Polish claims had covered some 6,678,000 people: 3,189,800 Poles and 2,937,600 Germans. In the plebiscite areas, some 263,300 Germans and 279,600 Poles were said to be affected.

The Commission also recommended that the north-eastern frontier of East Prussia should run along the Niemen river downstream from Schmalleningken, which involved the cession of the Memel district of some 945 square miles. This proposal affected some 148,000 people, half of whom spoke Lithuanian, compared with the 304,000 Germans and 94,900 Lithuanians embraced by the Lithuanian claims. Two main justifications for this transfer of territory were advanced: the Niemen river marked almost exactly the ethnic frontier between Germans and Lithuanians in the region; and, the Niemen valley, including the port of Memel, constituted the natural trade outlet for a hinterland inhabited chiefly by Lithuanians and White Russians.

The pre-conference views of Balfour and of the Foreign Office scarcely found full expression in the Commission's recommendations. Its proposed eastern frontier for Germany hewed fairly closely to the ethnical principle, modified by geographic and other factors when necessary, as Balfour and the Foreign Office had advocated. The most important deviation was in Upper Silesia where Balfour had advocated a strictly ethnical line and the Foreign Office had recommended the exclusion from Poland of Leobschutz and Ratibor. The Commission advised the transfer to Poland of all of Upper Silesia. In the north, Balfour had been prepared to see Danzig given the status of a free port to protect Poland's commercial interests but he opposed handing the city to the Poles. The Foreign Office took the same stand, while recommending a Polish enclave around Neufahrwasser and Putzig, separated from Poland proper by a German land connection with East Prussia. The Poles would have transit rights across this German corridor. The latter had been all that Balfour was prepared to cede to the Poles to give them access to the sea. In sharp contrast, the Commission on Polish Affairs, with the British members in agreement, supported a Polish corridor and the award of Danzig to Poland. In December, the Foreign Office had advised a plebiscite to determine the fate of Mazuria; this proposal was embodied in the report of the Commission, although no agreement had been reached on how to conduct the vote. In the Upper Silesian, Danzig, and corridor questions then the British representatives on the Commission had gone considerably farther than the Foreign Secretary, the Foreign Office, and the General Staff had earlier been prepared to go.

As the debate on the report quickly revealed, however, Lloyd George, for one, refused to follow the Commission. Behind him, there stood Sir Henry Wilson and Smuts with their grave reservations about the reconstruction of eastern Europe upon the basis of small national states. Balfour presumably had not changed his views.

Two further observations should be made before we turn to the debate on the report. Before the Commission met, the British advisors had veered away from their earlier attitude under the influence of their American counterparts to establish, as far as possible, a common Anglo-American front on German territorial questions. In so doing, they were carrying out a well-defined policy of their government: to work as closely as possible with the Americans in the peacemaking. Secondly, if the Howard-Lord agreement had promised a stiff battle with the French over the German-Polish border, and Pichon's stand during the armistice negotiations had suggested that the French would fight for Poland's historic frontiers, the Commission's proceedings did not quite develop that way. Le Rond did stress strategic factors far more than did Kisch and Bowman. He did press harder for Polish claims than did his English and American colleagues. But, the basic French line appeared very close to the proposal of Kisch and Bowman and Le Rond's amendments were not major in character.

The Council of Ten discussed the report on March 19,[1] following its presentation by Jules Cambon. Vigorous opposition came from Lloyd George, who viewed some of the proposals as immoderate, unwise, and contrary to the Fourteen Points. Contending that too many Germans were being assigned to Poland, he singled out for specific criticism the provisions respecting Danzig and Marienwerder. Lloyd George spoke of two basic principles which were endangered: the principle of fairness to the Germans and the principle of seeking a durable peace settlement. To assign, because of a railway, the German-populated areas west of the town of Marienwerder to the Poles would be unfair and imprudent. Their cession would sow the seeds of war. He drew a parallel with Alsace-Lorraine; Danzig and Marienwerder would become *Germania Irredenta*. He doubted whether the United States, Great Britain, and France would, in the future, be prepared to back up the proposed settlement with force if, for instance, the Germans in these areas revolted against Polish rule and German forces intervened to aid them. He posed a further objection: if the Allies demanded huge indemnities and the cession of a large German population to Poland, the present German government might collapse and the German people hesitate to accept such a treaty. Clearly Lloyd George was gravely concerned about the overall character and impact of the treaty which was shaping up in mid-March.

He urged: let the Polish railway lines be cut, if necessary. The Poles could have access to the seas by guaranteed transit rights, like those being provided for the Germans. In any case, not only would it be easy to move railways—much easier than to transfer people—but also Poland would still be linked to the Baltic by the Vistula.

In sum, Lloyd George thought that the Commission's proposals in part had violated the Fourteen Points, overlooked the German reaction, imperilled the future peace of Europe, and given the Poles more than they required.

[1] *P.P.C.*, IV, 413-19.

Against Lloyd George's objections, Jules Cambon undertook a stubborn, though rambling, defense.[1] His arguments were mainly directed against Lloyd George's objections to Polish acquisition of Marienwerder. Danzig tended to be ignored. He tried to meet Lloyd George's charge that the proposals were immoderate by comparing them with the frontiers of Poland before the partitions of the eighteenth century. The Poles had claimed their historic frontiers, but the Commission on Polish Affairs had, after study, decided upon a much more moderate line.

To assert that the Commission could have been more drastic scarcely met the criticism that it had been immoderate.

An attack had been made upon the proposed German-Polish frontier in the name of justice and the Fourteen Points. How did Wilson respond? In his first intervention, he misunderstood the area to which Lloyd George referred. Later, Wilson remarked that if Germans were transferred in areas historically German, the shift could only be justified on the basis of reciprocity. With reference to Marienwerder, Wilson admitted 'he had not reached a definite conclusion in his own mind on the particular point under discussion'.[2] Granting the inclusion of two million Germans in Poland violated one principle, he pointed out Germany had been notified that free and safe access to the sea would be demanded for Poland. The difficulty was how to balance conflicting considerations. It was necessary to consider the strategic as well as the economic needs of the new Poland. Moreover, mixed populations in the border regions were unavoidable. The Council had to decide which mixture offered the best prospects of security. He was afraid of drawing the line as near the Danzig-Thorn railway as had been suggested by Lloyd George; at the same time, he felt some of the anxieties which Lloyd George had entertained, including the danger of a future German attempt to rescue German minorities from Polish rule. Altogether Wilson's initial reaction was confused, hesitant, and indecisive.

After Balfour intervened to suggest an ethnical line in the Marienwerder region (which he realized would cut the Mlawa-Warsaw railway in several places), Wilson countered with the suggestion that they consider the 1772 boundary of the province

[1] *Ibid.*, pp. 415-18. [2] *Ibid.*, p. 417.

of East Prussia. This was between the Commission's line and the one proposed by Balfour. Wilson argued that this frontier would not cut the railway line and might offer sentimental justification to Germany for the loss of some Germans.

To end the discussion, Lloyd George proposed that the report be referred back to the Commission on Polish Affairs for reconsideration 'with a view to readjustment of the boundaries of East Prussia in such a manner as to exclude from the new Polish State territory historically as well as ethnologically Prussian while ensuring to Poland secure access to the sea'.[1] Opposing such a precise instruction, Wilson moved for reconsideration in the light of the discussion. His colleagues accepted his suggestion.[2]

The Commission on Polish Affairs set to work again on the morning of March 20.[3] Illustrating the cleavages at Paris within delegations as well as between them, the initiative in resisting Lloyd George was taken by Kisch, who urged that they adhere entirely to their recommendations. He read a draft note addressed to the Supreme Council embodying this intransigent

[1] *Ibid.*, p. 419.

[2] A sequel to the meeting of May 19 was the publication in French newspapers, particularly *Le Temps*, *Le Journal*, and *L'Echo de Paris*, of a full report of the findings of the Commission on Polish Affairs accompanied by maps and an account of what Lloyd George had said. On March 21, before the Council of Ten, Lloyd George protested in terms so strong that even the official minutes convey their vigour. He threw the blame primarily on someone around the Council table, demanded a strict French enquiry to discover the culprit, and threatened to take no further part in their discussions until the final Conference took place. Wilson backed him, while Balfour pointed out that similar leakages were taking place in the case of other commissions and the committees of the Conference.

[3] A.C.N.P., 140, 181.213201/13 contains the printed minutes of this session in French; also a semi-verbatim report in English of the remarks of the English-speaking representatives. Mr. Paton has explained privately that the official minutes were kept by French secretaries, some of whom did not understand English very well. As a result, the official minutes were frequently inaccurate as far as English speeches were concerned. They were not closely edited by the English-speaking members because they were too busy to have time for such a chore. It may be then that the U.S. delegation decided to keep semi-verbatim reports of the remarks of English-speaking members of the Commission for the sake of a more accurate record of the negotiations. As we shall see later, this practice was applied to other commissions as well.

position. During a lengthy discussion, Bowman stressed the ethnographic difficulties involved:

> It is not a question as Lloyd George emphasized yesterday of two million Germans within the Polish state; . . . but it is a question of where you can modify your proposed lines so as to get rid of the Germans, and the same time, meet the other practical considerations of a boundary. The nearer we can come to answering his point specifically and the other points raised by other gentlemen yesterday, the more chance we have to meet the argument that will be raised at the next session of the Council of Ten.[1]

Changes were made in Kisch's draft to meet Bowman's point. Finally the Commission adopted its reply to the Supreme Council.[2] Concerning itself only with the Marienwerder question, it explained that the Warsaw-Mlawa-Danzig railway had been assigned to Poland for three reasons: first, to secure Polish access to the sea; second, the railway could be economically valuable only if it served Poland; third, the railway was the shortest line from the port of Poland to its capital. In their opinion, these considerations outweighed the fact that Kreis Rosenberg and part of Kreis Marienwerder were predominately German in population and had formed part of Ducal Prussia for centuries. With minor exceptions, all other territories east of the Vistula which they proposed giving to Poland had been historically Polish territory. Although, in the last analysis, the Commission based their stand upon the railway line, it submitted other considerations. To follow the historic frontier of East Prussia seemed impossible because of its intricate and abnormal character. To assign this entire region to East Prussia was impractical because the Germans would have complete command of the Vistula.

If the members of the Polish Commission were stubborn, Lloyd George was not less so. When the Council of Ten on March 22 took up the Second Report of the Commission on Polish Affairs,[3] Lloyd George repeated in substance his argument of March 19. Although he was not so sure that the ethnical results of the proposed settlement could be avoided, he was alarmed still about the political consequences: if this demand

[1] A.C.N.P., 140, 181.213201/13.

[2] *P.P.C.*, IV, 452-454.

[3] *Ibid.*, pp. 449-50.

upon Germany were added to the others which were in the making, the effect upon German public opinion could be deplorable. He cautioned:

> The Conference must avoid presenting such a Treaty that no Government would dare sign it, or such as would cause the immediate collapse of any government that undertook the responsibility of accepting it. These observations were not levelled at the Committee on Polish Affairs, but the recommendations of that Committee were a considerable element in the difficulty just mentioned. . . .[1]

Lloyd George would only accept the Commission's solution provisionally. Wilson agreed and proposed that the second report of the Commission on Polish Affairs be reserved for final examination in connection with subsequent boundary determinations affecting Germany. Under this powerful prodding, the Council suspended final judgment on a German-Polish frontier. The first attempt at Paris to solve the Polish Question had failed.

[1] *Ibid.*, p. 449.

VII

'DINNER INSTEAD OF DANZIG'

THE fate of Danzig and of Marienwerder now dominated the negotiations over the German-Polish border. An arrangement had to be devised which would if possible be satisfactory to Germans and to Poles, provide Poland with secure access to the seas, protect the right of national self-determination, give promise of durability, and reconcile the different interests of the principal Allied Powers.

The German and Polish positions were far apart. Evidence of German attitudes came from General Hammerstein, the President of the German Armistice Commission. His wire of March 26 protested against any violation of the provinces of West Prussia and Posen.[1] According to Hammerstein, '. . . all political parties, even the revolutionaries, vie with each other in protests against the Polish claims. . . . The majority is German and wishes to remain German. . . .' Warning that Germans were contemplating the use of force if necessary, the message ended impudently with the plea that Wilson's principles be not treated as scraps of paper. On March 27, Hammerstein informed General Nudant, head of the Permanent Inter-Allied Armistice Commission, that a map was being sent which showed that Posen and East Prussia, not counting the Cassubes, were inhabited by a German majority. Protests were also being forwarded over the proposed disembarkation of Polish troops at Danzig and asserting the necessity for recognizing historical

[1] A.C.N.P., 299, 185.1127/107.

rights in these regions.[1] The German attitudes described by Hammerstein were sharply opposed to the Poles and to the settlement recommended by the Commission on Polish Affairs. It was extremely doubtful whether the gap could be bridged by negotiation or both parties satisfied with a judgment rendered by the Council of Four.

The Poles and the principal Allied and Associated Powers sought an independent, viable state which could stand between Germany and Russia. Economic independence meant secure access to world markets and sources of supplies, especially those of states friendly toward the Poles. For goods to move, railways and waterways are required. Harbour facilities are necessary, including navigable channels, docks, cranes, warehouses, rail and road connections with the wharves, customs houses, and a labour force. These elementary needs can be manipulated in many ways, short of deliberate and open blockade, to hamper the movement of goods and peoples. Discriminatory tolls and fiscal charges can be employed. There can be an unwillingness to provide adequate facilities—to repair docks, to keep channels dredged, etc., as illustrated by the Russian attitude towards navigation along the Lower Danube before the Crimean War. These are frequently normal problems in the relations of friendly states. They are accentuated when basic animosities exist between two countries, such as were likely to exist between Germany and Poland after the First World War. Therefore, the Poles and their major associates were justified in being anxious about the conditions of Poland's access to the seas.

It was also reasonable to argue that Danzig and the surrounding region was of greater importance to Poland than to Germany, especially economically. Germany had many outlets to the sea; German trade would not be restrained or stifled by the loss of Danzig. For Poland, what other port was readily at hand? Since ethnical considerations narrowed the land and coast available to Poland to the strip east of Pomerania to the Frisches Hoff, Danzig, in 1919, was the only port available with adequate facilities. Besides, with its water and rail communications, Danzig was Poland's natural outlet to the sea.

In themselves, these considerations did not dictate a single solution to the problem of Polish relations with Danzig. They

[1] *Ibid.*

did seem to rule out a solution leaving Polish trade at the mercy of German governments. They did reasonably suggest either Polish acquisition of the city and region, or limitations upon German sovereignty under international guarantee, or autonomy for the city together with extensive Polish economic privileges. In short, mixed solutions aiming at a just compromise between competing Polish and German interests.

The relatively greater economic importance of Danzig to Poland than to Germany was not the only major consideration. Durability had to be sought in a situation where emotion was likely to prevail over reason and a sense of accommodation. Lasting arrangements depended in part upon a settlement acceptable to all parties. In view of the depth of German and Polish feeling, the prospects for agreement were doubtful. And, considering the psychological attitude of the victors, they were not impartial mediators between Germans and Poles. Lloyd George showed his qualities as a statesman when he asked the Council of Ten to bear in mind what the Germans were likely to accept in the long run. The weakness of his position was the existence of powerful forces in Germany which would not be appeased by slight shifts in the German-Polish frontier because they were not in the long run willing to accept the existence of an independent Poland. Still, arrangements which came closer to meeting the German viewpoint on the eastern borders could influence the balance of political forces within Germany and thus affect the durability of the settlement by helping to keep German moderates in power.

If Lloyd George's instincts were sound in this respect, they were well grounded also in prompting him to raise a question of equal importance: in the long run, would the Allied and Associated Powers back the proposed settlement, with force if necessary? Since Poland, despite Warsaw's pretensions, would be a small Power, it would need Allied support to survive. Would governments and public opinion in Great Britain, France, and the United States be prepared in the foreseeable future to render aid to Poland in an emergency such as Lloyd George depicted? This question can only be answered in the light of the situation in Paris in 1919. While it is impossible to say that Lloyd George was right or wrong, it can be said, perhaps, that he had good reason to be apprehensive. Lloyd

George and his associates were uncertain about the future course of the United States in European and world politics.[1] If the United States returned to isolationism, American power would not be available to uphold a Polish-German settlement unacceptable to the stronger party, Germany. Undoubtedly, Lloyd George also had in mind British reservations about Poland. As we have seen, disapproval of the Poles and doubts about the wisdom of resurrecting Poland were deep-rooted attitudes on the part of many British statesmen. When linked with the public pressures for rapid demobilization and the traditional insularity of British opinion, reasonable grounds can be discerned for Lloyd George's doubts. It was a moot question whether in the long run Great Britain would be prepared to uphold an unstable settlement in an area of little direct interest which seemed unfair to the Germans in the light of the Fourteen Points, as popularly understood.

The Danzig issue was part of a much broader debate: how to deal with Germany over the entire range of the peace treaty. The Big Three sought a durable settlement, with security from aggression. What was the best way of treating Germany to accomplish these ends? When Lloyd George retreated to Fontainebleau to size up the Conference and to prescribe for its ills, he became preoccupied with the fear that dangerously harsh terms were being prepared. Designed by their authors to weaken and restrain Germany; they could be self-defeating if they succeeded only in permanently antagonizing Germany and driving it into union with the Russian Bolsheviks. Moderation, fair-play, even-handed justice, however, might convince the Germans that the settlement was reasonable, just, and hence acceptable. These views were persuasively expressed in Lloyd George's Fontainebleau declaration of March 25.[2] In dealing with the German-Polish borderlands, the Prime Minister agreed that Poland should have a corridor to Danzig but the passageway should be drawn irrespective of strategic and economic considerations so as to minimize the number of Germans placed under alien rule.[3]

[1] Nicolson, *Peacemaking, 1919*, pp. 205-6.

[2] See chap. VIII, pp. 223 *et seq.*, for further discussion of the Fontainebleau memorandum.

[3] Lloyd George, *Truth*, I, p. 413.

The basic premises of the peace plainly preoccupied the Council of Four which now dominated the Paris negotiations. On March 27, Wilson backed Lloyd George's appeal for moderation. The President warned that it would be a grave error to give the Germans strong reasons for seeking revenge by imposing excessive terms upon them and leaving them with a sense of injustice. He said: 'Je ne crains pas dans l'avenir les guerres préparées par des complots secrets des gouvernments, mais plutôt les conflits créés par le mécontentement des populations.'[1] Germany must be treated with moderation and equity.

Clemenceau claimed 'Mes principes sont les votres; je ne discute que l'application.' But his impassioned reply to Lloyd George belied his assurance. Paying homage to the Prime Minister's desire to be fair to the Germans, Clemenceau accused him of being too frightened about possible German resistance to signing the treaty. They must not abuse their triumph; neither must they throw away the fruits of victory. Turning to Wilson, Clemenceau challenged the practicality of his idea of doing justice to Germany. What they regarded as justice in that room would not necessarily be accepted as such in Germany. 'Je puis vous dire que leur idée de la justice n'est pas la notre.' Clemenceau assured Wilson that he and all Frenchmen knew the Germans:

> Hier encore, je recevais un nouveau dossier sur les atrocités commises en France. Nous avons appris malheureusement à connaître les Allemands à nos dépense et nous savons que c'est un peuple qui se soumet à la force pour impose lui-même la force au monde. . . . Les Allemands sont un peuple servile qui a besoin de la force pour soutenir un argument.[2]

Clemenceau feared the German spirit would not quickly change. The problem would be how to persuade the Germans that the victors had been just. Clemenceau inferred that sweet reason would be insufficient; to restrain the aggressive tendencies of Germany would require a combination of force and justice.

He offered Danzig as one example. Here, in Clemenceau's

[1] Mantoux, *Délibérations*, I, pp. 41 *et seq.* Since Mantoux renders Wilson's and Lloyd George's remarks in French, I have not translated quotations from this French language source into English.

[2] *Ibid.*, p. 43.

eyes, justice had to be done—justice to the Poles for the historic crime of partition. Justice to the Poles for German crimes in recent decades: 'Nous nous rappelons les enfants fouettés pour avoir prié Dieu en polonais, les paysans expropriés, chassés de leurs terres, pour faire place à des occupants de race germanique.' German wrong obligated the victors to give the Polish state the means of existence. Bluntly, Clemenceau rejected Lloyd George's advice that economic and strategic considerations be laid aside in delimiting the Polish Corridor: 'Il faut accepter des accrocs inévitables au principe du droit des peuples à disposer d'euxmêmes, si nous voulons sauvegarder ce principe même.'[1]

In his rebuttal Lloyd George stressed that they were imposing a hard peace upon Germany. The Reich was losing arms, colonies, six or seven million people, many natural resources. It was shouldering a heavy reparations bill. 'Si vous ajoutez à cela des conditions secondaires qui puissent être considérées comme injustes, ce sera peut-être la goutte d'eau qui fera deborder le vase.'

Lloyd George defended the Germans against Clemenceau's criticisms: they had a certain quality of character; they had fought bravely; they would accept the just penalties of defeat:

> . . . mais ce qui les blessera le plus est l'idée d'abandonner des millions d'Allemands à la domination polonaise. Il a été très pénible pur la France de voir des Français passer sous la domination allemande; mais les Français considéraient du moins les Allemands comme des égaux. Il n'en est pas de même des Polonais dans l'esprit des Allemands. C'est cette sorte de sentiment qui peut les empêcher de signer le traité de paix.[2]

Lloyd George shared this view of Polish inferiority as the following sentence reveals: '. . . il ne faut pas instituer une Pologne séparée dès sa naissance par une querelle inoubliable de son voisin le plus civilisé'. Earlier he had remarked: 'J'avoue mes

[1] Austria, the military limitations of the League, and the insecure geographic position of France were also dealt with in Clemenceau's speech. He concluded with an appeal to the Council of Four not to ignore military advice completely and with a warning about the perils of Bolshevism in their own countries in case public opinion felt they had thrown away the victory. *Ibid.*, pp. 42-5.

[2] *Ibid.*, p. 47.

grandes craintes au sujet de Dantzig. Nous allons donner à la Pologne 2 millions d'Allemands. Les Polonais gouverneront mal et mettront longtemps à prendre la pratique des affaires à la manière occidentale.'[1]

He defined his preferred solution for Danzig: a free port, and arrangements leaving Poles in Poland, Germans in Germany. To support his stand he read to the Council a letter from General Smuts in which the South African described as unstatesmanlike the proposed cessions to Poland.[2] It appears that Smuts's influence was one reason why Lloyd George was defying some of his advisors and others in his resistance to Polish claims to Danzig and Marienwerder.

After the end of this dramatic debate in the Council of Four, Dr. S. E. Mezes, who was director of the staff of technical experts on the American delegation, and J. W. Headlam-Morley, who was in the political section of the British delegation as a special advisor on German territorial questions, concocted several plans for the disposition of Danzig. On March 31, Mezes presented three possibilities to Wilson: an independent state of Danzig, including the Marienwerder region; the settlement recommended by the Commission on Polish Affairs; and the assignment of Danzig to Poland and of the territory east of the main branch of the Vistula, including Marienwerder, to Germany.[3]

Under the first plan, the free state of Danzig would stretch from a line five miles west and south of the city to the east branch of the Vistula, an area containing some 310,000 Germans. Seventy-three thousand Germans and half that number of Poles could be added if the region east of the Vistula to the southernmost point of the pre-1770 boundary of East Prussia was included in the free state. The Council of the League would elect the chief executive. Internally, the state would have a wide measure of self-government; externally, it would be neutral in its relations with Germany and Poland.

[1] *Ibid.*, p. 48.

[2] Smuts expressed his alarm about excessively heavy terms on Danzig, the Rhineland, and indemnities. Poland could not exist without the goodwill of Russia and Germany. Europe would have to live with Germany after the war and the treaty should take this into account, according to Smuts. See p. 226 below for a further discussion of Smuts's influence.

[3] Wilson Papers, VIII-A-31, April 1, 1919.

Mezes made some pungent comments upon this plan. The addition of the Marienwerder region to the free state would be unjustified because it would damage 25,000,000 Poles far more than 73,000,000 Germans. Otherwise, the first plan accorded well with the existing population distribution, and could, for the moment at least, give Poland 'a good chance' of access to the Baltic. But it had, in his opinion, serious disadvantages. Germany would have a powerful weapon in any peaceful struggle for the economic and consequently the political subjugation of Poland. Under this arrangement, Danzig would also be a fruitful field for German exploitation; a way-station on the road to the riches of Russia and the East. German agents in Poland could receive invaluable aid from the over 300,000 independent Germans in and about Poland's only port. Such a solution would probably not be durable. The solid block of Germans in Danzig would steadily press for union with East Prussia; this demand could not, and would not, be long denied. In conclusion, while granting this plan had current attractions, he asserted the verdict of history would probably be that, when Poland was reborn, it had been denied an essential port and doomed to vassalage to Germany.

As for the second plan, Mezes told Wilson that all the United States' and British specialists preferred it. He tried to woo the President by advising him that the second (and the third) plan left them with a free hand in the negotiations over Fiume. According Danzig to Poland was similar to assigning Fiume to the Yugoslavs; and, he commented, anything else for Fiume would, relatively speaking, be a favour to the Italians. Mezes counselled Wilson that the United States' specialists believed that Danzig, as the port for twenty-five million ardently patriotic Poles, would quickly become a Polish city. 'History would approve Plan II as a brave and sound solution of a distressingly knotty problem.'

According to Mezes, the third plan recognized the presence of many Germans near the mouth of the Vistula. To the Poles, the disadvantage would be that they would lose about forty thousand of their nationals, would be deprived of unhampered control of their river artery, and would be without the shortest and best railway connecting Warsaw and their only port. For the Germans' part, they would lose a German city and its surroundings. About this Mezes observed: 'What significance should be accorded the fact that city and environs were made German by German political devices and at infinite pains, I confess I don't know. But no doubt many German functionaries, their families and dependents, would leave.'

A refinement of the third plan was suggested by Headlam-Morley and worked into a proposal by him and Mezes which they took to their respective chiefs for comment.[1] Under this scheme, Germany would cede Danzig and the region west of the Vistula to the League of Nations, which in turn would give the territory to Poland as a free port. The League would guarantee the city a wide measure of autonomy. East of the main Vistula, Germany would transfer to the League territory as far as a designated line. After examining conditions on the spot, the Council of the League would draw the boundary in this area between East Prussia and Poland. Both Germany and Poland would be granted transit rights on the necessary railway lines.

Mezes told Wilson that this scheme had three advantages. It gave time to consult the people concerned. It tied the League into the treaty of peace. It would avoid delay in drafting the treaty 'by postponing difficult questions for the further examination they need'. He asked Wilson for his opinion before the next meeting with Headlam-Morley.

Wilson presented the four projects to the Council of Four on April 1,[2] comparing the idea of a free city with the Hanseatic towns of the Middle Ages. He criticized the first plan because it might tempt the Germans of Danzig to seek reunion with Germany. The Headlam-Morley scheme had the advantage of placing the settlement under League guarantee, but had the disadvantage of postponing important decisions. Lloyd George suggested an amalgamation of the first and fourth plans. He favoured an independent Danzig joined economically to Poland by a customs union which would link the Danzigers to the economic future of Poland. Their interest in the economic prosperity of Poland, against the background of independence of Germany, could gradually attach them to Poland by economic ties. At the same time, for as long as the Danzigers wished, they would enjoy German laws and institutions. The League, in his view, would be represented in Danzig by a

[1] *Ibid.*

[2] Mantoux, *Délibérations*, I, pp. 109 *et seq.*

governor-general whose role would be similar to that of British governors-general in the Dominions. Wilson did not immediately accept the free state solution, although he clearly leaned towards it.

As for Marienwerder, Lloyd George reiterated: 'ma grande préoccupation est d'éviter de mettre trop d'Allemands en Pologne'.[1] Marienwerder, with its 420,000 Germans, should be left in East Prussia, while giving the Poles full rights over the railways. Wilson suggested a plebiscite, to which Lloyd George agreed.

The first difficulty was how to persuade Clemenceau to accept a settlement falling short of the Polish claims. While Clemenceau reluctantly inclined towards the proposed settlement of the Danzig and Marienwerder questions, he successfully resisted a formal decision by the Council on this occasion.[2]

On April 2, Lloyd George and Wilson agreed that a free, autonomous city of Danzig should be established with a High Commissioner appointed by the League of Nations.[3] The city would be linked to Poland by a customs union. In addition, the fate of Marienwerder should be determined by plebiscite. Mezes and Headlam-Morley were instructed to prepare draft articles embodying the proposed arrangements.

The Lloyd George-Wilson plan was then evidently submitted to a special committee consisting of Haskins, Headlam-Morley, and Tardieu, who reached agreement on Danzig and Marienwerder.[4] In addition to the features described above, the Vistula was to come under the regime for international rivers in case Marienwerder voted for union with East Prussia. To protect their communications, in peacetime the Germans should have the right to establish rail lines across the territory of Danzig toward East Prussia and Russia. When the experts' proposals came before the Council of Four on April 3, Lloyd George insisted that the Poles should have similar rights of communication between Danzig and Warsaw since the Mlawa line crossed Marienwerder.

Clemenceau gave his consent to the plan, remarking:

[1] *Ibid.*, p. 111. [2] *Ibid.*

[3] Headlam-Morley Memorandum on Polish Settlement, Danzig, etc., April 7, 1919, House Papers, 31/153.

[4] Mantoux, *Délibérations*, I, pp. 125-6.

'L'essentiel est d'arriver à une solution acceptable pour les Polonais. Je ne veux pas rompre avec eux et vous savez qu'ils ne sont pas toujours commodes.'[1] Orlando agreed. The decision had been taken! Danzig was to be a free city, a solution which had been envisaged, if not preferred, by the French Foreign Office in December 1918, and by Balfour much earlier.

All that now remained was to work out the details and to withstand the vigorous, even furious, assaults of the proponents of the Polish claims, before meeting the German protest.

Following the instructions of the Council of Four, Mezes and Headlam-Morley prepared draft clauses providing for the establishment of a free city, for a plebiscite in Marienwerder, and for special railway privileges to Germany and Poland. During these negotiations, doubts arose as to the meaning of the instructions: was Danzig to be sovereign or autonomous under Polish sovereignty? Headlam-Morley consulted Lloyd George, on April 5, who advised him that Polish sovereignty over the city was excluded. Thereupon, Mezes and Headlam-Morley proceeded with their draft, confining its provisions to what was necessary for the treaty with Germany, on the assumption that many details should be left for later and fuller discussion with representatives of the city.

Under their draft proposals, Germany was to renounce all sovereignty over Danzig in favour of the Allied and Associated Powers. The latter would set up the independent city of Danzig and arrange the relations in which the city would stand towards Poland. These relations would be defined in a treaty between Danzig and Poland which, while based upon the city's possession of sovereignty, would secure to Poland its just and legitimate interests by the grant of three main rights: customs union, Polish ownership of the railways, and free use of the port by the Poles. They also considered it essential to place control of the foreign relations of Danzig in Polish hands. This provision which severely limited the sovereignty of the city was explained thus: '. . . if it were not done, we might have a German minister resident at Danzig, a Danzig Minister resident in Berlin, and in this way very dangerous intrigues might be started between Germany and Danzig'.

Headlam-Morley suggested that the plebiscite in Marien-

[1] *Ibid.*, p. 125.

werder be dropped since the predominantly German population would undoubtedly vote decisively for union with East Prussia. Otherwise delay and inconvenience would result.

Headlam-Morley and Mezes at this stage of the negotiations drew the frontier between Poland and Danzig-Marienwerder along the right bank of the Vistula, instead of following the thalweg. The purpose was to secure Polish control of the Vistula.[1]

By April 9, texts relative to Danzig (along the lines of the Mezes/Headlam-Morley project) and to Marienwerder were ready for the Council of Four.[2] Lloyd George noted that the free state of Danzig would only have 16,000 Poles out of a total population of 324,000, and that Marienwerder, which would probably go to East Prussia, had 160,000 people, of whom only 26,000 were Poles. He claimed, therefore: 'Ceci justifie la politique que nous avons deféndue.' Orlando promptly punctured Lloyd George's argument by pointing to the 1,800,000 Germans still assigned to Poland. Wilson was satisfied that Poland's access to the sea had been guaranteed by the proposals. He upheld the ethnic results as unavoidable because the Germans involved were so dispersed and as justifiable because these Germans occupied their lands largely due to the systematic colonization schemes of the Prussian government. Lloyd George agreed that a large German minority in Poland was inevitable.

On this occasion, the Big Four summoned Paderewski to present their conclusions to him. His intransigent attitude must be seen in the light of a strenuous campaign by the Poles and their supporters to reverse the decision of the Council of Four.

The Polish Delegation levelled a heavy paper barrage in early April against Lloyd George and Wilson.[3] The recurring motif of the Polish argument was: 'Danzig est la clé de la Pologne.'

[1] The foregoing is based upon Headlam-Morley's memorandum of April 7, 1919, House Papers, 31/153. Two sets of draft clauses are appended to the memorandum in this file: one set in original typed copy, with handwritten amendments; and a carbon copy which incorporates these changes. The latter resembles, as far as it runs, Wilson's draft of April 22.

The former included the provisions: '9. The Free City of Danzig will have the right to be united to Poland should a majority of its citizens at any time by free vote express a desire to that effect.'

[2] Mantoux, *Délibérations*, I, pp. 197 *et seq.*

[3] The memoranda are in A.C.N.P., 299, 185.1127/49.

An effort was made to place the issue on moral grounds by charging that the partitions of Poland were a crime, for which redress should be made. It was argued that the isolation of East Prussia was necessary for the maintenance of a durable peace. The balance of naval power in the Baltic was invoked, possibly to attract British favour: without a Polish navy and Polish ports, the Baltic would become a German sea; only a free and powerful Poland could oppose Germany in the Baltic; '. . . tous les Etats de la mer Baltique trouveront dans la Pologne *un appui contre* l'Allemagne'. Coupled with references in the memoranda to the rebirth of Poland as a great power, this dream of Polish naval might gave a measure of Polish aspirations.

A strong barrier still had to be demolished: Danzig's German character and the principle of the right of nationalities to self-determination. Boldly and defiantly the Poles charged against the wall which Lloyd George and Wilson were erecting between them and full possession of Danzig. Their pens scrawled out this pronunciamento: 'Le principe des nationalités ne peut être appliqué sans restrictions, il doit, dans certaines circonstances, céder a dès considérations d'ordre superieur.' In any case, so they argued, the German element in Danzig was artificial. It had been implanted by brute force. Under Polish rule, Danzig would gradually become a Polish city without oppressive or vexatious measures being used. Again the refrain was sounded: how could the vital interests of 28,000,000 people be sacrificed to some 250,000 Germans, only a minor fraction of the total German population? 'Il est inadmissible qu'on refuse pour de telles considérations l'incorporation à l'état polonais de l'embouchure de son fleuve principal.' Finally, they maintained, proof existed that it would be contrary to the interests of the people of the city and to their desires to make an 'application mécanique du principe des nationalités à Dantzig'. The only proof of this desire of the Germans in Danzig to come under Polish rule was the opinion of the Polish authors of the appeal. In short, the considerations of a superior order which must modify the principle of national self-determination and prevent its mechanical application to Danzig were simply the national interests and feelings of the Poles.

Special attention was paid in the Polish memoranda to the fate of Elbing. The Poles had lost the city when the Commission on Polish Affairs reached its final conclusions. Now, they returned to their demand: Poland must control all the mouths of the Vistula to assure its political and economic independence.

As these appeals circulated around the Conference, some support came from the Inter-Allied Commission on Poland. At a meeting on the morning of April 8, Noulens, the President of the Commission, and his French colleague, Niessel, and Montagna, one of the Italian representatives, spoke in favour of a large stretch of Baltic coast-line for Poland. Their figures varied from 80 to 110 kilometres. Open support for this proposal was not forthcoming, apparently, from other members of the Commission. A similar division of opinion occurred over the disposition of Elbing. Lord, of the American delegation, and Sir Esme Howard, of the British delegation, opposed Polish acquisition of the city. Romel, of Italy, and Noulens supported the Polish demand for Elbing. But on the issue of Danzig, except for Kernan, the other American member of the Commission, they were unanimously agreed that Danzig as well as the Danzig-Mlawa-Warsaw railway, with a corridor to the sea, should go to Poland.[1]

On the same day the British, Italian, and French military members of the Inter-Allied Commission addressed a memorandum to it on military questions concerning Poland. Their views undoubtedly reflected the thinking of Polish supporters at Paris. Advising the sending of war materials, instructors, and food supplies to Poland, the three generals felt that the Poles should have received immediate and energetic support in the interests of the Allies themselves. Why did the generals feel concerned? The final paragraph of their memorandum gave their reasons:[2]

> It is absolutely necessary that we should similarly support all the States allied with us which lie between Germany and Russia. But it is especially urgent that such help be given to Poland (*a*) because all necessaries are lacking in that country; (*b*) because her geographical position is such that it would be possible, with her co-operation, to separate Germany from Hungary and Russia, and to isolate the most dangerous sources of Bolshevism.

[1] Howard, de Wiart, Noulens, Neissel, Lord, Romel, and Montagna took this line. Kernan does not seem to have been present. Wilson Papers, 166.

[2] A.C.N.P., 456, 860C.00/63.

In this estimate of the strategical importance of Poland, there lay a powerful argument for giving aid to the Poles in the form of strategic frontiers and well-developed port facilities.

Paderewski knew then that he had many friends at court when on April 9 he presented an uncompromising front against the Danzig-Marienwerder proposals of the Council of Four.[1] Wilson described the plan, concluding with an affirmation of their wish not to create a *Germania Irredenta*. Paderewski, in reply, spoke in the name of the Polish Diet. It wished close relations with the Entente. It wanted territorial guarantees for the security of Poland. For seven hundred years, the Poles had been neighbours and victims of the Germans. They knew the Germans better than did Wilson or Lloyd George, whom he solemnly informed: 'Soyez persuadés que, si peu l'on prenne à l'Allemagne, ce sera toujours la *Germania Irredenta*.'[2]

The core of his argument was 'La question de Dantzig est pour nous une question de vie ou de mort'. If Poland did not obtain the city, he threatened disaster in eastern Europe, where he depicted Poland as a fortress of political order. Should Polish confidence in the peacemakers be shaken, the resultant despair and disappointment could lead to catastrophe and open the gate to Bolshevism.

The Council of Four failed to retreat before this spectre of communism. It would be unwise, however, to dismiss the Polish Prime Minister's fears as entirely without substance. The danger was very real that outraged nationalism could produce violent convulsions. Bolshevism, however, was not the sole alternative.

Paderewski attacked the proposed plebiscite in Marienwerder where he held the presence of German soldiers and officials, in effect, would give an artificial pro-Reich result. Nor would he accept a plebiscite for Danzig, despite his unsupported assertion 'je suis persuadé qu'elle votera pour l'annexion à la Pologne; il y va de son intérèt économique'. Rather mischievously perhaps Lloyd George asked: 'S'il vous est impossible d'annexer purement et simplement Dantzig, accepteriez-vous comme un pis aller une consultation populaire?' At first, Paderewski dodged a direct answer by replying that the Polish Diet and the Polish people wished to acquire Danzig which, together with Upper

[1] Mantoux, *Délibérations*, I, pp. 197-202. [2] *Ibid.*, p. 199.

Silesia, they viewed as a *sina qua non*.[1] Later, he flatly rejected any settlement of differences with enemies by means of plebiscites.

Wilson tried to persuade him that Danzig would be entirely at the disposal of Poland. Lloyd George attempted to back up the President by explaining: 'C'est une sorte de Home Rule pour Dantzig. Les relations extérieures étant entre vos mains, Dantzig a moins d'autonomie vis-à-vis de la Pologne que le Canada n'en a vis-à-vis de l'Angleterre.' If Paderewski knew anything about the trend in relations between Great Britain and the Dominions, Lloyd George's analogy could scarcely have been less reassuring. Be that as it may, Paderewski would not be persuaded. Under the free city arrangement, Danzig would remain in German hands and would end up by returning to Germany. When Wilson reminded him of the argument that economic ties would draw the Danzigers to Poland, Paderewski answered honestly if contradictorily: 'Il faut tenir compte du sentiment national: l'Allemagne n'est pas encore hors de combat,' provoking the simple and perhaps alarmed exclamation from Lloyd George: 'Truly?'[2] Here was fuel for the fear that the Germans might not sign the treaty!

Paderewski also refused to be satisfied with special guarantees for the use of the railways. Like everyone else in the room he knew that the Marienwerder plebiscite was going to have one outcome: German retention of the region. The vital Danzig-Warsaw railway would inevitably pass through German territory and 'Nous connaissons trop les Allemands pour nous fier aux garanties qu'ils auront acceptées.'

The conflict among the victors over the fate of Danzig now neared its climax. Within the ranks of the American delegation, General Kernan, aided by Lansing, sought to arouse Wilson on what they regarded as militarism and feverish nationalism in eastern Europe. On April 11, Lansing, in forwarding a memorandum by Kernan on the Polish-Ukrainian situation and on general conditions in Poland, drew the President's attention specially to the General's observations on French, Polish, Czech, and Rumanian 'imperialistic designs'.[3] Kernan thought that

[1] *Ibid.*, pp. 199-200.
[2] *Ibid.*, p. 200.
[3] 'Memorandum by General Kernan on the suspension of arms between Poles and Ukrainians in eastern Galicia and some general observations on conditions in Poland', Paris, April 11, 1919, Wilson Papers, VIII-A-35.

militarism represented a greater threat to Poland's future than did Bolshevism. Although he did not relate his beliefs to territorial questions, they could lead to the conclusion that Polish claims to Danzig, Marienwerder, Elbing, etc., were simply the manifestations of an extravagant nationalism backed by the imperialistic, militaristic ambitions of France on the continent. From this position, opposition to Polish demands could be logically and emotionally based. Wilson himself shrewdly commented in a private conversation on April 7: '. . . The only real interest of France in Poland is in weakening Germany by giving Poland territory to which she has no right.'[1] Kernan's charges, if read by the President, would doubtless have strengthened him in continuing to uphold the Danzig proposals.

On the other side, the Poles in Paris and their supporters within the delegations of the Great Powers sought, in growing desperation, to persuade the Council of Four to revoke its decision on Danzig. On April 12, the Commission on Polish Affairs heard the Polish Prime Minister fervently appeal for Danzig.[2] He claimed that if German officials were eliminated from Kreis Stuhm and Kreis Marienwerder, the Poles would predominate. (He granted Kreis Rosenberg would vote 70 per cent. German.) And he exclaimed:

> . . . it could not be possible that the time honoured aspirations and the economic life of a population of thirty millions[3] could ever be sacrificed for the doubtful wishes of a part of the inhabitants of the small district of Rosenberg. Even Dantzig herself would today vote for attribution to Poland, to which its economic life was so clearly allied.

In reply to this appeal, Jules Cambon, the chairman, moved that they once again inform the Supreme Council of the necessity of assigning Danzig to Poland. The Commission

[1] Baker, *Woodrow Wilson and World Settlement*, II, p. 60. On April 1, the President said in the Council of Four: 'La paix avec l'Allemagne ne fait pas disparaître toutes les causes de difficultés possibles. Je crains beaucoup celles qui peuvent surgir de la situation de toutes ces nationalités en formation dans l'Europe Centrale. Il y a là une source inépuisable de desordres et de guerre, si nous n'y prenons garde.' Mantoux, *Délibérations*, I, p. 113.

[2] A.C.N.P., 135, 181.213201/17.

[3] The Polish population had increased by two millions in a fortnight.

agreed, stressing in their note to the Council of Four that any other solution would imperil peace in Europe.[1]

Clemenceau that day tried in the Council of Four to secure Marienwerder for Poland to make it easier for the Poles to resign themselves to the independence of Danzig.[2] Apparently, he had had a trying interview with Paderewski; as he told Lloyd George and Wilson: 'Vous ne pouvez imaginer l'emotion de Paderewski; elle est allée jusqu'aux larmes.' Clemenceau's effort was shrugged off by Lloyd George and Wilson. They agreed to write Paderewski a nice letter explaining they were seeking to protect Poland's best interests.

Although Colonel House's role in the controversy remains obscure, he was entertaining some of the disputants, as the etiquette of conferences requires. With evident relish, the Colonel noted in his diary for April 14: '. . . We are giving a dinner tonight of thirty-five covers and a reception afterward in honour of the Prime Minister and Madame Paderewska. One of the newspapermen remarked, "I suppose you are giving him a dinner instead of Dantzig"!'[3]

Despite the journalist's cynicism, an effort was being made to offer some compensation to the disappointed Poles; not dinner, but Marienwerder. Clemenceau, on April 15, in the Council of Four, returned to Marienwerder declaring: 'Je partage entièrement sur cette question le point de vue des Polonais.'[4] Wilson advised that the matter be left until Lloyd George returned,[5] adding the cryptic comment: '. . . c'est lui surtout qui s'y est intéressé', which suggests that the President was not so firmly set on the Marienwerder solution.

Next day, the Inter-Allied Commission on Poland renewed its pressure for a reconsideration of the proposed Danzig-Marienwerder settlement.[6] Noulens, the French Chairman of the Commission, took the initiative, proposing that they tell the Big Three: 'Poland must constitute a state as powerful from the military as from the economic point of view; so as to form to the east of Germany a counterweight indispensable to the equili-

[1] Sir William Tyrrell, who was present, is not recorded as having dissented from this decision.

[2] Mantoux, *Délibérations*, I, pp. 231-2.

[3] House, Diary, XV, p. 158.

[4] Mantoux, *Délibérations*, I, pp. 248-9.

[5] He had had to visit England on governmental and political matters.

[6] Wilson Papers, VIII-C-166.

brium of Europe since the disappearance of Russian power.' Both Howard and Lord opposed so strong a statement and secured a modified declaration affirming the need to establish a Polish state with sufficient power to become independent and viable. Unanimously, but in vain, the members wrote into their report that Poland should acquire Danzig and the railway connecting the city with Warsaw via Mlawa.

On April 18, the Council of Four considered another revision of the provisions for Danzig, Marienwerder, and railway rights.[1] The basic principles were left untouched. Clemenceau reaffirmed his desire to satisfy the Poles, but he did not see how it was possible and refrained from reopening the Marienwerder question. On this occasion, the Big Four also unanimously adopted the original recommendations of the Commission on Polish Affairs concerning the East Prussian-Lithuanian frontier.

Kisch, Headlam-Morley, and Mezes now made a last-minute attempt to persuade Lloyd-George and Wilson to assign Marienwerder to Poland. On April 20, the two British advisors submitted the following argument to Lloyd George.[2] The terms of the Danzig settlement, when understood, would go far to satisfy Polish public opinion. This would not be true of Polish officialdom, but that did not matter. The establishment of a free state entirely altered the basis of the Council of Four's opposition to awarding Marienwerder to Poland. Why? If a plebiscite were held in Marienwerder, the results were a foregone conclusion. If the paramount consideration was the wishes of the inhabitants, the area should be decisively awarded to Germany. If other considerations made allocation to Poland necessary, this should be done. Kisch and Headlam-Morley supported the latter course, contending that Marienwerder was vital to the life and trade of Poland.[3] Nothing could show more clearly that the battle over Polish claims was not simply between Lloyd George and Wilson on the one hand and 'immoderate' French and Polish delegates on the other. Within both the

[1] Mantoux, *Délibérations*, I, pp. 271-3.

[2] 'Note Relative to the Settlement of the Danzig Question and the Polish Frontiers in East and West Prussia', Paris, April 20, 1919, Wilson Papers, VIII-A-38.

[3] They assumed the final line would depend upon the modification made necessary by the establishment of the free city and that the rights of cultural minorities would be guaranteed in the peace treaty.

GERMAN - POLISH BORDERLANDS
BALTIC SEA
POMERANIA
BRANDENBURG
WEST
PRUSSIA
EAST
PRUSSIA
POSEN
RUSSIAN POLAND
SILESIA
UPPER SILESIA
Putzig
Neustadt
Lauenburg
Neufahrwasser
Danzig
Elbing
Marienburg
Stargard
Rosenberg
Schlochau
Konitz
Schwetz
Kulm
Flatow
Wirsitz
Schneidemühl
Thorn
Kolmar
Kreuz
Czarnikau
Filehne
Vistula River
Birnbaum
Schwerin
Meseritz
Tirschtiegel
Posen
Bentschen
Oder River
Bomst
Schmiegel
Gostyn
Lissa
Fraustadt
Krotoschin
Rawitsch
Militsch
Adelnau
Wartenburg
Schildberg
Namslau
Breslau
Kreuzberg
Bromberg
Lublinitz
Oppeln
Neisse River
Neisse
Friedland
Neustadt
Kosel
Leobschütz
Rybnik
Ratibor
Pless
SCALE OF MILES
0
50
QUAI D'ORSAY PROPOSED AWARD TO POLAND
QUAI D'ORSAY LINE
INTERNATIONAL BOUNDARY, 1914
PROVINCIAL BOUNDARY
ANGLO-AMERICAN LINE
U.S. RECTIFICATION
FRENCH RECTIFICATION
FOREIGN OFFICE LINE

Map 2.

British and American delegations, the two leaders' stand was contested down to the end.

Mezes forwarded this note to Wilson on April 21 with the advice: '... The Danzig decision is major, this minor; and here the need of Poland is greater.'[1] But Mezes, Kisch, and Headlam-Morley met with failure.

On April 22, Wilson submitted the final draft of the Danzig and Marienwerder settlement to the Council of Four. The Council approved.[2]

The settlement provided for Germany's cession to the Allied and Associated Powers of the city of Danzig and adjacent territory, as defined in detail in the proposals. Under these terms, Elbing remained under German sovereignty. A Free City of Danzig was to be established. Representatives of the city were to draft a constitution in agreement with a High Commissioner appointed by the League of Nations. The constitution would be under the guarantee of the League. The first duty of the High Commissioner was to handle all differences arising between Germany and Poland out of the treaty of peace and related agreements. An agreement was to be negotiated by the Allied and Associated Powers between Danzig and Poland to secure the following objectives: a customs union between Danzig and Poland; full and unhampered Polish use and service of all waterways, docks, and other port facilities necessary for the conduct of Polish trade through Danzig; Polish control and administration of the Vistula and of the railway system within Danzig, and of postal, telegraphic, and telephonic services between Poland and Danzig, including the right to develop these services and to lease or purchase the necessary property; the conduct of Danzig's foreign relations by Poland; and equal treatment for Poles in Danzig. The usual provisions were made respecting the rights of nationality. When the treaty came into effect, all German nationals ordinarily resident in Danzig were, *ipso facto*, to become nationals of Danzig. Such nationals were

[1] Wilson Papers, VIII-A-39, April 21. Mezes said: 'I concur in their conclusions (*a*) that a plebiscite in the Region east of the Vistula is unnecessary and inadvisable, and that the region should be assigned either to East Prussia or to Poland, and (*b*) that assignment to Poland is preferable. The Danzig decision is major, this minor; and here the need of Poland is greater.'

[2] *P.P.C.*, V, p. 114.

to have the right of opting for German nationality within two years. If they so opted, they would have to transfer their place of residence to Germany. There would be no restrictions upon the transfer of movable property and their immovable property was to be protected. On the other hand, German public property in Danzig was to pass to the Five Great Powers for transfer to Danzig or to Poland as the Five might equitably determine.

The settlement also provided for a plebiscite by communes in Kreise Stuhm and Rosenberg and in the portions of Kreise Marienberg and Marienwerder which lay east of the Vistula. No detailed provisions to secure freedom of transit for Poland and Germany across one another's territory were written into the final draft, but the Five Great Powers undertook to negotiate agreements between Poland and Germany to secure adequate railway facilities for the two states.[1]

The Council of Four had not yet finished with the Danzig question. On April 24, Headlam-Morley had communicated the proposed settlement to Paderewski. Although obviously upset by the news, the Polish Prime Minister accepted the principle of the settlement. He asked for two additional provisions: actual Polish ownership of the docks, etc., especially those at the mouth of the Vistula and outside the city walls; and Polish power of protection of the city against the possible unorganised attacks of German 'freebooters'. In the latter connection, he agreed that there should be no Polish military force in Danzig itself.

Headlam-Morley reported this talk to the Council of Four on April 26. Wilson opposed both requests. Lloyd George suggested a compromise: Paderewski might be satisfied if Poland were given power of development of the Port of Danzig. The proposals of April 22 had tacitly left this important power in the hands of the city. Lloyd George's suggestion met with approval. A compromise was also effected respecting Paderewski's second request: the Big Four decided to vest in the League of Nations the power of protecting the Free City against external attack.[2]

Having thus driven the last nail into its Danzig contrivance, the Council of Four had finished for the moment with the issue of the German-Polish border. It remained to present the settlement to the Germans and to the world.

[1] *Ibid.*, pp. 114, 118-22.

[2] *Ibid.*, pp. 293-4.

VIII
THE RHINE FRONTIER

À présent, pour nous comme pour nos ancêtres de tous les siècles, notre destinée est de repousser, encore une fois, l'invasion germanique et de prendre les mesures qui doivent nous en préserver dans l'avenir. Quelle barrière, quelle frontière devons-nous établir?

ERNEST BABELON'S answer sonorously resounded—le Rhin! 'Oui! de par la nature, l'histoire et l'attraction instinctive des populations, depuis les Pyrénées jusqu'au Rhin, c'est le *regnum Francorum*, notre France éternelle, *domus aeterna*.'[1]

At the Paris Peace Conference, Foch, Clemenceau, and Tardieu re-echoed the publicist's demand. With the unopposed restoration of Alsace-Lorraine, France returned to the line of 1870. (See Map 3.) But its plenipotentiaries at the conference sought more. Their claims confronted the Conference with the central problem of the postwar settlement: how to treat Germany so as to ensure a durable peace in Europe. The west European elements of this problem have become only too familiar: the clash between German and French aspirations; the imbalance in power between Germany and France; the French assumption that Germany would remain aggressive in the foreseeable future; the French fears of German power and ambitions. Hence the French efforts to redress the balance by weakening Germany and by organizing a West European defensive system.

[1] Ernest Babelon, *La Grande Question d'occident: le Rhin dans l'histoire*, II, p. 499.

Marshal Foch, in his note of January 10, 1919, to the heads of the principal delegations, resumed his offensive to gain the Rhine frontier. His plan to secure western Europe from German aggression had not changed since November 1918. Germany should relinquish sovereignty over the territory west of the Rhine. The bridgeheads across the Rhine should be occupied and a neutral zone established along the right bank.[1] While the ceded areas would enjoy a measure of autonomy, they should be integrated into a West European alliance, including France, Alsace-Lorraine, Belgium, and Luxembourg, providing for a single military organism and a common foreign policy. Each member should also be bound by a common economic policy. The final feature of his defensive system was an entente between western Europe and Great Britain.[2]

The Foch plan had important, if varied, implications for British statesmen and policy. For men like Balfour who thought primarily in terms of imperial interests and a continental balance of power, a stronger military and political grouping of the West European states including the Rhineland had certain advantages. If Russia remained weak and Germany continued to be powerful and aggressive, a strong West European security system associated with England would provide a postwar counterpoise against Germany. Because of the uncertain future course of the United States, such a grouping offered a possible alternative to America as a stabilizing influence on the continent.

On the other hand, numerous objections were possible. Under the Foch plan, France would be the leader of a closely united West European bloc. If both Germany and Russia remained almost powerless, France would then be the dominant power in Europe. French hegemony might not menace British security as seriously as had Imperial Germany. None the less, the historic and existing rivalry between Britain and France could neither be forgotten nor entirely submerged in the *bonne entente*. If it was a fundamental British interest to maintain a balance of power on the continent, the principle applied to France as well

[1] Ostensibly as a guarantee of German execution of the other clauses of the treaty of peace.

[2] Marshal Foch, Note of January 10, 1919, House Papers, 30/162; Wilson Papers, VIII-A-24; Mermeix, *Le Combat des Trois*, pp. 210-19.

as to Germany. From the standpoint of traditional concepts of British national interests, the problem in 1919 was how to contain Germany without dangerously strengthening France.

A further difficulty was whether opinion in the United Kingdom and in the Empire would accept the European commitments entailed in British association with the proposed security system. Popular opinion in the British Isles demanded demobilization of the forces. The General Staff worried about the lack of manpower and sought to conserve British military strength for the danger spots—Ireland, Egypt, the North-West Frontier. The Canadian Prime Minister had expressed his hostility towards European entanglements and alliances.[1] These and other signs pointed to the difficulties of securing political support within England and the Empire for a policy of entente or alliance with France.

Then, too, the Lloyd George government was committed to the principles of nationality and of national self-determination. If Great Britain supported a Rhineland settlement which violated these principles, as Foch's plan appeared to do, the government would face charges of bad faith, and be exposed to debilitating political attack in Great Britain.

The question also arose whether a departure from the national principle in the treatment of the Rhineland would make for stability or instability in western Europe. After all, neither Balfour nor the Foreign Office were prepared to apply the principle universally and in a doctrinaire manner. To be applied, the principle had to be submitted to the test of practicality. In western Europe they had hoped that adherence to national lines and wishes would help to alleviate discords and thus contribute to regional stability. From this viewpoint the Foch plan could be condemned as a scheme for perpetuating discords. In an era of nationalism, German sentiment was unlikely to accept the loss of the Germanic peoples and resources of the left bank. Thus the Teutonic desire to reunite the Rhineland with Germany would be a constant irritant and potential cause of war in western Europe.[2] National sentiment would in

[1] See p. 139, above.

[2] Some members of the British delegation were arguing at this time that a real 'change of heart' had occurred in Germany. See for instance 'Memorandum on the Inner Political Change in Germany', Political Intelligence

any case make the Rhinelanders an unreliable element in Foch's proposed security system. It could be doubted whether a departure in this case from the principle of nationality would be realistic politics.

Finally, the American factor had to be considered. Woodrow Wilson had opposed special security arrangements apart from the League of Nations. Nor would it seem likely that the President who had so staunchly advocated the principle of national self-determination would approve the severance from Germany of over 5,000,000 Germans presumably against their will. British support for the Foch scheme could lead to conflict with Wilson, thereby endangering the policy of seeking American co-operation in the maintenance of the peace.

Generally, plans for solving the problem of West European security along lines proposed by Foch placed British leaders in an awkward position. They could not afford to underwrite a settlement which British opinion was unlikely to support. They dare not alienate the United States lest both Britain and France might have to resist alone renewed German aggression. Yet France and western Europe had an acknowledged right to security. French friendship and co-operation were essential for the future security of the British Isles themselves. Would British diplomacy be equal to reconciling these divergent elements so as to avoid choosing between alignment with Paris or with Washington?

The initial reaction within the British delegation to the Foch proposals remains obscure. Sir Henry Wilson, Lloyd George's chief military advisor, who was concerned about the imbalance of power between France and Germany, agreed on January 26 with Foch and Weygand that it was impossible effectively to limit German arms and military manpower and that the best guarantee of security was to hold the line of the Rhine.[1] On February 19, while opposing French annexation of the Rhine-

[1] Callwell, *Wilson*, p. 166.

Department, Foreign Office, February 1, 1919 (*circa*), A.C.N.P., 484, 862.00/163.

This argument led readily to the conclusion that advantage should be taken of this conversion to strengthen the moderates and to weaken the chauvinists and militarists in Germany by treating the defeated power with moderation and fairness.

land, he urged his government to seek its detachment from the German military system.[1] But he considered it was impossible politically to hold the Rhine permanently.[2] He later advised the British Cabinet that the demilitarization of the Rhineland would protect French security.[3]

Early in February, the British plenipotentiaries were advised by some of their experts that their object '. . . should be to arrive at a settlement which may as far as possible be permanent, and insure not only the security of France but also the best interests of the populations concerned, thus obtaining a solution which may be generally accepted as an equitable and durable settlement'.[4] Lloyd George himself evidently opposed the Foch plans as a violation of principle and as a potential cause of war.[5] Tardieu has confirmed that the French encountered firm British resistance from the beginning.[6]

According to Tardieu, House and Wilson reacted far less sharply. Initially, House opposed a Rhineland buffer state. In a conference with Balfour on February 9, the Colonel accused the French of suffering from an *idée fixe*. In his opinion, the creation of a Rhineland republic against the wishes of the inhabitants could not be a permanent solution because the Rhinelanders would have the right, according to the principle of self-determination, of reunion with Germany. Believing that dismemberment would mean 'treating Germany in one way and the balance of the world in another', he feared 'we would run the danger of having everything from the Rhine to the Pacific, perhaps including Japan, against the Western powers . . .', because the Germans would try to form a strong anti-Western bloc. According to House, Balfour agreed with him. At the same time, both felt genuinely concerned with the prolebm of French security, about which House wrote in his diary:

> My thought was that the only hope France has for the future is the League of Nations and the spirit we hope to bring about through it. If after establishing the League, we are so stupid as to

[1] See p. 108, above.

[2] Callwell, *Wilson*, p. 172. He expressed this opinion in his diary on March 1 after a talk with Foch.

[3] *Ibid.*, p. 172.

[4] British memorandum 'The Western and Northern Frontiers of Germany, February 4, 1919', Miller, *Diary*, V, pp. 30 *et seq.*

[5] Lloyd George, *Truth*, I, pp. 395-6.

[6] Tardieu, *Truth*, p. 171.

> let Germany train and arm a large army and again become a menace to the world, we would deserve the fate which such folly would bring upon us. Germany will be suspect for a century or more, and I take it she will not be permitted to run amuck again.[1]

But he saw no effective solution in the Foch plan.[2] By mid-February, House was willing, however, to go further. In addition to disarmament, he thought France might hold the Rhine bridgeheads until the Germans had honoured the peace treaty.[3]

Woodrow Wilson, on the contrary, maintained a hostile attitude towards Foch's Rhineland concepts. On February 21, the Colonel reported that Foch favoured an immediate preliminary peace in which the military terms, indemnity, and German frontiers would be defined, including the Rhine as Germany's western frontier (without prejudice to decisions on the future Rhineland regime). The President suspected a French effort to hurry 'us into an acquiescence in their plans with regard to the Western bank of the Rhine, a plan to which I could, as I now see the matter, in no case accede. I know that I can trust you and our colleagues to withstand such a program immovably. . . .'[4]

The Foch programme was also opposed by the British and American technical experts who met on February 21 to concert their views on Germany's frontiers. In the west, they assumed the restoration of Alsace-Lorraine. They agreed 'it would not be necessary to secure to France a strategic frontier in advance of the former (1870) frontier of Alsace-Lorraine', if the French eastern border was protected 'by the removal of all military establishments, fortifications and strategic railways from the left bank of the Rhine'. 'It was considered undesirable to give to France the Landau salient . . .' north of Alsace-Lorraine. The experts, however, agreed on rectification of the northern

[1] House, Diary, XV, p. 42.

[2] *Ibid.*, XV, p. 44; Seymour, *Intimate Papers*, IV, p. 345.

[3] House, Diary, XV, p. 60; Seymour, *Intimate Papers*, IV, p. 346.

[4] House to Wilson, February 21, 1919, Wilson Papers, VII-A-21; Seymour, *Intimate Papers*, IV, pp. 332-4; Wilson to House, date uncertain, February 21 or later, Wilson Papers, VII-A-21; paraphrase in Seymour, *Intimate Papers*, IV, pp. 335-6.

frontier of Alsace-Lorraine, to give France strategic security, 'if the left bank of the Rhine was not militarily sterilized'. Thus, German territorial cessions to France in the Rhineland were held to depend on the military arrangements to give the French security along their eastern frontier.[1]

Since December, Clemenceau and Tardieu in conversations with members of the British and American delegations, had sought to prepare the ground for a favourable settlement of the Rhineland Question.[2] Clemenceau came out in support of the essentials of the Foch proposals. On February 22, just four days after the attempt on his life, the 'Tiger' insisted, during a conference with House, upon the establishment of a Rhineland buffer state which would be prohibited from rejoining the Reich whatever the inhabitants' wishes. In contrast with Foch's plans, Clemenceau proposed that the buffer state have no armed forces.[3]

Tardieu consistently pursued a more moderate line than did his chief. Obviously fearing that Clemenceau's disregard for the principle of self-determination would strengthen opposition to French proposals, Tardieu on February 23 assured Colonel House that the French government would accept the establishment of a Rhenish buffer state for a period of a few years after which the inhabitants could decide their future status. He explained: '. . . in this way a breathing space would be given us all and France would secure protection until she recovered from the present war'. In House's judgment, Tardieu had removed

[1] 'Minutes of meeting in Hotel Crillon between Great Britain and United States representatives to consider the changes in the frontiers of Germany which should form part of the preliminaries of Peace, February 21, 1919', House Papers, 30/165.

The British representatives were: A. Akers-Douglas, Lt.-Col. J. H. M. Cornwall, J. W. Headlam-Morley, and H. H. Paton. The Americans were: I. Bowman, C. H. Haskins, S. Mezes, C. Seymour, and Major D. W. Johnson.

It should be noted that they 'agreed . . . the territorial proposals which they drew up should be maximum terms, so that if any negotiation took place with the Germans, the result would be to reduce and not to increase the amount of territory to be ceded by Germany'.

For other phases of this meeting, see the relevant chapters.

[2] Tardieu, *Truth*, p. 171; Lloyd George, *Truth*, I, p. 386.

[3] House to Wilson, February 23, 1919, House Papers: House-Wilson Correspondence, 1919-24.

one of the most undesirable elements in Clemenceau's plan—the denial of the right of self-determination.[1]

But the French government did not formally advance such a proposal at that time. In Tardieu's powerful, persuasive memorandum of February 25,[2] three key recommendations were made: the western frontier of Germany should be drawn along the Rhine; the bridgeheads of the Rhine should be held by an inter-Allied force; and no territorial annexation should occur against the will of the inhabitants.

The supporting arguments were a mixture of those in the Foch memoranda and of new ones to refute counter-arguments which had developed since early January. In addition, Tardieu made a stronger effort than had Foch to link French interests with general interests, while stressing the vital necessity of the proposed regime to France. French demands were related to British and American attitudes towards sea power:

> In other words, with no territorial ambitions, *but deeply imbued with the necessity of creating a protection both national and international,* France looks to an inter-Allied occupation of the Rhine for the same results that Great Britain and the U.S. expect from the maintenance of their naval forces; neither more nor less.

Tardieu also pointed out the implications for the new states of eastern and southern Europe: 'The occupation of the bridges is also necessary in order that, should Germany attack Bohemia and Poland, the help to be extended to those nations should not be stopped by the Rhine.'

Tardieu rejected the assurance that German disarmament and the League of Nations would provide adequate security for France. Germany could not be trusted to observe its obligations. Action under the League would be too cumbersome to save France from sudden invasion by much superior German forces. The promise of final victory was not enough. According to Tardieu, France wanted a physical guarantee in the form of a Rhineland buffer state and of an inter-Allied shield along the

[1] House to Wilson, February 24, 1919, *ibid.*; Seymour, *Intimate Papers*, IV, pp. 346-7.

[2] Tardieu, *Truth*, pp. 165-84; *Papers Respecting Negotiations for an Anglo-French Pact*, Cmd. 2169, 1924, pp. 25-57, 'Memorandum of the French government on the fixation at the Rhine of the western frontier of Germany and on inter-allied occupation of the Rhine bridges, February 25, 1919'.

Rhine. Demilitarization of the Rhineland was rejected as an adequate guarantee of physical security; if the bridges were not held they could easily be seized by German forces in the first stage of a lightning attack against France.

Perhaps the French delegates had already been exposed to Lloyd George's axiom that no new Alsace-Lorraines should be spawned in Europe because Tardieu also contended that the proposed Rhineland settlement would help to create conditions of permanent stability in western Europe. Germany, he said, would always be tempted to attack France as long as a dangerous disproportion of power existed between the two countries and the economic heart of France lay temptingly close to its Teutonic neighbour. Such conditions would be removed if the Rhineland were detached from Germany. The Rhine itself would be an additional stabilizing factor because it was a natural frontier equally defensible by all. With Gallic ingenuity Tardieu pointed out that these considerations placed the French proposals in accord with the League's principles for the prevention of war. Presumably he meant that a settlement which contributed to regional stability would aid rather than hinder the League of Nations in maintaining peace.

Whether the creation of a potential German *irredenta* would have a stabilizing effect was a question not effectively answered, although Tardieu radiated confidence about the political and economic prospects of the proposed buffer state. Its German inhabitants were depicted as anti-Prussian although German by tradition and tongue. If Germany proper fell into disorder, the peoples of the left bank would welcome stability within a West European system because they placed the maintenance of order above everything. They could be offered many inducements to accept a new status: exemption from military service, tax relief, special facilities for trade, customs union, banking reforms, and most glorious of all, independent government under the League of Nations.

Thus Clemenceau and Tardieu on February 25 formally advanced the essentials of the Foch plan for the Rhineland. Why did they adopt this position? This question cannot be firmly answered as yet because too many uncertainties surround the French government's calculations and actions at Paris. It might be assumed that the programme of February 25 embodied the views of a united country and delegation. This, however, is doubtful. Neither French bureaucratic nor political opinion appears to have been in accord on a single solution of the Rhineland question.[1] Although muted, a moderate view existed which recognized the strength of German nationalism and viewed as unrealistic any effort to turn the clock back to the Germanic Confederation of 1815-66. This school of thought stressed physical guarantees of security along France's eastern border and the necessity of winning Anglo-American support in the postwar world. Whether Clemenceau and Tardieu belonged to this school out of either conviction or necessity in 1918-19 is hard to judge. Perhaps the two men differed in their approach. Tardieu certainly appeared more conciliatory in February 1919 than did Clemenceau. Yet, speaking retrospectively, Clemenceau is reported to have said: 'Foch's and Poincaré's policy was a bad one in itself.'[2] But whatever Clemenceau's and Tardieu's preferred solution of the Rhineland question may have been, their proposals of February 25 were not necessarily what they were bargaining for at that stage of the negotiations.

Both Frenchmen were pragmatic statesmen. Their conduct in the Rhineland negotiations does not suggest that they believed France could in the long run single-handedly maintain a Rhineland buffer state against a resurgent and revengeful Germany. Instead, they were anxious to protect the interests of France in concert with England and America which meant finding a solution *à trois* to the problems of France's eastern frontier. When viewed in this way, the adoption of the extreme position of February 25 appears as a probable tactical manœuvre prompted by considerations of domestic political expediency and based on the immemorial customs of bargainers. If they realized that a Rhineland buffer state constituted an impractical solution of the problem of West European security, they had first to take a strong position to protect the government against the politically powerful bloc of French generals, admirals, diplomats, politicians, and publicists who sought the complete severance of the Rhineland from Germany. After February 25, Clemenceau and Tardieu could always defend moderation and compromise on the ground that they had sought a Rhineland

[1] See chap. IV. [2] Martet, *Georges Clemenceau*, pp. 149-50.

buffer state but had to retreat because Anglo-American resistance was so strong that to persist in the demand would have risked leaving France in perilous isolation. On the other hand, Lloyd George and Woodrow Wilson had to be strongly impressed with the need for effective guarantees of French security and with the inadequacy of their initial proposals for the protection of western Europe. The adoption of an extreme position, vigorously advanced, might succeed in wresting greater concessions from the English and American statesmen.[1]

If these were the considerations governing Clemenceau's and Tardieu's tactics at this time, the substance of their programme probably was: secure the Rhine as a strategic frontier; win an Anglo-American commitment in Europe in the form of (*a*) a permanent or long-term inter-Allied occupation of the Rhineland and of the bridgeheads, (*b*) a military alliance with England, and (*c*) an understanding with America; and other guarantees including the demilitarization of the Rhineland and strict supervision of German disarmament. If these objectives could be realized, the separation of the Rhineland from Germany, while preferable if supported by England and America, was expendable. At least, the demand for separation was a good talking-point which enabled French negotiators to reiterate their thesis about the dangers of the imbalance of power between Germany and France and of the weaknesses of the initial Anglo-American proposals for countering those dangers.

Undoubtedly, the French government's note of February 25 impressed the British and American delegations. Among the British, the response to Tardieu's case, while reserved, was not entirely unsympathetic. Balfour concluded, after talks with Tardieu, that the French were prepared to make their proposals more palatable to the British and Americans by abandoning the permanent dismemberment of Germany if they could secure a temporary administrative separation between the left bank and Germany proper and an inter-allied occupation of the region. This regime would exist for an interim period until the League of Nations was functioning effectively and until Germany was no longer suspect and was admitted to the League. Should the Rhinelanders at the end of the probationary period desire permanent separation from Germany, that could be considered

[1] See, however, *ibid.*, p. 150, where Clemenceau disparages this view.

at the time. While his tone was sympathetic, Balfour did not make clear whether he would support such a compromise.[1] Sir William Wiseman noted on March 2 that Tardieu had presented 'a very able paper' which 'made considerable impression with House and Balfour, but, although moderately stated, does not present very practical solution'. At the same time, Wiseman hinted that opposition to Tardieu's scheme within the British delegation was not based entirely on its intrinsic merits but was taken for bargaining purposes. He commented: 'We cannot, however, make final settlement with France until Syrian and Morrocan claims are settled, and these cannot be settled until we know whether Americans will accept mandatory in Turkey.'[2]

Lloyd George conferred with Clemenceau and House in an attempt to reach agreement. On March 7, House complained in a wire to Wilson that the French Premier took the 'unreasonable position that the Left Bank should never be allowed to rejoin Germany'. Because of Clemenceau's obduracy, they reached no 'tentative agreement', but Tardieu undertook to persuade his chief to alter his stand.[3] The wire contained the suggestion that if Clemenceau did so, House might tentatively approve the buffer state and occupation proposals. Alarmed by this hint, Wilson instructed House on March 10 to give not even provisional consent 'to the separation of the Rhenish provinces from Germany under any arrangement' and to reserve the American stand until his return to Paris.[4] In British and American circles the hope persisted that German disarmament, coupled with Rhineland demilitarization and the League of Nations would constitute a satisfactory solution to the problem of West European security.

There was general agreement on removing the instruments of aggression from German hands. Already the Council of Ten had set the military, naval, and air experts to work on German disarmament. On March 6, Foch presented to the Council the

[1] Balfour to House, February 25, 1919, House Papers: Balfour-House Correspondence.

[2] Wiseman to Reading, March 2, 1919, Wiseman Papers, 90/21.

[3] House to Wilson, March 7, 1919, House Papers: House-Wilson Correspondence, 1919-24.

[4] Wilson to House, March 10, 1919, *ibid.*

first full report of the Committee of Military, Naval, and Air Experts. It contained several proposals which bore directly on the Rhineland question.[1]

The report advocated the draconian disarmament of Germany which would thereby lose its advantages of superior manpower and economic strength. Article 8 provided for the dismantling of all German fortifications in the territory west of a line drawn 50 kilometres east of the Rhine. Article 9 prohibited the maintenance of military forces or establishments on the left bank of the Rhine. The Allied forces would possess the power of police control in this zone. While German forces in the unfortified zone east of the Rhine were not expressly forbidden by these draft regulations, a demilitarized buffer region between Germany and western Europe was envisaged which would strengthen the French military position *vis-à-vis* Germany.

Lloyd George objected to the provisions regarding the strength and organization of the future German army. On March 7, in advancing his counter-proposals regarding the size, recruitment, and service term of the German land forces, he urged that this force be kept as weak as possible because the 'permanent limitation of armaments was an illusion'.[2] This was a damaging admission which weakened the argument that German disarmament would be an effective guarantee of French security.

The Council of Ten—with Lloyd George, Balfour, Clemenceau, Lansing, and House present—discussed at length on March 10 the proposed military terms of peace. Article 8 was adopted without question. Wilson approved on March 17. Article 9 had been considerably strengthened since March 6. It now read:

> All territory on the left bank of the Rhine which may remain as part of Germany after the ratification of the Treaty of Peace will be 'demilitarized'. That is to say, the inhabitants of this territory will not be permitted to bear arms or receive any military training or to be incorporated in any military organization either on a voluntary or compulsory basis, and no fortifications, depots, establishments, railway construction or works of any kind adapted to military purposes will be permitted to exist within the area. Nor will this territory be allowed to contribute directly or

[1] *P.P.C.*, IV, pp. 232-3.   [2] *Ibid.*, p. 263.

indirectly in money or in material of any description towards the armies of Germany.[1]

In effect, this provision would have weakened Germany militarily while avoiding further territorial dismemberment in the west. A buffer zone, but not a buffer state, would exist. This solution, however, was not yet acceptable to the French government. The clause was struck out, subject to reconsideration later, because the fate of the left bank had not been determined.[2]

On this same occasion, Lloyd George eloquently upheld France's right to special consideration along its eastern frontier. Foch had advised that if a German long-term service force was accepted, its strength should be reduced to 100,000 instead of 140,000 or 200,000 as had been suggested. Clemenceau backed him with the argument that if British and American forces were withdrawn from the continent, France alone would bear the burden of containing Germany. Therefore, the German army should be kept to an essential minimum. Lloyd George replied:

> France was . . . entitled to a decisive voice in the matter. It was inevitable that this interest should affect France more closely than Great Britain, and Great Britain more closely than America. Twice in living memory invasion of French soil had come from the same quarter. France was therefore entitled to consider her fears. Germany would have no good cause for complaint. Twice she had misused her military machine, and on this occasion its misuse had led to the death of 20,000,000 young men. . . . The Associated Powers were therefore entitled to say that they would not allow Germany the use of a machine that could again be the cause of similar disaster. As between the figures of 100,000 and 140,000 he had no very clear predilection, but he did not feel that he could resist the Military Advisors of France, unprotected by the sea as England and America were, and with only the Rhine as a defence. . . .[3]

Lloyd George thus recognized that the problem of French security differed, because of geographic circumstances, from that of Great Britain and of the United States. He gave special weight to French demands, but obviously only within carefully circumscribed limits: the problem of security was to be solved

[1] *Ibid.*, pp. 307-8. [2] *Ibid.*, p. 300. [3] *Ibid.*, 297-8.

by disarming Germany, by severely limiting the size of its land forces, and by forbidding German fortifications and forces in the Rhineland. Also, while not ruling out an occupation of German soil, he contended at this stage that France would have to bear this responsibility if it were decided upon. Having granted that a special security problem existed and if it could be shown that the measures which he advocated were insufficient to provide security for France and western Europe, Lloyd George was now in a position on the Rhineland issue which would be difficult to hold—especially since he had admitted that permanent disarmament was illusory.

That morning, Lloyd George, Clemenceau, and House established a secret committee to delineate the boundaries of Germany. Their purpose probably was to speed up the work of the conference and to have some definite plan ready on German territorial questions for Wilson to consider upon his return to Paris.[1] As members, they named Philip Kerr, André Tardieu, and Sydney Mezes.[2] In Kerr, his private secretary, Lloyd George had chosen a strong champion of Anglo-American cooperation and of American involvement in postwar world politics.

When the committee met on March 11, Tardieu submitted a Rhineland project which provided for German renunciation of sovereignty over and of the right to customs union with the territories of the Reich west of the Rhine river. It stipulated that the line of the Rhine, including the bridgeheads, would be occupied by an inter-Allied force under mandate from the League of Nations. Germany also was to accept the demilitarization of its western frontier within a zone fifty kilometers wide. The detached territories, with the exception of Alsace-Lorraine, would be organized into one or more independent states under the protection of the League of Nations. German economic interests in the left bank region would be liquidated. Germany

[1] Three sources on the proceedings of this committee on March 11 and 12 are available: (1) 'Notes of Discussion between Mr. P. H. Kerr, M. Tardieu and Dr. Mezes', *Papers Respecting Negotiations for an Anglo-French Pact*, Cmd. 2169, 1924, pp. 59-67 (these are notes by Mr. Kerr); (2) 'Rhine Questions', House Papers, 30/166, Wilson Papers, VIII-A-21 (although unsigned, this memorandum seems to br Dr. Mezes' report on the discussions); (3) Tardieu's account, given in his book *La Paix*, pp. 190-95.

[2] House, Diary, XV, p. 89.

also would be obliged to supply coal to the industries of the left bank, for which Germany would receive credit on reparations account.[1]

Kerr, to whom Tardieu's arguments were entirely strategic in character, gave Lloyd George the following picture of these important conversations.[2]

Kerr agreed that the military frontier of Germany had to be drawn east of the Rhine while holding that the permanent maintenance of even token British forces on German territory could not be countenanced. His government could accept the demilitarization of the Rhineland and the disarmament of Germany including the reduction of the German forces to 100,000 men. In addition he promised that the English, having experienced the dangers of German militarism, would be prepared, if it showed any signs of reviving, 'to nip the attempt in the bud'. He assured Tardieu '. . . the real security of France lay in maintaining a complete understanding with Great Britain and America; that these three Powers had already defeated Germany once and that if they maintained their solidarity with adequate preparations Germany would never dream of attacking them again'. To ask for more, he threatened, would weaken the security of France. His broad hint that the British government would favour helping, in some form or other, France against German militarism and aggression opened up a promising line of negotiation.

Mezes assured Tardieu of American concern for French security. The American government could more easily meet the French point of view if Allied troops were not maintained on German soil proper and if the proposed Allied occupation was only temporary. The use of the words 'German soil proper' was possibly significant because later in the discussion a distinction was drawn between the Rhineland provinces and Germany proper. Mezes, perhaps, was hinting that the American delegation might accept the buffer state idea under limitations such as he had defined.

Tardieu conceded that Allied troops might not have to be quartered on German soil proper but they would have to be stationed along the Rhine in immediate contact with the bridges. After leaving for a brief talk with Lloyd George, Kerr

[1] *Cmd. 2169*, pp. 67-8. [2] *Ibid.*, pp. 59-67.

returned to say that from 'the British point of view'—i.e. Lloyd George's—there was as much objection to an inter-Allied occupation of an independent Rhineland state as to that of Germany proper. This statement suggested that the buffer state idea might be acceptable if not tied up with an army of occupation.

Tardieu threatened that if the left bank was not detached from Germany, France would demand a strategic frontier from south of Treves to the Rhine north of Landau, which would place 1,300,000 Germans under French sovereignty.

What mainly divided Tardieu and Kerr, the principal protagonists, at this meeting? Of the four main points in Tardieu's project Kerr had given unqualified support to none, but the gulf can be exaggerated. They agreed on the Rhine as the military frontier and on German disarmament. As for an occupation, Kerr had only said that British support for a permanent occupation could not be expected. He told Tardieu near the end of the meeting: 'So far as I could see the difference between our views centered upon the question of the occupation of the Rhenish provinces.' In other words, they were not necessarily divided over the question of the separation of the Rhenish provinces, although Kerr had made clear British apprehensions about this solution. Tardieu moved closer to the British position by granting that the bridgeheads need not actually be occupied and by suggesting a temporary separation of the Rhenish provinces with the inhabitants ultimately deciding their future status. Was it possible that, if the British were not required to station troops in the Rhenish provinces, they might agree to the proposed separation?

At their second meeting on March 12, according to Tardieu, Kerr announced the complete opposition of the British government to the idea of separation.[1] In his account, Kerr reports telling Tardieu that the British delegation, after reconsidering the question, was more opposed than before to an Allied occupation of the Rhenish provinces and to 'any proposals which committed them to keeping those provinces from the rest of Germany if they wished to rejoin it by the use of force'.[2] Reiterating the British government's doubts about undertaking long-range military commitments on the continent, Kerr

[1] Tardieu, *La Paix*, p. 193. [2] *Cmd. 2169*, pp. 62-5.

invoked the views of certain Dominion leaders to the effect that if Germany violated its disarmament obligations

> they would be able to call upon their people to help to force Germany to fulfil its undertakings, but that they were not going to leave a man in Europe or to bind themselves to interfere in any way in purely European questions such as the future of the Rhenish provinces.[1]

Kerr failed to see why the French government could not accept the alternative proposal for security: German disarmament, the demilitarization of the left bank, and confidence in joint action by Great Britain, the United States, and France to uphold these arrangements. Under this plan, so the Englishman optimistically predicted, if Germany broke her obligations, French armies could advance immediately on German soil, the British would be in the field within three weeks, and the Americans within two months. Thus there would be no danger 'if France, Great Britain and America stood together as a united bloc at the center of the League of Nations'. He urged upon Tardieu:

> This surely gave France practical security against a repetition of 1914. I repeated that it seemed to me that the essential point was that the Allies or the League of Nations should insist on the observance by Germany of the military terms of peace. So long as they were observed there was no menace to France. What mattered, therefore, most of all, was making a settlement which would obtain the whole-hearted support of the public opinion of the British Empire and of America, so as to ensure that if Germany began to break it these overseas people would instantly insist at whatever cost on Germany respecting her bond.[2]

There were large 'ifs' in Kerr's proposals. What assurance was there that British and Dominion opinion would regard the perpetuation of German disarmament as any less a purely European affair than an inter-Allied occupation of the Rhineland and the bridgeheads? Moreover, important members of the British delegation doubted the probable efficacy of the League of Nations. In December 1918, not long after Wilson's repudiation in the congressional elections, the Foreign Office had expressed reservations about the League. In advising the

[1] *Ibid.*, p. 62. [2] *Ibid.*, pp. 63-4.

British government to support a League of Nations and to seek a territorial reconstruction of Europe based partly on the assumption that the League would be a success, the Foreign Office had also recommended that the traditional means of ensuring British security should not be neglected in case the League failed. The Chief of the General Staff, Sir Henry Wilson, believed that 'to build on the League of Nations was to build on shifting sands'.[1] Hughes and Curzon doubted the potential security value of the League. While such views were not held unanimously by members of the British government and delegation, they were sufficiently widespread to provide an audience within British ranks which could react sympathetically to French criticisms of the League and thus create pressures from within the British delegation for some form of additional guarantee to France. Certainly, the British delegation at this time appeared divided over the proper response to the French Rhineland demands.

At first sight, indeed, Kerr in his talks with Tardieu and Mezes, had not entirely closed the door upon British support for the separation of the left bank from Germany. His remarks suggested that if a new Rhineland regime allowed for peaceful revision of the status of the region, the British government might entertain such a plan. Nor was a short-term occupation necessarily ruled out. But the substantial significance of his position was inescapable. If a buffer state were established and then a strong movement for reunion with Germany developed which only force or the threat of force could stay, France would have to battle Germany without its Entente partner—and probably without America too. A France isolated against Germany would be, in terms of the strategical logic of Foch and Tardieu, doomed to defeat, either militarily or diplomatically. Tardieu clearly recognized the gloomy implications for France of the position which Lloyd George had taken.

What then was the British Prime Minister seeking? The answer would appear to be that he and his intimate associates were now working towards a more special guarantee against German aggression than the Covenant promised to afford. Kerr on March 12 had again hinted at an American-British guarantee to resist by force any German attempt to rearm or militarily

[1] Callwell, *Wilson*, p. 176.

to reoccupy the left bank territories. Significantly, the form of the proposed guarantee was left open ('. . . the Allies or the League of Nations should insist upon . . . observance . . .'), but, in either case, the substance of the guarantee would be the overwhelming military superiority of the three Great Powers. Such an arrangement embodied the vital goal of securing a firm American postwar commitment in Europe. Viewed in the latter light, Kerr's proposal of some form of guarantee was addressed as much, if not more, to the Americans as to the French. It was part of a British campaign to secure Wilson's consent to special guarantees of Anglo-French security in Europe.

During the conversation of March 12, Tardieu scarcely budged from his initial position. Recalling Lloyd George's reference to the illusion of permanent disarmament, he repeated the French objection to depending for security on German disarmament and on the demilitarization of the Rhineland. As for a guarantee against German aggression, he doubted that Anglo-American aid would be timely enough to save France from invasion. Expressing disappointment with the British position on an Allied occupation and on Rhineland separation, which, he hinted, diverged from an understanding reached between Lloyd George and Clemenceau, Tardieu insisted that the French government 'held with firm tenacity' to the demand for a Rhineland buffer state 'at any rate so long as Germany had 4,000,000 men who had practical training in war'. The separation could be for a ten-, fifteen- or twenty-year period, but it was an absolute necessity. France could never feel safe, moreover, if an Allied force did not physically control the Rhine frontier. Near the end of the meeting, Kerr queried whether military occupation of the left bank was an integral part of the French plan for a Rhineland buffer state. Tardieu replied: 'The three parts of this scheme, the drawing of the German frontier on the Rhine, the constitution of an independent Rhenish state and the Allied command of the bridges, were three legs of one plan and stood or fell together.'[1]

On the American side, the initial French proposals also received a rebuff at this meeting. The possibility of American support for the temporary severance of the left bank from Germany had opened up in the talks with Colonel House. If the

[1] *Cmd. 2169*, p. 64.

Americans approved a scheme which would give the French five years or longer to build a position of strength in the Rhineland, the British might be induced to accept it. However, to Tardieu's evident surprise, Mezes asked that decisions on the Rhineland question be postponed until the President's return. Thus, the Kerr-Tardieu-Mezes talks of March 11-12 ended in virtual deadlock.[1]

[1] Mezes' short report summarized the situation at the end of the two meetings:

'Tardieu, after seeking the Premier, yielded the bridgeheads proposal, accepting, as a substitute, rigid military inspection in Germany.

'Kerr was holding out against *political independence and inter-Allied occupation* of the Rhine Provinces if intended as any more than a very short-lived measure winding up the war.

'Tardieu was holding out for *both*, mentioning first a fifteen- to twenty-year term, later a ten-year term, and later alluding to, but not accepting (he would) a five-year term.' House Papers, 30/166.

IX

THE TREATY OF GUARANTEE

LLOYD GEORGE had evidently resolved to seek an Anglo-American promise to aid France against unprovoked German aggression, as a substitute for the French Rhineland proposals which, as Kerr had indicated, the British Prime Minister believed would perpetuate tensions. Lloyd George also doubted whether British and Dominion opinion would in the long run support so drastic a dismemberment of Germany. A treaty of guarantee on the other hand would give France the assurance of not having to stand alone against an aggressive Germany. The chances of war in western Europe would be minimized not only because the militant forces of German revisionism would have lost a major potential rallying cry—return the Rhineland to the Reich!—but also because no German government or general staff would likely contemplate war with a powerful Anglo-American-French combination. Thus, a treaty of guarantee, together with German disarmament and demilitarization of the Rhineland, would more effectively further the British policy of German containment and European stabilization than would the French proposals.

Also, if the United States participated in the proposed guarantee, the British government would have realized its objective of persuading that country to throw its weight into the postwar European balance. Lloyd George sought to use the traditional American sentimental attachment to France and the evident desire within the American delegation to satisfy French demands for security as a fulcrum on which to lever Wilson and his colleagues into acceptance of a precise political and military commitment by the United States in western Europe.

The British effort to secure a guarantee began in the secret Committee of Three on the frontiers of Germany, without, however, closing the door upon alternative solutions. Lloyd George on March 12 told House the French proposals were unacceptable 'upon the terms they had in mind'. The Prime Minister suggested that a Channel tunnel could be built to put British troops in France within forty-eight hours. The ebullient Welshman surely jested! More practicably, he affirmed his readiness to pledge British aid to France in case of unprovoked German aggression. House's reaction is not recorded, although he did agree the French proposals could lead to another war.[1]

Clemenceau, for his part, felt aggrieved. That evening he complained to House that the British Prime Minister had broken his word over the Rhineland, Syria, and the division of reparations.[2]

On the following day, Kerr advised Lloyd George and Balfour that Tardieu's propositions came from shell-shock, lacked widespread support within France, and were unnecessary for the security of France. To supplement the proposals already made, Kerr recommended the occupation of the Rhine bridgeheads for a year or so 'until certain of the fundamental terms of peace are concluded'. Kerr warned that if these territories remained German, it would be 'difficult to refuse' French demands for strategic annexations, provided the local inhabitants were exempted from military service and enjoyed local autonomy similar to that proposed for the Saar. Kerr suggested that such a temporary regime could be envisaged, subject to revision by the League of Nations.[3]

Although Kerr did not suggest an Anglo-American guarantee, his advice may have encouraged the pursuit of this objective partly by its attack on Tardieu's proposals, partly by the unpalatable alternative which was posed.

Lloyd George moved quickly to win Wilson's approval of a guarantee. The President returned to Paris during the morning of March 14. By noon, he and the British Prime Minister were

[1] House, Diary, XV, pp. 92-3. [2] *Ibid.*, p. 93.

[3] *Papers Respecting Negotiations for an Anglo-French Pact*, Cmd. 2169, 1924, p. 68. Cited below as *Cmd. 2169*.

closeted together. Lloyd George proposed a joint guarantee to aid France against unprovoked German aggression. Wilson agreed.[1]

Wilson's commitment constituted a signal success for Lloyd George's diplomacy. If the promise became reality, American power would bolster the peace settlement in the vital sector of western Europe. Russia's successor in the European equilibrium would have been found. British and French security would be protected without drastically dismembering Germany and subjecting the Germans to a lengthy military occupation.

The success, however, was only tentative. Would the French accept? Would Wilson himself have second thoughts about the idea? Could he persuade his delegation and country to support the proposed guarantee?

Having formed a common front, Lloyd George and Wilson faced Clemenceau during the afternoon of March 14. While opposing the original French programme for the Rhineland, they approved a short occupation to guarantee German payment of reparations. Their main counter-proposal was an Anglo-American promise to resist a German attack upon France. Clemenceau asked for time to consider their offer.[2]

Beset by perplexing and sometimes conflicting considerations, Clemenceau and his colleagues decided to accept the Lloyd George-Wilson proposal while demanding additional physical guarantees of security. Clemenceau defined this policy in the forceful French memorandum of March 17. While paying homage to the historic importance of the suggestion of March 14, Clemenceau cogently contended it replaced the positive physical guarantee desired by the French with a political guarantee. The latter, to be effective, should be supplemented and made very precise. Thus, the German act constituting aggression or the threat of aggression, the defensive rights which France would then enjoy, and the nature of the consequent military obligations of Great Britain and the United States should be clearly defined. As well, some of the physical guarantees earlier demanded would have to be incorporated into the new system of security. France, so Clemenceau argued, could not 'renoncer pour des espérances à une sécurité positive'.

[1] Lloyd George, *Truth*, I, p. 403.

[2] *Ibid.*; Tardieu, *La Paix*, p. 195; Mermeix, *Le Combat des Trois*, p. 198.

The note proposed a Rhineland settlement upon the following basis: an Anglo-American pledge to aid France and Belgium in case of German aggression; occupation of the line of the Rhine and of the bridgeheads; demilitarization of the left bank of the Rhine and of a zone fifty kilometres wide along the right bank; in this zone, Germany to be debarred from having military forces and organization, holding military manœuvres, recruiting troops even by voluntary means, maintaining fortifications, and manufacturing war materials; a permanent Anglo-American-French Commission of Inspection to ensure German observance of these provisions; any German movement or attempted movement into the zone to be considered an act of aggression; recognition of a French right to reoccupy the Rhineland and bridgeheads with a radius of twenty kilometres if the Inspection Commission determined that Germany had violated the demilitarization and disarmament provisions of the treaty of peace. The final stipulation involved the French government's claims to the Saar.[1]

Thus the French delegation dropped the demand for a separate Rhineland in return for an Anglo-American guarantee reinforced by stringent physical securities. The latter in effect made the Rhine the military frontier between Germany and France and withdrew the Rhineland, strategically, economically, and demographically, from the German war-making machine. After insisting that these proposals represented his maximum concessions, Clemenceau learned on March 18 that Lloyd George and Wilson found them unacceptable.

More than a month of hard negotiations ensued. They formed a tangled skein which is hard to unravel, partly because of its complexity, partly because numerous strands remain hidden or obscure. It should be remembered that initially Lloyd George and Wilson had agreed in principle to (1) a military guarantee to France, (2) the limited demilitarization of the Rhineland, and (3) a brief military occupation of the region. On March 17, the British Prime Minister faced the vigorous French contention that this programme was inadequate. How did he and his associates respond?

His stand was influenced by the sentiment within his delega-

[1] 'Note sur la suggestion presentée le 14 mars 1919', Tardieu, *La Paix*, pp. 197-200; Wilson Papers, VIII-8-24, March 17, 1919.

tion in favour of a moderate peace with Germany. It was felt that German morale should not be crushed and that a fairly strong Germany had a constructive role to play in postwar Europe. Already some members of the British delegation were worrying about the German reaction to the peace terms.[1] Criticism was directed particularly against the system of 'small untried European States' which was appearing. It was feared this system would produce economic controversies and armaments competition. Opinion within the delegation favoured disarmament and the reduction of trade barriers to help solve these prospective conflicts. At the same time a final British decision evidently had not been taken about policy towards Germany. There were two alternatives: 'We must either squeeze all we can out of Germany, or help her to her feet again. It is impossible to do both.' Lloyd George, alarmed by the settlement in the making, left for Fontainebleau 'to think out the possibility of drastic changes which [would] give the whole Peace Settlement a more inspiring appearance and one more in sympathy with the progressive forces making themselves felt all over the world'.[2] Whether Lloyd George's sojourn at Fontainebleau resolved this dilemma may be questioned.

The Fontainebleau conference was planned as early as March 21. In his choice of advisors, Lloyd George revealed whose opinions he most valued at that stage: General Smuts, General Sir Henry Wilson, Lord Cunliffe—the Governor of the Bank of England, J. M. Keynes—the economist, Sir Maurice Hankey—Secretary of the Imperial War Cabinet and Secretary-General of the British Empire Delegation, and Philip Kerr.[3] Apparently Balfour and Foreign Office staff were not present. By no means was the Fontainebleau coterie marked by unanimity of views. Smuts and Henry Wilson differed over the League; Cunliffe and Keynes disagreed over reparations. Yet, with the exception perhaps of Cunliffe, they had in common a moderate approach to the German Question.

Only Henry Wilson has given a glimpse of their three-day proceedings. Like Smuts, he criticized the appearance of 'numberless small nations'. Viewing the proposed terms as

1 Wiseman to Reading, March 21, 1919, Wiseman Papers, 90/21.
2 Wiseman to Reading, March 23, 1919, *ibid.*
3 Lloyd George, *Truth*, I, p. 403; Riddell, *Intimate Diary*, p. 38.

crushing and as probably impossible for the Germans to sign' he feared they would drive Germany into alliance with Russia.[1] The influence of the latter ideas can be clearly seen in Lloyd George's note embodying the results of their talks.

In the Fontainebleau memorandum,[2] which was directed mainly to Clemenceau, the keynote of Lloyd George's argument was they should forget the passions of the war and act like impartial arbiters. His appeal was for a far-sighted peace which later generations would accept without a sense of patriotic exasperation or injustice.

Seven main principles were advanced. The treaty must be just both to the Allies and the Germans. The different nationalities should as far as possible be allocated to their motherlands, a principle which should take precedence over considerations of strategy, or economics, or communications. Reparations should be paid within a generation. Germany should have a peace which would be preferable to Bolshevism.[3] The peace terms must be such that a responsible German government could execute them. Otherwise, an unpalatable alternative existed. The victors would have to coerce Germany by blockade, by force, by occupation. Lloyd George doubted that Great Britain and America would uphold an occupation of the whole country; he questioned whether France could bear such a massive burden. Blockade 'would inevitably mean Spartacism from the Urals to the Rhine, with its inevitable consequence of a huge Red Army attempting to cross the Rhine'. Peace, too, must rest upon disarmament and an effective League of Nations strengthened by the immediate admission of Germany. Finally, the Prime Minister saw an Anglo-American guarantee to France as another pillar of peace.

Lloyd George's appeal was a mixture of common sense and impractical idealism. The former element can be seen in his

[1] Callwell, *Sir Henry Wilson*, II, p. 176.

[2] Lloyd George, *Truth*, I, pp. 404 *et seq.*

[3] He played up the danger that Germany might throw its lot in with Bolshevism, thus creating a mighty bloc of peoples and resources under the directing genius of German brains and organizing ability. His picture in this respect of Europe in revolution or on the verge of revolution did not appear exaggerated in March 1919. Bela Kun had just seized power in Hungary. The fear of a Bolshevik sweep into central and western Europe was current and alive in Paris.

contention that German irredentism could undermine any settlement and in his advice that the terms should be such as to enable a reasonable German government to carry them out. The latter aspect of his views can be seen in his naïve belief that victors and vanquished could agree upon the substantial meaning of justice, particularly when the 'just' settlement was imposed and not freely negotiated.

What terms for the western boundaries of Germany were drawn from these principles of peacemaking? His position here remained unchanged. The Rhineland provinces should not be separated from Germany. They should be demilitarized. No troops should be sent into the demilitarized area 'for any purpose whatsoever without previous notification to the League of Nations'. The British Empire, a phraseology which covered the Dominons as well as the United Kingdom, and the United States should undertake to aid France if Germany militarily invaded the Rhineland 'without the consent of the Council of the League of Nations. This guarantee to last until the League of Nations had proved itself to be an adequate security.'[1]

These terms did not permit the French to enter the demilitarized zone without the consent of the League of Nations, i.e. no occupation. The guarantee was not necessarily to be permanent. Furthermore, demilitarization might be temporary because by inference the situation might arise when Germany would have the consent of the League Council to move troops across the Rhine.

On March 27, the Council of Four debated Lloyd George's memorandum.[2] Clemenceau made a moving appeal to Lloyd George and Wilson to understand the French need for and right to security. On the oceans, the destruction of German naval power gave security to England and America. 'Il nous en faut une équivalente sur terre.'[3] He accepted the League of Nations as one means of giving security to France, but if the League could not be backed by military sanctions they would have to be provided by other means.

Lloyd George, who cautioned the Council that the Rhineland Question, along with Danzig, Silesia, and reparations, aroused

[1] Lloyd George, *Truth*, I, p. 414.

[2] This discussion has been reviewed above. See pp. 180 *et seq.*

[3] Mantoux, *Délibérations*, I, pp. 41-8.

the greatest concern within Germany, stressed the possibility of a German rejection of the victors' terms if they failed to take German sentiment into account. To reinforce this plea, he read a letter from General Smuts who, expressing alarm over the excessive conditions being imposed upon Germany, especially in the Rhineland and in the east, predicted that Germany would remain a dominating force on the continent and warned they would be foolish to attempt to reconstruct the world without German collaboration.

The injection of the South African's view into their deliberations was not a new manœuvre on Lloyd George's part. It would appear that Smuts' ideas enjoyed a wide currency throughout the British delegation. Of all the Dominion leaders, Smuts had most to say on the deeper issues of the peacemaking. Lloyd George personally seems to have been strongly influenced by Smuts, whom he had taken to Fontainebleau. At the same time, his influence went beyond the British delegation. Wilson was apparently attracted by him as both the League negotiations and the issue of war pensions had illustrated. Clemenceau also seems to have respected Smuts. None the less, on this occasion, he sourly remarked that he hoped General Smuts would keep the French in mind as well as the Germans.

On March 31, French counter-blasts attempted to demolish Lloyd George's case. In the first place, Marshal Foch, in a note[1] and before the Council of Four,[2] developed, with devastating logic, and with much emotion, the thesis that the Rhine should be the military and political frontier between Germany and the Western Powers. His major point was that France and the other Western Powers would not be secure if the Rhineland provinces were only neutralized, even if a powerful Anglo-American-French alliance existed to back up this neutrality. An alliance would not overcome the disadvantages of space and of time as far as France was concerned. Even a Channel tunnel, Foch pointed out, could not move troops more quickly than they had been moved in 1914; in any case it could be blown up. As for American aid, 'It is not weeks but months

[1] French text in Mermeix, *Le Combat des Trois*, pp. 219-22; English text in Bliss Papers, 241; extracts in: Tardieu, *La Paix*, 184-5; Lloyd George, *Truth*, I, pp. 422-3.

[2] Mantoux, *Délibérations*, I, pp. 92 *et seq.*

that it will require.' In German disarmament he had no faith. The restrictions could easily be evaded and Germany might find resources in Russia—an accurate forecast. And he repeated his earlier argument that the Russian counterpoise against Germany had disappeared and indeed might even in the future be on the side of Germany. The strategic situation, he contended, along the eastern frontier was graver for France than in 1914. He pessimistically predicted:

> Under these conditions, therefore, the battle which we will have to face in the plains of Belgium will be one in which we shall suffer from a considerable numerical inferiority, and where we shall have no natural obstacle to help us. Once more, Belgium and Northern France will be made a field of battle, a field of defeat.... Once again those same countries will fall a prey to havoc and devastation.[1]

He concluded that these dangers could be avoided only if the Western Powers physically and politically held the line of the Rhine.

Significantly, Sir Henry Wilson, General Bliss, and General Diaz did not support Foch. Despite the Marshal's logic and eloquence, Lloyd George and Woodrow Wilson remained hostile to political separation of the Rhineland from Germany.[2]

On the same day, Clemenceau formally answered the Fontainebleau memorandum.[3] To think that Germany could be appeased by easing the territorial terms of peace in Europe was, Clemenceau asserted, 'a sheer illusion and the remedy is not equal to the disease. . . . This kind of appeasement will be vain once we cut Germany off from world policy.' In other words, Clemenceau accused Lloyd George of trying to protect British interests at the expense of France and the smaller Allied nations in Europe. In many respects, it was a fair criticism of Lloyd George's position although, as Lloyd George quite

[1] Foch memorandum on Rhine, Bliss Papers, 241.

[2] Mantoux, *Délibérations*, I, pp. 92-5. Lloyd George asked why Marshal Foch played down the Channel tunnel idea. Sir Henry Wilson undertook the reply pointing out that the existence of a tunnel and of sea transport would not necessarily double the number of the forces which could be transported to France in a given time compared to transport by sea alone.

[3] Wilson Papers, VIII-A-29, March 28, 1919. Actually sent to Wilson on March 31.

rightly pointed out in his response of April 2, Clemenceau had overlooked many substantial points in France's favour such as the proposed Anglo-American guarantee and the thoroughgoing disarmament of Germany.

Lloyd George, in reply, threatened to reverse his stand on the disarmament of Germany and reparations, which was sheer bluff, and on the guarantees for French security. Despite the sharpness of his letter, Lloyd George was trying to treat Clemenceau rather lightly, as his handwritten note covering the copy sent to Wilson indicated:

My Dear Mr. President

I enclose reply I am sending to Clemenceau's paper.
I thought on the whole it was better not to take it too seriously.

Ever sincerely

D. Lloyd George.[1]

For Lloyd George, the Rhineland negotiations remained deadlocked.

On the American side between March 14 and April 2, Colonel House's efforts to arrange a compromise dominated the Rhineland negotiations. As he defined his purpose, 'My main drive now is for peace with Germany at the earliest possible moment.'[2] Initially, the Colonel suggested on March 17 a temporary Rhineland buffer state. Events, however, had outrun this idea. After Clemenceau sent House a copy of the French note of March 17,[3] the Colonel bent his efforts towards seeking a solution along the general lines drawn by Tardieu. Although absolute proof is lacking, apparently House did not know until March 27 that Woodrow Wilson had committed himself to a special guarantee of American aid for France. This was the first major breach in the intimate relationship between the two men.

Although Lloyd George had broached the idea of a guarantee to him, House on March 19 appears to have presented it to White and other members of the United States delegation as coming from Clemenceau. White believed Clemenceau had asked for the insertion in either the Peace Treaty or the

[1] Wilson Papers, VIII-A-31. [2] Seymour, *Intimate Papers*, IV, p. 384.
[3] House Papers, 30/168; Seymour, *Intimate Papers*, IV, pp. 393-4.

Covenant of a special pledge of Anglo-American assistance to France in case of unprovoked German attack. He further understood that Lloyd George had agreed to the proposal but evidently White was not aware of Wilson's undertaking.[1] It seems unlikely, as Birdsall suggests, that the American Commissioners, Lansing, Bliss, and White knew of Wilson's offer to Clemenceau at that time.[2] Was House misleading them or was he himself ill-informed?

Undaunted by the first manifestations of hostility within the American delegation towards a treaty of guarantee, House prepared on March 20 a formula for a pledge of mutual Anglo-American-French assistance.[3] The Colonel approached Clemenceau with his draft in the hope that France, Great Britain, and the United States might agree 'provided Lloyd George and the President thought the American and British people would sustain such action'. Clemenceau accepted with slight verbal change.

At the time, House wrote:

> I have my doubts as to the Senate accepting such a treaty but that is to be seen. Meanwhile, it satisfies Clemenceau and we can get on with the real business of the Conference. It is practically promising only what we promised to do in the League of Nations, but since Clemenceau does not believe in the League of Nations, it may be necessary to give him a treaty on the outside.[4]

Nothing showed more clearly the compromising nature of Colonel House. He had quickly accepted the French proposal, as he understood it to be, while recognizing that it did not entirely accord with the League system. He doubted whether the promise would be implemented by the United States but to reach agreement on the Rhineland question at any price he was willing in effect partially to mislead Clemenceau. While he thus treated as secondary a matter of primary concern to the French, the Colonel sincerely believed that ample provision for

[1] White to Root, in Allan Nevins, *Henry White: Thirty Years of American Diplomacy*, pp. 410-12; also White to Lodge, *ibid.*, p. 415. Both letters were dated March 19. White reported to Root: '. . . we do not see how it is possible to insert in the Treaty or the League of Nations Covenant any such guarantee on our part which the Senate will, or ought to, accept. . .".

[2] Birdsall, *Versailles Twenty Years After*, p. 209.

[3] Miller, *Diary*, VI, pp. 474a-b.

[4] House, Diary, XV, p. 105.

French security was being made entirely apart from the proposed treaty of guarantee.

Having secured Clemenceau's approval for his draft, House turned to Lloyd George and Balfour. Both accepted it without amendment. Then House turned to his own delegation again.

The three American Commissioners, Lansing, White, and Bliss, were decidedly cool in their reaction to House's proposed treaty of guarantee. They viewed it as prejudicial to the League of Nations and to the purposes for which the United States had entered the war.[1] On March 21, 'They all expressed themselves very strongly against the principle involved in concluding such an agreement. . . .' Urging a showdown with the French, White favoured a separate peace with Germany if amicable agreement proved impossible.[2]

In the meantime, House had received, on March 20, a note from Tardieu combining the Colonel's formula for the guarantee with French demands for physical securities. The latter were the same as in the French note of March 17 except for the omission of the provision barring German recruiting in the demilitarized zone. In addition, the note of March 20 called for League approval of the guarantee and the ancillary arrangements '. . . in the interests of the general Peace, the maintenance of which will be the essential aim of the League'.[3]

House turned Tardieu's latest proposal over to Miller, one of the American delegation's legal advisors. Miller, with the aid of his American colleague, Gordon Auchinloss, and of Sir William Wiseman of the British delegation, drew up a paper on the Rhine Question which neatly defined the dilemma confronting them: 'The problem is to satisfy the French that they have adequate security against another German attack and at the same time put nothing into the Peace Treaty which is likely to be the cause of future wars.' If the Rhineland buffer state were given up, the three experts saw two alternatives remaining: the United States and Great Britain could guarantee to aid France in case of German attack; or the League Covenant could contain a provision committing the League to help France in such

[1] *P.P.C.*, XI, p. 126, Minutes of the American Commission, March 20, 1919.

[2] *Ibid.*, p. 130, Minutes of the American Commission, March 21, 1919.

[3] Wilson Papers, VIII-A-24; Miller, *Diary*, VII, p. 29.

a contingency. They criticized the former because it would be a declaration of non-confidence in the League, weakening the organization from its very inception, and the latter because it would cast the League in the role of an alliance system directed against Germany.

In their opinion, the French basically desired to prohibit all military operations in a territory stretching from 50 kilometres east of the Rhine to the eastern borders of France. Any entry of German forces into this area should be treated like an invasion of France itself. To preserve this vital security zone, France should have the legal right to resist a German military movement into it as well as enjoying the assurance of effective British and American support.[1]

Miller and his associates suggested a plan for achieving this result. After discussing their proposals with House, Gordon Auchinloss prepared a similar plan which omitted the guarantee formula while providing for an inspection committee of civilians named by the League of Nations.[2] House submitted the Auchinloss memorandum to Lansing, Bliss, and White. Lansing and White approved; Bliss only tentatively.[3] The Colonel gave the scheme on March 24 to Wilson who appears to have accepted it. Thus House secured substantial support for a Rhineland demilitarization plan which differed in major respects from Tardieu's proposal of March 20.

On March 27, the Colonel learned that Wilson was prepared *in addition* to support a treaty of guarantee for France. About this important conversation House wrote:

> He surprised me by saying that he was willing to guarantee with Great Britain that we should come to France's rescue in the event of an attack by Germany. I had not shown him the memorandum on this subject which I had drafted, and which Lloyd George, Balfour and Clemenceau had accepted. . . .

House continued:

> . . . In thinking about this matter today, I thought I ought to call the President's attention to the perils of such a treaty. . . . it would

[1] 'The Left Bank of the Rhine', March 21, 1919, House Papers; copies also in Miller, *Diary*, VII, and Wilson Papers, 90/96.

[2] Miller, *Diary*, VIII, pp. 50-2.

[3] House, Diary, XV, p. 109; Wilson Papers, VIII-A-27, March 23.

> be looked upon as a direct blow at the League of Nations. The League is supposed to do just what this treaty proposed, and if it were necessary for the nations to make such treaties, then why the League of Nations? I did not shake him for in a moment of enthusiasm he committed himself to Clemenceau and he does not wish to withdraw his promise, a position which I thoroughly commend.[1]

These words strongly suggest that House did not know between March 14 and March 27 that Wilson had accepted the idea of an Anglo-American guarantee of French security. According to Tardieu's note of March 17, the idea had come from the allies of France; the United States was an 'associate', not an 'ally'. Therefore, the Colonel may well have believed that Wilson had not associated himself with it. But, as we have seen, House was willing to explore the possibilities of the idea. Securing the approval of Lloyd George, Balfour, and Clemenceau to a guarantee formula, he then tried it out on the American Commissioners, Lansing, White, and Bliss, before approaching Wilson. Their increasingly vigorous reaction against the proposed treaty of guarantee evidently induced House not to suggest the guarantee formula to Wilson but to seek his approval for a solution of the French desire for security along the lines of the Auchinloss memorandum. But, to his surprise, and without his having discussed a guarantee formula with Wilson before, the President revealed to House on March 27 his willingness to support the proposed treaty. Quite rightly, in view of his own reservations and of the attitude of the other Commissioners, House warned the President of the pitfalls of this course.[2] Wilson, so House suggests, may have regretted by then the promise made to Clemenceau on March 14, but having given his word, he would not break it.[3]

[1] House, Diary, XV, pp. 114-15; compare with House, *Intimate Papers*, IV, p. 395.

[2] House told White about the President's acceptance of the guarantee and added, incorrectly, perhaps, 'England was resolved to give this guarantee whether the United States did or not.' White in turn reminded House that Lansing, Bliss, and he believed the guarantee 'would be extremely unfortunate, and absolutely fatal to the success of the League of Nations'. House promised to forward their views to Wilson. Minutes of the American Commission, *P.P.C.*, XI, p. 133. According to House's Diary, he did so but perhaps without mentioning the three Commissioners.

[3] Compare this reconstruction of events with Birdsall, *Versailles Twenty Years After*, pp. 209-10.

That afternoon (March 27) the Council of Four debated the Rhineland problem. Wilson summed up the measure of agreement reached thus far: all military works, strategic railways, and assembling of armed forces to be prohibited in the Rhineland west of a line running fifty kilometres east of the river. German violation of these provisions would be regarded as an hostile act. Finally, France would have the protection of a British and an American military guarantee.

Clemenceau emphasized the unacceptability of a temporary guarantee. He suggested that the Anglo-American guarantee be inserted in the Covenant of the League. To this, Wilson objected; to provide permanently for action by a small group of states would be an admission that the League's guarantee would never be sufficient. Nor could they insert in the Covenant a provision envisaging action against a single state. That would violate the principle of collective security. On the other hand, Wilson recognized that any solution of the problem of French security was closely linked with the question of the future effectiveness of the League of Nations. To ease Clemenceau's fears, the President was willing to accept a formula permitting two or more states to act against an unjustified aggression pending enforcement action by the League itself. He would also agree to planning in advance for such contingencies as an unprovoked German attack upon France.

While professing to be satisfied, Clemenceau wanted the movement of German forces into the demilitarized area to be defined ahead of time as an act of aggression. Tardieu still insisted on a French right to move up to the Rhine in case of hostile German acts. Wilson demurred: extreme nervous tensions would last for a generation or more in Franco-German relations; such a situation could lead to premature French action. In reply, Clemenceau urged that the French proposal for an Anglo-American-French commission of inspection took these possibilities into account. If the Council of the League performed this task, as Wilson and Lloyd George had suggested, dangerous delays would occur.[1]

Next day—that famous March 28 on which Wilson and Clemenceau exchanged spirited verbal blows—the President

[1] Mantoux, *Délibérations*, I, pp. 50-1.

formally initialed a proposition on the Rhineland[1] which almost completely coincided with the stand taken by Lloyd George in the Fontainebleau memorandum of March 25. As on other German territorial questions at the end of March, Clemenceau faced an almost solid Lloyd George-Wilson front.

Compared with the French position of March 17 and 27, Lloyd George's and Wilson's stand differed in several important respects. The treaty of guarantee depended upon the approval of the Council of the League and its duration was to be limited. Neither of these ideas was contained in the French proposals. In stipulating that violations of the demilitarization provisions be regarded as hostile acts, Lloyd George and Wilson specifically excluded the French proposal that German violations of the military, naval, or air clauses of the treaty should be so treated. Also rejected was Clemenceau's request that German troop movements into the demilitarized zone be defined in advance as an act of aggression, thus bringing the treaty of guarantee into operation. Neither were Lloyd George and Wilson willing to concede to France the right to occupy the Rhine line and bridgeheads in case of German violations of the demilitarization and disarmament clauses of the treaty. A substantial gap still existed between the French and the Anglo-American positions.

The French counter-proposals to the Fontainebleau memorandum of March 25 and to Wilson's note of March 28 came on April 2. They were a mixture of old and new demands. Instead of a 50-kilometre-wide demilitarized zone east of the Rhine, a line east of the river 'at a distance very nearly equal to the distance from the Rhine to the Franco-Belgian border' was proposed. Clemenceau urged the widening of the neutral zone, because if the German army was only fifty kilometres from the river it would be twice as close as the French forces which in most places would be some one hundred kilometres away.[2] Another new proposal was that a local police force should be permitted in the demilitarized zone.

As for inspection, the French now suggested a compromise. Instead of a commission of inspection, each signatory power should have the right to notify the Council of the League that Germany had violated one of the above provisions. The Council should be obligated immediately to proceed to examine the

[1] Wilson Papers, VIII-A-29, March 28, 1919. [2] *Ibid.*, April 2, 1919.

charge. If it were proven, Germany should be bound to accept the decision. As Clemenceau later explained to the Council of Four, while a disarmed Germany represented no serious threat, they had to ensure Germany remained disarmed, and for this, inspection was necessary. France must be able instantly to inform England and America of German violations of the disarmament clauses so that effective counter-action could be taken. Otherwise France would hold a valueless guarantee.[1]

The French note also stipulated that German violation of the disarmament or demilitarization provisions of the treaty of peace should be regarded as an act of aggression, bringing the guarantee into operation. The amendment was thus explained: Foch had shown that the Germans could successfully invade France and Belgium if they reached the Rhine first. A renewal of German aggression would be made impossible by German disarmament, but

> It must be recognized just the same that if Germany ceases to respect the military clauses which disarm her, the danger pointed out by the Marshal would exist. It is therefore necessary that the guarantee given should apply not only to a violation by Germany of her agreements in the neutralized zone, but also to the military terms of peace in general.

It was further argued that the circumstances bringing the guarantee into operation should be precisely defined:

> Marshal Foch's note of March 31 has demonstrated the grave risk to which France might be exposed, under certain circumstances. It is therefore highly necessary that the guarantee suggested as a substitute for the definite occupation of the Rhine should be very precise so that no doubt may exist regarding the nature of the facts under which it would be set in motion.

Another amendment provided for the treaty to remain in force until the *contracting parties* had agreed the League offered an adequate substitute. This defined more clearly how the decision to abrogate the agreement should be reached and would give to France an effective veto over such a decision.[2]

Wilson and House during the evening of April 2 discussed relations with the French. Complaining that Clemenceau was

[1] Mantoux, *Délibérations*, I, pp. 139-45.

[2] 'Amendments Proposed by France', House Papers, 29/47.

stubborn, the President asked House to press Tardieu to persuade his chief to be more reasonable. On the morning of April 3, House spoke strongly to Tardieu, charging unfairly that the French delegation had made no effort to meet the American point of view. House fastened particularly upon the French attitude over the Saar. In return, Tardieu dwelt upon the political difficulties facing the French delegation, depicting Clemenceau as under strong pressure from Marshal Foch, who had threatened to resign unless a permanent occupation of the Rhineland was secured. Tardieu promised to do what he could, being hastened on his way by House's threat that the President would return home if decisions were not reached.[1]

Clemenceau conceded little. On April 4 in the Council of Four he abandoned the idea of a demilitarized zone of variable depth. At the same time, since Wilson opposed the establishment of permanent commissions of inspection in Germany, he proposed, as an alternative, precise machinery of enquiry available in case of need. Colonel House, who represented the ailing Wilson, made clear his disagreement with the President on this point. Lloyd George, however, resisted Clemenceau. Thus, the Rhineland negotiations simply marked time.[2]

In what may have been an inspired move on Lloyd George's part, Sir William Wiseman on April 5 wrote House on the general impasse and offered a solution. The gist of his argument was: it was impossible to think of peace terms which could meet the national aspirations of the Allies and give the vanquished a chance to save themselves from ruin. Wilson should threaten to return home and at the same time make a bold proposal to the Council of Four, including terms based upon a strict interpretation of the Fourteen Points accompanied by the proposition that the United States postpone payment of its war loans to the Allies in return for their doing likewise among themselves. The existing loan agreements should then be converted into new obligations payable at pleasure and not bearing interest. According to Wiseman, if Wilson followed this course, he would be master of the Peace Conference and the territorial disputes would fade into proper perspective. He saw this as the only way

[1] House, Diary, XV, pp. 128, 130-1. See also Nevins, *Henry White*, pp. 435 *et seq.*, for White's role at this time.

[2] Mantoux, *Délibérations*, I, pp. 139-45.

of inducing the Allies to draft terms which would leave room for negotiation with the Germans. This bold if impractical plan had its attractive features as an answer to the British search for a more moderate peace and for a rapid conclusion to the deadlocked conference. Splendid, generous, and imaginative though the concept was, it proved abortive.[1]

Meanwhile, friction had been developing within the British delegation. Not without satisfaction, House noted in his Diary:

> Sir William Tyrrell had an interview with Clemenceau yesterday. He told Clemenceau that in his opinion he had made a great mistake in trying to have an understanding with Lloyd George rather than with President Wilson. He also told him that he had 'prostituted his friendship with Colonel House in making such an attempt'. I mention this in order to show how completely the British are in revolt against Lloyd George. It starts with Balfour and runs down through Cecil, Tyrrell, Wiseman, Montagu and many others. The only people who uphold Lloyd George, as far as I know, are his immediate secretariat. . . .[2]

Although this tells little about the substance of the disagreement, Lord Hardinge has confirmed the existence of hard feeling among the British delegation and attributed it at least to Lloyd George's failure sometimes to consult Balfour 'on the most weighty and important matters', such as, allegedly, the text of the treaty of guarantee.[3] If a 'revolt' was under way in the British delegation in early April, it probably had received its main immediate impetus from the Fontainebleau affair when Lloyd George ignored the Foreign Office advisors. Undoubtedly we see here an important stage in the growth of the conflict between the Prime Minister and his secretariat on the one hand and the Foreign Secretary and Foreign Office on the other which reached its climax under Curzon's secretaryship.

Tensions within British ranks in early April must also have been a reflection of the general impasse in the negotiations. As Wiseman reported to Reading on April 8

> Last week was the worst since the Conference began. It looked as though an absolute deadlock had been reached. . . . Since

[1] Wiseman to House, April 5, 1919, House Papers, 16/6.
[2] House, Diary, XV, p. 139, April 5, 1919.
[3] Hardinge, *The Old Diplomacy*, p. 241.

> Saturday last the position has substantially improved. . . . In general, everyone is tired of the Conference and nerves are on edge. This applies to public press, members of delegations, and leading statesmen.[1]

The deadlock soon broke. The Council of Four first made progress on reparations and the Saar. In both cases, Lloyd George and Wilson retreated.

On the Rhineland question, Wilson and Lloyd George tried to maintain a firm stand. The Prime Minister informed a meeting of Dominion leaders that the Council of Four was returning to the earlier British position of a demilitarized Rhineland under German sovereignty. Claiming to have interviewed French statesmen outside Clemenceau's government Lloyd George said he had 'found no desire that France should absorb the west bank of the Rhine'.[2] On April 12, the President instructed House to hand Tardieu his reply to the French note of April 2

> with the very solemn warning that it is necessary for him to induce his chief to accept these terms as drawn, pointing out to him that this is an extraordinary step for the United States to take, and that there will be no possible hope of my obtaining the proposed treaty, if the additions he suggested were made.
>
> It would be well for him to understand that this is the only obtainable solution of the problem of the protection for France of her eastern frontier.[3]

Wilson asserted that his proposals of March 28 had been definite and constructive and 'made after the most mature consideration of all the circumstances involved'. In recapitulating his proposals, the President omitted Clause 3 of his earlier stipulations and added to the guarantee formula the words 'That I should lay before the Senate of the United States and urge for adoption a treaty with France. . . .' In this, he wisely

[1] Wiseman Papers, 90/21.

[2] 'Notes of a meeting of the Dominion Prime Ministers . . . Friday, April 11, 1919, at 9 a.m.", *Cmd. 2169*, pp. 92-3. Law, Borden, Hughes, Botha, and Massey were present. This source gives no record of the discussion, if any.

[3] Wilson Papers, VIII-A-35; House Papers, Wilson-House Correspondence, April 12, 1919. House noted in his Diary: 'At the request of the President, I asked Tardieu to call in order to read the riot act to Clemenceau, through him, regarding the left bank of the Rhine and the protection of France. . . .' House, Diary, XV, p. 153.

qualified the nature of the promise being made to Clemenceau. He affirmed his close association in the Rhineland negotiations with Lloyd George: 'Both Mr. Lloyd George's proposals and my own were made after repeated consideration of all other plans suggested, and they represent the maximum of what I myself deem necessary for the safety of France or possible on the part of the United States.'

The President then explained his attitude towards the proposed French amendments of April 2. It would be an error to go beyond the military terms provisionally agreed upon regarding German destruction of all fortifications on the east bank of the Rhine. 'It is my clear judgement that we should adhere to the fifty kilometers stipulated in the military terms.' The proposal regarding a local gendarmarie was termed unnecessary 'because the point was already covered in the general military terms which had been provisionally accepted'. He continued:

> I am sorry to say I cannot at all agree to include in the third paragraph the military, naval, and air clauses of the Treaty of Peace. With regard to the added paragraph concerning the right of the signatory powers to notify the Executive Council of the League of any violations of these regulations which might have been observed, it is clear that right already exists on the part of members of the League if any action is taken anywhere which threatens to disturb the peace of the world, and that it would be unwise to connect it with this special agreement and treaty. . . .

In fact, Wilson accepted only one French amendment: that the guarantee treaty remain in force until the contracting parties agreed the League provided an adequate substitute.[1]

Still backing Lloyd George, Wilson thus refused to deviate substantially from his stand of April 2 on the Rhineland question. The timing of his statement, April 12, seems to rule

[1] Wilson Papers, VIII-A-33; House Papers, 29/47, 'Memorandum on the Amendments Proposed by France to the Agreement suggested by President Wilson regarding the Rhine Frontier', April 12, 1919. Wilson's basic objection to a clause regulating the size of the local police force in the demilitarized zone probably was that to be enforced it would require inspection which 'would breed friction and would promote not safety but antagonism'. Wilson Papers, VIII-A-33, April 8, 1919. This appears to be an early draft of the definitive note.

out the suggestion that the French had made a bargain with Wilson in which they exchanged acceptance of his Monroe doctrine amendment to the Covenant for his approval of a Rhineland occupation.[1]

Within two days, the President retreated. Early in the evening of April 14 Clemenceau told House he accepted the President's Rhineland terms. Since, however, he would have to battle the French generals, he asked for one concession to enable him to fight more effectively: France should be allowed to occupy three zones in the Rhineland—the first, including Coblentz, for five years; the second, including Metz, for ten years; and the third, lying close to the French frontier, for fifteen years.[2] Next day, Wilson accepted Clemenceau's offer so reluctantly that House urged: 'We had better do it with a *beau geste* rather than grudgingly. . . .'[3] House rushed to tell Clemenceau. Now, Lloyd George was to face a Wilson-Clemenceau front in the Rhineland negotiations.

The main task now was to put their decisions into draft form. On April 18, the Council of Four reverted to the demilitarization scheme of March 10. Lloyd George objected to depriving Germany of the right to raise Rhineland volunteers for the Reichswehr and to prohibiting the imposition of taxes in the Rhineland for the maintenance of the German military establishment. His colleagues agreed, although Clemenceau did so unwillingly. They scarcely could have done otherwise, for the two provisions would have been almost impossible to enforce.[4]

On April 20, Wilson and Clemenceau approved draft agreements on the demilitarization and occupation of the Rhineland. The former corresponded in substance with the earlier Anglo-American stand. It included the provision that the Anglo-American guarantee would continue 'until it is agreed by the contracting powers that the League itself affords sufficient protection'. In addition, the demilitarization agreement compromised on inspection. Clause 6 read, in a clipped style: 'As long as the present treaty remains in force, a pledge by Germany to respond to any inquiry that the Council of the League of

[1] See Birdsall, *Versailles Twenty Years After*, p. 213.

[2] House, Diary, XV, p. 156; Seymour, *Intimate Papers*, IV, pp. 406-7.

[3] House, Diary, XV, pp. 159-60.

[4] Mantoux, *Délibérations*, I, p. 271; *Cmd. 2169*, pp. 93-4.

Nations will deem necessary.' Clemenceau and Tardieu had thus failed to secure the precise inspection machinery for which they had striven.[1]

The occupation agreement was described as a guarantee for the execution of the peace treaty. Article 1 provided for a fifteen-year occupation of the Rhineland and the bridgeheads by an international force. Article 2 defined the three zones which would be successively evacuated at five-year intervals if Germany executed the conditions of peace. Article 3 declared that if, during or after the fifteen-year period, the Inter-Allied Commission of Reparations recognized that Germany refused to execute, in whole or in part, the peace conditions, the international reoccupation of all or part of the areas defined in Article 2 would immediately take place. Article 4 provided for the immediate withdrawal of the occupation forces if Germany carried out all its treaty engagements before the end of the fifteen-year period.[2]

On April 22, Clemenceau submitted these drafts to the Council of Four. Lloyd George accepted the proposals on demilitarization. To the end he remained hostile towards the occupation. In a strictly military sense, perhaps, the Rhineland occupation was unnecessary. For the French, however, if the Germans should attack, British and American as well as French forces would be engaged—a solid guarantee of Anglo-American assistance. A 'battalion and a flag' would also be a symbol of American and English repudiation of a policy of isolationism.

It may be wondered why Lloyd George was not more willing to ensure this tangible expression of a new American role in European and world affairs. In defending his position, Lloyd George emphasized the difficulties which British governments would encounter in maintaining a large occupation force because of the widespread opposition in the United Kingdom to compulsory military service. Another reason for opposing an occupation force may be seen in Henry Wilson's letter of April 11 to Admiral Cowan in the Baltic:

[1] 'Stipulations to be Embodied in the Treaty', Wilson Papers, VIII-A-38, April 20, 1919.

[2] 'Articles concerning Guarantees of Execution of the Treaty', *P.P.C.*, V, pp. 117-18.

> You want me to send a general to help in the Baltic Border States. Yes, on one condition. That is that the Big Four lay down a broad policy. Otherwise—No. Since November 22 of last year I have been trying to get a policy—trying, trying, trying, and not a shadow of success.
>
> That being so, my whole energies are now bent to getting our troops out of Europe and Russia, and concentrating all our strength in our coming storm centres, viz. England, Ireland, Egypt and India. There you are, my dear. Since the statesmen (?) can't and won't lay down a policy, I am going to look after and safeguard our own immediate interests, so that when all the hot air now blowing about Leagues of Nations, Small States, Mandatories, turns to the icy cold wind of hard fact, the British Empire will be well clothed and well defended against all the bangs and curses of the future.[1]

Woodrow Wilson suggested that the word 'international' be deleted, but Clemenceau opposed. If he did not have 'votre drapeau' beside the French flag in the Rhineland, he could not face the French Parliament. Finally, Lloyd George enquired whether fifteen years would be the absolute limit or would the period vary with Germany's payment of reparations? Clemenceau in reply mistakenly pointed out that prolongation would depend upon a League decision. In other words, Britain could veto a prolongation.

Lloyd George finally consented. Clemenceau then tabled a draft treaty between France and the United States which he and Wilson had agreed to on April 20. Under its terms, German violation of certain, unspecified terms of peace would be treated as hostile acts. The United States would be pledged to aid France immediately in case of unprovoked German aggression. This pledge was subject to the approval of the Council of the League and to continue until the signatories agreed that the League offered sufficient protection. After Wilson explained to Lloyd George that he preferred separate American and British treaties with France,[2] the British Prime Minister provisionally

[1] Henry Wilson to Admiral Cowan, April 11, 1919 (*circa*), in Callwell, *Sir Henry Wilson*, II, p. 182.

[2] On April 16, Henry White had written Wilson warning him that the proposed treaty of guarantee would encounter opposition in the United States from League supporters who would see it as weakening the League, from those who opposed overseas commitments, and from those who

agreed to the formula. Balfour accepted after the meeting.[1]

A Rhineland compromise had been effected with one major loophole remaining: the United States Senate or the British Parliament might not approve the treaty of guarantee. In return for the promise of aid, Clemenceau had retreated from the original demand that the Rhineland be separated from Germany or at least that France have the physical protection of a permanent military occupation of the area. The danger existed that the French delegation had made concessions in return for an empty promise. To guard against this contingency, Clemenceau and Tardieu decided to secure a legal basis for the prolongation of the Rhineland occupation after fifteen years if the Anglo-American treaties of guarantee fell through.[2]

Clemenceau broached this problem first with Wilson, on April 23: if the treaties of guarantee never materialized, what guarantees of French security would replace them? Wilson agreed to discuss this delicate problem.[3] On April 25, Clemenceau and Wilson presented a draft formula to Lloyd George. The original agreement on the occupation regime had simply provided for the evacuation of the last stratum of German territory at the end of fifteen years. To this provision, Clemenceau and Wilson suggested adding a sentence reading: 'If at that time the guarantees against unprovoked aggression by Germany are not considered satisfactory by the present Allied and Associated Governments, Germany consents to accept such similar guarantees as they may require.' Lloyd George, while aware of Clemenceau's problem, termed this clause 'very dangerous' and withheld approval.[4] Certainly, Germany, under this provision, would have been undertaking a loosely-defined obligation, not necessarily limited only to accepting a longer occupation if the victors so decided.

[1] *P.P.C.*, IV, pp. 114, 118; Mantoux, *Délibérations*, I, p. 319.

[2] Tardieu, *La Paix*, pp. 225 *et seq.*

[3] *Ibid.*, p. 234.

[4] *P.P.C.*, V, pp. 244, 247-8.

attacked Wilson's policies in general. White advised the President to separate the American agreement from the British to lessen opposition within the United States by critics who would condemn a joint alliance with Great Britain. Next day Wilson replied: '. . . You are quite right about the whole thing, and I can assure you that I never had in mind the joint arrangement with Great Britain, but only a separate treaty with France, and, as you know, all that I promised is to try to get it. . . .' Wilson Papers, VIII-A-37.

Finally, on April 30, the Council of Four accepted the following text: 'If at that date the guarantees against unprovoked aggression are not considered sufficient by the Allied and Associated Governments, the evacuation of the occupying troops may be delayed to the extent regarded as necessary for the purpose of obtaining the required guarantees.'[1] This draft clearly provided for a prolongation of the occupation in case the treaty of guarantee was still-born. It also opened up the prospect that the compensating 'required guarantees' would not necessarily have to be exacted from Germany alone. They could take the form, for instance, of the later Locarno agreement or of the Pact of Paris of 1928. This was a more flexible and statesmanlike proposal.[2] To Tardieu, the significance of the clause was simple and satisfactory: '... pas de traités de garantie, pas d'évacuation en 1935'. His claim seems exaggerated. France alone would not make the decision that the guarantees against unprovoked aggression were insufficient; any delay in evacuation was made permissive, but not mandatory. At least, however, the door was open for substitute measures in case the treaties of guarantee failed to materialize.[3]

Criticism of the occupation regime now came from several

[1] *Ibid.*, p. 357.

[2] Since the two secretaries, Hankey and Mantoux, were asked to withdraw when the Council considered this matter on April 30, we do not know the substance of the discussion.

[3] Two days after the German delegation received the text of the treaty, a brief flurry occurred in the Council of Four over article 3 of the proposals of April 22 which had found its way into the treaty as article 430. Wilson pointed out that the treaty article would permit a reoccupation of the Rhineland if Germany 'failed to observe' its obligations under the treaty. The wording in the draft proposal had been more specific—should Germany 'refuse to execute' the agreed conditions a reoccupation could take place. The President also pointed out that their intention had been to restrict this provision to Germany's refusing to execute the reparations clauses of the treaty, not the entire treaty. He also wanted the wording to be permissive rather than obligatory in nature. His amendments were accepted. The final form of the provision was: 'In case either during the occupation or after the expiration of the fifteen years referred to above, the Reparation Commission finds that Germany refuses to observe the whole or part of her obligations *for reparation as provided in* the present Treaty, the whole or part of the area specified in Article 429 will be reoccupied immediately by the Allied and Associated Forces.' *P.P.C.*, V, pp. 519-20, 542, 576.

directions. Sir Henry Wilson, Chief of the Imperial General Staff, criticized it on the grounds that the first withdrawal should be in the south, not in the north. About his interview on the subject with Lloyd George, Henry Wilson wrote:

> (I said he) must now decide whether he was going to be a European or an American, and that in my opinion, he must be European. I declared that my Cousin was Boche, and that we never could have peace in Europe without the goodwill of the Italians, that we could not have Orlando and Wilson in the same room at the same time, and that therefore Wilson had better clear out. It is quite clear to me that Lloyd George is out of his depth and in these matters is weakly following my Cousin, who himself has no idea where he is going.[1]

Nothing came of his criticism of the withdrawal system.

Poincaré and Foch also attacked the Rhineland occupation provisions. On April 28, the former sought to persuade the Council of Four to prolong the occupation at least until Germany had discharged its reparations obligations. On[2] May 6, the latter asked the heads of governments to re-submit to the military experts the three questions: guarantees, occupation, and Kehl.[3] Both Poincaré and the Marshal failed to overcome Lloyd George's objections.

One item of the Rhineland settlement remained incomplete: Lloyd George and Wilson had still to define the precise guarantee being offered to France.

The British Prime Minister laid the proposed agreement before the British Empire Delegation on May 5, explaining that the guarantee against unprovoked German aggression had been necessary 'to satisfy the French' and to enable Clemenceau to overrule French militarists.[4] His surprising description of the agreement ran: 'The guarantee was for a period of fifteen years, co-terminous with the period during which the Army of Occupation would exist. He was apprehensive lest the United States Senate might refuse the guarantee. A clause had been added providing for reconsideration of the length of the period

[1] Callwell, *Sir Henry Wilson*, pp. 183-7.

[2] Lloyd George, *Truth*, I, pp. 427-32.

[3] *P.P.C.*, III, pp. 384-8. Foch opposed leaving Kehl in German hands.

[4] 'Minutes of the British Empire Delegation, No. 30, Monday, May 5, 1919, 5:30 p.m.', Foster Papers.

of occupation. . . .' The Prime Minister's reference to the American Senate clearly explains the British reservation that the guarantee would only come into force for Great Britain when the United States had also ratified. But what was the significance of his reference to the fifteen-year term? Later in the meeting, when the text of the proposed guarantee was read (the Wilson-Clemenceau text of April 20), Borden rightly pointed out that the formula made the guarantee binding as long as France wanted it. Had the Prime Minister intended to mislead, or had he inadvertently revealed a private understanding, or was he simply confused?

The subsequent discussion revolved around the Dominions' attitudes towards the guarantee and its implications for the League.

Barnes enquired where the guarantee differed from the safeguards in the Covenant. Lloyd George went straight to the point: The Germans might be in Paris before the League took action. Both Borden and Botha commented, as had Lansing, White, and Bliss, that this cast doubt upon the effectiveness of the League.

Towards the guarantee itself, the reactions of the Dominion leaders varied. Hughes, of Australia, preferred a simple pledge of assistance to France against unprovoked German attack. Massey agreed. Borden, while unsure of the probable effect in Canada, 'feared that Canadians would be reluctant to accept such a commitment'. Botha 'feared that there were so many Frenchmen who wanted permanent militarism, and would take a provocative attitude towards the Germans, that such a commitment would be a very dangerous affair'. On the latter point, Bonar Law sought to be reassuring by noting that the phrase 'unprovoked aggression' protected them since the British (and Americans) would be the final judges of whether the aggression was unprovoked. The discussion made clear that while Great Britain would probably approve the guarantee, and possibly Australia and New Zealand as well, Canadian and South African support was doubtful.

Next day, Lloyd George and Balfour handed Clemenceau a letter embodying the British government's undertaking. After repeating the stipulations for the demilitarization of the Rhineland, it read:

> As these conditions may not at first provide adequate security and protection to your country, H.M.G. agree to ask Parliament to authorize a treaty with France by which Great Britain shall be bound to come immediately to her assistance in the event of any unprovoked movement of aggression against her being made by Germany.
>
> The Treaty will be in similar terms to that entered into by the United States and will come into force when the latter is ratified.
>
> The Treaty must be recognized by the Council of the League of Nations as being consistent with the Covenant of the League, and will continue in force until on the application of one of the parties to it, the Council of the League agrees that the League itself affords sufficient protection.
>
> The obligation imposed under this Treaty shall not be binding on the Dominions of the British Empire until the Treaty is ratified by the Parliament of the Dominion concerned.[1]

This text made British participation in the guarantee dependent upon that of the United States and upon the consent of the Council of the League. It also relieved the British Dominions of any commitment without their consent, a recognition of the right of the Dominions to pursue an independent foreign policy in relation to the United Kingdom. This reservation also constituted a further weakening of the guarantee from a French viewpoint. In the Council of Four on May 6, on Wilson's initiative, Clemenceau accepted the Lloyd George-Balfour text in preference to one suggested by Tardieu.[2]

Upon signing his pledge to submit to the Senate a guarantee treaty which would come into effect with ratification of the British undertaking,[3] Wilson, in a comment to Miller, revealed

[1] *P.P.C.*, V, pp. 494-5.

[2] Tardieu's draft closely followed the Clemenceau-Wilson agreement of April 20. His draft defined any German violation of articles 42 and 43 of the draft treaty as 'an act of hostility'. Wilson objected that this wording suggested that if Germany built a railway line in the demilitarized zone which might be described as strategic, the United States would be obligated to take action. The President stressed that American troops 'were only to be sent in the event of an act of aggression'. Tardieu's draft had also provided that the League Council's decision to approve the guarantee should be taken by majority vote. In the final pledge made by Lloyd George and Wilson, no mention was made of voting procedure, thereby implying that the decision would depend upon unanimity. *P.P.C.*, V, pp. 485-6.

[3] *P.P.C.*, V, p. 495.

his effort to square the guarantee with the Covenant: '. . . he (Wilson) considered this practically an advance determination by the Council in place of the determination which they might make if there was such an aggression'.[1]

At the end of the plenary session on May 6, Lloyd George and Wilson presented Clemenceau with their written promise to seek a treaty of guarantee for France. For British diplomacy the agreement was a signal, if not final, success for the policy of securing an United States' commitment to uphold European peace and stability.

[1] Miller, *Diary*, I, pp. 293-5.

X

LLOYD GEORGE, WILSON, AND THE SAAR DILEMMA

'BOTH the American and British delegations opposed (the French claims to the Saar Basin) on the ground that another Alsace-Lorraine problem would be created which would cause trouble in future.'[1] In this statement Lloyd George at least oversimplified the actual situation at Paris. Both he and Woodrow Wilson received advice from within their own delegations to support a settlement favourable, in greater or lesser degree, to French aspirations for control of the Saar.

On the British side, the Political Intelligence Department of the Foreign Office had reported on the economics of the Saar Question in tones favourable to the French.[2] The Imperial General Staff supported cession to France for economic and strategic reasons,[3] although the CIGS, Sir Henry Wilson, advised Balfour in early February '. . . to bargain the grant of the Saar Valley against the Sykes-Picot (agreement)'.[4] Certain British territorial advisors recommended on February 4, 1919, that French claims for a revision of the frontier in the Saar area be upheld. Explaining that coal gave the Saar its importance, they commented that the population was purely German and the German title perfectly valid.

> Revision can accordingly be recommended only on the ground that completely new factors have been introduced, such as the

[1] Lloyd George, *Truth*, I, p. 401.
[2] See p. 106, above.
[3] See p. 108, above.
[4] Callwell, *Sir Henry Wilson*, p. 168.

> ruthless destruction of the French coal mines in the north of France, and the service to which with the help of the Saar Valley coal, the Briey-Longwy iron mines were actually put by Germany in her strategical offensive.

If the Saar in whole or in part were transferred to France for these reasons, they urged that the transaction be credited to Germany's reparations account. At the same time, they favoured awarding France most of the coalfield with the frontier so drawn as to ensure maximum security. They recognized this meant giving France more territory than it had possessed either in 1792 or 1914. The latter, they believed, '. . . could probably be so arranged that without strategic considerations being mentioned, all that France claims in virtue of such strategic considerations would be conceded to her'.[1] This position coincided closely with that of the American territorial advisors, although their British counterparts were prepared to concede more to France regardless of the fate of the Rhineland.

Wilson's technical advisors favoured as a minimum the line of 1814, which would give France two-thirds of the Saar coal production of 1913, some 8,000,000 tons. This quantity constituted only 3 per cent. of Germany's total prewar coal production but 18 per cent. of France's and, together with the large untapped reserves in the Saar, would reduce the chronic French prewar coal deficit which would now be augmented by the return of Alsace-Lorraine. In addition, the 1814 line would add important metallurgical, glass, and pottery industries and a skilled labour force to the French economy. Strategically, French control of the middle Saar Valley would add to the security of northern Lorraine, although neither the 1814 nor the 1815 lines provided good defensible frontiers which probably called for strategic modifications in both lines. Indeed, the American territorial experts were prepared to approve the cession of the entire Saar Basin for strategic reasons. They advised that, if the left bank of the Rhine was not demilitarized, both the Saar Basin and the 1814 line in the region between the Lauter and the Queich should go to France.

[1] 'Memorandum Submitted to British Plenipotentiaries. The Western and Northern Frontiers of Germany. February 4, 1919', Miller, *Diary*, V, pp. 30 *et seq.*

They conceded their recommendations subordinated the sentiments of 350,000 Saarlanders to considerations of justice, economics, and strategy. But 'the present desires of these people should not prevent a just disposition of this important coal deposit in favour of a country whose limited coal supplies have been much reduced by unlicensed German exploitation and destruction in the present war'.[1] These recommendations reflected particularly the thinking of Charles Homer Haskins, the West European specialist of *The Inquiry*.[2]

When the British and American advisors met on February 21

[1] 'Outline of Tentative Report and Recommendations Prepared by the Intelligence Section, in accordance with instructions, for the President and the Plenipotentiaries, January 21, 1919', Wilson Papers, VIII-A-13; Miller, *Diary*, VI, pp. 43-52.

[2] Two of his reports underlay this section of *The Outline* of January 21: (1) *Alsace-Lorraine—Report on the Problems of Alsace-Lorraine*, C. H. Haskins, November 14, 1918, American Inquiry: No. 210, A.C.N.P., 303, 185.1135/1; (2) *The Eastern Frontiers of France*, C. H. Haskins, American Inquiry: No. 208 (no date, but clearly after the Armistice), *ibid.*

In the former report, Haskins attempted to justify French annexation of the Saar to the 1814 line even though it savoured of imperialism and would be against the wishes of the inhabitants: '. . . if the Saar Valley were simply a given portion of the earth's surface, this (the charge of violation of popular rights) would be hard to answer. But the Saar Valley is also a great mining area, comparable on a lesser scale to the neighbouring *minette* field, and the control of key deposits of minerals by the small population which happens to live over them might well be held to carry too far the principle of self-determination. Let the people be free to control their own destinies, but let the mineral deposits beneath them be governed by consideration of relations to the outside world. If this principle of the separation of mines from people be accepted, it will put the question of the Saar in a different light. This will then be viewed in the first instance as a mining area rather than a certain number of people. If the area were transferred to another flag, full opportunity should be given to the people to retain their allegiance and to receive adequate compensation for any property they might leave behind. The people might remain German, and the mines become French.

'If the question of the coal mines can thus be dissociated from that of the inhabitants, the problem takes on a different aspect. There can be no doubt that France needs the coal; what is her claim to it? . . . Its chief occasion is economic, the French need of coal. But its international justification must be primarily as an indemnity. . . . The Saarbrucken mines are, with one exception, the property of the Prussian state, not of private companies, so that individual rights and adjustments are not involved. It is a simple question of seizing the property of a public wrongdoer.'

to establish a common front on German territorial questions,[1] they decided to oppose the outright cession of the Saar to France, but agreed to French management, administration, exploitation, and ownership of the Saar coal-mines as compensation for the damage to the French mines. They were prepared to establish French 'supremacy and administration' over the valley while protecting the local inhabitants from subjection to French institutions. The main features of the proposed regime were: local linguistic and religious freedom; exemption of Saarlanders from German or French conscription; a special school system free from ordinary French educational administration; a local assembly for local matters; no representation in either French parliament or German national assembly; inclusion of the Saar within the French customs union and fiscal system. The question of the judiciary was expressly left open. It was further agreed that the frontier of the Saar should be drawn well beyond the coal basin itself for strategic, economic, and administrative reasons. While vague on the question of sovereignty over the Saar, the American and British territorial experts envisaged its virtual absorption by France by means short of outright annexation.

The Anglo-American experts agreed to let the French take the initiative in making proposals. Tardieu did so near the end of March. His minimum demand was the 1814 frontier; the maximum, the entire Saar Basin.[2]

Tardieu, basing the former demand upon the principles of juridical and historical restoration, argued that the French claim to the Saar rested on the same historic, moral, and national grounds as the Polish and Czech cases which had already been favourably received by the Conference. This was a patent exaggeration.

The principles of economic reparation and of the natural economic unity of the Saar Basin were the main basis of his maximum claim. Tardieu, however, went beyond reparations

[1] 'Minutes of meeting in Hotel Crillon between British and United States representatives to consider the changes in the frontier of Germany which should form part of the preliminaries of Peace, February 21, 1919', House Papers, 30/165.

[2] 'Mémoire présenté par la délégation française', Tardieu, *La Paix*, pp. 279-89. No date is given. He drew heavily upon L. Gallois' report to the Comité d'études, *Le Bassin Houillère de Sarrebruck: étude économique et politique.*

to reveal a profound concern for the balance of economic and political power between France and Germany. His argument was crystal-clear: the acquisition of Alsace-Lorraine would accentuate the chronic French coal deficit; even after the mines of northern France had been restored to production, France would have to import 30,000,000 tons of coal annually; 'En d'autres termes, la France serait économiquement tributaire de l'Allemagne, qui, par le charbon, contrôlerait les prix de tout notre métallurgie de l'Est et dominerait ainsi toute notre politique.' For France, this could mean defeat despite victory. While advancing his powerful argument, Tardieu consciously avoided basing the French claims on grounds other than reparations. In the light of the French government's obligations under the pre-armistice agreement, the problem of deciding how to present the claim must have posed serious difficulties for the French delegation. Tardieu's solution was most skilful. Although the 'historical-juridical' argument was thin and unconvincing, the economic case, both on grounds of reparations and balance of power was strong indeed.

Tardieu presented his government's Saar claims to the Council of Four on March 28.[1] At bottom, the French appeared to seek the entire Saar Basin. Alternatively, they sought to acquire the 1814 line and to establish a special political-economic regime over the remainder of the Saar Basin, including full ownership of the mines. Neither Lloyd George nor Woodrow Wilson accepted these proposals.

Fluidity also characterized Lloyd George's position. Three days earlier in the Fontainebleau memorandum, he had been prepared to accept the 1814 line. As an alternative, he had suggested the existing frontier of Alsace-Lorraine together with French use of the Saar coal-mines for a ten-year period to compensate for the destruction of the French coalfields, after which Germany would guarantee to impose no restrictions upon the export of Saar coal to France.[2] Someone seems to have drawn his attention to the understanding reached by the Anglo-American territorial advisors on February 21 because on March 28 the Prime Minister advocated the substance of their solution. Lloyd George opposed French annexation of any part of the

[1] Mantoux, *Délibérations*, I, pp. 63-5.

[2] Lloyd George, *Truth*, I, p. 414.

Saar Basin but he proposed to detach the territory from Germany and to erect an autonomous, neutralized state under the suzerainity of France. Full ownership of the mines would pass into French hands. Under this regime, he envisaged a relationship between the Saar and France similar to the position of the Isle of Man or the Channel Islands to the United Kingdom. In short, the Saar would become a French possession. Based primarily on consideration for the balance of power, this solution came close to French annexation and would have given the French government the substance of its demands. Clemenceau admitted the plan merited examination.[1]

Wilson, invoking the letter and spirit of the pre-armistice agreement, supported not only German retention of the Saar but also German ownership of the mines. Recognizing a French right to and need for compensation, he advocated arrangements for ensuring French use of the mines for the reconstruction period based on the principle of the economic unity of the Saar, which ruled out Tardieu's second alternative. Thus, the President opposed both Clemenceau and Lloyd George and broke with his own advisors.

His basic position was that the Saar Question could be treated as one of the numerous economic problems caused by the war and its aftermath. France needed coal while its own mines were restored to production. What could be simpler than to oblige the German mineowners of the Saar to supply coal to France during this interim period? If this principle were admitted, then the question of who owned the mines would become only a matter of sentiment. The bond of the pre-armistice agreement would have been fully honoured; the principle of national self-determination would have been preserved. No lasting German grievance would unsettle European affairs after the war.

Wilson became embroiled in a stormy argument with Clemenceau. The former's solution did not meet the French claims in at least two major respects. Tardieu had argued without contradiction that the Saar and Alsace-Lorraine were closely tied economically. The acquisition of Alsace-Lorraine thus seemed to imply the necessity of gaining the Saar's economic resources as well. An interim economic relationship

[1] Mantoux, *Délibérations*, I, p. 67.

would be inadequate. Wilson had no effective answer to this problem. But, did the need for such an economic relationship between France and the Saar necessitate the establishment of a special political relationship as well, either through annexation or through the establishment of a special Saar regime? Here the French Prime Minister differed sharply with Wilson. His general argument ran: Politics and economics are inseparable; the Germans can be expected to utilize the economic resources of the Saar for political ends. Thus, economic limitations upon German use of the Saar's resources will be insufficient; stringent political guarantees will be necessary as well.

The argument that politics and economics are inseparable is hard to assail, but the Frenchman's premise about future German political behaviour was open to question. German political action would be conditioned to some extent by the conduct of the victors. This contention lay at the root of Wilson's and Lloyd George's positions. The gist of Wilson's appeal to Clemenceau was that if they violated the letter or the spirit of the pre-armistice agreement—in which the Saar was not mentioned and the principle of self-determination seemed enshrined—they would embitter the Germans and spark the very search for revenge which Clemenceau sought to render harmless. Wilson also conjured up the picture of people universally being moved by the spirit of justice; if they ignored such idealism, public opinion everywhere would become cynical and hostile towards any settlement which they devised, thus undermining the peace from the very beginning. Wilson advised the French delegation to forget historic grievances, abandon their desire for revenge, treat the fallen enemy justly and generously and expect in return, goodwill and co-operation on the Germans' part.

Clemenceau's responses combined the resignation of a tired old man with the resolution of a strong patriot. 'Je ne changerai pas votre opinion, je le crains; vous vous considérez comme lié par votre parole.' The French Premier accused Wilson of eliminating sentiment and memory from the scales of judgment. 'Le fait de la guerre ne peut être oublié,' he said, pointing to the desire in France for material and moral reparation following the hardships of a war which they regarded as provoked by Germany. Thus, '. . . il faut arriver à une justice non mathématique, mais qui tienne compte du sentiment'. According to Clemenceau, the world was not governed by abstract principles and not all peoples accepted the same principles. In seeking to do justice to the Germans, 'Ne croyez pas qu'ils nous pardonneront jamais; ils ne chercheront que l'occasion d'une revanche; rien ne détruira la rage de ceux qui ont voulu établir sur la monde leur domination et qui se sont crus si près de réussir'. Finally, Clemenceau pointed out that in the Polish and Czech settlements they were making exceptions to principles. So why not in the case of the Saar, where at least 150,000 of the inhabitants were French!

Lloyd George intervened strongly to support Wilson's declaration of principle. In a striking phrase, he asserted they could not substitute appetites for principles. At the same time, Lloyd George took the stand that equally respectable principles were at issue; to reconcile them, some compromise was necessary. The British people did not lack sympathy for France, but they were haunted with the fear of creating new Alsace-Lorraines in Europe. Having once again strummed his old refrain, Lloyd George urged that the regime proposed by the Anglo-American experts would give to the French government the substance of its claims. But Wilson remained adamant. France had a right to the use of the mines; no more. And in the spirit of the Covenanters the President declared he recognized only one principle—the principle of self-determination. He had unfortunately recognized others—the principles of the economic unity of the Saar Basin and of French use of the mines.

The meeting ended in embittered feelings between Wilson and Clemenceau. Lloyd George rather ineffectually played the role of peacemaker, more on Clemenceau's side than on Wilson's. He did succeed in persuading Wilson to consult the Anglo-American advisors who had proposed autonomy for the Saar, but the suspicious President insisted that the consultation be unilateral in form.[1]

That afternoon, Clemenceau met with Tardieu and Loucheur,[2] to plan their next move. Since both Lloyd George

[1] *Ibid.*, pp. 63-75.

[2] Loucher was Minister of Industrial Reconstruction in Clemenceau's Ministry and one of his intimate advisors at the Conference on economic questions.

and Wilson had opposed the frontier of 1814, they decided to abandon this claim overtly at least. But what should they press for? In their opinion, Lloyd George's proposals offered inadequate guarantees for the operation of the mines and for the 'freeing' of the French inhabitants of the Saar. On the other hand, Wilson had opposed both Tardieu and Lloyd George. He had, however, accepted the French right to the use of the mines and the three Frenchmen decided to use this as a *point d'appui*. They decided to press a threefold case: perpetual French ownership of the mines; a special economic and political administration to permit French exploitation of the Saar; safeguards for the rights of the inhabitants, French or German.[1]

This new position was set forth in the *Note sur la question de la Sarre*, March 29. It conceded that the population of the Saar in 1919 was German in majority, but explained this in terms of 'Germanization' over a hundred years. The Note insisted upon a solution which would give France time to undo what had been done by force a century ago.[2]

The proposed scheme was ingenious. Temporarily the Saar would be under neither German nor French sovereignty, but under the protection of the League of Nations; the League would confide a mandate over the Saar to France. While the Germans of the Saar would retain their German nationality, they would not vote in elections for German assemblies, although they would vote for local governmental bodies. Officials appointed by the German government would be dismissed. German nationals would be given every facility to leave the area. The mandate would give to France the right of military occupation and powers over the local administration. In this connection, the system of education was specifically mentioned.

A remarkable system for deciding sovereignty over the Saar was described. In the first place, French nationality was to be conferred individually on those who requested it and who passed inspection. Whenever the majority of the voters in any major administrative division acquired French nationality in this way, that district would legally be annexed to France after approval by the League of Nations. An alternative method of initiating the process of annexation would be for a *Kreis* assembly to

[1] Tardieu, *La Paix*, p. 294. [2] *Ibid.*, pp. 294-6.

request union with France. Then, at the end of fifteen years, the Saarlanders remaining would be consulted about whether they preferred German or French sovereignty! Truly the principle of national self-determination was being stretched to persuade a people to declare themselves for France in the absence of any well-defined, indigenous movement among the Saarlanders for union with France and by a system open to many abuses.

Clemenceau and his associates clearly hoped that a French stranglehold over the economy, polity, and educational system could Gallicize the Saar or a substantial proportion of it within less than one hundred years! The French negotiators had not abandoned by one jot or tittle their aspirations for French control, even French acquisition, of the Saar Valley.

Meanwhile Colonel House seemed the centre of almost frenzied activities to secure a compromise. On March 28, House urged Wilson to come into line with the British position so that, by yielding a little, the tactical mistake could be avoided of taking a stand unsupported by Lloyd George when his and the American delegations were almost in agreement. Next day, after numerous consultations among the three delegations, House instructed Haskins to seek a solution involving unrestricted French control of the Saar mines but not the transfer to French sovereignty of a large German population. With Tardieu, Haskins reached a tentative agreement on a French occupation of the Saar for ten or fifteen years, followed by a plebiscite. At the time, House inclined towards this solution; he saw difficulties ahead if the French owned the Saar coal-mines while the valley remained under German sovereignty.[1]

Wilson himself consulted Isaiah Bowman, Chief of Territorial Questions in the Technical Experts' section of the American delegation, Major D. W. Johnson—another American expert, and C. H. Haskins near noon on March 29. Afterwards Haskins and Johnson, aided by J. W. Headlam-Morley of the British delegation, drafted a statement which was sent to Wilson. They proposed agreement in principle that full ownership of the Saar coal-mines should pass to France and their value credited to the German reparation account; that the fullest economic facilities be accorded to France, including exemption from German

[1] House, Diary, XV, p. 121, March 29, 1919; Seymour, *Intimate Papers*, IV, p. 396.

taxation (including export and import duties), full mobility of foreign and native labour, and freedom of development of communications; and that the necessary political and administrative arrangements to secure the above ends 'be enquired into'.[1]

Haskins, who thought Wilson too severe on this issue, reinforced the pressures upon Wilson to modify his initial position in a letter to the President on March 30.[2] Recalling earlier memoranda on the Saar, Haskins explained that the 'special form of political regime' envisaged by the Anglo-American experts had been intended to limit rather than to extend French control. He also denied the American advisors had agreed to an autonomous state, as Lloyd George had alleged. In his effort to budge Wilson, Haskins affirmed his opinion that the 1814 line represented a peace of justice, that of 1815, a peace of violence. But he left to Wilson to determine whether the 1814 frontier fitted the Fourteen Points. He advised that if they accepted a French right to reparation in the Saar, 'the question becomes one of the degree of political ownership which should go with it'. He posed two alternatives: full French ownership and control of the mines and their adjuncts, with minimum political authority; or, French use of the mines for a set period under French occupation with a plebiscite at the end to decide the question of sovereignty. Thus Wilson was counselled to reject Lloyd George's proposal of an autonomous Saar state and to move closer to the French position while avoiding territorial annexation, at least immediately. Haskins did not suggest a system of League supervision or control.

Privately, Haskins believed it was impossible to devise a regime ensuring France the use of the mines and entrusting Germany with political control. The only result would be

[1] A.C.N.P., 302, 185.1134/4 and 185.1134/34. Item /34 is a three-page typed memorandum entitled 'The Saar Basin' and described in handwriting as a docket. The text refers to annexes, maps, etc., which are not attached, but elsewhere in vol. 302 are undated memoranda and maps which seem to line up with the references in the memorandum. Item /4 is marked 'A' and appears to contain the statement of points which were sent to Wilson and then by him to Clemenceau. There is no way of telling whether Wilson specifically approved them at this time.

[2] Haskins to Wilson, March 30, 1919, Wilson Papers, VIII-A-30, March 30.

'constant friction, undesirable in the interest of both the population of the region and of the growth of a good understanding between France and Germany'. Instead, Haskins thought, the Franco-German conflict of interests could best be reconciled by permitting the mines to be exploited for fifteen years or so by France under the auspices of the League of Nations, with the inhabitants assured of local liberty. At the end of the period, a plebiscite could be held by the League and the mines could be sold to the highest private bidder with the proceeds going to Germany less any balance due on reparation account.

Haskin's view of the advantages of this scheme was illuminating if only because this plan closely coincided with the final solution. France would secure the direct benefits of the mines during the reconstruction era. Their ultimate sale would help to liquidate Germany's reparation debt to France. Also, France would have a chance of acquiring the territory by free, popular vote. As for Germany, it would retain sovereignty, until the Saarlanders decided otherwise. Since Haskins believed that the permanent economic interests of the Saarlanders required association with the French economy, he probably hoped that material interests would influence them to prefer political union with France.[1]

When the Council of Four met on March 31, Wilson, submitting the proposals drafted by Haskins, Johnson, and Headlam-Morley two days before, accepted French ownership of the coal-mines and a special economic regime to facilitate French exploitation of their resources. Although the President did not make clear whether he favoured permanent ownership, he had retreated considerably from his initial position. His defense was simple: the plan was necessary to ensure that France received just compensation. Reiterating his opposition to annexations and to an autonomous Saar state, Wilson stressed the importance of not imposing governments of the victors' choice upon unwilling people and of not detaching them from their national group except where the intermingling of populations made this inevitable.

Lloyd George supported the proposals in principle. Clemen-

[1] Based upon a memorandum entitled 'The Saar Basin' bearing the notation 'Unofficial memo. C. H. Haskins 30 Mar. 19', A.C.N.P., 302, 185.1134/13.

ceau reserved his position. He sought in addition a special *political* regime.[1]

A fortnight of intense, wearing negotiations followed the decision to establish a special economic regime in the Saar. While the details of this regime had to be worked out, the major problem became the issue of sovereignty. Should the Saar be governed by France, by Germany, or under the League of Nations? If by Germany, would the special economic regime work? If by France, would not the charge of hypocrisy and *de facto* annexation be laid? How, too, should the rights and interests of the inhabitants be protected? These questions and ancillary ones like the issue of perpetual French ownership of the mines now preoccupied the Four and their advisors. Throughout, Lloyd George supported a special political regime for the Saar, with a preference for an autonomous state detached from Germany and linked to France as closely as possible.

To study the economic proposals, the Council appointed a special Committee on the Saar consisting of Headlam-Morley, Haskins, and Tardieu. As they worked, they and their chiefs were not concerned with the Saar alone. A complex series of issues faced the tiring negotiators, as House noted in his Diary: 'Saw Mezes, Haskins, and other of our experts many times during the day trying to work out some solution of the Dantzig, Sarre and the reparation controversies.'[2] The Rhineland, the Covenant, the carping press and other difficulties like the Bela Kun revolt could have been added to the Colonel's list.

Following the first meeting of the Saar Committee, Haskins advised Wilson that the strongest French point was the possibility of consulting the Saarlanders after having time to offset a hundred years of Prussification. He also predicted that friction would be more likely in a regime based upon French use of the mines under Prussian administration 'than in a temporary administration by France under a definite mandate with ample guarantees of all local liberties, especially in view of the obvious French interest to conciliate the population in view of an ultimate plebiscite'.[3]

Attached to this letter were proposals based upon Haskins'

[1] Mantoux, *Délibérations*, I, p. 89.

[2] House, Diary, XV, pp. 126-7.

[3] Haskins to Wilson, April 1, 1919, Wilson Papers, VIII-A-31.

conversations with his English and French colleagues. France would have permanent ownership of the mines, with full facilities for their exploitation. The mining area would be held by the League of Nations for fifteen years during which France would administer the territory as a mandatory power. Under the mandate, France would maintain law and order, including the authority to appoint officials. The area would be demilitarized. As for the local inhabitants, they would retain German citizenship, except for any who freely desired to become French nationals. The Saarlanders would retain their local representative assemblies, religious arrangements, law, language, and schools. They would be exempt from military service. On the other hand, they would not vote for representatives in the German Reichstag or the French Parliament. If any should wish to leave the territory, their right to dispose of their property on equitable terms would be protected. At the end of the fifteen-year period, the League of Nations would conduct a plebiscite, by communes or for the whole territory, to determine whether France or Germany would hold the Saar.[1] Haskins offered this programme to Wilson as a possible basis of agreement.

Haskins' advice was reinforced by other influences. Wickham Steed, of *The Times*, following a talk with Clemenceau, forwarded proposals to Wilson through House. House suggested to Wilson: 'Steed is a very old friend of Clemenceau's and it may be well to let him try his hand in this if you consider this (practical?).'[2] The striking feature of the Saar formula in Steed's letter was its similarity to Haskins' scheme, the major difference being that France should enjoy permanent ownership of the mines if time revealed the French mines had been permanently damaged by the Germans.

At the same time, the Saar Committee by April 6 produced an elaborate draft embodying the principle of French ownership of the Saar mines. The proposals were based upon Tardieu's initiative. Headlam-Morley and Haskins signed them. The Committee's draft plan for a special economic regime conferred ownership of all minerals in the Saar upon the French state 'which will have the perpetual right of working them or of not working them, or of transferring to a third party the right

[1] *Ibid.* [2] *Ibid.*

of working them, without receiving any previous authorisation or fulfilling any formalities'.

One can only admire the thoroughness of Tardieu's plan to ensure the effective functioning of the special economic regime. Among the provisions were the following. No differential tariffs or other obstacles were to be imposed on railways and canals for the transport of goods and persons connected with the mines. The French state was to have the right even to set timetables for workers' trains in the coal basin and adjacent districts. Germany was not to take measures regulating the recruitment, dismissal, or wages of employees of the French state in the Saar. The use of French or foreign labour was not to be impeded. As for schools, the French state was to have the right of organizing, incidental to its ownership of the mines, primary or technical schools and of providing instruction within the schools in the French language according to programmes and with teachers of its own choice.

In the article on the protection of labour and property, Tardieu provided for the right to appoint private watchmen for the surveillance of the properties. The mines, their subsidiaries and accessories were to be free from all German mining, industrial, or social regulations unless the French government specifically consented to them. In addition, the Saar was to enter the French customs system. Article XVI, contained the only recognition in the whole draft of any German interest in these arrangements: the French state was not to levy an export tax upon metallurgical products of the Saar basin which were exported to Germany. The final article forbade any restriction upon the circulation of French money in the Saar or its use in connection with the mines.[1]

Haskins advised House and Wilson:

> While the draft is subject to changes in technical detail, it appears to contain in substance the just and necessary basis for working these mines, regard being had not only to the greatest efficiency of operation but also to the interests of the workmen and the general prosperity of the basin.
>
> If these articles, the substance of which appears economically and socially necessary, were to be applied without the establish-

[1] Wilson Papers, VIII-A-33, April 6, 1919; A.C.N.P., 302, 185.1134/16; Miller, *Diary*, VIII, pp. 26-33.

ment of some special political and administrative regime, serious friction and conflict would inevitably arise.[1]

The Saar Committee's report was condemned as impractical by Lloyd George in the Council of Four on April 8. The combination of French ownership of the mines and German sovereignty would only produce disputes. Instead he favoured an independent state under the League of Nations but joined to the French customs union. The latter Lloyd George justified by contending that without Alsace and Briey the Saar could not exist economically. In his view, this solution had other advantages. The Saarlanders would not be made French against their will. They would retain their linguistic, legislative, and administrative rights. At the same time, a buffer state larger than Luxembourg would have been formed.

Indeed, Lloyd George was in an expansive mood as he envisaged applying the regime to the entire industrial region up to the Moselle whose economic life depended upon the mines. According to the Prime Minister, Haskins was impressed by this solution and Headlam-Morley, who strongly opposed French annexation of the Saar, believed the Basin could not live unless established as an independent political unit. Lloyd George breezily hoped that after a few years a plebiscite would show the Saarlanders were unwilling to return to Germany.

House, representing the ailing Wilson, seemed to react favourably.[2] Clemenceau was non-committal, merely observing Wilson had granted that the political and administrative implications of a special economic regime required study.

Lloyd George finally submitted three different plans, expressing a preference for the second: local sovereignty under the League's authority; a local parliament; *a mandate given to France which would name the governor;* absorption within the French customs union; and neutralization. Was this the scheme

[1] Wilson Papers, VIII-A-33, April 6, 1919.

[2] House's reaction appears in another light in this confidence to his Diary later that day: 'George wished to read several plans which he said he had in mind for the settlement of the Sarre Basin. He started in to read them but since they were of no earthly value, I asked to be excused, alleging that I had an urgent engagement with the President. . . .' House, Diary, XV, p. 144, April 8, 1919.

he had had in mind earlier in the meeting: 'Je donnerais à ce pays l'indépendance, sous l'autorité de la Société des Nations'?[1]

The three draft schemes had been drafted by Headlam-Morley.[2] Scheme A left sovereignty with Germany while transferring all rights of administration and exploitation to France. Scheme B transferred sovereignty to the League of Nations while giving all rights of administration and exploitation to France. Otherwise, Scheme B was identical with Scheme A except in two details. Scheme A did not specifically forbid the new territory to contribute directly or indirectly to the armies of Germany. Scheme B omitted a provision whereby German nationals inhabiting the Saar Basin would *ipso facto* lose their German nationality and when outside the Saar Basin would have French diplomatic protection.

The identical provisions called for a French mandate to administer the demilitarized Saar Basin on behalf of the League of Nations. The French government would appoint the governor who would be responsible to it. The governor was to preserve the customary system of government, as far as possible. There would be a legislative assembly elected by universal manhood suffrage. Among its powers, the assembly would legislate in educational matters, but the execution of the educational laws would be in the hands of the governor. Facilities were to be provided for the education of children in the language of their parents. Freedom of worship was to be assured and the hierarchical organization of the different communions or their relations with their spiritual leaders were not to be interfered

[1] Mantoux, *Délibérations*, I, pp. 181-3. *P.P.C.*, V, pp. 60-1, contains a much shorter minute on the discussion which reads in part: 'Mr. Lloyd George said that the report prepared by M. Tardieu, Dr. Haskins, and Mr. Headlam-Morley on the Saar Valley was to the effect that no really workable scheme could be drawn up on the basis that they had been given.

'He thought therefore that it would be necessary to adopt some other scheme. He then read extracts from three alternative schemes which had been submitted to him at an earlier stage by Mr. Headlam-Morley. The scheme which attracted him most was scheme C, which would create a new state in the Saar Valley, somewhat larger than had hitherto been proposed, in customs union with France and for which France would have a mandate from the League of Nations. . . .'

[2] *P.P.C.*, V, pp. 69-71. The three schemes are also in Wilson Papers, VIII-A-33, April 8. Here drafts A and B are reversed compared to the titling in *P.P.C.* Confusion compounded!

with. No inhabitant was to be hindered from leaving the territory if he so wished.

The economic clauses of Scheme B provided for a Franco-Saar customs union. Former German public property was to pass to the Administration of the Saar. France would have an exclusive right to exploit the mines, to operate and develop the railways and waterways. Workmen were to be treated equally. Towards the expense of administration, the French government was to pay a fixed sum per ton of coal determined, along with other outstanding matters, in subsequent negotiations.

Scheme C provided for an independent Saar Republic linked to France by a customs union and whose foreign relations would be controlled in Paris. Within the Republic, the French government would have a privileged position, including the exclusive right to operate the mines, railways, and waterways. Title to these properties would, however, be vested in the Republic unless the French government purchased the railways and the waterways outright. Otherwise the Republic would be autonomous and demilitarized. An elected consituent assembly would draft an organic law providing for a legislature, for the judiciary, and for the administrative system. Freedom of worship would be guaranteed. Habitual inhabitants could opt for German citizenship.

What scheme did Lloyd George commend to the Council? He clearly rejected Scheme A. It would appear equally clear that he urged Scheme C: the independent Saar state. Indeed, the Hankey minutes read: 'The scheme which attracted him the most was scheme C. . . .' But according to both Hankey and Mantoux, Lloyd George referred to details in Scheme B, not in Scheme C. The conclusion seems inescapable that Lloyd George was confused. Probably he had hastily read or had had explained to him the two schemes shortly before he entered the meeting. Considering the pressures under which these men worked and the wide variety of unfamiliar matters coming up for decision, some confusion was understandable. Still, it was disorder at a high level on critical issues.

How far had Lloyd George moved since March 28? On each occasion the core of his position remained the same, although he had moved slightly away from the French position. Whether he proposed an autonomous or an independent Saar under the

League or under French mandate, his views ran counter to both Clemenceau's and Wilson's current opinions. The former wanted the Saar within France; the latter saw the establishment of a separate Saar state or special political regime as a violation of the right of self-determination. Lloyd George's ideas seemed open to a cool reception.

In the meantime, how was Wilson reacting to the proposed special economic regime? Around this time he wrote:

> SUGGESTION regarding the mines of the Saar district:
>
> Absolute control by the French of the entire output of the mines of the whole region for the period that will be required to put the mines of Northern France in complete working order; that period to be calculated upon a liberal basis by an inter-allied commission. No taxes or charges of any kind either by the German Government or by the private owners during that period.
>
> After the expiration of that period French consumers to be supplied with coal from these mines on exactly the same terms and under the same conditions as German consumers, without payment of any government charge or duty and without discrimination of any sort.[1]

He was clearly struggling with how to meet the short-run claim of France to reparations and the long-run claim to Saar coal to strengthen its political and economic position in relation to Germany. Wilson's opposition to perpetual French ownership of the mines appeared clearly, as well as his concern to limit French claims and to tie the proposed special arrangements closely to the principle of reparation. The final paragraph, which reflected the third of the Fourteen Points, foreshadowed the final solution of the long-run supply problem.

Wilson's resistant attitude may have been strengthened by Bernard Baruch, who queried why the Saar mines should go to France and termed the report of the Saar Committee unfair to Germany.[2] Baruch, alone of the President's advisors in the next few days, resisted the settlement which was being worked out.

[1] Wilson Papers, VIII-A-33, April 6, 1919. This is a typed note on paper embossed WOODROW WILSON. No date is typed in. On top a pencilled note reads '(c.Apr. 6, 1919?)' and on the back a note reads '(Written by W. W. on his own typewriter)'. These notes were probably written by Ray Stannard Baker. They do not establish April 6 as the definite date on which Wilson wrote this memorandum.

[2] Wilson Papers, VIII-A-33, April 7, 1919.

After Wilson had studied the report of the Saar Committee, he made two amendments. By the first, the President sought to limit the scope of the original provision which seemed to give the French a general right to control the entire educational system of the Saar Valley on the primary and technical levels and thus open the way to the Gallicization of the Saar population. The other amendment applied to article XI which read:

> In case of disorder or conflict the German Government shall have the obligation to assure protection to the employees and the property of the French State. Reparation for damage to the one or the other shall be at the cost of the German Government.

Wilson inserted the words at the beginning of the second sentence: 'If it fails in that duty, etc. . . .' The President's wording limited the obligations of the German government. If the German government did all in its power to avert damage and yet damage occurred, under Wilson's amendment it would not be responsible for reparation. His concern for just treatment seems very evident in these instances.[1]

The report and Wilson's amendments, together with a note on Baruch's criticisms, were handed to Miller by Colonel House with the comment: '. . . the President was willing to take this and to agree to it if I (Miller) possibly could. . . .'[2] After consulting Haskins, Miller prepared a draft embodying the principle of German sovereignty over the Saar and the maintenance of the political and civil rights of German subjects in the area. To settle conflicts arising out of the special economic regime, Miller advised a Permanent Commission of Arbitration. His proposal also provided for a plebiscite at the end of fifteen years to determine the issue of sovereignty. In articles V and VI we may see the origins of the clause in the draft treaty of May 7 which the German delegation so tellingly excoriated:

> V. On such of the said territory as shall remain German . . . the property rights of the Government of France under these articles shall be taken over as a whole by Germany at a price payable in gold which shall be determined by three appraisers, or a majority of them. . . .
>
> VI. The price so fixed shall be payable within . . . after the determination thereof and unless the said price so fixed shall be

[1] Miller, *Diary*, VIII, Documents 715 and 716. [2] *Ibid.*, I, pp. 227-8.

> then paid by Germany to the Government of France, the territory which would otherwise remain German shall thereafter be occupied and administered by France as an integral portion of French territory.

The immediate importance of the two articles was their affirmation of the principle of temporary French ownership of the mines in areas remaining German after the plebiscite had been held. Other amendments proposed by Miller sought to protect the rights of the individual against the French state, to assure equality of treatment for Saar workers, and to allow local importation from Germany into the Saar without customs duties.[1] He assured House and Wilson that the plan as a whole was '. . . in accordance with the principles of the President and in particular in accordance with those stated in the Fourteen Points and that these provisions would be so generally regarded'.[2]

At the afternoon meeting on April 8 of the Council of Four, Wilson rejected Lloyd George's proposal, made that morning, for a semi-independent Saar state and advanced Miller's proposals for a Permanent Arbitration Commission and a plebiscite.[3]

Both Clemenceau and Lloyd George objected to the retention of German sovereignty and to the arbitration commission. The French Prime Minister doubted that Wilson's plan would give France security of exploitation. Wilson contended his proposal would eliminate the political difficulties of an immediate transfer of sovereignty. Lloyd George remarked that, according to his advisors, the successful working of the economic regime proposed by Tardieu was incompatible with German sovereignty. Wilson, in reply, stressed that France would have police powers. Lloyd George agreed the scheme amounted to virtual French annexation, but feared that if Germany retained sovereignty and could intervene in the Saar, it could cause trouble. Wilson firmly repeated his opposition 'à l'idée de créer arbitrairement un Etat indépendant de la vallée de la Sarre'. In his opinion, the difficulties foreseen were largely imaginary: the commission of arbitration would prevent or regulate

[1] Ibid., VIII, pp. 21-5; see also A.C.N.P., 302, 185.1134/3.

[2] Miller, *Diary*, I, pp. 228-9, and VIII, Document 136.

[3] These proposals took the form of a 'Note du President Wilson sur la Sarre'.

differences; and the plebiscite would decide the fate of the basin.

The session ended with this sharp exchange:

M. CLEMENCEAU. Nous examinerons cela; mais je crains qu'un tel système ne puisse conduire qu'à des disputes sans fin.

LE PRESIDENT WILSON. Je vous demande instamment de ne pas suspendre la paix du monde à cette question de la Sarre.

M. CLEMENCEAU. Non, mais la paix du monde exige que nous éstablissions d'abord la justice entre nous.

LE PRESIDENT WILSON. Nous avons passé, à mon avis, beaucoup trop de temps à discuter les questions qui intéressent exclusivement les quatre puissances représentées ici.

M. LLOYD GEORGE. Ce sont, après tout, celles qui ont porté ensemble le fardeau de la guerre.[1]

Tardieu worked through the night to prepare a rebuttal which was handed to Wilson and Lloyd George during the morning of April 9. In this forceful riposte, Tardieu sought to strike through a chink in the President's armour by pointing out that Wilson, in his note of April 8, had recognized the inevitability of conflicts between France and Germany under the proposed Saar regime. According to the French argument, an arbitration commission would facilitate disputes and delays because, if the German administrative organization remained intact, each economic measure taken by the French government could be indefinitely held up by the German authorities, who, among other things, could simply start an action before the arbitral tribunal.

His Note accused Wilson of bad faith in promising, on March 31, perpetual French ownership of the mines while envisaging, on April 8, the loss of this right within fifteen years. Tardieu bluntly asserted: 'La France ne peut pas y souscrire.' Moreover, if the Saarlanders were to vote freely in fifteen years, the minimum condition was freedom from 'l'oppression de l'administration prussienne qu'elle subit depuis cent ans'. As Tardieu pointed out, Wilson's note of April 8 withheld this freedom.

The Note thus rejected any solution which would enable Germany to checkmate the exercise of a French economic mandate in the Saar. What, then, would the French govern-

[1] Mantoux, *Délibérations*, I, p. 194.

ment accept? It supported any one of the three schemes advanced by Lloyd George, supplemented by Wilson's suggestions—a plebiscite at the end of fifteen years and an arbitral tribunal.[1]

Thus the French delegation, dropping the system for piecemeal annexation, accepted a plebiscite conducted by the League to decide the ultimate fate of the Saar. Simultaneously, the French held fast to the claim for permanent ownership of the mines. Perhaps the emphasis on Wilson's alleged acceptance on March 31 of perpetual French ownership may have been intentionally exaggerated to give the acceptance of a plebiscite the appearance of a major concession in return for which a complementary gain could be made. By accepting the British alternatives, the French delegation attempted to secure British support in the drive to win Wilson's consent to a special administrative and political regime for the Saar.

Wilson now stood isolated on this issue. His position was difficult. He had adamantly opposed a semi-independent Saar state and was equally unwilling to accept the idea of a French political mandate. But he had conceded first the French right to use the mines and then a special economic regime. Both logic and the combined pressure of Lloyd George, Clemenceau, and of men like Haskins within his circle of advisors were pushing him towards accepting special political-administrative arrangements. Wilson probably had not thought the issue through. Obviously he depended upon Miller, for example, for substantial counter-proposals to the idea of a full-fledged special administrative-political regime for the Saar. The concept of an arbitration commission to bridge the gap between French economic rights and German political rights in the Saar seems to have been Miller's, not his. Wilson filled the vacuum in his thoughts with it, and, fortified with Miller's sheet of paper, went grimly forth to the council room determined, stubborn, but brittle. Under the almost overwhelming logicality of Tardieu's case and the bland persuasiveness of Lloyd George, Wilson dropped the idea of an arbitral commission and gradually moved closer to the French position.

Lloyd George, at the morning meeting, April 9, of the Four,

[1] Wilson Papers, VIII-A-34, April 9, 1919; Miller, *Diary*, VIII, p. 148; House Papers, 30/169.

called upon his colleagues to take the French note seriously. Wilson replied:

> Ce qui rend malaisée la solution de ce problème, c'est que la seule justification certaine de tout ce que nous pouvons faire dans le bassin de la Sarre est le droit de la France à la réparation de ses pertes économiques: cela ne justifie pas un changement de souveraineté territoriale.

Lloyd George countered: 'Il y a le fait qu'une partie de la population de ce district a gardé des sentiments antiprussiens.' Lloyd George brought forward no evidence to sustain this claim, which had not been proven on this or on previous occasions; the French spokesmen had simply repeated the pretension so often that, it seems, Lloyd George had accepted their claim as true. He pressed Wilson to accept a special political regime for the Saar in return for the French concession in accepting a plebiscite.[1]

Wilson at last agreed although Baruch had advised him to provide in the reparations settlement for the distribution of Saar coal. Perhaps Baruch's strong feeling that a division of rights between France and Germany would be 'a constant source of turmoil and unending friction'[2] helped to turn Wilson away from his position of April 8. He had conceded too much, however, to go in the direction urged by Baruch. After the morning meeting on April 9, Wilson instructed Miller and Haskins to draft articles providing for a Commission of Administration for the Saar and for a plebiscite at the end of fifteen years. Wilson consulted Haskins by telephone about their work.[3] Probably his substantive proposals at that meeting reflected this conversation.

The afternoon session of the Council of Four proved decisive.[4]

[1] Mantoux, *Délibérations*, I, p. 196.

[2] Baruch to Wilson, Wilson Papers, VIII-A-34, April 9, 1919.

[3] A.C.N.P., 302, 185.1134/34. Miller and Haskins worked through the afternoon to prepare a draft letter and a memorandum in reply to the French note of April 9. These documents did not reach Wilson, evidently, because as Miller explains: '. . . the President telephoned to Dr. Haskins and as they could not be gotten ready by 5 o'clock, and in the meantime Dr. Haskins had a meeting with Tardieu, Aubert, and Headlam-Morley, the latter representing the British, we decided to hold the papers until we saw whether we could agree with them or not.' Miller, *Diary*, I, pp. 230-1.

[4] Mantoux, *Délibérations*, I, pp. 203-7.

Wilson began by criticizing the three British projects because they implied German renunciation of sovereignty over the Saar and thus prejudged the result of the plebiscite. He believed any plan which placed sovereignty in League hands, and confided a mandate to France 'ne donnerait au problème qu'une solution ambigué'. And he added:

> De plus, comme je l'ai déjà dit tres franchement, j'ai peur d'une solution de ce genre pour des raisons de principe. Je ne veux cependant pas m'attacher avec raideur à la lettre du principe, si l'on peut arriver à une solution raisonnable. Ce que je repousserais, c'est un système qui préjugerait du resultat du plébiscite.

He put his objection more directly later: 'La dernière solution proposée donnerant en réalité le pays à la France, avec un plébiscite qui ne serait plus guere qu'une formalité. Il y a là une objection qui est pour moi insurmontable. . . .'

The President plainly feared that the British schemes kept open the way towards the gallicization of the Saar. While Wilson had come to accept a special economic and political regime in the Saar, he was unconvinced that the Saarlanders sought to leave the German for the French fold. He suspected that the French would take advantage of a special economic and political regime to coerce the Saarlanders into accepting permanent French rule. Such a course would be a more subtle but none the less just as substantial a violation of the right of national self-determination as would immediate and outright annexation. Wilson opposed such a violation of principle not just because he held firmly to principle *per se* but also because he feared the undermining, corrosive and 'cynicizing' effects of a settlement which patently contradicted the promises and legal obligations of the victors. On the other hand, Wilson sympathetically accepted the French claim to Saar coal especially during the period of reconstruction. Even if he was not impressed by the claim that the Saar was French as well as German in character, he could not ignore the emotional strength of the French plea and he had to search for a way of satisfying the French by giving them an opportunity of securing the Saar by the free vote of its inhabitants.

Thus in place of the British projects he proposed

d'obliger l'Allemagne à laisser pendant quinze ans ce pays sous l'administration d'une commission nommée par la Société des Nations et responsible devant elle. La population conserverait ses lois, ses institutions actuelles, la commission ayant le pouvoir d'y apporter les modifications rendues nécessaires par le régime économique spécial institué par le traité. Je donnerais en même temps à cette commission les fonctions d'un tribunal d'arbitrage pour régler tous les litiges auxquels pourrait donner lieu l'application du traité, en même temps qu'elle aurait le pouvoir législatif et le pouvoir éxecutif dans toute la region.

Des règles fondamentales seraient établies pour assurer à la population l'entière liberté religieuse, le respect de ses institutions scolaires, etc. . . . En somme, la souveraineté de l'Allemagne serait suspendue pendant une période de quinze ans, et à la fin de cette période, la population déciderait elle même de son sort par un plébiscite.

Lloyd George's immediate reaction was favourable, but Clemenceau asked why, if German sovereignty were suspended and administration confided to the League of Nations, the League should not give a mandate to France? Wilson made this strong response to Clemenceau's embarrassing question:

je cherche de toutes mes forces une solution qui vous satisfasse et qui me satisfasse: je n'en vois pas d'acceptable avec l'abolition de la souveraineté allemande. Les déclarations que nous avons faites, les engagements que j'ai pris promettent à la France la réparation du tort qui lui a été fait en 1871. Peut-être aurait-il mieux valu dire: 'Le tort fait à la France en Alsace-Lorraine', ou toute autre formule qui aurait compris la violation des droits de la France en 1815. Mais il n'a été parlé que du traité de Francfort et nous sommes liés par ce que nous avons dit. . . .

Je vous demande de m'aider à trouver une voie dans votre direction. J'ai fait beaucoup de pas à votre rencontre; ne me rendez pas impossible de vous aider autant que je puis.

The British Prime Minister now began strongly to support Wilson.

M. LLOYD GEORGE. Ce qui importe avant tout pour la France c'est d'avoir la houille de la Sarre.

M. CLEMENCEAU. Cela dépend du public auquel vous pensez: pour les industriels français, évidemment. Mais le reste de la France attache à la région de la Sarre une autre importance.

M. LLOYD GEORGE. Il faut arriver à une solution qui donne à la France la houille de la Sarre sans créer pour l'avenir de nouvelles causes de conflit. Le document critiqué par M. Tardieu ne remplissait pas cette condition et les critiques de M. Tardieu étaient justes. Mais les mêmes objections ne portent pas contre ce que vient de proposer le Président Wilson. La souveraineté de l'Allemagne serait suspendue pendant la période de quinze ans qui doit precédér le plébiscite. Pendant ces quinze ans, la France aura le temps de se rétablir économiquement, et, à l'expiration de ce délai, la région de la Sarre sera tellement liée à la France par ses intérêts qu'elle ira volontairement vers elle.

M. CLEMENCEAU. Je ne fais pas d'objection à ce projet. Je voudrais seulement qu'il fût examiné attentivement par mes conseillers.

To get a quick decision, Lloyd George proposed that they consult their experts immediately. The exchange with Headlam-Morley and Tardieu led Wilson to suggest no mention be made of the word 'sovereignty'; they need only to say that administration of the Saar passed into the hands of the League for fifteen years. And he summed up his position as follows:

> Le point essential, à mes yeux, est de ne pas trancher la question de souveraineté et d'assurer le respect des institutions locales, sauf dans la mesure où il est peut-être nécessaire de les accommoder aux nécessités du nouveau régime économique.

Lloyd George urged local autonomy on the ground that nothing would aid more to detach the Saarlanders from Prussia because 'une population qui a acquis ce genre de droits ne veut plus en être privée'. Unfortunately for this liberal faith, the Saarlanders, like many people, were to prefer values other than those of freedom!

Throughout the meeting Wilson appeared acutely self-conscious, apparently aware of having been driven from position to position and now anxious to be both conciliatory and firm. Having accepted the idea of a special political regime, he sought to limit its scope to the functions solely necessary for the operation of the special economic regime. He also was working to square the proposed settlement with the principle of national self-determination by avoiding all appearance of prejudging the final decision on sovereignty and of conferring undue power upon the French to influence that decision.

Particularly striking was Lloyd George's pragmatic, balancing role. Initially, he had taken a position favourable to the substance of the French claims, partly under the influence of the Anglo-American experts. Possibly surprised by Wilson's first position on the Saar Question, Lloyd George had pressed moderation and concessions upon him. Now, after Wilson had come a long way towards meeting the French viewpoint (and the British) Lloyd George, quick to perceive that differences had been reduced almost to the vanishing point, backed Wilson and sought to persuade Clemenceau to accept the President's proposals for a special political regime. How simple and attractive the Welshman made the prospects seem for Clemenceau: you will get your coal and your valley too!

Instructed by the Four to prepare a report based on the discussion, the Saar Committee worked until midnight.[1] It justified French ownership and exploitation of the mines on compensatory grounds and as part payment of Germany's reparation debt. The economic, administrative, and political articles were upheld as necessary to assure the rights and welfare of the population and to ensure to France the essential conditions for effectively using the mines. Annex I established a special economic regime as envisaged by the Saar Committee on April 7, with the proviso that amendments would be required if Annex II were approved. The latter provided for the Commission of Administration and related politico-judicial matters.

[1] Miller, *Diary*, I, pp. 231-2. Headlam-Morley, Miller, and Tardieu each had a working paper which formed the basis of their negotiations. The British draft left sovereignty in German hands while providing for German renunciation of the right of administration over the Saar which would be administered by a commission appointed by the League of Nations. In these as in other respects, it was close to Miller's plan. More detailed than the Headlam-Morley and Miller working papers, the Tardieu draft was identical in certain major respects. It differed in such details as providing for majority decisions in the procedure of the Commission and in specifically barring the Saarlanders from choosing representatives for either German or French parliamentary assemblies.

The most substantial difference lay in article XV which described the mines as the perpetual property of the French state. If any of them fell within German territory after the plebiscite Germany and France would arrange under the auspices of the League for their exploitation under conditions favourable to France. On this issue Miller maintained the position taken in his proposals of April 8. Miller, *Diary*, VIII, pp. 159-61.

In substance it followed Tardieu's working paper. Article I, however, preserved German sovereignty over the Saar. Another significant change from the Tardieu memorandum was in article VIII which expressly prohibited the Commission of Administration from imposing new taxes without consulting the elected representatives of the Saarlanders. Annex III elaborately spelled out the arrangements for the plebiscite. Reluctantly and tentatively, Tardieu accepted the American delegation's position on the transfer of the mines from French to German ownership in any areas remaining to Germany after the plebiscite. In this eventuality, according to the Annex, the property rights of the French government should be taken over by Germany at a price determined by appraisers and payable in gold. The way was left open for another type of property settlement between France and Germany before the deadline for payment in gold.

Next morning, Wilson approved the report of the Saar Committee, but Clemenceau wanted sovereignty transferred to the League of Nations. Lloyd George suggested that the word 'sovereignty' be not mentioned and that they simply stipulate that Germany abandon administration to the Allied and Associated Powers as trustees of the League. Wilson objected that the Allied and Associated Powers lacked juridical personality whereas the League would; therefore, have Germany renounce its administrative rights in favour of the League. Lloyd George accepted this, but Clemenceau turned it down since it left sovereignty in German hands. At this point, Orlando suggested that it was a question of words; in Italian and French 'administration' had a narrower meaning than in English; therefore, why not use the word 'government'? The Four agreed to avoid specifically posing the issue of sovereignty. The word would be dropped, and 'administration' changed to 'government'.[1]

While the giants played with words, their technical advisors waited in the anteroom, where Tardieu told Haskins and Miller that his delegation had rejected the tentative proposals covering German re-purchase of the mines.[2] This aroused intense debate among the Four. Clemenceau insisted France must retain the right of ownership. Lloyd George opposed, with a cogent

[1] Haskins saw no objection to this. Mantoux, *Délibérations*, I, pp. 209-10.

[2] Miller, *Diary*, I, p. 233.

argument against which Clemenceau and Tardieu had no effective defense. The Council had already accepted Tardieu's argument that the economic and the administrative arrangements were inseparable. Clemenceau's proposal opened the way to continual conflicts resulting from French ownership under German administration. Tardieu weakly retorted that Franco-German relations might be very different in fifteen years compared to 1919. Moreover, he contended gold could never replace the coal which France needed so badly: '. . . il faut que nous puissons assurer notre fourniture de charbon et qu'une stipulation en ce sens figure dans le traité'. To this, Wilson, who backed Lloyd George, replied that the normal play of economic forces would make Saar coal available to Lorraine. Lloyd George concurred, adding that within fifteen years the French would have regained the use of the mines in northern France. These contentions led Tardieu to suggest imposing the obligation upon Germany to continue supplying France with coal. Wilson objected to transforming an economic relationship into a political obligation. He asked: 'Que feriez-vous si l'Allemagne prenait un engagement et refusait ensuite de le tenir? Lui déclareriez-vous la guerre pour cela?' Finally, Clemenceau asked for twenty-four or forty-eight hours to make up his mind.

Probably the French delegation insisted upon the right of ownership of the mines after the plebiscite to have a powerful weapon in later economic-political negotiations with Germany. In any efforts to pry pre-plebiscitary promises from Germany to supply coal to France at reasonable prices and in adequate quantity after the fifteen-year period, the right of ownership could be a powerful lever. But on April 10 the prospects of securing this right were dim in view of Lloyd George's and Wilson's combined opposition. Indeed, could the French even secure a provision obligating Germany to supply Saar coal after a plebiscite unfavourable to France?

Before adjourning, they decided that the frontiers of the Saar would be drawn to the limits of the coal basin itself, with the modifications necessary to have the boundary coincide with the limits of existing administrative entities.[1]

[1] Mantoux, *Délibérations*, I, pp. 209-13. Miller gives a list of the amendments to the draft proposals of April 9 in his *Diary*, VIII, pp. 202-3. In addition to the major changes which Mantoux noted, article III of annex II

Thus, by noon on April 10, the Four had reached agreement on all substantive issues except the problem of ownership of the mines after the plebiscite. In the Council next day, Loucheur, as French spokesman, dropped the demand for perpetual ownership of the mines. Instead, he requested the right of option to supplies of German coal equivalent to the average annual French consumption of Saar coal in the three years preceding the plebiscite and at the same price as on the internal German market.

Typically, at least in these negotiations, Wilson's initial reaction was negative: execution of such a clause would be difficult; the danger of conflict was present. Naturally, Loucheur doubted this; Germany was not being wronged by such an arrangement and had coal to spare; besides, the danger of halting French industrial production was graver than the possible conflicts which might arise. Lloyd George tended to favour Loucheur's proposal. He saw nothing humiliating or abusive in it; it avoided the tensions inherent in any settlement resting upon French ownership and German sovereignty. And if Germany had a legitimate reason to complain about the execution of the arrangement, it could appeal to the League of Nations. Wilson continued to argue against the proposal, while Lloyd George upheld it, until, finally, the President hesitated: . . . he did not see a principle involved; . . . nor did he fear an injustice; . . . he simply sought the best and most pacific

---

was changed from 'The Commission will consist of five members chosen by the Council of the League of Nations, of whom one shall be . . . a German subject, the latter an inhabitant of the Basin of the Saar . . .' to 'The Commission will consist of five members chosen by the Council of the League of Nations of whom one shall be . . . a *native* inhabitant of the Basin of the Saar (not French) . . .'.

A new clause was also to follow after article V of annex II to the effect: 'The value of the property ceded to France shall be credited as part payment of the amount due for reparation from Germany to France. This value shall be determined by the Reparation Commission.' Miller had evidently suggested a separate mixed commission, but Wilson advised that the Reparation Commission be given the chore. This was the substitute, evidently, for the original proposal which read: 'The use of the property in the Saar Basin belonging to the Imperial German Government, or the Government of any German State will pass to the Administration of the Saar Basin, subject to reasonable compensation.' Miller, *Diary*, I, p. 233, and VIII, pp. 209 and 168.

practical solution; . . . but he was no prophet, . . . etc. Finally, on Wilson's own suggestion, the French were to prepare a draft embodying Loucheur's formula and then to reach agreement on it with the other technical advisors.

Having sharpened his lance in this encounter, Lloyd George returned to the lists to joust with unflagging persistence for the cause of an independent Saar. The plebiscite, he said, should offer a third choice: a separate Saar state under the League of Nations. Lloyd George's calculation seems obvious: while the Saarlanders probably would not accept French sovereignty, they might vote for semi-independent status under international auspices. France, thereby, would permanently gain the substance of its aims in the region and Germany correspondingly weakened.[1]

During the afternoon of April 11, in the Saar Committee, Headlam-Morley, personally opposed to Lloyd George's plebiscitary proposal, supported it in pursuance of his instructions. Loucheur made clear that his government wanted the coal-supply agreement with Germany to be perpetual and assured the Committee that the French government was ready to buy the agreed quantity of coal on a permanent basis. But not until the next day did Loucheur and Baruch reach agreement on a formula.[2]

On the evening of the 13th the Saar Committee's report to the Four was accepted. The coal-supply formula ran as follows:

> If the ownership of the mines, or a part thereof, passes to Germany, it is understood that France or French nationals will have a just claim to the use of such coal of the Sarre Basin as their industrial and domestic needs will be found at that time to require. An equitable arrangement regarding amounts, time of contract and prices will be fixed at that time by the Council of the League of Nations.[3]

Lloyd George's proposal was also adopted, thus providing the voters in the plebiscite with three choices: maintenance of the treaty regime; union with France; or union with Germany. In each case, the decision could apply to all or part of

[1] Mantoux, *Délibérations*, I, pp. 224-8.
[2] Miller, *Diary*, I, pp. 241-3.
[3] A.C.N.P., 302, 185.1134/5.

the territory.[1] Finally, they decided the Saar frontier would follow administrative lines.[2] (See Map 3.)

At the beginning of this chapter Lloyd George's assertion was noted that the British delegation opposed the French claims to the Saar for fear of creating another Alsace-Lorraine. Few better examples could be found of the sometimes tendentious and unreliable character of *The Truth About the Treaties*. Within the British delegation there was much support for the cession to France of all or part of the Saar. Lloyd George's own attitude was ambivalent as he gyrated among the contending elements, especially between Wilson and Clemenceau. He came basically to support an autonomous, neutralized Saar state, detached from Germany and placed under French suzerainty. Thus he would give France the substance if not the form of its claims in an effort further to redress the balance between France and Germany without violating the principle of self-determination. It may be doubted whether this solution would have avoided a new 'Alsace-Lorraine'. In any case Lloyd George failed to sever the Saar permanently from Germany, largely because Woodrow Wilson fought a stubborn defensive battle which succeeded not only in rebuffing the extreme French claims but also in deflecting Lloyd George from his goal. Although Lloyd George had to accept the plebiscite and other Wilsonian features of the final Saar settlement, he and his delegation kept open the possibility of maintaining the separation of the Saar from Germany.

[1] *Ibid.* The Committee's formula read: '(*a*) Si le vote conclut (pour tout ou partie du territoire) au maintien du régime establi par le présent traité, l'Allemagne s'engage à faire, en faveur de la Société des Nations, toute renonciation que celle-ci jugera nécessaire. La Société des Nations prendra les mesures appropriées pour adapter le régime nouveau à l'intérêt permanent du bassin et au bien général . . . .'

[2] *Ibid.*

XI

CZECHOSLOVAKIA, AUSTRIA, AND GREATER GERMANY

THE settlement of Germany's southern frontier raised two important questions at Paris: the German-Czech boundary and whether to permit the union of the Austrian and the German Republics. Unlike the west and the east where territory was being taken from Germany, in the south as a result of the dissolution of the Dual Monarchy German-populated lands could be attached to the Reich. For Germany, the addition of some ten million German-speaking peoples and of valuable resources and industries would partly counter-balance territorial losses elsewhere. For the principal Allied and Associated Powers, the southern boundary question obliged them to strike a balance between conflicting national, strategic, and economic considerations.

I

The problem of the German-Czech frontier graphically illustrated the difficulties of applying the principle of nationality. The Allies had adopted a policy of reconstructing south-central Europe upon the basis of nation-states. Thus, a strong, durable Czechoslovak nation-state was to be founded to give the Czechs and the Slovaks control of their own internal and external affairs. Their new independent status would be largely a sham if the settlement of their frontiers subjected them strategically and economically to a powerful neighbour. Yet a strategic and economic frontier was unattainable without including the fringe areas of Bohemia and Moravia with their German-speaking majorities. *If* these peoples preferred union with Germany rather than with Czechoslovakia, a viable Czech nation-state could only be created by violating the principle of national self-determination. Yet, the new state would lack internal cohesion if it included a large, hostile German-speaking minority which sought the protection of and even union with the Reich. A German irredentist movement in Bohemia and Moravia would imperil the security of the Czech nation-state as well as constantly endangering the peace and stability of south-central Europe. In attempting to reconcile conflicting promises and considerations, the technicians and statesmen at Paris faced a difficult task indeed.

The Czechs demanded the historic frontiers of the ancient Czech kingdom, comprising the three provinces, Bohemia, Moravia and Silesia, with certain additions for which they were prepared to make minor territorial concessions.[1] According to their general argument, these claims were justified by the principle of nationality and would not adversely affect the vital interests of Germany.

Since they could not avoid the problem of the German-speaking minority in Bohemia and Moravia, the Czechs at Paris set out to prove that it was 'at bottom, a very easy one to solve'.[2] Their argument ran smoothly. Over 1,000,000 Germans in Bohemia were conjured away by charging that the Austrians had systematically falsified the language statistics and had exerted pressure upon Czechs to declare themselves German. Further, it was alleged, few purely German districts existed because the Czechs and Germans were so intermixed. The Bohemian Germans, moreover, in the frontier areas were divided into three geographically separated groups, which could neither be formed into a self-governing German province within the Czech state nor be united with German Austria. If

[1] 'The Territorial Claims of the Czecho-Slovak Republic'. Délégation Tchécoslovaque, Mémoire No. 2, A.C.N.P., 298, 185.1126/2. The Czech *mémoires* 1-11 are reproduced in A. G. de Lapradelle, *La Documentation internationale: la paix de Versailles*, vol. 9, pp. 18-138.

[2] 'Problems Touching the Germans of Bohemia', Délégation Tchécoslovaque, Mémoire No. 3, A.C.N.P., 298, 185.1126/3.

the Bohemian Germans did not remain in the Czech state, they could only join Germany.

The latter solution was attacked on several grounds. Economically, the Czechs contrasted the geographic and economic isolation of the highly industrialized fringe areas from Germany with the links between them and the interior of Bohemia. To sever the border regions from Czechoslovakia would weaken its economy and threaten Czech subordination to Germany, while if the German Bohemians joined Germany they would face economic ruin. As a result, the Germans would seek to extend their influence over Prague. As the memoire put it:

> The fatal consequence, then, of the separation of these German regions from Bohemia would lead to the whole of Bohemia being coveted by Germany who might take possession of it without violence, through her economic expansion and penetration, or else through the force of arms.[1]

If the Germans held the belt of natural mountain fortresses around Bohemia '. . . they could at any moment, invade the whole of Bohemia and no Czech government could offer the least resistance'.

After arguing that the Czechs had the better historic right to these areas because the Germans in Bohemia were 'mere colonists', the memoire glossed over or explained away the opinions and aspirations of the Bohemian Germans. The Peace Conference was assured:

> 1. That the Germans of Bohemia do not represent united element [*sic*], properly organized and led towards a definite aim.
> 2. That they have no leaders enjoying the confidence of the people, and that there is in Bohemia no really strong popular movement entitled to invoke the principle of the rights of nations to decide their own fate.
> 3. That, on the contrary those among the Germans of Bohemia who are at present capable of clearly expressing a political idea, declare, willy-nilly that their economic interests urge the Germans of Bohemia to prefer the Czecho-Slovak State to a great Germany; and that the union of German Bohemia to Germany is an illusion.[2]

The protests of the Bohemian Germans were dismissed as the

[1] *Ibid.*, No. 3. [2] *Ibid.*

product of a noisy, Pan-German minority. The numerous, 'reasonable' German peasants, industrialists, and workers 'who are aware of the real political and economic necessities of the situation' were ready, it was alleged, quietly and fearlessly to remain within Czechoslovakia.

Only one argument could be seen in favour of the separation of the Bohemian German regions from Czechoslovakia: 'The principle of nationality applied to the limit, taking language as the criterion.' In this instance the Czech delegation rejected this principle on the grounds of higher necessity—that of the survival of the Czech nation—and appealed: 'It is then necessary to make sacrifices in favour of those who deserve it and to offer sufficient guarantees of their honest desire of peace, above all in a case like this one where it is a question of Czechoslovaks and Germans.'

Recognizing the need for assurances on minority rights, the Czech memoire claimed that the Czechs were too sensible to risk a policy of violence and injustice towards the German minority. While promising to accept any international regime to safeguard national minorities, they said the Czech state was ready to forestall such provisions by giving the Bohemian Germans privileges under which '. . . the Germans in Bohemia would have the same rights as the Czechoslovaks themselves. The German tongue would be the second tongue of the land and no vexatious measures would be taken against the German population. The regime adopted would be similar to that of Switzerland.'[1]

On February 5, 1919, Beneš, the Czech Minister of Foreign Affairs, presented his government's territorial claims to the Council of Ten.[2] In his particularly adroit introduction, the

[1] The Czech portfolio of written claims contained additional memoranda which need not be analysed here. For example, in *Le Problème de la Région de Glatz*, the Czech delegation advanced maximum and minimum claims. Under the former, it sought 490 square kilometres of the frontier area of Glatz, including 68,000 people, of whom 48,000 were admittedly German. In compensation, the delegation was prepared to cede the salient of Javornik with 30,000 inhabitants. Based upon economic and strategic considerations, the maximum claim covered the entire Glatz region. Although over 120,000 more Germans and no Czechs were involved, this difference was quickly passed over. Délégation Tchécoslovaque, Mémoire No. 9, *ibid.*, 298, 185.1126/7.

[2] *P.P.C.*, III, pp. 877-87.

Czech leader reminded Lloyd George, Wilson, and Clemenceau that the Czechoslovak people had shown 'a practical sense of politics', had supported the Allies 'without asking for any guarantees or weighing the probabilities of success', and had raised three armies on the Allied side. He declared the Czechs considered themselves 'a member of the Society of the Western States', and that in developing their state, they 'would adopt the European and human point of view, and base their claims on the very principles the Conference was assembled to establish'. He assured the Big Three that the Czechs, if only for their own good, would be 'prudent, reasonable and just' toward their neighbours.

Wittingly or not Beneš had adopted an approach well-designed to impress Lloyd George. The Prime Minister believed that big battalions bolstered any claim to territory; the French were to be constantly taunted about their big claims and little armies in the Near East. Beneš' stress on practical politics was not wasted either. The Foreign Office had shown a high regard for these Czech qualities while, in contrast, the Prime Minister viewed the Poles as political incompetents. Perhaps different British estimates of the Poles and of the Czechs partly account for Lloyd George's inconsistent attitude at Paris on the territorial claims of the two delegations.

Beneš also pictured the Czechoslovaks as the opponents of Pan-Germanism. 'Hence', he said, 'the special importance of the Czecho-Slovak frontiers in Central Europe . . .' where the Czechs '. . . had always felt they had a special mission to resist the Teutonic flood.' During the war they had fought hard because of the 'constant feeling . . . that they were the protectors of democracy against Germanism, and that it was their duty at all times to fight the Germans'.

Having cleverly appealed to the sympathies of the Big Three, Beneš then submitted the Czech territorial case on the frontier with Germany, closely following the demands and arguments of the printed memoranda. Bohemia, Moravia, and Austrian Silesia were claimed, with modifications in the existing frontier for strategic, economic, and ethnographical reasons. Ratibor was coveted for economic considerations; Glatz for sentimental, military, and economic ones. No debate developed, although Lloyd George and others asked questions on points of detail.[1] In reply to Lloyd George's query about whether the German Bohemians, if given the opportunity, would vote for exclusion from Czechoslovakia, Beneš candidly replied that they would for political and national rather than economic reasons.

To examine the questions raised by Beneš and to recommend a just settlement, the Council of Ten established a committee of two representatives each from the American, British, French, and Italian delegations. The British delegation appointed an Australian, Sir Joseph Cook, Minister of the Navy, and Harold Nicolson, of the Foreign Office, as the British representatives. Sir Joseph was not known for his grasp of Central European affairs, but the appointment did give another Dominion politician something to do at Paris.

The Commission on Czechoslovak Affairs was authorized to consult representatives of the peoples concerned. In questions affecting the German-Czech frontier, the Commission consulted Czechs but not representatives of the German Bohemians. Both the British and French members claimed that they had received almost no indication of German opinion in Bohemia. The British government did have a Chargé d'Affaires at Prague, Cecil Gosling, who reported in March about German complaints of mistreatment by the Czechs. Through the Coolidge Mission to the former territories of Austria-Hungary, the American delegation had much information on current attitudes among the German Bohemians. What indication did this evidence give of their reaction to the Czech territorial claims?

The basic contention in these Bohemian German petitions and memorials was that the Allies had committed themselves to the principle of national self-determination. The Germans in Bohemia demanded the impartial application of the principle there. They claimed to be a sufficiently large and well organized community to be consulted about their future status. Thus, a

[1] Lloyd George, writing in 1938, claimed: 'The questions I put to Dr. Beneš show that I viewed his proposed incorporation of territory occupied by German and Magyar majorities with serious misgiving. It was a departure from the principles laid down by the Allies during the War. . . .' He was 'so much disturbed by Dr. Beneš' proposals' that he instructed General Smuts, during his Hungarian mission, to visit Prague to investigate and report on their effects. The main concern, however, seems to have been the Danube frontier. Lloyd George, *Truth*, II, pp. 941-2.

memorial from representatives of Germans in the district of Teplitz asserted:

> We understand that the new regulation of things is to be founded upon the principle of self-determination of nations and not on 'historical' remembrances. . . .
>
> The historical boundaries of Bohemia, as well as those of former Austria, convey a mere geographical and political idea but not a *national* one. . . .
>
> In order to be durable, peace is to be based on the XIV articles of president Wilson. Among these XIV articles one of the most important is the self-determination of nations.
>
> We are not aware that these XIV articles have been abandoned . . . nor did we hear anything as yet, that these XIV articles were meant to prevail only in favour of the conquerors and not where their application would help the vanquished to their rights.

Claiming to speak for all German Bohemians, the signers demanded a vote to determine the fate of German Bohemia.[1]

Another petition, entitled *The Cowland. German Settlement. Thou must stay German, my native country!*, appealed for the application of Wilsonian principles, claiming that the capital of Kuhlandchen, the city of Neutitschein, had only 14·6 per cent. Czech inhabitants 'in which number are included 2 or 3 per cent. prisoners in jail and in the house of correction'.

Another memorial from the Academic Senate of the German University of Prague asserted that if the principle of national self-determination was not to be merely a phrase, 'then political and cultural self-expression must be granted to the Germans living in Bohemia, Moravia and Silesia'. The summation of the argument was

> We may say that the bulk of the German element in these territories amounts to three and a half millions, that these Germans live in widespread and closely connected settlements, that they have their own culture—economic, social and political. Thus they are perfectly entitled to form an independent political community, and to freely decide upon what state they are in future to belong to.

It warned that if the Germans in Bohemia were brought under Czech rule against their will the result would be continued

[1] 'Memorandum by the Representatives of the district of Teplitz to the American Commission of Peace', January 24, 1919, A.C.N.P., 180, 184.01102/110.

discord.[1] One declaration ended with the threat that a peace imposed by force would never be accepted: 'We know that power will be forced [*sic*] by power and we will not be alone.'

An effort was made to refute the Czech economic arguments. Thus a memorandum[2] by Dr. Rudolph von Auen, Governor of German Bohemia, and Dr. Robert Freissler, Governor of the Sudetenland Province, took the line that the industries of Bohemia, Moravia, and Silesia had lost their foundation with the collapse of the Dual Monarchy and that the Czechoslovak state could not provide the same basis for them as had the domestic market of Austria-Hungary. Simultaneously, they tried lamely to refute the argument that the new Czech state would perish without these industries, but they could not deny the economic importance of the region to the new country.

Many petitioners sought to deal with the Czech argument that the three provinces were historically Czech and that the Germans were mere colonists. For instance, Dr. von Auen rather forcefully pointed out that it was not just or practical to choose a particular time in history for determining the future partition of land in Europe. The German districts of Bohemia had been settled, improved, and owned by Germans for centuries.[3]

As the spokesmen of 'Cowland' put it:

> We all know that our ancestors did not come in this land as conquerors, but as pioneers in the swamp and wilderness. We all know that the German people came here two hundred years before the discovery of America. Two hundred years before the first European foot has been put on the ground, whose president now sends us the great sublime words of the freedom and spontaneous direction of self-determination to all people of the whole world. There is no right which can be stronger than ours. What are the sacrifices of the Czechs compared to the sacrifices wrought by our ancestors to make this country, which was a swampy wilderness, civilized. All the culture here was made by

[1] 'Memorial upon the number and the political and cultural position of the Germans in Bohemia, Moravia and Silesia, Prague, February 20, 1919', *ibid.*, 184, 184.01102/258.

[2] *Ibid.*, 298, 185.1125/23.

[3] 'The Right of the Germans of Bohemia to Dispose of Themselves. A Speech delivered by Dr. Rudoph Longman von Auen, Governor of German Bohemia, in the German-Bohemian National Assembly, held in Vienna, 28, December, 1918', *ibid.*, 180, 184.01102/110.

> the Germans, the prospering farms and villages, the flourishing industry are all German labour. This has been the work of 600 years.[1]

It might be objected that the Czechs were not proposing to steal the lands and the homes of the Germans in Bohemia. What was involved was a transfer of political sovereignty. Why then did these spokesmen of the Bohemian Germans not accept Czech assurances on minority rights and seek to work within a Czech state for the greater prosperity and progress of all? In these memorials, the answer was brief: we have no faith in Czech promises and in an international regime to protect minority rights. It was charged that the Czechs had ruled oppressively since they had gained control of the three provinces in November 1918. The representatives of the District of Teplitz charged: 'Under the present circumstances there is no freedom whatever. We are not able to hold electoral meetings, our press, our letters, telegrams and telephones are most severely controlled by the Czecho-Slovaks, who forbid every utterance in behalf of our independence.' In their memorandum von Auen and Freissler charged that the Czechs had closed German schools, had imposed language restrictions of incredible severity, and had arbitrarily removed officials. As for a liberal Czech regime for minorities, they said they knew nothing except wordy pronouncements and contrary deeds. Most of these memorials and petitions claimed that the overwhelming majority of the Germans in Bohemia, Moravia, and Silesia opposed incorporation in the Czechoslovak state and explained that this sentiment was suppressed by Czech repression and censorship. These statements reflected the acute tension between Czechs and the Bohemian Germans which reached a peak on March 4, 1919, when German demonstrations in Eger, Carlsbad, Aussig and other centres ended in bloodshed.[2]

The same grim warning ran through all these materials—to incorporate the Bohemian Germans into Czechoslovakia would

[1] *Ibid.*, 180, 184.01102/115.

[2] See Coolidge to A.C.N.P., March 5, 1919, *ibid.*, 182, 184.01102/184; also Czech view, *ibid.*, 185, 184.01102/266. Gosling reported on March 26 that German men and women had been flogged and otherwise mistreated by unruly Czech soldiery. *Documents on British Foreign Policy, 1919-1939*, Series I, vol. VI, pp. 1-2, n. 3.

create a dangerous *Germania Irredenta* which would threaten the stability of the Czech republic and the peace of Europe.

To what extent did these views represent widespread and durable Bohemian German sentiment or, as Beneš claimed, a noisy minority? Some evidence supporting the latter interpretation reached the American delegation. The German Austrian director of an important iron and coal works in the vicinity of Oderberg in Silesia was reported as agreeing that Bohemia must keep its industries, mines and coalfields if it was to have an economic future. The new Czech state would have great difficulty in competing with Germany because of the inferior quality of its coal and iron mines and because its geographical position made it expensive to import ores from Sweden. 'This view, he claimed, is held by many of the German Austrian manufacturers, who, like himself, believe that it will be more to their advantage if Bohemia remains part of the Czech state.'[1] Later, Robert von Mayr, professor of Roman Law at the German University in Prague, wrote: '. . . Notwithstanding that I am a German (Austrian) by birth, through conviction and with pride, I and with me numerous Germans of the old monarchy don't want a union to Germany, neither for national motives nor for those of culture or economy. . . .' In his opinion, 'reasonable Germans' in *Deutschböhmen* would accept incorporation within Czechoslovakia if the Czechs would adopt a thoroughly liberal minorities policy. Von Mayr, it should be added, looked forward to a broader union of the states which had emerged from the ruins of the Dual Monarchy.[2] Cecil Gosling who was highly critical of the Czech treatment of the Bohemian Germans and who feared disturbances in *Deutschböhmen* when the frontier settlement was announced, none the less believed: '. . . All that the Germans really desire is a guarantee that they will be allowed to use their language in the courts, schools and parliaments and that they shall have proper representation. . . .'[3] Such intelligence suggested that the 1914 frontier coupled with a regime effectively protecting minority rights could provide a durable settlement of the German-Czech Question.

[1] A.C.N.P., 177, 184.01102/31, January 17, 1919.

[2] King to Coolidge, April 3, 1919, *ibid.*, 186, 184.01102/330.

[3] King to Coolidge, Prague, April 5, 1919, *ibid.*, 186, 184.01102/330.

It is hard to imagine a sharper contrast than that between the Czech and the extreme German-Bohemian claims as they appeared in the records of the American delegation. In examining the effort made by Charles Seymour, Allan Dulles, and Major Johnson to reduce the number of Germans being assigned to Czech rule, this almost daily flood of evidence on the German outlook must be kept in mind. In part it compensated for the failure of the Commission on Czechoslovak Affairs to consult all the peoples concerned. Considering the atmosphere in Paris, perhaps this was as close as any delegation could come to hearing 'the other point of view'.

At the first meeting of the Commission on Czechoslovak Affairs on February 27,[1] Jules Laroche, director of the European Section of the French Ministry of Foreign Affairs, proposed adoption in principle of the historic frontiers of Bohemia and Moravia. He had been instructed by Philippe Bertholet, then acting director of Political and Commercial Affairs in the Quai d'Orsay, to support Czech demands.[2] Charles Seymour, Austro-Hungarian expert on the American delegation, believed the disadvantages for Czechoslovakia of a large German minority would be outweighed by the advantages of a natural geographic and economic frontier. Sir Joseph Cook agreed. Only the Italian representative, the Marquis Raggi, a plenipotentiary delegate and a former ambassador to Paris, questioned whether the Czechs would find the German minority too large. Laroche countered: the Czech nation had a great vitality; it posed an obstacle to German expansion, and if the German districts were excluded, the Czechs would lose a vital frontier. Raggi agreed: Strategical considerations were of the greatest importance and if the Commission took into account historical, ethnical, and economic factors as well, they would satisfy the Czech aspirations and the just wishes of the Allies. Doubtless, the Italian representative had in mind the Italian claims in the Adriatic.

Thus, with very little discussion, particularly of the dangers of German irredentism, the Commission on Czechoslovak Affairs at its very first meeting easily and unanimously reached

[1] 'Minutes of the Commission on Czecho-Slovak Affairs', English and French versions, the latter being much fuller, *ibid.*, 135, 181.21202/1 *et seq.* Unless noted otherwise, all references to its sessions are based on this source.

[2] Jules Laroche, *Au Quai d'Orsay avec Briand et Poincaré, 1919-1926*, p. 72.

the major decision to be made in the German-Czech boundary question.

The decision was scarcely surprising. It was in accord with the pre-conference attitudes of the Foreign Office, the American Inquiry, and the French government. On February 3, the Political Section of the British delegation had reaffirmed the earlier Foreign Office position and had recommended acceptance of the Czech claim primarily for geographic and economic reasons. As for Silesia, apart from the Teschen question, the Czech claim to central Silesia south of Troppau was upheld for ethnical reasons but on the same grounds the Czech claim to Western Silesia was rejected by the Political Section. The Czech claim to Glatz was opposed as was the claim to Ratibor.[1]

The Commission established a sub-committee to work out an actual line for the Czech frontiers. The British members were Harold Nicolson and Lieutenant-Colonel Cornwall; the American, A. W. Dulles and Major D. W. Johnston; the French, General Le Rond; the Italian, A. Stranieri, Captain Romagnoli, and Commander Pergolani.

The sub-committee first met on March 1.[2] Its only acute controversy arose out of the American delegation's proposed rectifications in the Bohemian frontier. These covered four districts: Eger, Rumburg, Friedland, and Fridwaldau, which the Americans proposed to assign to Germany.[3] A common thread ran through this plan: the reduction by almost 500,000 of the number of Germans to be incorporated within Czechoslovakia. This seemed to be both a just and a practical solution which might ease while not eliminating the seriousness of the German problem in Czechoslovakia. A parallel could be drawn between this policy and the attitude taken later in March towards Danzig and Marienwerder by Lloyd George. It was a policy of eliminating pin pricks by means of pin concessions. Was it worth the game?

1 'The Cheko-Slovak Case', Political Section, British Delegation, Foster Papers.

2 'Minutes of the Sub-Committee on Czecho-Slovak Frontiers', English and French version, A.C.N.P., 136, 181.212101/1 *et seq.* Unless otherwise noted all references to the sub-committee's meetings are based on these records.

3 'Memorandum Regarding the Rectifications, Proposed by the American Delegation, of the Bohemia Frontier, which will affect German Territory', *ibid.*, 298, 185.1126/18. No date.

On March 4 the Czech Foreign Minister, Beneš, explained the Czech demands. The Glatz salient was desired because Czech control of the city would facilitate communications between Poland and Czechoslovakia and help to make Prague instead of Berlin a key communication centre between eastern and western Europe. Also, since the Czechoslovak state could be quickly cut in two by armies driving on Brunn and Olmutz, its northern frontier required strengthening through the acquisition of Glatz.

The Czech government wanted the coal-mines of the Neurode salient. It sought to advance the Czech frontier in the Schmiedeberg region to satisfy national sentiment and to strengthen Czechoslovakia strategically.[1] While the Czechs were willing to exchange part of Rumburg for the Friedland salient, they opposed giving up the city of Rumburg itself. It was an important communications and textile centre, and economically was oriented towards Aussig, the river port of Bohemia on the Elbe. Moreover, the Czechoslovak government wished to have territory bordering on Lusatia.[2] Beneš also stressed the importance of the communications system of the Rumburg salient.

When questioned about the possible dangers of incorporating more Germans in the Erzgebirge-Böhmerwald regions, Beneš denied being apprehensive. He made the rather ridiculous assertion that the Bohemian Germans almost unanimously did not share the 'pan-Germanic agitations' of a few. In the words of the procès-verbal,

> M. Benes affirme que cette agitation a été tout artificielle et qu'elle n'a jamais correspondu aux sentiments de la grande majorité des Allemands de Boheme. En réalité, 99 p. 100 d'entre eux seraient partisans du rattachement de leur pays à la Bohême. Mais ils sont terrorisés par quelques agitateurs et ils n'osent pas le dire.

He added that the economic life of this region was oriented

[1] Next day Major Johnston pointed out that the rectifications demanded by the Czechs in the Schmiedeberg region actually weakened their strategic position, besides cutting the railway so as to hinder communications between Landeshur and Hirschberg. Le Rond agreed.

[2] For a brief discussion of the Lusatian Question see Temperly, *History of the Peace Conference of Paris*, IV, p. 275. Nicolson termed the Czech policy on Lusatia 'mere rubbish'. *Peacemaking*, p. 252.

towards Prague rather than Vienna and that in the postwar period these economic ties would be reinforced.[1] Beneš opposed the cession of Eger, a heavily populated region with a highly developed textile industry, whose spinners worked for the merchants of Pilsen. Three main railway lines linked Eger and Pilsen. Thus economically the region was attached to Bohemia, according to Beneš.

The Commission itself on March 8 had a fruitless session on the German-Czech frontier. Le Rond raised a question of principle: could former Austrian territories be given to Germany if Czechoslovakia did not request such a 'transfert de souveraineté'? The transfer of former Austrian territory to Germany could set a precedent for the reunion of German Austria with Germany. Upon Allan Dulles' initiative the Commission declined to discuss this question.

Inadvertently perhaps, Sir Joseph Cook raised another question of principle. He suggested that after tracing a frontier they could, in accord with the principle of self-determination, enquire into the wishes of the peoples who were left beyond this proposed boundary. Sharp opposition came from Jules Cambon: if one part of the Austrian population was consulted, this privilege could not be withheld from the remainder of Austrian territory.[2]

Sir Joseph denied that he had had a plebiscite in mind; he had only wished to indicate that they should be acquainted with information on the sentiments of the populations concerned. Laroche turned the conversation back into safer channels by warning that if they talked about plebiscites and consultations they would raise not only the issue of German Austria but would revive that of the Germans of Bohemia. The Commission decided to continue drawing frontier lines while calling the attention of the Supreme Council to the questions of principle which had been raised.

On March 11, at its sixth session the sub-committee turned to

[1] Areas like those of Teplitz and Brux had important lignite mines which were linked to Prague by railway.

[2] Raggi supported Cambon. In so doing, he was following the general policy of the Italian delegation as far as all the territorial commissions were concerned. Cambon's attitude contrasts with his later acceptance of the recommendation of the Commission on Polish Affairs that a plebiscite be held to decide the fate of Mazuria.

the unsettled problems. In Glatz, Dulles and Stranieri opposed any change in the existing frontier on the grounds that the actual frontier was not strategically hopeless and that the region was inhabited predominantly by Germans. General Le Rond dissented: the historic and administrative frontier in the Glatz salient should be altered so as to give neither Czechoslovakia nor Germany an offensive advantage. After much detailed discussion, Le Rond and Major Johnston reached agreement on a boundary equally defensible on both sides and excluding the town of Glatz from Czechoslovakia. Nicolson committed his delegation to this line. Stranieri accepted in principle. Dulles had no personal objections.

After quickly agreeing not to award Schmiedeberg to Czechoslovakia, the sub-committee turned to its contest over Rumburg. Allan Dulles proposed that the salient be severed from Bohemia for three reasons. Geographically, the existing frontier did not coincide with natural lines. Economically, the railway lines in the salient did not lead into Bohemia proper. Ethnically, a large German majority populated Rumburg. And as he remarked later if they could reduce the number of Germans in the new Czech state, they would make its tasks easier. Nicolson and Cornwall supported Dulles. Cornwall added the argument that from the strategical point of view this salient menaced the German city of Dresden.

Pergolani defended the Czech claim. Le Rond, while he agreed that strategically the Rumburg salient was not defensible, supported its retention by Czechoslovakia. As for Dulles' argument about reducing the German minority, Le Rond cogently remarked that no matter what they did, strong minorities would exist within the Czech state. If it were well administered its citizens, whatever their ethnic origin, would quickly develop a loyalty to the new state and would be assimilated. If it were badly administered, it would not live. Indeed he argued that the stronger the German minority the better because it would force the Czech government to pursue an equitable minorities policy. In any case, since Bohemia formed a historical and political entity, the less they altered its outlines the better.

On Rumburg the French and Italian delegates thus initially opposed the British and American members.

They now turned to a long and involved discussion of the Eger Question. For ethnical, economic, and political considerations, Dulles favoured severing the Eger salient from Czechoslovakia. In explaining the political reasons, he pointed out that Eger formerly had been an independent duchy and that the Czechs themselves were prepared to cede the Asch region in the salient.

Cornwall tried to link the Rumburg and the Eger Questions. He proposed that only the Asch salient be removed from Czechoslovakia, which would leave the town and area of Eger itself within Bohemia. At the same time he proposed cutting the Rumburg salient from Bohemia along a line north of Schonlinde.

Stranieri supported the American position, but Le Rond could not accept. In his opinion, they should adopt the modifications proposed by the Czechs themselves, namely the elimination of the Friedland and Asch salients, while otherwise maintaining the existing frontier, subject to detailed rectifications made by the boundary commission.

At this point, the British and French representatives were in agreement on the Eger Question, but the British had linked it with a proposal to eliminate part of the Rumburg salient from Czechoslovakia. Without actually rejecting the latter, although indicating disapproval, Le Rond demanded whether the American delegation accepted the British proposition. Dulles fought shy of this. He pointed out the American members had already sacrificed ethnical principles for economic and geographic considerations. When they saw the possibility of drawing a line which reconciled economic and ethnical factors it would be painful to renounce that opportunity. Besides, he wanted to know exactly the French and the British positions on Rumburg. He succeeded in forcing Le Rond to take a definite stand. The general declared, reluctantly, that his delegation would accept the severance of the Rumburg salient despite the economic disadvantages. In reserving his position, Dulles was either unable or unwilling to take advantage of this offer which would probably have led to agreement on denying part of Rumburg, and Asch, if not all of Eger, to the Czechs. At this point the American delegation faced two choices: either to accept the proposed Franco-British line or to revert to its earlier position that both salients should be severed. Le Rond made clear that if agreement was not reached on the former basis the French delegation would return to its original position that the existing frontier should be maintained. The Italians, who had been supporting the Americans, reserved their stand.

The entire seventh session of the sub-committee on March 13 was devoted to a vain attempt to find common ground on the Eger and Rumburg Questions. Harold Nicolson explained his delegation had preferred the existing administrative frontiers but to reach unanimity it was prepared to compromise by abandoning the Rumburg salient in the hope that the American delegation would concede on the question of Eger. If the American delegation did not compromise, his delegation would return to its original position that the two salients remain within Czechoslovakia, with the exception of Asch which the Czechs themselves had proposed to renounce. In backing Nicolson, Le Rond considered they had been underestimating the military importance of Eger, where by the use of the rail lines, the Germans could quickly concentrate forces in the area and turn the natural defenses of the Czechs. But Le Rond's main problem was to handle Dulles' argument that it was in the interests of the Czechs themselves to exclude or reduce other ethnic groups whenever possible. The general pointed out that the Czechoslovakian government was confident that Czechoslovakia could absorb an extra hundred or two hundred thousand non-Czechs. Moreover, if some Bohemian German groups were joined to Saxony or to Bavaria, they might become dangerous centres of irredentist propaganda among the remaining Germans in Bohemia.[1]

Dulles held that the exclusion of Eger from Czechoslovakia would probably have no more adverse influence upon opinion in Karlsbad and other German cities than the exclusion of Asch would have upon the town of Eger itself. If the Commission

[1] Referring to petitions received by other delegations from German Bohemia demanding union with Germany, Le Rond, not surprisingly perhaps, said he had not seen such pleas, but had received reports from Bohemia which gave an entirely different estimate of the situation. Nicolson said that the only report received by the British delegation had come from Prague and it had referred to the prevalence of Bolshevism among the workers of Rumburg. This prompted Le Rond to remark that the American proposition would give Eger to Bavaria which at that time was governed by Spartacists.

was willing to accept the exclusion of Asch, why could it not equally accept the severance of Eger from Czechoslovakia? Le Rond effectively countered that once the principle of transfer was accepted there were no logical reasons for stopping at certain points. The people of Karlsbad could argue in the same way as the people of Eger. Irredentism would spread throughout Bohemia.

The main fact was that as long as a large German minority existed in Czechoslovakia a German irredentist movement was likely to exist whether the frontier was drawn south of Asch or south of Karlsbad. Both Dulles and Le Rond were seeking to avoid the inevitable; but at least the French basic line was readily explainable in terms of history and usage. Cornwall tended to support Le Rond's position: the people of Eger had no better reasons than the people of Karlsbad and Marienbad for demanding separation from Czechoslovakia.

Thus, the British, French, and Italian members agreed to recommend that the existing frontier be maintained between Zittau and the Böhmerwald, while noting that the Czechoslovak government had proposed the severance of the Asch salient. Nicolson's and Cornwall's attempt to effect a compromise over Eger and Rumburg had thus failed.

The Commission on Czechoslovak Affairs, on March 13, approved the sub-committee's recommendations on Glatz, Schmiedeberg, and Reichenberg. Seymour maintained his delegation's position on Eger and Rumburg.

In the ensuing discussion, Sir Joseph Cook urged that military experts decide the issues from the standpoint of Czech security. Evidently fearing this stand could lead to support for the American line in Eger, Le Rond explained that, while the Czech line of defence in this region lay east of Eger and the frontier proposed by the American delegation ran through this defensive line, if they left Eger and its approaches to Germany they would facilitate a German military concentration in front of the Czech defences. Thus, the loss of Eger would weaken Czechoslovakia whereas the cession of Asch would not. After he reviewed the economic arguments, the Commission agreed unanimously to return the question to the sub-committee.

On March 14, when the Commission debated its first draft report, Seymour asked for the inclusion of an explanation of the American attitude towards Eger and Rumburg. This read:

> The American Delegation has never lost sight of the advantages of maintaining as international limits, the national and historical clearly-defined frontiers and of conserving the existing economic and industrial relations. After close study, it is persuaded by excluding the salients of Rumburg and Eger from the Czech State Bohemia will have excellent natural frontiers, will not suffer any serious economic disturbance and will be freed of three hundred and thirty thousand persons of the German race whose influence on the Czecho-Slovak State might lead to grave political difficulties.[1]

Later Allan Dulles, on the other hand, advised adding to the report a statement to the effect that the Commission had been unanimous in recognizing the dangers to the Czech state and the potential difficulties for the Germans themselves of separating from Czechoslovakia all the territories inhabited by the Bohemian Germans; '. . . the only admissible solution therefore consists in reattaching them to Czecho-Slovakia'.

The report of the Commission on Czechoslovak Affairs[2] was ready for the Supreme Council on March 20. In explaining the principles upon which they had determined the frontiers of the new state the report asserted: 'The Committee have been principally guided in their discussions by ethnical considerations, and it is upon these considerations that they have endeavoured to base their conclusions as a whole.' By no stretch of the imagination could the Commission be said to have been so guided in determining the Czech-German frontier. Historic, economic, and strategic principles, not ethnical, had been the primary criteria. The Commission justified deviations as follows:

> The Committee have found it necessary, however, in certain cases to take into account certain important considerations other than those of nationality. It became evident, indeed, that whereas it was extremely desirable to give the new Tchecho-Slovak State the greatest possible ethnic unity, it was above all essential to provide

[1] A.C.N.P., 135, 181.21201/6.

[2] 'Report Submitted to the Supreme Council by the Committee on Tcheko-Slovak Questions', *ibid.*, 136, 181.21202/3. French text in Lapradelle, vol. 9, pp. 139-62.

for the new State conditions which would satisfy its economic needs; and for this purpose it was considered important, on the one hand, not to destroy the existing unity of economic life, and on the other hand to assure to the Tchechs such means of communication as were indispensable to their economic development, as well as a frontier line providing the necessary guarantee for their national security.

In defining the proposed German-Czech boundary, the report recommended that it should in principle follow the 1914 line between Germany and Austria-Hungary from a point about eight miles east of Neustadt to the junction with the former administrative boundary between Bohemia and the province of Upper Austria. Along this line two major modifications were unanimously suggested. In the region of Glatz a new trace reduced but did not eliminate the German salient. This would improve the Czech strategic position in the north-west portion while leaving the German town of Glatz within Germany. In the area of Reichenberg, the report proposed an adjustment transferring the Pollaun re-entrant to Czechoslovakia for strategic reasons and adding the Friedland salient to Germany. Concerning the line from the Neisse at Zittau to the Böhmerwald, the report could only note the difference of views: the British, French, and Italian representatives recommended the 1914 frontier except for the cession of the Asch salient to Germany; the United States delegates advised the transfer of Eger and Rumburg to the Reich.

In concluding its report, the Commission advised that the situation created by the alien minorities included within the new state 'appears to merit special consideration in the general study which will be made of the measures to be taken to ensure the protection of ethnic minorities'.

The Council of Foreign Ministers debated the proposed Czech-German frontier on April 1.[1] Balfour did not disagree with the Commission's recommendations or support the American stand on Eger and Rumburg, although in October 1918 he had had his doubts about deviating from the ethnographical principle in Bohemia and the Foreign Office had advised this type of change. Lansing and Cambon tangled heartily with one another. Lansing, without debating the

[1] *P.P.C.*, IV, pp. 543-7.

question of Glatz, spoke bluntly: '. . . the fixing of frontier lines with a view to their military strength and in contemplation of war was directly contrary to the whole spirit of the League of Nations, of international disarmament, and of the policy of the United States as set forth in the declarations of President Wilson'. Cambon argued that Wilson himself had recognized that the new states must be viable. He also misleadingly commented that the American members of the Commission had made no general reservations of the kind advanced by Lansing.[1] In his opinion the ethnological principle alone could not be applied: 'If a nation was to be composed strictly according to the national sentiments of each village, the result would be a country as discontinuous as the spots on a panther's skin. Such, he presumed, was not the result the Conference desired the Commission to recommend.'

Lansing, after repeating the American objections to the incorporation of Eger within Czechoslovakia, provoked Pichon to declare heatedly:

> He could not allow Germany to be fortified by populations taken from what had been Austrian dominions, taken, moreover, from Bohemia, which, he trusted, would remain an Ally of France, and handed over to Germany, which, as far as he was concerned, still remained a country to be feared. If America refused to take into account considerations of national defence, France was not in a position to neglect them.
>
> Mr. Lansing asked whether M. Pichon had noted that in yielding Friedland to Germany the Commission had reinforced Germany by 60,000 inhabitants.[2]
>
> M. Pichon said that he was not prepared to generalize this practice.

Once again Cambon attempted to explain that this had been done to compensate for the readjustment of the frontier near Glatz. Clearly they had become mired in the difficulties created by departing from the 1914 line.

The dispute then moved to the Council of Four. The Council

[1] The American members had inserted the following statement in the Report of the Commission: 'The United States wish . . . to make it quite clear that they were principally guided in their decisions by geographic, economic, and political considerations.' Cambon's statement was not entirely correct.

[2] *P.P.C.*, IV, p. 545.

was being racked by the controversies among Clemenceau, Lloyd George, and Wilson. The latter was in the midst of his fight for the League and a moderate peace. Would he choose to do battle over Eger and Rumburg or even along the wider front of German Bohemia? And Lloyd George. What of him? Despite their differences, he and Wilson were combatting Clemenceau over the western and eastern frontiers of Germany. He wanted no new Alsace-Lorraines in Europe. Not many days before, the Prime Minister had taken an adamant stand against the recommendations of the Commission on Polish Affairs. He had feared the likely dangerous effect of including too many Germans within Poland. He had fastened particularly upon Danzig and Marienwerder as examples of purely German districts which were being placed, by the Polish Commission, under non-German rule primarily for strategic and economic reasons. On the very day that the Central Committee on Territorial Questions was dealing with the German-Czech draft settlement, the British Prime Minister was finishing the Fontainebleau memorandum defining his policy of a moderate peace. Would he then take a similar stand either on German Bohemia with its potential irredenta of over 3,000,000 German-speaking people or on the narrower questions of Eger and Rumburg with their populations of 256,634 Germans and 1,235 Czechs compared to Marienwerder with its total population of only 138,000?

It is difficult to determine the British Prime Minister's basic thoughts on the problem of the German-Czech frontier. On March 11, in the Council of Ten, Lloyd George had depicted the nationalities of the former Dual Monarchy as all scrambling for territory:

> In his opinion, the Allies were here to do justice to all those peoples. . . . He thought great care should be taken to show complete fairness to all parties. The new map of Europe must not be so drawn as to leave cause for disputation which would eventually drag Europe into a new war.[1]

These words could convey the suggestion that the German Bohemian Question was one of those problems involving the future peace of Europe which called for moderate treatment of

[1] *Ibid.*, p. 317.

the vanquished. The possibility of rectifications in the 1914 boundary between Germany and Bohemia was referred to in the Fontainebleau memorandum of March 25.[1]

When the issue came up in the Council of Four on April 4, Clemenceau complained that the proposed German-Czech boundary was complicated and involved cessions of territory to the Germans about which he commented 'cela me parait bien inutile'. He proposed instead that the prewar frontier between Germany and Bohemia be maintained. The Germans and Czechs could then negotiate territorial exchanges as they pleased. And, he added, with monumental blandness, that the question of the Bohemian Germans had nothing to do with the German treaty which they were then alone considering.

Lloyd George agreed, remarking that it was in effect a question related to the division of the former Dual Monarchy. That was that! No fight! Lloyd George had faithfully followed the basic advice of the Foreign Office. On the American side, Colonel House, the indefatigable conciliator, sat that day in the Council of Four in place of Wilson. He agreed that Clemenceau's solution was the best, subject to the opinion of President Wilson.[2] Wilson apparently felt less strongly than Lansing, Seymour, and Allan Dulles for he accepted the decision.

The draft treaty of May 7 when handed to the Germans defined the Czech-German frontier as the line of August 3, 1914, between Germany and Austria from its junction with the administrative boundary between Bohemia and the province of Upper Austria to a point about 8 kilometers east of Neustadt. (See Map 3.) Germany was also to renounce in favour of Czechoslovakia sovereignty over the territory of Prussian Silesia between the old Austro-German frontier and a point to be fixed later. Finally, Czechoslovakia was obligated to accept an international regime for the protection of national and religious minorities.

II

The dissolution of the Dual Monarchy had left German-Austria in a difficult position. Three main alternatives faced Vienna: independence, entrance into a Danubian Confedera-

[1] Lloyd George, *Truth*, II, p. 951. [2] Mantoux, *Délibérations*, I, p. 148.

tion, or union with Germany. The latter had been the official policy of the Austrian government since November 1918. On the German government's part, the idea was heartily espoused. Chancellor Ebert in the Weimar Assembly on February 7, 1919, had declared 'German-Austria must be united with the mother country for all time'.[1] A week later, Brockdorff-Rantzau, the German Foreign Minister, proclaimed to the Assembly, 'The German people is beyond all state boundaries, even beyond the boundaries of the old Empire, a living unity . . .'[2] He envisaged *anschluss* between Austria and Germany. In view of these sentiments, a situation apparently existed where the principle of national self-determination should come into play to unite the two states.

Although the evidence available to the British delegation remains inaccessible, the information available to the American delegation indicated a different situation prevailed compared to the public impression of a keen popular desire in Austria and Germany for *anschluss*. Examples of these reports shed some light upon the conditions under which the decision was taken to maintain the historic frontier between Germany and Austria proper.

On January 30, Professor A. C. Coolidge, who headed the American field mission to the former Habsburg lands, reported from Vienna that Austrian opinion was divided over the future political relationships of German-Austria. He found it hard to estimate the relative strength of the partisans of a Danubian confederation and the proponents of union with Germany. 'A prominent official said to me recently that if everyone in Austria were to vote out loud the great majority would favour the union; but if they were to vote secretly everyone would vote against it.' His judgment was that Austrian public opinion on the issue remained in a highly fluid state.[3]

Hugh Gibson, as might be expected, took a more positive position. Reporting from Vienna, on February 1, he found the desire to join Germany prevalent mainly among the Austrian socialists, but in his opinion even many socialists opposed *anschluss*. The war had intensified traditional feelings of dislike

[1] *P.P.C.*, XII, pp. 10-11. [2] *Ibid.*, p. 21.

[3] Professor A. C. Coolidge to the Commission to Negotiate Peace, Vienna, January 30, 1919, *ibid.*, pp. 240-4.

for Germany and the general opinion was that in a fair election the proposal for union would be defeated.[1]

On the other hand, on February 10, Coolidge reported Austrian sentiment for *anschluss* had gained strength during the previous two weeks for a number of reasons, including the hostile attitude of the Czech government and the excitement of the elections in Austria itself.[2] Five weeks later, Coolidge observed that pro-union sentiment had perceptibly cooled down. Events in Munich and Berlin had alarmed the propertied and conservative classes and the fear was gaining ground that if Austria joined Germany it would be subjected to severe treatment under the terms of peace.[3]

H. H. Field, of the Gherardi mission, wired from Zurich on March 19 that most politically prominent Austrians whom he had interviewed in Switzerland were 'stoutly opposed' to German-Austrian union. He also described the general attitude of the 'masses' in Bavaria as profoundly indifferent to the question of union. Two very different groups in Munich favoured *anschluss*, the socialists largely as a matter of party tactics and the militarists to whom 'it is a matter of power; to offset the losses in Alsace-Lorraine, Poland and Schleswig, the adjunction of a compact German population seems a godsend'. Intellectual circles were divided while liberal opinion seemed opposed to the union. Field warned 'no step could foster the movement for union and particularly its expression in public assemblies more than a veto proclaimed in advance by the Entente'.[4]

On balance, these field reports must have strengthened those in the American delegation who opposed, at the very least, a hasty approval of union between Austria and Germany.

Five days after Ebert proclaimed the German government's policy towards *anschluss*, three members of the American delegation, A. W. Dulles, F. R. Dolbeare, and E. L. Dresel, the Chief of Division of Political-Diplomatic Questions, circulated within their delegation a written appeal against determining at that time the question of German-Austrian union. They argued that a clear case for the application of the doctrine of self-

[1] *Ibid.*, p. 231. [2] A.C.N.P., 179, 184.01102/85.

[3] *Ibid.*, 184, 184.01102/224; also *P.P.C.*, XII, p. 278.

[4] A.C.N.P., 196, 184.01402/19.

determination did not exist because it was not evident that the *anschluss* campaign reflected 'the genuine desire of the majority of the German-Austrian people'. They then brought forward ten reasons why the United States should think twice about approving *anschluss*. Union would more than compensate Germany for its losses elsewhere. It would supply further arguments to France and Italy in their demands for strategical frontiers. Bohemia would be almost completely encircled by Germany. Germany would be in an admirable position to undertake economic and political penetration of the smaller states of south-eastern Europe, etc. They advised that the policy of the Austrian government as well as Austrian public opinion could be influenced by lifting in whole or part the Allied blockade and by other preferential treatment. Or the Allies might issue a direct statement opposing *anschluss* for the present. Or, informal expressions of opposition might be made.[1]

Dresel recommended that the Council of Ten issue a public statement disapproving 'of all precipitate action to bring about the incorporation of German Austria into Germany'.[2] This proposal was considered by the American Commissioners on March 3. Lansing opposed any American initiative 'in this question of an European territorial settlement, especially in view of the fact that such an initiative might appear to be in contradiction to the President's principles'.[3]

The reader will recall the pre-conference debate within French official circles over the proper solution of the Austrian Question. During the Peace Conference, the French government came out in favour of an independent Austria. As early as February 22, Clemenceau urged that the Allies take a firm stand against *anschluss*.[4] When the Kerr-Tardieu-Mezes' secret boundary committee met on March 11, Tardieu formally proposed that Germany be obligated to accept the frontier of August 1, 1914, with Austria. Further, Germany should

[1] 'The Union of German-Austria with Germany', a memorandum by A. W. Dulles, Dolbeare, and Dresel, February 12, 1919, forwarded by Bullitt to Lansing, *ibid.*, 303, 185/1136/1.

[2] *Ibid.*, 185.1136/3.

[3] A. W. Dulles to Joseph Grew, March 3, 1919, *ibid.*, 185.1136/4. Compare with Minute in *P.P.C.*, XI, pp. 87-8.

[4] House to Wilson, February 23, 1919, Wilson Papers; Seymour, *Intimate Papers*, IV, p. 335.

recognize the independence of German-Austria and agree to do nothing, politically or economically, which directly or indirectly would violate this independence. Germany too should accept the neutrality of German-Austria under a League guarantee.[1] Tardieu raised the subject again at a meeting of the Central Territorial Committee on March 15. According to Tardieu, in the light of events at Weimar they should impose on Germany the pledge to adopt no measures which would affect the independence of German-Austria. Tardieu thought that this pledge need not be perpetual, but it would stop the existing intrigues. Mezes 'willingly' supported Tardieu although he did not think the Territorial Committee needed to include such a provision in its report on the Austro-German frontier. Raggi questioned the Committee's competence to make such a recommendation while Sir Eyre Crowe had no objection to Tardieu's motion but had to reserve his stand. They agreed to inform the Supreme Council:

> The American and French Delegations to the Central Committee on Territorial Questions, suggest that it would be expedient to impose on Germany, in the preliminaries of peace, a pledge to take no step, political or economic, which can infringe the independence of Austria.
>
> The Committee does not think itself competent to express an opinion on this suggestion, which goes beyond the question of frontiers so-called. It simply observes that there is an Austria independent of Germany, and recommends the maintenance, between German-Austria and Germany, of the frontier existing on the 1st of August, 1914, reserving such changes as may result, for either state, from the Czecho-Slovak Republic.[2]

The French government at this time did not confine its anti-*anschluss* efforts to the Paris talks alone. On March 23, Pichon informed French diplomatic missions in London, Washington, Rome, and elsewhere of the despatch of the Allizé mission to Vienna. Ostensibly an information mission and economic

[1] *Papers Respecting Negotiations for an Anglo-French Pact*, Cmd., 2169, p. 67.

[2] 'Minutes of Central Territorial Committee', March 15, 1919, A.C.N.P., 135, 181.2102/1. Seymour's statement about union. 'This was, on the whole, approved by the American Delegates, as it was requested by the Austrians themselves' (*What Really Happened at Paris*, p. 108), seems to create a wrong impression of opinion in the American delegation from at least January on.

enquiry, the main purpose of the undertaking was to exert influence in Austria, primarily through the political parties, against the *anschluss* movement and Pan-German ideas. The Allizé mission was also to study the economic requirements for the establishment of a viable, independent Austrian state. A further objective was to strengthen French prestige in Vienna by counterbalancing the existing Italian, British, and American missions there.[1] In subsequent reports, the Allizé mission drew a picture of conflict between Vienna and other urban centres on the one hand and the rural areas on the other, between the Socialist government under Otto Bauer and the country conservatives represented by the Social Democrats and the Christian Socialists respectively. The provinces and the Christian Socialists were seen as opposed to union with Germany. In May, Allizé reported that Christian Socialist gains in the Styrian elections had set back Otto Bauer's effort to rally Austrian public opinion behind union with Germany.[2] Generally, this analysis coincided with the reports of the Coolidge mission, and with the later reports of Sir Francis Oppenheimer, who visited Vienna in May as British Financial Commissioner.[3]

During the spirited conversation in the Council of Four on March 27 in which Lloyd George, Wilson, and Clemenceau debated the basic approach to be taken in the German Peace Treaty, the French Prime Minister defended French policy on grounds of the balance of power. If the victors reduced their armaments and simultaneously added some 7,000,000 Austrians to Germany, the power of Germany would be dangerously increased. He questioned whether it was 'an outrage' to insist that the Austrians remain independent and not enter into a German bloc to participate in plans of *revanche*.[4] Neither Wilson nor Lloyd George took up this point in the discussion.

A month later, when Wilson and Clemenceau agreed on the clauses of the Rhineland settlement, they also approved an article on the independence of German Austria: 'Germany

[1] Klotz Archives, No. 19.

[2] *Inter alia*: General Hallier, chef de mission militaire, to Ministry of War, May 5, 1919; Allizé to Pichon, May 12, May 14, 1919, Klotz Archives, No. 19.

[3] *D.B.F.P.*, Series I, vol. XI, pp. 40-53; see especially p. 43.

[4] Mantoux, *Délibérations*, I, p. 44.

recognizes the independence of German Austria within the frontiers as defined by the present treaty.' On April 22, the Council of Four accepted this provision.[1]

When this article came back better polished by the Drafting Committee, Clemenceau proposed that Germany be committed to respect the inalienable independence of Austria. Without this stipulation, the first use Austria could make of its independence would be to join Germany. Wilson, while he considered it desirable to prevent the immediate union of Austria and Germany, preferred to withdraw the word 'inalienable'. He did not believe they could refuse a country the right to unite with another if it wished. Thus he faced a dilemma: he did not wish to impose a permanent obligation upon Austria but on the other hand to fix a time limit during which *anschluss* would be forbidden would in effect invite Austria to join Germany at the end of that period. Lloyd George had no objection to insisting upon permanent separation if it was indispensable to the security of Europe. He suggested that the German government should be obliged to abstain from manœuvres designed to lead to *anschluss*. Clemenceau rejected this on the grounds that the Germans could not be trusted. Finally, Wilson came up with a solution: Germany should recognize and respect Austrian independence which would remain inalienable except by consent of the Council of the League of Nations. 'Trés bien,' exclaimed Clemenceau. It was a clever piece of diplomatic ingenuity and resourcefulness.[2]

The Council of Four had taken its final basic decision on the Austro-German border which the draft treaty of May 7 defined as the line of 1914 between the two countries. (See Map 3.) Germany was to respect the inalienability of Austrian independence, within the frontiers drawn by the Austrian Treaty, unless the Council of the League decided otherwise. Thus the long-standing views of the British Foreign Office on *anschluss* were not embodied in the treaty, although fusion at a later date was not formally prohibited. Lloyd George had accepted the opinion that Austro-German union could have dangerous strategic consequences. Germany would be given a favourable military and economic position from which to renew the *Drang Nach*

[1] *P.P.C.*, V, pp. 114, 118.

[2] Mantoux, *Délibérations*, I, pp. 461-2; *P.P.C.*, V, pp. 421, 425.

Osten. Union could facilitate a German-Italian rapprochement at the expense of France and the new Slav states in eastern Europe. Czechoslovakia would be perilously exposed and isolated. Such strategic considerations, combined with the absence of strong popular demand in Austria for union, seemed to dictate a policy at Paris of maintaining Austria as an independent, buffer state. Paradoxically, Lloyd George and the other Allied statesmen then proceeded to draft a treaty of peace with Austria which, in combination with Czech and Yugoslav opposition to Danubian Federation, seemed diabolically designed to drive German Austria into union with Germany.

XII

THE LOW COUNTRIES: ZINC, STRATEGY, AND COMPENSATIONS

THE Belgian Minister of Foreign Affairs, M. Hymans, presented his government's claims to the Council of Ten on February 11. Primarily Belgium sought a revision of the Treaties of 1839, the free use of and sovereignty over the western Scheldt as far as the sea in time of peace and war, and a friendly rapprochement with Luxemburg. As for German territory, Hymans laid claim to Malmedy and other Walloon districts which he did not define and Neutral Moresnet. He suggested that Holland could be compensated for the loss of the left bank of the Scheldt by the German cession of Prussian Guelderland, eastern Friesland, and the County of Bentwich between Guelderland and Emden. At the end of his speech, Hymans reserved the right to raise questions of Belgian economic and political interests in the Rhineland if the fate of that area was discussed at the Conference.[1]

On the following day, Balfour moved that an expert commission be established to study the proposed transfer of Malmedy and Moresnet and possible rectifications in the German-Dutch frontier only along the lower Ems. Sir Eyre

[1] Some Belgian groups had wider aims in mind; the Comité de Politique nationale, for example, which in the west sought Luxembourg, then the line of the Kyll, Urft, and Roer rivers, including Roermonde; a long, narrow salient to the Rhine opposite Duisburg; all of south Limbourg; and at sea, a line to the north shore of the Scheldt. A.C.N.P., 425, 755.5615/20.

Crowe and J. W. Headlam-Morley were named as the British representatives; Tardieu and Laroche, for the French; Haskins and Colonel Embick for the United States; Bussatti and Count Vannutelli-Rey for Italy; and Kato for Japan.[1]

Before the Commission first met, the Anglo-American experts on February 21 agreed to support the cession of Moresnet and Malmedy to Belgium. If a large minority so requested, some form of popular consultation would be arranged. Significantly, their agreement excluded Eupen.[2]

When the committee, which ultimately became the Commission on Belgian and Danish Affairs, assembled on February 25, the fate of Neutral Moresnet posed no serious problem.[3] This area of only 900 acres inhabited by some 3,500 Belgians, Prussians, and others, had been jointly administered by Belgium and Prussia since 1815 because of vagaries in the Final Act of the Congress of Vienna. Economically, this tiny area was important because the works of a Belgian zinc mining company, the Vieille Montagne, were located there. The Belgians wanted full political control of Neutral Moresnet to facilitate the operations of the mining company. Part of the works of the company were also located in Prussian Moresnet which led to a Belgian demand that this area be annexed as well. As partial compensation for wartime damage to Belgium's forests, the timber resources of Neutral Moresnet and Prussian Moresnet furnished further grounds for the Belgian claims.

With relatively little discussion the Commission on March 6 agreed to the cession of Neutral Moresnet and of the communal and domainal woods of Prussian Moresnet to Belgium. The latter transfer was justified on grounds of reparations. On March 8, the Commission approved the transfer to Belgium of that part of Prussian Moresnet in which the works of the Vieille Montagne were located. This was justified on grounds of economic practicality.[4]

The Belgian claims to Malmedy and other districts caused

[1] *P.P.C.*, III, pp. 1006-7. [2] House Papers, 30/165.

[3] Verbatim reports and *procès-verbaux* of their sessions are in A.C.N.P., vols. 145 and 146. Except where otherwise noted, this chapter is based on this source.

[4] See 'Memorandum on the Belgian Forests', by the Director-General of Waters and Forests, Brussels, February 25, 1919, A.C.N.P., 301, 185.1131/20.

the Committee more difficulty, partly because the Belgian claims were only gradually unfolded, partly because the members continually had to seek more information. Generally speaking, the Belgians claimed the German Kreise of Malmedy and Eupen. The former had a population of some 34,768; the latter of 26,156. Economically both regions were valuable because of their forest reserves. Eupen also was the centre of a small textile industry and contained many of the mines which were exploited by the Vieille Montagne.

The Belgian demands depended also upon strategical considerations. The Belgian General Staff submitted a maximum and a minimum line. In effect, the former would have given to Belgium control of the Eifel Highlands. The latter, which followed fairly closely the linguistic line between the Walloons and the Germans, embraced most of the Kreise of Malmedy and Eupen. It might be added that the minimum strategic line in the Eupen region went beyond the location of the zinc mines.

On March 5, the Commission heard a report by Colonels Cornwall, Embick, and Requin. The best strategic frontier in their opinion was the maximum line advocated by the Belgian General Staff. It would give to Belgium control of the only natural defensive position between the Rhineland and Belgium and would enable that country to dominate the Rhine plain, including Aachen. On the other hand, this line would embrace a rather large number of Germans. As for the approximate ethnic line, embracing most of Eupen and Malmedy it was less strong militarily but quite defendable in their opinion. In the ensuing discussion Tardieu favoured the best strategic line, the same type of stand which he and other French representatives took on the other territorial commissions. Sir Eyre Crowe preferred the more limited line, while Haskins held a final decision depended largely on how the question of the Rhineland was settled.

Agreement on the cession of Malmedy to Belgium was quickly reached. Tardieu wished to stress in their report the military and the ethnical reasons for this decision; Haskins wanted the economic reasons emphasized more. The main debate was over the disposition of Eupen and St. Vith. The latter area around the town of the same name, while in Kreis Malmedy, had been excluded from the minimum line recommended by the military experts.

Headlam-Morley, on behalf of the British delegation, opposed the cession of Eupen because it was entirely populated by Germans. Sir Eyre Crowe doubted that the economic reasons for the transfer could counterbalance the potential danger to Belgium of annexing Germans. He suggested that a special regime could be established to protect the rights of the Vieille Montagne to exploit the mines of Eupen. On this occasion, Haskins, hesitant about approving the proposed transfer, wanted to know more about the economic relations between Belgium and Eupen. He did agree to the Belgian annexation of St. Vith. Tardieu strongly supported the Belgian claims to Eupen. The Italian and Japanese members of the Commission lined up behind him.

Later, the Committee had more detailed information about the economic relations between Belgium, Moresnet, and Eupen. The Belgian argument was that Moresnet would be valueless without the works of mines located in Eupen. Tardieu urged the simplest solution was to attach the mining territory to Belgium. At first, he faced the combined opposition of Sir Eyre Crowe and Haskins. Crowe argued that since mines almost everywhere straddled frontiers it was impossible to alter boundaries to suit each special interest involved. Haskins, treating the question as essentially political and economic, proposed (1) that the Vieille Montagne should enjoy free use of the mines remaining in German territory and (2) the cession to Belgium of the small area in which the works of the company in Eupen were located. Tardieu rejected this solution.

Possibly they were in effect fighting a preliminary battle over the Saar Valley. If Tardieu established that economic connections between the works and the mines justified a transfer of political sovereignty and thus overrode the ethnic principle, a precedent would have been set for the French claims to the Saar mining basin. On the Anglo-American side, Crowe and Haskins were possibly attempting to protect their delegations against this tactical danger.

The Belgians continued to fight hard for Eupen. In a note on March 12, the Belgian government formally laid claim to Eupen and Montjoie. It was pointed out that Eupen possessed certain rights in the Belgian forest which gave rise to continual litigation which could only be ended by the return of Eupen to Belgium.

Also, according to the Note, unless Belgium had control over the entire Vesdre river basin, which had its source in Eupen and Montjoie, it would be impossible to develop flood-control plans, to prevent pollution, and to supply local Belgian industries and canals with water. It was argued as well that there were many family ties between Belgium and these regions. Finally, the Note laid claim to the forests of the Eupen area as compensation for the ruthless Prussian exploitation.[1]

Apparently the Belgian note had a decisive effect. At the Commission's session on March 12 the Anglo-American opposition to the Belgian claim to Eupen collapsed. Tardieu had the satisfaction of a minor triumph. Headlam-Morley saw the close economic ties between Eupen and Belgium as the main justification for the transfer, provided that the majority of the inhabitants were not opposed.

In its final report, the Commission recommended: (1) cession to Belgium of Neutral Moresnet, the domainal and communal woods of Prussian Moresnet, and the territory adjacent to the highway from Liège on which was located some works of the Société de la Vieille Montagne; (2) the annexation by Belgium of Kreis Malmedy—'. . . unless a majority of the population makes formal protests'; (3) Belgian acquisition of Kreis Eupen —provided 'no protest shall be made by the majority . . .'. These proposals were limited by the French reservation that a final decision depended on how the Rhineland Question as a whole was settled. The Commission also stipulated that if Eupen was not annexed to Belgium the Belgian companies concerned should have the unrestricted right of exploiting the mineral deposits of the Kreis and of exporting their products without hindrance.[2]

Before the Report was considered by the Council of Four, the Belgian delegation in a note dated April 1 proposed to advance the frontier in northern Eupen along the Moresnet road and the Vervier railway where a small salient existed. This would place the new line along the hills dominating the city of Aachen.

[1] 'Note Concernant Eupen', Belgian Delegation, Paris, March 12, 1919, A.C.N.P., vol. 301, 185.1131/40.

[2] 'Report (with Annexes) Presented to the Supreme Council of the Allies by the Commission on Belgian and Danish Affairs', March 19, 1919, A.C.N.P., 147, 181.21802/8.

Secondly, the Belgian delegation pointed out the proposed frontier severed the railway between Eupen and Malmedy. 'It would not be logical to fail to incorporate the railway into Belgian territory.' Customs control would be difficult and a small enclave would exist west of the River Our. This 'slight' request meant the annexation of the westerly portion of the Kreis of Montjoie.[1]

In the Commission, Haskins, Crowe, and Tardieu finally agreed that the Belgian demand was not justified. Although Sir Eyre Crowe discounted the number of Germans involved, he felt that annexation would strengthen the German element in the Belgian population to the detriment of Belgium. Bussatti and Kato supported the Belgian claim, the former quite forcibly for a time, but they finally bowed to the majority. Montjoie remained German. Similarly, the Commission followed Haskins in opposing the proposed rectification near Aachen because it would pose a threat against the city.

Upon the suggestion of the French jurist, M. Fromageot, the Commission accepted a more precise definition of the method of making known the wishes of the inhabitants of Malmedy and Eupen. Originally, no specific system for registering any protest was provided for in the draft articles. Now the Belgian government was to open, during the six months after the treaty of peace came into force, registers at Eupen and Malmedy in which the local citizens could record their desire to have the territories remain in whole or in part under German sovereignty. Their views were to be communicated to the League of Nations by the Belgian government; Belgium would undertake to accept the decision of the League. The minutes of the discussions throw little light upon why the members of the Commission accepted this travesty upon the exercise of the right of self-determination.[2]

[1] 'Note from the Secretary-General of the Belgian Delegation to the American Delegation', Paris, April 1, 1919, A.C.N.P., 301, 185.1131/47.

[2] British and American initiative was evidently responsible for the original reference to popular wishes. During the seventh session of the Commission, Haskins betrayed a sensitivity for public sentiment by suggesting a reference in their report to the pro-Belgian petitions which had been received. Crowe suggested a formula safeguarding popular rights which would avoid a plebiscite which, he said, some feared. This led to their adopting the phrase 'Sauf protestation formelle de la part de la majorité . . .' which was used in the case of Malmedy.

The Commission's final report came before the Council of Four on April 16. Hymans pressed for the two modifications which the Commission had turned down: the strategic rectification near Aachen and the adjustment giving Belgium control of the Eupen-Malmedy railway and of part of the forest of Hertogenwald (as he now revealed). Balfour and Clemenceau questioned the practical wisdom of adding more Germans to the 'plebiscite' area. Wilson, doubting that Belgian interests would be served by incorporating into the newly acquired territories 'un élément de fermentation', raised the question of principle: 'Ne vous semble-t-il pas que, malgré le petit nombre des intéressés, 4,000, nous risquerons de nous départir à leur égard du principe que nous cherchons à appliquer à des problèmes plus vastes? Ne devons-nous pas avoir autant de de scrupules qu'il s'agisse de 4,000 Allemands, ou de 4 millions?' Hymans conceded that Belgium wanted as few Boches as possible and that no great economic interest was involved. Without amendment, the Council approved the proposed settlement.[1] (See Map 3.)

In discussing the territory which Holland might receive from Germany to compensate for the possible Dutch cessions to Belgium, the members of the Commission did not take their task very seriously. As the British representative, Sir Eyre Crowe commented:

> Nous sommes en ce moment dans les nuages en ce moment [*sic*] et nous faisons un travail auquel bnous [*sic*] n'attachons pas grande importance. Il me semble peu vraisemblable que la Hollande cède le Limbourg à la Belgique et je vourdrais trouver, pour notre rapport, des formules vagues qui ne nous entrainent pas à des principes que nous ne pourrions soutenir.[2]

Generally, the British position as represented by Crowe and Headlam-Morley was cool towards the whole idea of transferring German territory to Holland in the regions of the lower Ems, Prussian Guelders, and Cleves. They were willing to

[1] Mantoux, *Délibérations*, I, pp. 258-61.

[2] Verbatim report of sixth session of the Commission on Belgian and Danish Affairs, A.C.N.P., 146, 181.2180/6. Tardieu ended the meeting with this comment: 'déjà, quand j'ai parlé de cette question au Conseil suprême, je n'ai pas eu l'impression qu'on attendait grand chose de notre commission et j'ai déclaré que nous n'apporterions au Conseil presque rien.'

support as a just Dutch claim a rectification of the frontier at the mouth of the Ems to give the Netherlands free access to the port of Delfzijl. Otherwise, Crowe held that changes required the consent of the populations concerned which provoked the honest reaction from Laroche:

> . . . si on envisage sérieusement l'idée d'une compensation, il ne faut pas parler de plébiscite; ce serait retirer d'une main ce que nous donnons de l'autre; il y a des chances que le plébiscite soit contraire au rattachement à la Hollande et les Hollandais répondraient aux Belges qu'ils subordonnent la cession du Limbourg à un plébiscite semblable.[1]

On these issues, Haskins and Crowe were close together while Tardieu and Rey viewed compensations more leniently.

Their report of March 19[2] was vague, brief and cautious. A rectification at the mouth of the Ems 'should be kept in mind'. Territorial compensation along the right bank of the Ems was unanimously rejected because of the German character of the population. Compensation on the left bank of the Ems was said to be probably 'insufficient and unattractive' and the German character of the majority was noted. Actually this wording hid a difference of opinion: the American and British representatives had held that cession was virtually impossible; the French, Italian, and Japanese delegates were willing to consider cession but viewed the left bank areas as almost economically worthless. Unanimously, it was pointed out that *if* Holland was to receive equitable compensation it would have to be along the left bank of the Rhine in the districts of Prussian Guelders and Cleves. Then came the saving formula—'account being taken both of the economic and moral interests of the population affected and of the coal which it would be desirable to give to Holland'. Finally, the Supreme Council was reminded that, *if* the principle of compensations was granted, the form of application depended upon the final settlement of the Rhineland Question. This meant that the French delegates hoped that if a separate Rhineland state or states were set up, the inhabitants of Cleves and Guelders might be more willing to join Holland, and the Dutch more willing to receive them.

The latter consideration was most important of all, perhaps.

[1] *Ibid.*

[2] See above, p. 316, n. 2.

The Dutch government, in a statement to Parliament in February 1919, had rejected the idea of territorial cessions to Belgium.[1] It had also, according to Crowe, expressed no interest in gaining German territory although it had indicated a wish to solve the problem of the mouth of the Ems.

The Commission did recommend a conditional clause obligating Germany to cede territory to Holland if necessary. When the article reached the Council of Four on April 16, Wilson, in diplomatic language, said that rectification of the German-Dutch border was none of their business. Balfour saw the policy could only be justified if the people involved wanted union with Holland. Hymans tried to answer their arguments: his country would have difficulty in reaching a just settlement with the Dutch unless it had compensations to offer; Germany's conduct in 1914 had subsequently justified the obligation. The Council, however, on Wilson's suggestion, deleted the article.[2]

It was a sound decision. German and other critics of the terms of peace could have used the provision further to discredit the entire work of the conference. Nor was it a policy capable of effective implementation without strong and reprehensible pressure upon the Netherlands.

[1] 'Declaration of the Queen's Government to the Netherlands Parliament', communicated to the United States Minister in Paris, February 23, 1919, A.C.N.P., 301, 185.1131/37.

[2] Mantoux, *Délibérations*, I, pp. 261-3.

XIII

APPEASEMENT OR STATESMANSHIP?

THE fifty-two feverish days between the presentation of the draft treaty to Germany on May 7 and the signing of the final terms of peace on June 28 give, in retrospect, a microcosmic view of the 'German problem' between the First and the Second World Wars. The grounds of conflict and the divergent attitudes between victors and vanquished and among the victors themselves appeared very largely in the form which they assumed during the postwar years. One sees the classic statements of the case for and against the war-guilt clause of the Treaty of Versailles. One sees British leaders taking positions between France and Germany which some would praise as moderate and far-sighted statesmanship and which others would contemptuously and sadly describe as the seed-time of appeasement. In these and other respects, the negotiations with the German delegation and among the Allies in May-June 1919 provide an indispensable link between the war, the peacemaking, and the twenty years' crisis which followed.

On May 9, Brockdorff-Rantzau, first president of the German delegation to Paris, sounded the basic note of all subsequent German complaints about the treaty: '. . . on essential points the basis of the Peace of Right, agreed upon between the belligerents, has been abandoned'.[1] Thus was inaugurated the enduring controversy over the justice and soundness of the Treaty of Versailles.

[1] Luckau, *The German Delegation at the Paris Peace Conference*, p. 225.

I

In their initial response, the Big Three followed the leadership of Woodrow Wilson, who proposed they reply uncompromisingly that they would consider only practical modifications in the treaty.[1] Despite the Wilsonian firmness of their answer, Lloyd George anxiously asked if the Germans were likely to refuse to sign the treaty. When Clemenceau confidently replied that they would see reason, Lloyd George rejoined: 'Je crains qu'ils ne le fassent pas avant que nous ayons donné à nos armées l'ordre d'avancer.'[2] Did the British Prime Minister here let fall the vital clue to the explanation of his and the British delegation's conduct during the negotiations with the Germans? Was it pure funk, expediency, or principle which underlay the British effort to secure concessions for Germany and which embroiled Lloyd George in strenuous battles with Clemenceau, Woodrow Wilson, and Paderewski?

The first major German criticism[3] of the proposed territorial settlement grudgingly conceded that some cessions could be justified by the principle of national self-determination, but charged that the Allies had bartered German people and territories 'about from sovereignty to sovereignty as if they were mere chattels and pawns in a game for the purpose of giving guarantees for financial or economic claims of the adversaries of Germany'. The Note particularly condemned the Saar and Belgian boundary settlements.[4] Claiming that the Saarlanders were purely German, the Note made one of the most telling points in the entire German case at Versailles: that the future fate of the Saar's peoples would depend not upon free choice but upon payment in gold. Referring to paragraph 36 of the Annex to the Saar articles, the German delegation declaimed: 'In the history of modern times, there will very probably exist no instance whatever that one civilized power had obliged another to surrender its nationals to foreign sway as an

[1] *Ibid.*, p. 233. [2] Mantoux, *Délibérations*, II, p. 26.

[3] 'Note on the Territorial Provisions of the Peace Draft Relating to the West of Germany', German Peace Delegation, May 13, 1919, *P.P.C.*, V, pp. 817-20.

[4] The Schleswig Question was also raised.

equivalent for a sum of gold.' Acknowledging that France must be compensated for its damaged mines, the German Note proposed compensation in kind with 'terms of delivery on a business footing' from both the Saar and the Ruhr, thus avoiding the 'odious' regime devised in the draft treaty.

As for Belgium, the German delegation opposed the proposed cessions in view of Germany's willingness to make full reparation to the Belgians and of the 'undoubtedly non-Belgian' character of the population concerned. Attacking the proposed 'plebiscite' in Eupen and Malmedy as unjustified by the pre-armistice agreement, the Germans rightly described the method as 'inequitable'.

On the request of the Council of Four, the Sub-Commission on the Geographical Frontiers of Germany drafted a reply to the German Note. Under the chairmanship of Tardieu, Sir Eyre Crowe, Mezes, Haskins, della Torretta, and Ijuin met on May 15 to prepare their rejoinder.[1] Their debate was chiefly over the phrasing and tone of an uncompromising draft written by Tardieu.[2] The main problem was how to handle the German 'sum of gold' charge. Article 36 of the Saar Annex had provided for the transference to France of areas whose inhabitants had voted for Germany *if* the Reich had not paid in gold or its equivalent the agreed price for the mines in those districts. Haskins expressed most concern. Tardieu considered that article 38[3] of the Saar Annex partially answered Brockdorff-Rantzau on this point. His argument carried the sub-commission whose draft reply on this point read: '6. Para. 38 of the Annex

[1] The Council formed the Sub-Commission on the Geographical Frontiers of Germany, as one of several committees struck to deal with the German replies. For *procès-verbal* of May 15 meeting, see A.C.N.P., 152, 181.24201/1.

[2] For instance, Tardieu proposed the Allied and Associated Powers should affirm that an *important* element of the inhabitants was French in origin and aspiration. Haskins wanted the word 'important' deleted. Tardieu held to his point, but finally they reached agreement on the following specious phrasing: 'The Allied and Associated Governments deny that the population of this Basin is purely German. It is on account of the mixed character of this population that special provisions have been made. . . .'

[3] This read: 'It is understood that France and Germany may, by special agreements concluded before the time fixed for the payment of the price for the repurchase of the mines, modify the provisions of paragraphs 36 and 37.'

relating to the Basin of the Saar expressly reserves the possibility of a direct arrangement between France and Germany at the end of the fifteen years. The fears which you express on the subject of the possible consequences of paras. 36 and 37 are not, therefore, justified in fact. . . .' Ultimately, they asserted, any deadlock would be resolved by the League of Nations. In fact, this declaration contained little solace for the Germans; it left open the possibility of losing the Saar in whole or part, because of payment difficulties. Overall, the sub-commission's proposed answer contained no modification whatever of the Saar or Belgian terms of the draft treaty.

When the draft reply came before the Council of Four on May 22,[1] Lloyd George condemned the 'sum of gold' clause because under it the Saarlanders could remain in virtual political servitude for economic reasons. Wilson and Clemenceau saw the need for amending the embarrassing clause, but they had difficulty in finding the proper formula to protect German rights while simultaneously guaranteeing payment to France for the mines in areas which, as a result of the plebiscite, remained under German sovereignty. J. W. Headlam-Morley, of the British delegation, strongly recommended the complete recasting of the provision to avoid adverse reactions within Germany and neutral countries. Clemenceau, Wilson, and Lloyd George agreed. The latter emphasized that the revised article should refer only to the question of the ownership of the mines after the plebiscite; 'Il faut dire nettement que notre intention n'a jamais été d'échanger des populations contre de l'or.' It would, in his view, strengthen the hands of those Germans who advised signing the treaty.

Finally the Council of Four, following a formula suggested by Tardieu, adopted the following new clause:

> The obligation of Germany to make such payment shall be taken into account by the Reparation Commission, and for the purpose of this payment, Germany may create a prior charge upon her assets or revenues upon such detailed terms as shall be agreed to by the Reparation Commission.
>
> If, nevertheless, Germany, after a period of one year from the date on which the payment becomes due, shall not have effected the said payment, the Reparation Commission shall do so in

[1] Mantoux, *Délibérations*, II, pp. 165-7; *P.P.C.*, V, pp. 813-15.

> accordance with such instructions as may be given by the League of Nations, and if necessary, by liquidating that portion of the mines which is in question.[1]

Ultimately this became article 36 of the Saar Annex in the Treaty of Versailles.

Otherwise, the Council of Four refused to modify the Saar or the Belgian settlements.[2]

Throughout, Lloyd George had stood firmly by the original decision to institute a special system for the Saar, while pressing strongly for the type of concession which eventually emerged. In general, too, he had revealed a sensitivity about German reactions to the treaty and whether they would sign.

Formidable criticism of the draft treaty was developing within the British delegation. Smuts wrote Wilson about his intense dislike of the terms which, he warned, would not bring peace.[3] Singling out the territorial, reparations, and occupation provisions, Smuts urged drastic revisions to produce a more rational and moderate settlement. Advising Wilson to 'use your unrivalled power and influence' to those ends, he made this moving appeal: 'Democracy is looking to you who have killed Prussianism—the silent masses who have suffered mutely appeal to you to save them from the fate of which Europe seems now to be lapsing.'[3]

Wilson in his response to Smuts on May 16[4] revealed his attitude towards the draft treaty. Granting that it was 'very severe indeed' and 'in many respects harsh', he defended it as not 'on the whole unjust in the circumstances, much as I should have liked to have certain features altered'. Wilson appeared as the stern, avenging, conscientious judge:

[1] *P.P.C.*, V, pp. 828 and 917.

[2] 'Reply of the Principal Allied and Associated Powers on May 24, 1919, to Letters from Herr Brockdorff-Rantzau on May 13 and May 16, 1919', *P.P.C.*, V, pp. 915-17.

[3] Wilson Papers, VIII-A-49, May 14, 1919.

[4] Already Wilson was beginning to receive resignations, usually of minor officials, from members of the American Delegation who protested against the terms of settlement. On May 17, for example, William C. Bullitt wrote a cruel, emotional letter to the President which ended with this repudiation: 'I am sorry that you did not fight our fight to the finish and that you had so little faith in the millions of men, like myself, in every nation who had faith in you.' *Ibid.*, VIII-A-49.

[5] *Ibid.*, VIII-A-49.

> I feel the terrible responsibility of this whole business, but inevitably my thought goes back to the very great offense against civilization which the German State committed, and the necessity for making it evident once for all that such things can lead only to the most severe punishment.

Although stamped with sincerity and bearing the promise of an open mind, Wilson's response showed his attachment to the terms substantially as drawn.

A week later in a memorandum to Lloyd George, with a copy to Wilson,[1] Smuts undertook a wide-ranging critique of the proposed settlement. He told the Prime Minister: 'I think the two cardinal errors in policy of this Treaty are the long occupation of the Rhine, and the enlargement of Poland beyond anything which we had contemplated during the war.' The 'most dangerous provision of the whole Treaty' was the Rhineland occupation. If not dropped, as he preferred, at least the French forces should be restricted in numbers, the Rhinelanders should be under German civil administration and law, and the Rhineland (as well as the Saar) should be within the German customs union. Viewing French economic control of the Saar mines as sufficient, Smuts advised that at least the special regime should automatically end in fifteen years and German sovereignty restored 'as soon as Germany can repurchase the coal mines'.

As for Poland, Smuts advised that Upper Silesia and all 'real' German territory should remain with Germany, that the area of the Free City of Danzig be reduced and the city placed under German suzerainty, with the administration under League auspices. The South African's views on Poland were very strong:

> I am convinced that in the undue enlargement of Poland we are not only reversing the verdict of history, but committing a cardinal error in policy which history will yet avenge. . . . It is reasonably certain that both Germany and Russia will again be great Powers, and that, sandwiched between them the new Poland could only be a success with their goodwill. How, under these circumstances, can we expect Poland to be other than a failure, even if she had that ruling and administrative capacity which history has proven she has not? Even while the Conference is sitting, the Poles are defying the Great Powers. What is going to happen in future with

[1] *Ibid.*, VIII-A-51. Baker, *Woodrow Wilson and World Settlement*, III, pp. 458-65. Botha supported these views. See Buxton, *Botha*, p. 201.

> the Great Powers divided and at loggerheads? I think we are building a house of sand. . . .

Fearing that the German government might make revision of the eastern boundary settlement a condition for signing the peace, Smuts urged Lloyd George to consider the forthcoming German case on this issue very carefully.

Smuts also attacked the reparation provisions, the punishment clauses, the military and air terms, the international rivers and railways articles, and the 'pin pricks' of the Draft Treaty. He told Lloyd George:

> I am very anxious, not only that the Germans should sign a fair and good Peace Treaty, but also that, for the sake of the future, they should not merely be made to sign at the point of the bayonet. . . . The Treaty should not be capable of moral repudiation by the German people hereafter . . . that we should as far as possible carry the German Delegates with us, that we should listen to what they have to say, that we should give all necessary explanations to them, and that where our Clauses appear really untenable, we should be prepared to accept alterations or compromises. . . .

To accomplish these ends, the General recommended oral discussions with the German delegation.

The latter proposal came before the Council of Four at this time, although by another route. In response to a German suggestion, Baruch, Davis, and Lamont of the American delegation backed Loucheur's suggestion that Allied business experts meet with their German counterparts to explain the economic clauses and to listen to their complaints. They told Wilson: 'Loucheur thinks that M. Clemenceau and Mr. Lloyd George will adopt promptly *any* suggestion you make on this matter. . . .'[1]

Wilson accordingly proposed to the Council of Four on May 21 that Allied and German experts meet.[2] They had, he said, to show to the world their readiness to do everything reasonable to induce Germany to sign, otherwise public opinion would question a military advance to force the German signa-

[1] 'Memo for the President.' Initialled: B.M.B., N.H.D., T.W.L., undated. *Ibid.*, VIII-A-54.

[2] *P.P.C.*, VI, pp. 800-92; Mantoux, *Délibérations*, II, pp. 156 *et seq.*

ture. Clemenceau would have none of it: oral negotiations would aid the German game and divide the Allies. Lloyd George suggested they postpone a decision until the full German case had been received. Clemenceau agreed. Wilson acquiesced unwillingly, sourly remarking that 'he was afraid ten years hence we should find that nothing had been got out of the Treaty of Peace, and this would cause a reaction in Germany's favour'.

Wilson showed his great faith in the power of reason—in the ability of the Allied experts to persuade 'reasonable' Germans, like the financier Melchior, that their fears about the destructive powers of the Reparation Commission were not well founded. His attitude contrasted with Clemenceau's more adamant stand: the Germans would sign when the Allied troops moved; and with Lloyd George's prediction: the German delegation would sign if concessions were made.

What these concessions might be, Smuts had advised the Prime Minister; what the consequences of German rejection of the terms might be, Winston Churchill pictured for him.[1] The latter, having read Smuts' paper (and one by Barnes, the Labour member of the British War Cabinet), advised 'it is of profound importance to reach a settlement with the present German Government, and to reach it as speedily as possible'. His impressive argument ran: Doubtless the Allies can militarily overrun Germany but they will encounter serious political and social problems which will be worsened by the re-imposition of the blockade.

> It is one thing to keep a compact force for a long time in comfortable billets around Cologne in a well-administered and adequately rationed district. It is quite another to spread these young troops we have over large areas of Germany holding down starving populations, living in houses with famished women and children, and firing on miners and working people maddened by despair. Disaster of the most terrible kind lies on that road, and I solemnly warn the Government of the peril of proceeding along it. A situation might soon be reached from which the British moral sentiment would recoil. I consider that we shall commit a political error of the first order if we are drawn into the heart of Germany in these conditions. . . .

[1] 'Memorandum by Mr. Churchill', May 21, 1919, Foster Papers.

True, Churchill conceded, British opinion presently insisted upon stern terms. But all classes also pressed for demobilization and the lifting of wartime restrictions. 'The same crowd that is now so vociferous for ruthless terms of peace will spin round tomorrow against the Government if a military breakdown occurs through the dwindling forces which are at our disposal.' The latter point Churchill pressed upon Lloyd George and the Cabinet: 'Our military strength is dwindling every day . . .', 'our strength is ebbing every day . . .'. And he related military weakness not only to enforcing terms upon Germany but also to maintaining Britain's imperial interests: 'the formidable pre-occupations which are arising in the East, where British interests are so pre-eminently engaged, must be taken into consideration before a policy which commits us to a long occupation of Germany if force is resorted to'. After sketching a harrowing picture of British youths firing on the German masses and of Britain floundering in a German morass, he asked: 'Meanwhile, what is going to happen in India, in Egypt, in the Middle East, and in Turkey?'[1]

Thus he advised Lloyd George:

> . . . I strongly urge settling up with the Germans now. . . . the present German Government is sincerely desirous of making a beaten peace and preserving an orderly community which will carry out its agreement. It seems to me quite natural that they should put forward a series of counterpropositions, and we ought to take these up seriatim with patience and goodwill and endeavour to split the outstanding differences.

Churchill warned against '. . . following too far Latin ambitions and hatreds . . .', which could lead to the dissipation of the strong position then enjoyed by the British Empire. He exhorted: 'Settle now while we have the power, or lose perhaps for ever the power of settlement on the basis of a military victory.'

Lloyd George immediately responded to Smuts' and Churchill's advice. On May 29 Lloyd George insistently sought a reconsideration of the occupation regime.[2] Clemenceau refused to reconsider.

[1] These ideas coincided with those of Sir Henry Wilson. Churchill added at the end of his paper that the CIGS concurred with the views it contained.

[2] *P.P.C.*, VI, pp. 108-11.

Wilson struck an adroit, constructive third note by urging that 'we must insist upon the civil life of the people continuing without interference'. To this Clemenceau agreed. Under the aegis of Lloyd George and Wilson, the Council of Four established a four power commission to prepare a new draft convention on the Rhineland occupation. The commission was to provide particularly for complete self-government for the Germans in the occupied area, with certain necessary exceptions, and for the fewest possible troops, concentrated in barracks or reserve areas, with no billeting except perhaps for officers. At least, therefore, if the occupation was retained, it would be limited and ameliorated in the direction sought by Smuts, Noyes, and other moderates.

That same day, the Allies received the main observations and counter-proposals of the German delegation.[1] A twofold note was sounded by the Germans: the victors had broken their promise of a just peace; the Treaty was impossible to carry out. They argued a contradiction existed between the draft treaty and the agreed legal bases of peace negotiations, the wartime assurances of enemy statesmen,[2] and the general idea of a League of Nations. They saw *no* recognition of these principles in the draft treaty, which, according to the German memorandum, embodied a moribund, imperialistic, and capitalistic world outlook. In these introductory passages the essential character of the entire German case against the conditions of peace was well represented: righteous indignation, telling blows, half-truths, flagrant misrepresentation, and patent exaggeration.

On territorial issues, their bitterest attack was directed against the eastern settlement: '. . . it is incompatible with the conception of national self-determination that two and a half million Germans should be torn from their Mother-country against their will . . .' so as to give Poland railway lines and strategic frontiers. Upper Silesia raised the most intense feeling:

[1] 'Observations of the German Delegation on the conditions of peace', May 29, 1919, *P.P.C.*, VI, pp. 759-901.

[2] Namely, no war against the German people, a peace not of violence but of right, peace in the spirit of the League of Nations, no destruction of Germany's position as a world power, and strict observance of the right of self-determination.

'The abstraction of Upper Silesia would remain for Germany an ever-open wound, and the recovery of the lost land would be, from the first hour onward, the glowing desire of every German. . . . Germany cannot spare Upper Silesia; Poland does not need it.' West Prussia was claimed as 'old German territory' with a German population superior to the other inhabitants, numerically, socially, culturally, and economically. The loss of a portion of Pomerania was protested as was the territorial severance of East Prussia from Germany proper. The latter, it was alleged, was being delivered 'economically speaking' into Polish hands; Germany, the Allies were told, could never permit the loss of East Prussia. Also contested were the plebiscites in Mazuria, Marienburg, and Marienwerder: their populations were German; no serious separatist movements existed; therefore, a vote was uncalled for. The cession of Memel was 'rejected by the German government'.

The Danzig settlement was harshly condemned as standing 'in the sharpest opposition to all the assurances given in the statements of President Wilson'. Charging that the economic regime was intended to Polonize 'purely German Territory', the German delegation threatened the proposed settlement 'would lead to violent resistance and to an enduring state of war in the East'. 'The German Government must accordingly reject the proposed rape of Danzig and must insist that Danzig and its environs be left to the German Empire.'

A number of specific points were also raised by the German delegation: the loss of part of Guhrau and Militsch (49,000 Germans and only 3,700 Poles); the cession of the towns of Schneidemuhl and Bromberg (the latter, no more than 18 per cent. Polish population); the purely German district of Netze; the assignment of Leobschutz and Ratibor to Czechoslovakia.

Altogether, the list of rejections and protests was formidable. What were the Germans conceding to the Poles?

They conceded most of Posen, including the capital, in view of the province's 'indisputably Polish character', although they alleged that the Allied boundary proposals were dictated 'not by considerations of nationality, but by those of a strategic preparation for attack on German territory'. In West Prussia, they would give up the 'unquestionably' Polish areas, *except* for a territorial link with East Prussia. The German delegation offered to grant to Poland, under defined international guarantees, free and secure access to the Baltic, by ceding free ports at Memel, Koenigsberg, and Danzig, by an agreement regulating the Vistula, and by special railway conventions. In the free ports, the Germans assured the Allies that Germany and Poland could reach agreement whereby 'every facility could be assured the Polish State by contract for the erection and use of the requisite installations (docks, landing-places, storehouses, quays, etc.)'. Transit rights on railways and waterways would be on a reciprocal basis. On the vital question (for the Poles, to whom it was also a matter of national sentiment) of the Vistula, the Germans, observing that the river constituted an important element in their system of waterways, promised '. . . the German Government is prepared to enter into negotiations with Poland concerning the establishment of regulations for the Vistula'.

In the south, according to the German note, 'Germany demands that the right of self-determination shall also be respected where the interests of the Germans in Austria and Bohemia are concerned'. While renouncing the use of force to alter the German-Austrian frontier, the German government declared: 'Germany cannot pledge herself to oppose the wishes of her German brothers in Austria.'

In the west, the German delegation rejected the Allied proposals of May 24 on the Saar. As for Alsace-Lorraine, the Germans renounced German sovereignty while protesting French acquisition of this 'ancient German territory' which was being 'torn from the nation to which 87 per cent. of its inhabitants belong by virtue of language and customs . . .' and which had economic ties with Germany of 'still greater importance'. The counter-proposal was for a plebiscite with three choices: union with France, union with Germany as an autonomous state, or complete independence with freedom to enter into special economic relations with one of the neighbouring states. The Germans again rejected the cessions to Belgium and made the counter-proposal that Germany would contract to deliver timber to satisfy Belgium's 'not unjustifiable claims'. Zinc was not mentioned!

The Rhineland occupation was also attacked. The German counter-proposal called for evacuation of the bridgeheads and other occupied territories within six months of the signing of the peace treaty. In the interim, the Allied occupation should be regulated by an agreement with Germany which would protect German sovereignty, the rights of the inhabitants, etc. At the same time, the destruction of fortifications in the west and the establishment of a zone 'unoccupied by any military forces' (and other measures of disarmament) were accepted if Germany was admitted with equal rights to the League of Nations.

Any comparison of these and the other positions adopted by the Allies in the Draft Treaty and by the Germans in their Counter-Proposals reveals, on balance, a wide divergence in both spirit and specifics. So wide was the gap, so deep were the passions, so vital the issues for all parties that agreement by negotiation and mutual consent seemed out of the question. Yet, some, at least, of the German positions coincided with those taken by the English and Americans during the interallied negotiations: Wilson had originally believed that the Saar question could be handled as a purely economic affair; Lloyd George had favoured the complete neutralization of the Rhineland. Would it then prove possible for Lloyd George and Woodrow Wilson effectively to take the lead after May 29 in revising the terms of peace so as to bring victor and vanquished closer together?

II

British deliberations on the German counter-proposals began with a meeting of the British Empire delegation on Friday, May 30.[1] Lloyd George believed the Germans' best point was: 'You have a set of principles which, when they suit you, you apply, but which, when they suit us, you deny.' Picking up this comment, General Smuts contended the draft treaty contained provisions which were not included within the Fourteen Points (like the chapter on rivers and railways), or went beyond them, or even contravened them. 'The Allies must be most careful not to treat the Agreement of the 11th November as a scrap of paper. . . . [They] had to consider the effect upon the world of the terms of the Treaty.' A long and involved discussion ensued over the nature of the pre-armistice commitment. Hughes put the opposing point of view most clearly and vigorously:

[1] British Empire Delegation, May 30, 1919, Foster Papers.

> All the facts must be looked at, not merely the Fourteen Points, but also the subsequent addresses and the general circumstances. Certain of the principles laid down by President Wilson were very wide, and had to be applied in such a way as would ensure a just and lasting Peace. If the provisions relating to rivers were necessary in order to make a lasting Peace, then they were justifiable.

In general, the meeting agreed more with this argument than with Smuts'.

Lloyd George, indirectly, accused Smuts of being too technical: 'The real question for consideration was whether the Germans had made out any case of injustice.' In his opinion, two injustices had been committed: the eastern settlement and the Rhineland occupation. About the former, he said: '. . . the Germans had made out a strong *prima facie* case on the Eastern boundaries'. If the Germans had stated the facts correctly, the national consciousness of Upper Silesia was not Polish. In Posen and elsewhere, German districts had been assigned to Poland. 'It might be wise,' Lloyd George thought, 'to suggest a plebiscite. If the Germans refused a plebiscite, they would put themselves out of court.'

As for the Rhineland occupation, Lloyd George stressed not so much injustice to the Germans but cost to the Allies. He complained that the size of the forces had not been fixed and that the costs would in the end be borne by the Allies since they would be subtracted from the reparation payments.[1]

This inconclusive meeting was followed on Saturday, May 31, by a meeting of the British Cabinet in Paris and on Sunday, June 1, and Monday, June 2, by two meetings of the combined British Cabinet and the British Empire delegation. At present, our only insight into these historic sessions is through Lloyd George's revelations, which are not always reliable.[2]

The British and Dominion Ministers formally authorized

[1] Reparation was the fourth main subject of debate. Barnes particularly objected that an undefined liability, which would become heavier the harder the Germans worked, would be demoralizing. While he saw merit in the German counter-proposals in this respect, the Prime Minister 'had not been shaken in his views' on reparations by them. He feared Great Britain would get little or nothing out of the German scheme. Opinion was divided over the issue.

[2] Lloyd George, *Truth*, I, pp. 689-720. Lloyd George quotes extensively from the records of the sessions of June 1 and 2.

Lloyd George to propose four concessions to the Germans: (1) the eastern boundary settlement: revision leaving 'to Germany the districts where the population was predominantly German in cases where there was no overwhelming reason for transferring such districts to Poland . . .' and providing for 'plebiscites being held in doubtful cases'; (2) the League of Nations: a promise to admit Germany earlier than envisaged in the treaty if Germany was 'making a real effort to perform her obligations'; (3) the Rhineland occupation: reduction in the size of the occupying forces and in the period of occupation; (4) reparations: revision in the direction of fixing the amount of Germany's liability. For leverage in the negotiations with Clemenceau and Wilson, Lloyd George was authorized

> to use the full weight of the entire British Empire even to the point of refusing:—
>
> 1. The services of the British Army to advance into Germany.
> 2. The services of the British Navy to enforce the Blockade of Germany.

It was further agreed that Lloyd George should enjoy latitude in negotiating within the above limits.

The long debate leading to these conclusions cannot be adequately reviewed nor understood in the absence of a full record. Opinion does not appear to have been as unanimous as the Prime Minister later made out in the Council of Four.

Differences existed over the eastern frontier. Lloyd George, relaying the advice of expert advisors, recommended conceding a plebiscite in Upper Silesia, and boundary changes elsewhere where the Germans undoubtedly predominated over the Poles, without a plebiscite unless the Poles objected. Against Barnes, Lloyd George actively defended the Polish corridor. Smuts repeated his criticism of the eastern settlement, showing almost complete disdain for the Poles: 'Poland was an historic failure, and always would be a failure, and in this Treaty we (are) trying to reverse the verdict of history.' Balfour, in accepting Lloyd George's recommendations, thrust hard at Smuts and his general viewpoint: 'He had no sympathy whatever with the attacks on the Eastern frontier. It was a very difficult problem and on the whole it had been well handled.' Calling the Germans 'impudent' for complaining about the incorporation of German minorities within Poland, he effectively pointed out that national minorities were inevitable in that part of Europe if new states were to be erected and that the Germans themselves, in insisting upon a land link with East Prussia, sought to retain purely Polish areas. While admitting the past failures of Poland, Balfour accused some of his colleagues of assuming that Germany had suddenly been converted to ways of peace and he asked: '. . . why should there be faith in Germany altering her course, and no hope of—he would not go so far as to say confidence in—Poland behaving as a reasonably civilized State?' Balfour dwelt on the continued danger of German aggression: 'Germany was no unhappy victim of circumstances; she was suffering, and ought to suffer, for her crimes; and there was no sign whatever that Germany was repentant. . . . If the Germans were to be given an army to-morrow, . . . they would immediately start a war of revenge.' Hughes appeared hostile to the German case on Upper Silesia; Fisher urged Lloyd George to reconsider the corridor settlement, if the issue was pressed.

The leaders of the British Empire generally agreed on revising the occupation provisions. In varying degrees, Balfour, and Lloyd George supported Smuts' view that the least they should settle for was a shorter period and strict controls over the size and authority of the occupying forces. The Prime Minister echoed Balfour's comment that the Rhineland occupation really meant support of the French army by the British taxpayer.

Strong opposition evidently developed against the Saar proposals. In his defense. Lloyd George admitted that they 'could not be defended upon any definite principle. They were acknowledged to be a compromise.' But, he pointed out, the alternatives were worse: as the maximum, the French had wanted the Rhineland; as the minimum, they had demanded the 1814 frontier of the Saar. 'On the whole, . . . they had done the best for Germany that reasonably could be achieved. . . .' He expressly asked that, since he had to press so many concessions upon the French, 'he should not be required to place the Saar Valley among them'.

The sentiment dominated the meeting that the French were intransigent. Balfour early in the debate warned that the French would oppose revisions which the British desired. Later he said that he 'recognized also that the British Representatives had been driven into a peculiar state of mind by the greed of France, Belgium and Italy'. But it was Lloyd George who put the problem, from a British viewpoint, bluntly: 'The French (will) give up nothing unless they (are) forced.' Sympathetically he referred to the devastation France had suffered as underlying the savage French hatred of the Germans which had been revealed in the peace negotiations. Yet, though he queried whether the British attitude would be different in the same circumstances, '. . . he did not think that the British Empire would allow the future peace of the world to be tied to the chariot of French fury—legitimate and justified though it might be'. Therefore, he asked the British and Dominion leaders to back an ultimatum (as Hughes rightly described it) to the French: agree to revision or march on Berlin without us. With Winston Churchill in the lead, the imperial ministers agreed.

In retrospect, the British programme of concessions appears restricted in character. On territorial questions it left intact the bulk of the settlement contained in the draft treaty. In another sense, too, the programme was limited. Nowhere did it adversely affect British and Dominion interests. The imperial ministers were not freely offering to sacrifice anything of importance to themselves either to encourage French concessions or to meet the German counter-proposals. Territorially, the Poles were to give way; but no question of agreeing to the demand for return of the German colonies under a League mandate. Each item in the programme contained a solid, calculated kernel of imperial and national interest. The reparations proposal was intended to ensure that Britain and the Dominions received their due share of German payments. The occupation proposals were designed to keep Britain's hands freer to protect imperial interests and to avoid, so it was alleged, the British taxpayer's indirectly subsidizing the maintenance of the French army.

Yet, to see nothing but narrow, selfish British and Dominion interests underlying the programme of concessions would be to distort and misunderstand the Imperial Cabinet's actions. In the first place, that body did not possess a single mind, a single level of ability and comprehension, or a single standard of judgment. The dozen or so men gathered in the Hotel Majestic approached the problem of responding to the German counter-proposals from many different angles. Smuts and Balfour differed profoundly in their approach to the treatment of Germany. Barnes and Hughes saw the problem of reparations and of Germany's admission to the League of Nations in contrasting lights. Similarly, each seems to have supported the common programme for varying reasons. Milner and Austen Chamberlain, for example, on reparations at least, viewed it as a minimum step towards a more enlightened and businesslike handling of the economic and financial settlement; Hughes, probably, looked at its restrictive features. As a result of such differences, the Imperial Cabinet as a body was probably unable to come closer to a more pliant attitude towards the German counter-propositions particularly on economic issues. Another brake upon a broader programme was the necessity of maintaining inter-Allied unity in the face of the enemy. The French were to be pressed, but not too far; hence the acceptance of Lloyd George's plea to drop proposals for a change in the Saar regime.

British and Dominion interests by no means existed in a watertight compartment. If the proposed territorial concessions facilitated the signing of peace and in the long run bolstered the forces of stability in Europe, they served European as well as British interests; they cannot be criticized as the first act of appeasement of Germany at the expense of the east Europeans. Similarly, if amelioration or even elimination of the Rhineland occupation would increase the sums available for reparations and lessen the prospects of renewed war in Europe, these results would be in the French and the general European interest as well as to the advantage of the British Empire. In sum, the British programme of concessions embraced complex considerations: narrow national and imperial concerns, anxiety about the consequences of German refusal to sign, a sense of moderation and justice mingled with expediency, a conviction that the French were intransigent, and some comprehension of the general, long-range interests of Europe and the world.

Armed with a programme and with sanctions, Lloyd George confronted Clemenceau and Wilson in his own flat at 4 p.m., Monday, June 2.[1] The ultimatum was presented: the British

[1] *P.P.C.*, VI, pp. 129-46; Mantoux, *Délibérations*, II, pp. 265-74. The two accounts are basically the same, although Mantoux sharpens points of detail and clarifies certain statements in the Hankey minutes.

'. . . were not prepared to continue the war and march on Germany or join in the reimposition of the blockade unless certain defects in the Peace Treaty were put right'. In the east, Lloyd George proposed a plebiscite in Upper Silesia and frontier adjustments favourable to Germany in the Guhrau, Militsch, Schneidemuhl, Konitz, and north Pomeranian regions. In defending the plebiscite, he prophesied that a German war of revenge would be averted if the results favoured Poland. He soothingly assured the Council: 'His personal view was that Upper Silesia would vote in favour of Poland.' Memel, he dismissed as a 'minor matter'. As for the Rhineland occupation, 'To this his Colleagues would not agree'. In a frank outburst, he told Clemenceau that the Imperial Cabinet considered European peace would be endangered if a large French army was stationed on the Rhine because of the dangers of incidents which could lead to war and to British involvement. His frankness had limits, however: no mention of the British taxpayer! If Clemenceau did not meet the British point of view, Lloyd George would place the entire matter before Parliament. Yet, there was no outright rejection of an occupation: a short-term occupation of no more than two years was at least acceptable to British military opinion. On the other issues, League of Nations, reparations, pin pricks, Lloyd George similarly unfolded the British attitude.

The session turned into a contest between the British and the French Prime Ministers. Wilson was non-committal: 'Dans l'ensemble, beaucoup de ses critiques me paraissent dignes d'examen.'

Although obviously upset, Clemenceau avowed his openness to reason. In general, he stood firm on the Rhineland occupation and on reparations while prepared to consider changes affecting the Polish frontiers and occupation costs. On the eastern question, he stressed they had re-established Poland to redress a historic wrong and to create a barrier between Germany and Russia: 'If Poland fell to Germany, the Allies would have lost the war.' As for the occupation, '. . . he could not agree to there being no troops on the Rhine . . .' because they would be the most effective guarantee of German execution of the entire treaty. On the other hand, he deplored the possibility of the just reparations claims of Britain or the other allies suffering as a result of the costs of the occupation; on that he would negotiate.

Clemenceau feared the implications of the British proposals in terms of French opinion, of inter-Allied unity, and of the success or failure of the vital negotiations with the Germans. In his opinion, a few concessions would simply encourage the Germans to seek more; only firmness would succeed in dealing with the Germans. Clemenceau also struck shrewdly at the element of narrow, selfish interest in the British case:

> Je suis convaincu que nous avons fait ce qu'ils était raisonnable de faire; mais si je recule d'une pas, je sais que j'aurai contre moi un soulèvement général. Peut-on, par une distribution meilleure, donner satisfaction à des critiques qui peuvent être justifiées, sans révolter l'opinion française? Je suis prêt à l'examiner avec vous. L'opinion britannique ne se plaint pas que l'Allemagne ait a donner toutes ses colonies, toute sa flotte. Cela est naturel, chaque peuple voit les questions de son propre point de vue. Un sentiment non moins naturel en France sera que les critiques britanniques se concentrent sur les questions continentales.[1]

Lloyd George rejoined that, if the Germans insisted upon their colonial counter-proposals as a *sina qua non* for signing the peace, he would cede German East Africa if Clemenceau gave up the Cameroons. Britain, Lloyd George remarked has, 'assez de colonies; beaucoup sont pour nous un fardeau'. Undoubtedly, while Lloyd George was bluffing, he was expressing his personal views about colonies. Whether he could have carried the British Cabinet and delegation with him was equally doubtful. In any case, Clemenceau did not accept Lloyd George's challenge.

The Allies had entered their final crisis in negotiating a German settlement. Between them and German acceptance of the terms lay the wide chasm of disunity into which they could plunge and take victory with them. Could they avoid this disaster without simultaneously renewing the war because they could not moderate the conditions already agreed upon?

Unfortunately, the French deliberations following the Council meeting on June 2 remain concealed. On the American side the agitation and reactions produced by the German observations and counter-proposals are more apparent. Here, both by virtue of his high office and of his egocentric personality,

[1] Mantoux, *Délibérations*, II, p. 270. The Hankey minutes make Clemenceau sound sarcastic and almost petty in this phase of his remarks.

Woodrow Wilson stood at the centre of activities, listening, lecturing, deciding.

Smuts appealed to him again. In a letter on May 30,[1] the General, reminding Wilson that they were committed to making peace within the 'four corners' of the Fourteen Points and subsequent addresses, contended that the Germans had struck at the basic weakness of the proposed settlement—the Allied failure to make a Wilson Peace. In at least three respects, according to Smuts, they had treated the pre-armistice agreement like a scrap of paper: the Saar regime, the internationalization of German rivers and railways, and the Rhineland occupation. He concluded: 'There will be a terrible disillusion if the peoples come to think that we are not concluding a Wilson Peace, that we are not keeping our promise to the world or faith with the public. But if . . . we appear also to break a formal agreement . . . we shall be overwhelmed with the gravest discredit, and this Peace may well become an even greater disaster to the world than the war was.'

Wilson's reply was cautious and non-committal: he appreciated the gravity of the situation; Clemenceau and Lloyd George seemed willing to re-study some of their former decisions; he was hopeful that the coming week would be fruitful.[2] In writing this letter, the President may have had Smuts, mandates, and pensions in mind. But basically, Wilson did not—and he could not—agree that *he* had accepted a settlement which substantially contravened his principles. While recognizing the importance of refuting the argument that the moral or legal basis of the peace negotiations had been ignored, he was firmly convinced: 'The real case [is] that justice had shown itself overwhelmingly against Germany.'[3]

Advice, very different in spirit and content, came from Haskins. In a long memorandum dated June 2,[4] the President's intimate counsellor on western territorial questions adopted a basically intransigent attitude towards the German case. Concentrating on territorial issues, the Harvard medievalist-turned-diplomat effectively criticized the weaknesses and misstatements in the German historical arguments. For example, he pointed

[1] Wilson Papers, VIII-A-54; Baker, *Wilson*, III, pp. 466-8.

[2] Wilson Papers, VIII-A-54. [3] See *P.P.C.*, VI, p. 159.

[4] '*In re* German counter-proposals', Wilson Papers, VIII-A-54.

out that it was historically unsound to claim that Upper Silesia had 'belonged to the German State since 1163' if only because this argument rested upon a false identification of the Bismarckian Reich established in 1870 with the loosely organized medieval Holy Roman Empire.[1] Haskins also rightly pointed out to Wilson that 'German speech is (not) a necessary test of political sympathy with the present German Empire . . .' but understandably of course he refrained from applying this argument to the Polish case for Upper Silesia. He also accused the Germans of trying to make 'one-sided use' of the plebiscitary device in their desperate effort to retain territory, although they had themselves never used the device when acquiring territory in the past. These and the other comments in Haskins' memorandum gave the President good debating points for the Council of Four and probably helped to stiffen his attitude towards the German case. On specific issues, the substance of Haskins' advice was: hold fast on the Belgian-German boundary; reject the German demand for a plebiscite in Alsace-Lorraine; resist any substantive changes in the Saar settlement. In the latter case, he dismissed the German observations thus: 'adds nothing definite', 'written for purposes of publicity', and 'contains many misrepresentations'.

Haskins did propose some minor modifications, including the system for consulting the people of Eupen and Malmedy. Here, he thought, the League of Nations instead of Belgium might be responsible and might have power to conduct a plebiscite if necessary.

Wilson's reply to Haskins[2] contrasted significantly with his response to Smuts:

> My dear Haskins:
>
> Thank you very much for your memorandum *in re* the German counter proposals with regard to territorial questions. It is illuminating and helpful, because it is true.
>
> Cordially and sincerely yours, . . .

The brief, inconclusive meeting of the American delegation on June 3[3] was productive of more, conflicting and even un-

[1] In this connection, we should bear in mind Lloyd George's constant reference to Upper Silesia's having been German for 800 years in justifying his attitude towards the proposed plebiscite.

[2] Wilson Papers, VIII-A-54, June 4, 1919.

[3] *P.P.C.*, XI, pp. 197-222.

welcome advice for Wilson. It dramatically revealed Wilson's own outlook on some of the outstanding issues.

Wilson's attitude before his delegation was similar to Lloyd George's before his. Both stressed justice. The British Prime Minister on June 2 had said to the Imperial Cabinet that the primary consideration was to have 'an absolutely just Peace . . .'. If they had based decisions upon the wrong or incomplete facts they should not hesitate to revise the terms. There was no disagreement here with Wilson but there was a difference in frankness at least about where to strike the balance between principle and expediency. According to Lloyd George, '. . . they must see that the terms imposed were expedient as well as just'. By this he meant that the victors were *entitled* to go to the *limits* of justice in dealing with the Germans but that they would be *unwise* in every instance to do so. This attitude provided two yard-sticks for measuring revision: (1) had they gone beyond the limits of justice; (2) had they been unwise or inexpedient in going to the limits of justice in any case? In the east, Lloyd George believed they had gone beyond the limits of justice; in the Rhineland occupation, he judged they had been inexpedient. Both he and Wilson were on common ground as far as the first yardstick was concerned, but in theory at least differed over the second one for as Wilson had said: '. . . if we regard the treaty as just, the argument of expediency ought not to govern . . .'.[1]

Wilson's position on June 3 is difficult to explain. There was a certain air of common experience, of camaraderie about the meeting. The President was seeking advice on possible revisions and yet at the same time he was in a defensive posture towards elements within (and without) his delegation who were critical of the terms of peace to which he had agreed.[2] Of course, in some cases he had agreed only after prolonged resistance, but he seemed to have convinced himself that no essential Wilsonian principle had been violated nor that justice had not been done.

[1] Hoover had asked Wilson where, apart from justice, expedience entered into revision of the draft treaty in order to induce the Germans to sign. Hoover also questioned whether they could be dogmatic about what was just and unjust in the prevailing atmosphere.

[2] See Herbert Hoover, *The Ordeal of Woodrow Wilson*, chap. 15. The author overlooks this aspect of Wilson's position on that occasion, even as between him and the President.

Moreover, he was aware of how hard it had been to reach inter-Allied agreement, he knew the depth of French feeling, and thus feared the divisive effects of reopening issues like the Saar, occupation, etc. Wilson was also moved by a firm anti-German bias—at least against the Weimar ruling class—and by a strong pro-Polish predilection. He placed much faith, too, in the future ability of the League of Nations to solve some of the difficulties facing the peacemakers. The result of these elements in his outlook, combined with his natural idealism and personal sensitivity, placed Wilson, on balance, in the anti-revisionist camp partly out of choice but probably largely through circumstance. The result—anguish, even despair, and a devastating sense of frustration which produced outbursts like that directed against the British delegation.

Wilson wound up the session by saying he was sick and tired of those people who 'overrode our judgment', put irrational terms into the treaty, and, in fear, were now falling over themselves to remove these obstacles lest the Germans refuse to sign. Having the British mainly in mind, Wilson complained:

> From the unreasonable to the reasonable, all the way round, they are all unanimous, if you please, in their funk. Now that makes me very tired. They ought to have been rational to begin with and then they would not have needed to funk at the end. They ought to have done the rational things, I admit, and it is not very gracious for me to remind them—though I have done so with as much grace as I could command.

Recriminations of this kind were inevitable and mutual at that stage of the Paris proceedings. They should be accepted sympathetically for what they were: not cool statements of fact but the emotional outbursts of tired men who had been under prolonged tension and strain and whose consciences pricked them for what they had done and who tried to shift the burden of guilt or responsibility to the shoulders of others.

Wilson's picture of the British role in the territorial and other negotiations leading to the draft treaty of May 7 was at once unfair, misleading, and partly true. Take, for example, the British programme of concessions. On reparations, the accusation applied even though the British delegation and Lloyd George himself had been of two minds on the issue; on Upper

Silesia, the minor German-Polish border adjustments, the Rhineland occupation, and German admission to the League of Nations, the indictment did not ring true. Similarly, on the issues not touched upon in the four-point programme, the British role in the negotiations was more complex than the President suggested. His remarks raised not only the issue of British conduct but also the question of the American delegation's and Wilson's own personal share of responsibility for the decisions taken. Wilson seemed very close to assuming a Pilate-like attitude. Of a lesser man one would say that on this occasion he was a stage-player; of an idealistic, sensitive and frustrated statesman one might comment that it was an unfortunate manifestation of a *crise de conscience.*

No formal decisions on territorial and related issues were taken. On the eastern frontier, Lord considered the Germans had made a poor case for revision. While cautiously conceding that minor readjustments might be made, he upheld the indisputably Polish character of Upper Silesia. He thought a plebiscite would favour Poland but only if it were held under fair conditions. These, he felt, would not be easy to obtain.

An inconclusive discussion took place on the relative importance of the Upper Silesian coal supply to Germany and Poland. Lansing's questioning and Lamont's answers seemed intended to bring out Poland's lack of need for this coal, which suggested they were partial to Lloyd George's proposal. Wilson revealed his approach in proposing that American and Polish economic experts meet to devise arrangements for supplying Germany with Silesian coal. The American economic experts also criticized the power given to Poland under the general economic articles to expropriate private German property in Upper Silesia and force the German, not the Polish, government to pay compensation.

In contrast with the British sessions, the American meeting came to no collective decision on the course to follow in the subsequent negotiations. Wilson had come. He listened. He gradually dominated the discussion—Lansing thought he talked too much.[1] He left to pursue his course in the Council of Four. This inconclusive result to the all too-brief American deliberations was not due entirely to the personality and

[1] Lansing Diary, Desk Book, June 3, 1919.

constitutional position of the President. It was also a reflection of the personal feuds and differences of opinion which underlay the discussion and which, if brought more openly to the surface, could have erupted and rent the American delegation.

III

That afternoon, in the Council of Four, Wilson and Lloyd George dueled, at times violently, over the issue of a plebiscite in Upper Silesia.[1] The Welshman appeared at his forensic best as he brilliantly and relentlessly drove the resistant Wilson from one position to another until finally the President himself proposed a plebiscite. If the German delegation rejected the offer, it should be withdrawn. They also agreed the Guhrau-Militsch region should remain with Germany, the railroad in the Schneidemuhl-Konitz region should be transferred to the German side of the boundary, and the Pomeranian line should be adjusted in Germany's favour. Wilson suggested the inclusion of safeguards for the protection of German property in the areas assigned to Poland; Lloyd George recommended a guarantee that Germany could purchase coal from any areas ceded to Poland on the same terms as the Poles. Clemenceau confined himself largely to brief interventions whenever Wilson seemed to weaken under Lloyd George's barrage. His position was to adhere to the treaty of peace as Wilson had originally suggested. Prophetically, he pointed out that if Allied troops were used in the plebiscite area, even American, the Germans would claim that they had exerted partisan pressure on the voters. Thus, nothing would have been solved: in peace, the same difficulties would be faced as in war; 'Il faut avoir le courage de dire "non", si nous croyons que nous avons raison.'

Perhaps the crux of the dispute between Lloyd George and Wilson was the latter's contention that under the 13th of the Fourteen Points all that had to be established was the indisputably Polish character of Upper Silesia. To this Lloyd George replied, 'this was exactly the challenge that the Germans made. They said that the population was not Polish in sentiment' even though they might be Polish ethnographically or linguistically. Only the people themselves, so the Prime Minister argued,

[1] *P.P.C.*, VI, pp. 147-56; Mantoux, *Délibérations*, II, pp. 275-83.

could determine the question for themselves, by free vote, under fair conditions. 'C'est absurde,' said Wilson in indignantly repudiating Lloyd George's inference that he was not upholding the principle of self-determination. Later, Lloyd George veered heavily in the direction of expediency:

> Nous pouvons faire aux Allemands une concession sans importance réelle si elle les amène à signer. Par exemple, si je suis persuadé que le plébiscite donnera la Haute-Silésie à la Pologne et aidera à la signature, pourquoi ne pas y consentir? Ce plébiscite fera disparaître tout élément de doute sur le sentiment de la population.[1]

But would it remove the element of doubt and hence of controversy? That problem bothered Wilson, as it did Clemenceau, but the President had no weapons left in his armoury with which effectively to combat Lloyd George's forcefulness, persuasiveness, and logic.

On June 4, the Council of Four appointed a Commission on the Eastern Frontiers of Germany.[2] The Commission was instructed to provide for the three frontier rectifications in Germany's favour, a plebiscite in Upper Silesia, German equality with Poles in coal purchases from mines in areas of Upper Silesia finally assigned to Poland, and modification of the economic clauses relating to the treatment of German private property in the transferred areas. Headlam-Morley, Lord, Le Rond, and della Toretta were appointed members of the Commission.

The Council also took a brave decision on the 4th: to invite Paderewski for a hearing next day.[3] For Lloyd George, it was a question of two down and one to go: Wilson, Clemenceau, and now the Polish Prime Minister. Paderewski conceded the frontier rectifications, protesting however, that the readjustments should be reciprocal. Lloyd George quickly supported this stand. The Council instructed the Commission on the Eastern Frontiers to examine the inclusion of the Schildberg-Kempen-Kreutzburg region within Poland. Regarding the proposed economic changes, Paderewski simply commented, 'We understand perfectly well.'

[1] Mantoux, *Délibérations*, II, pp. 280-1. [2] *P.P.C.*, VI, pp. 181 and 186.
[3] *Ibid.*, pp. 191-291; Mantoux, *Délibérations*, pp. 305-12.

What of his attitude towards the plebiscite?[1] Opposition, but resigned acceptance. He made perfectly clear the Polish conviction that a plebiscite would mean the ultimate failure of Poland to acquire the agricultural, western portion, for several reasons. Although ethnographically Upper Silesia contained, by Prussian statistics, 1,500,000 Poles and 700,000 Germans, the western portion was under strong German influence. Roman Catholic clerical influences were held to be strongly German in spirit and despite 'our majorities, amounting in many districts to ninety per cent. and more,—they would decidedly follow the orders of that German clergy. From that point of view a plebiscite is absolutely impossible.' In the eastern districts, Paderewski believed the vote would favour Poland, but the vital mining and industrial area would be too close to the frontier to enjoy security in case of German attack. It was significant that he advised communal voting, evidently fearing the overall result in Upper Silesia. He also had no faith that a delayed vote, following an inter-Allied occupation, would alter the final result by much: in the east, yes; in the west, German officials, landowners, and clergy would remain influential.

Lloyd George and Paderewski clashed frequently over Polish conduct in Galicia and towards the Ukraine, and especially following Paderewski's impassioned protest against the proposed plebiscite or any substantial changes in the boundaries publicly announced for Poland: '. . . I should immediately resign, because I could not return to my country. . . . You know that revolutions begin when people lose faith in their leadership. . . . Well now, if something is taken away from them, they will lose all faith in my leadership. They will lose faith in your leadership of humanity; and there will be revolution in my country.' His assertions were injudicious certainly but they were understandable and forgivable. They provoked a ferocious, even cruel riposte from the Celt, the final thrust being the devastating words: 'She (Poland) has won her freedom, not by

[1] The Polish delegation backed Paderewski with two formidable, formal memoranda on Upper Silesia and other issues: (1) 'Observations of the Polish Delegation with regard to the remarks of the German Delegation on the conditions of peace', A.C.N.P., 425, 760C.62/21; (2) 'Supplemental Remarks . . .', *ibid.*, 305, 185.11382/51 and /70.

her own exertions, but by the blood of others; and not only has she no gratitude, but she says she loses faith in the people who have won her freedom.' Both men quickly realized they had gone too far and the flame of dispute slowly flickered down. And Paderewski did get the Schildberg crumb from the table!

The Commission on the Eastern Frontiers of Germany began to work on June 6.[1] By June 10, its reports were ready and were presented to the Council of Four on the following day. It reached agreement on the financial and economic clauses without much difficulty. Headlam-Morley, backed by Lord,[2] submitted that the Polish treasury should pay for an injury done to German nationals whose property was expropriated by the Polish state in *all* the territories ultimately transferred from Germany to Poland. Le Rond demurred slightly. On the minerals question, Le Rond proposed that German imports from the mines in those parts of Upper Silesia which were assigned to Poland should be limited by a 25 per cent. quota and that the special arrangements envisaged to assure to the Germans Upper Silesian coal on equal terms with the Poles should exist for a ten-year period. Le Rond, however, faced the combined opposition of the British and American delegations. Headlam-Morley suggested that the transitional period last fifteen years, following the Saar precedent. The Commission finally recommended that Poland was to permit the sale to Germany of mineral products in the transferred areas of Upper Silesia for a fifteen-year period, free of export duties or other restrictions, and upon the same terms as for Polish or other purchasers.

More difficulty was encountered over the territorial readjustments. Le Rond advocated, on grounds of equity, that if the Council of Four wanted as strict an ethnical line as possible,

[1] This account of its work is based upon the English and French minutes in A.C.N.P., 143, 181.21501/1 *et seq.*

[2] Lord had circulated on June 5 to Wilson and the other American Commissioners a memorandum entitled 'Remarks on the Observations of the German Delegation on the Conditions of Peace', Wilson Papers, VIII-A-56. He vigorously examined each point on Poland in the German note, sometimes with elaborate sarcasm. A strong pro-Polish, anti-German bias appeared. His advice was the same as that tendered in the meeting of the American delegation on June 3.

modifications should be reciprocal.[1] Lord and Headlam-Morley were not unreceptive to this proposal, but, as the American representative put it, they opposed following the principle of compensations all along the line. The main British aim, as interpreted by Headlam-Morley, was to reduce the number of German-speaking peoples assigned to Poland.

There were two main types of cases discussed by the Commission: (1) those, four in number, specifically referred to the members by the Council of Four; (2) those not mentioned by the Council but raised by members themselves, usually by Le Rond, and favouring Poland.

The Commission spent little time on the Guhrau-Militsch and the Schildberg-Kempen-Kreutzburg regions. The former, with its 38,000 Germans and 2,000 Poles, was shifted from Poland back to Germany; the latter, with its 31,000 Poles and 11,000 Germans, was assigned to Poland. In the Schneidemuhl-Konitz question, Le Rond, Lord, Kisch, and Headlam-Morley agreed that Konitz should remain in Poland. They also suggested that Schlochau, with its 6,300 Poles and 1,500 Germans, should go to Poland.

[1] In this connection, it may be noted that Lord had asked for a meeting of the Commission on Polish Affairs on June 4. Under instructions, Kisch withdrew with the excuse that the Council of Four was seized of the problem of Poland's frontier with Germany. Actually Lloyd George regarded the Commission as impossibly pro-Polish and did not expect it to take a sympathetic attitude towards rectifications. The members remaining at the session, Lord, Jules Cambon, Le Rond, and Toretta, agreed: (1) that they should send a note to the Council of Four to the effect that the existing line took all factors into account and if changes were to be made they should be as favourable to the Poles as to the Germans; (2) that Germany should be assured of Silesian coal for a five-year transitional period. After a long discussion of the plebiscite question, it was clear they considered it would be unfair under the existing circumstances. The Council of Four should be advised of the necessity for delay and for an interallied occupation. Lord believed the 'practical difficulties [were] of an almost insurmountable character'. A.C.N.P., 139, 181.213201/25. Next day, Lord sent a note on the results of these discussions to Wilson (separate from the other memorandum of the same date) underlying how inequitable a plebiscite would be under existing circumstances. He advised: '. . . it would be necessary to transform the political, administrative, and religious organization of Upper Silesia to assure to the Poles, by prolonging the new regime for a considerable period, the time necessary to form a free and mature decision about their future'. Wilson Papers, VIII-A-56.

As for the Chottchow or Lauenberg region of Pomerania, the persistent Kisch remarked that here only 12,000 Pomeranians were transferred to Poland, compared to 900 Poles. Like Le Rond, Lord, and Toretta, Kisch was still an 'old hand' of the Commission on Polish Affairs. But despite the obvious reluctance of the French and American representatives and of his colleague, Headlam-Morley insisted they were bound by the instructions of the Council. They finally recommended that the former administrative boundary between Pomerania and West Prussia be followed except in the Lake Zarnowitz area where the administrative line would cut the Neustadt-Chottchow railway in three places. Their report pointed out that this adjustment favoured Germany and weakened Poland's seacoast position strategically by advancing the Germans to within twenty kilometres of the Gulf of Danzig.

Throughout Le Rond led a persistent French effort to secure other readjustments in Poland's favour. In the Bomst-Lissa district, Le Rond, supported by Toretta, whose delegation generally supported the French in these negotiations, proposed that the Fraustadt area, involving only 2,500 people, go to Poland. The English members opposed. Fraustadt remained German. Farther north, Filehne, with 9,708 Poles and 7,300 Germans, had originally been left in Germany. Le Rond urged Filehne's assignment to Poland. Initially, the British delegation rejected the proposal but on June 10, it agreed that Filehne could go to Poland. Still farther north, Le Rond and Lord favoured an adjustment in Poland's favour in the Batow-Prochlau region. Headlam-Morley opposed. He was prepared to accept a modification around Butow affecting 6,300 Poles and 1,500 Germans, but no such recommendation was made.

In its final report,[1] the Commission recommended rectifications which on balance subtracted 99,600 Germans from Poland and added 29,200 Poles.

The most substantial problem before the Commission was, of course, the plebiscite in Upper Silesia.[2] Four main issues arose: the principle of holding a plebiscite, the area to which it was to apply, whether to have an immediate or a delayed vote, and

[1] 'Report of the Committee on the Eastern Frontiers of Germany', June 10, 1919, A.C.N.P., 143, 181.21502/3.

[2] See also above, p. 350, n. 1.

the other general conditions under which the consultation should take place.

On the question of principle, Le Rond wanted the Commission to report why a plebiscite was unnecessary. In his opinion, no uncertainty existed about either the ethnical character or the national aspirations of the population. Headlam-Morley countered that he personally believed in the equity of a plebiscite. In any case the Commission had a mandate only to discuss implementation of the vote. Lord reluctantly agreed.

Various proposals were made about the area to be covered by the vote. Through Le Rond, the French delegation sought to exclude the five districts in the Regency of Oppeln which had sent Polish deputies to the Reichstag in the 1912 elections. To stage a plebiscite in indisputably Polish areas would be unjust to the Poles. Headlam-Morley avoided meeting this proposal head on by claiming the Commission had been instructed to deal with Upper Silesia as a whole. Lord saw the strength of the French argument, but sided with Headlam-Morley in side-tracking it. When Paton suggested extending the vote to Leobschutz and Ratibor, Le Rond turned the British legal point against them! The British delegation also failed to extend the plebiscite to those portions of Middle Silesia—Namslau and Gross-Wartenberg—which had been assigned to Poland.

In setting a voting date, the British representatives found themselves arrayed against the French, Americans, and Italians. Initially Le Rond proposed that no vote take place for three years at least, but later he agreed with Lord and Toretta on a period of one to two years. Against this, the British favoured balloting within six months. This proposition was defended by Paton on the following grounds. Because the period before the vote would be marked by antagonism between Germans and Poles, the general interest would be best served if it were held within the minimum period necessary to ensure an equitable result. Naturally, the Poles wanted a delayed vote because, so he admitted, Polish national sentiment was growing in Upper Silesia.

> But the duty of the Commission was to favour the expression of the present feelings of the population and not to allow this feeling to be modified in a direction favorable to Polish aspirations. It would doubtless be proper to prevent the German administra-

> tion from terrorizing the population, but this result would be easily obtained by the withdrawal of troops and officials and by an inter-allied occupation. Perhaps one might even require the departure of mine owners and of certain big landowners, which would represent only a small number of persons and could not materially change the result of the vote.
>
> It was not certain for that matter that the influence of German authorities and their means of applying pressure were as powerful as was generally admitted. The example of the 1912 elections . . . were sufficient proof in this direction.

He continued: In view of the rapid wartime growth of Polish national consciousness in Upper Silesia and of the attraction of an independent Poland, within six months, if elementary precautions were taken, the Germans would be incapable of preventing a free expression of opinion. He concluded:

> Thus a plebiscite in the near future, the practical advantages of which were evident, would very sufficiently satisfy the considerations of equity which all the Delegations were agreed to take into account.[1]

Speaking for the majority on the Commission, Lord felt that the Upper Silesians needed time to make a free expression of opinion possible. He could not agree 'that the Commission should seek only to bring about the expression of opinion of the population as this opinion existed at present'. A surprise vote favourable to the Germans within a six-month period would not halt the development of Polish sentiment in Upper Silesia. Within fifteen or twenty years a grave situation would exist: 'The existence of an unredeemed Poland would imperil the peace of Europe.' Toretta agreed with Lord, but Paton believed that the existing German 'terror' would arouse, not intimidate the population. Headlam-Morley comfortingly prophesied that existing national passions would likely abate. In any case, they were drawing other frontiers on the assumption that sizeable German minorities would reach a *modus vivendi* with the dominant

[1] Minutes of June 6, 1919, A.C.N.P., 143, 181.21501/3. Headlam-Morley thought 'that in Upper Silesia, as in Eastern Europe in general, the intimidation of property owners by the rural population is more to be feared than the opposite phenomenon'. Later, a lengthy British note constituted a 'minority report'. It simply spelled out Paton's arguments in detail.

Czechs, Italians, etc., in their respective states. 'Why could not a *modus-vivendi* succeed in establishing itself in the same way between Poles and Germans in Silesia?'

And so the argument ran on, the majority's view being finally summed up in the report of the Commission:

> The essential conditions for a just plebiscite are that the population in question should be able to form its decision on the basis of full and free discussion and a clear and intelligent conception of the issues placed before it, and that it should be able to express its decision without fear of the consequences.
>
> The situation in Upper Silesia is such that these indispensable conditions cannot be realised until the country has been under a regime very different from the present one for a considerable period of time.

Headlam-Morley drew the impasse over the timing of the plebiscite to the Council's attention on June 9.[1] The Four postponed a decision by instructing the Commission to draft schemes for an immediate and a delayed vote. Thus the final report contained two alternatives: a vote within six months; no vote for at least a year after inter-Allied control had been established.

In drafting the other conditions for the plebiscite, the Commission encountered no great difficulties over the right of suffrage and similar matters, including the subject of 'outvoters' which became so serious an issue later on. Their main concern was to provide for a fair expression of opinion. All members agreed that the minimum requirements were evacuation of German troops and officials and establishment of an inter-Allied occupation and administration. But how many and what classes of Germans with influence should be expelled? What should the power of the international commission be in this regard? What should its administrative authority be? Important differences of opinion arose over these issues. Le Rond wanted precise, detailed provisions to ensure freeing the Upper Silesians from German influences. Paton sought to reduce Le Rond's position to logical and practical absurdity: '. . . if the period which was to precede the plebiscite should last three years, and if not only German troops and Prussian officials

[1] *P.P.C.*, VI, p. 259; Mantoux, *Délibérations*, II, pp. 351-2.

were evacuated but also the landed proprietors and their personnel, as well as mine owners and their subordinates, without counting the clergy, in the end the life of the country would be completely paralyzed'. Lord agreed that mass expulsions were impossible.

On Headlam-Morley's advice, Lloyd George raised this matter in the Council of Four on June 9. Referring to the report that some members of the Commission wanted even to expel the German clergy from Upper Silesia, Lloyd George exclaimed it was impossible because: 'cela mettrait l'Eglise catholique contre nous'. The Council adopted his suggestion that the Commission be instructed to leave such details to the proposed International Commission for Upper Silesia.

More seriously, perhaps, from the British delegation's point of view, if the period were prolonged, the International Commission would have to assume a heavy role in the administration of Upper Silesia. Its problems would be akin to that of the Saar Commission. Its power would have to be commensurate and similarly carefully defined. In such a situation, the likelihood of friction with Germany would be greater. This was another reason why the British delegation favoured the shorter period: the International Commission administratively could 'make do' for six months or so.

In its report, the Commission for the Eastern Frontiers of Germany recommended *inter alia*. The evacuation within fifteen days after the treaty came into force of German troops and of German officials. The dissolution of all Workers' and Soldiers' Councils and evacuation of any of their officials who had come from other regions. They were held to exercise a German political influence in the area. The disbandment of all local military and semi-military organizations including the expulsion of any of their members who were not natives. This was designed to prevent Upper Silesian Germans from using force to promote their cause. As for the powers of the Four Power International Commission, the report contained two sets of articles, those appropriate for a delayed plebiscite and those for an immediate one, embodying Headlam-Morley's proposals. Since the Council of Four preferred the latter even for a delayed plebiscite, they are summarized here. The Commission's authority was to include: all powers exercised by the German and Prussian governments except for taxation and legislation; maintenance of order; measures necessary to ensure a free and secret vote, etc. In addition to designating German officials who should be evacuated and to providing for their replacement, the International Commission was to have authority to expel 'any person who may in any way have attempted to distort the result of the plebiscite by methods of corruption or intimidation'. Obviously these were elastic provisions which wisely left much to the discretion of the members of the International Commission. To prevent political reprisals, the Commission on the Eastern Frontiers also recommended that the Polish and German governments be obliged not to undertake prosecutions against anyone in their territories for political actions in Upper Silesia during the plebiscitary regime.

Before finally binding himself on the eastern frontiers Lloyd George consulted the British Empire delegation on June 10.[1] Although, as he told the delegation, difficulties had been encountered over Upper Silesia in the Commission on the Eastern Frontiers because its membership had been substantially the same as the pro-Polish Commission on Polish Affairs,[2] he was optimistic about acceptance of the British view on Germany's eastern frontier by Wilson and Clemenceau.

Backed by his colleagues, Lloyd George now faced the final showdown in the Council of Four on June 11.[3] Clemenceau reiterated his opposition to the Upper Silesian plebiscite. 'Soyez tranquille,' he advised Lloyd George who had said the plebiscite would avoid trouble in eastern Europe, 'vous aurez des troubles de ce côté, qu'il y ait un plébiscite ou qu'il n'y en ait pas.'

Wilson remained convinced the plebiscite was uncalled for by the Fourteen Points. Unsuccessfully he brought up Le Rond's suggestion that the vote be taken only in part of Upper Silesia. Very soundly, in a sharp dig at Lloyd George, he cautioned against sacrificing Polish interests while abandoning, on

[1] British Empire Delegation, June 10, 1919, Foster Papers.

[2] He referred to Lord as 'very strong advocate of Polish claims' and to Le Rond as 'dominated by the idea that it was necessary to take as much territory as possible from Germany in order to weaken Germany, not recognizing in any way, that in some cases this course would weaken the State to whom the territory was given'.

[3] *P.P.C.*, VI, pp. 303-5, 311-18; Mantoux, *Délibérations*, II, pp. 380-7.

reparations for instance, any sacrifice by the Allies. In reply to Lloyd George's accusation that the Poles were good propagandists and that in Paris the Council was hearing only one side of the case, Wilson heatedly answered that the Germans were in the superior political and propaganda position in Upper Silesia, and as 'against the Germans he was pro-Pole with all his heart'.

Lloyd George was adamant. It would cause serious turmoil if Germans, who considered themselves a superior race, were placed under Polish rule against their will. To back up his position Lloyd George repeated the ultimatum: British troops would not fight to uphold the original settlement. He promised, unreliably as events turned out, they would be used to defend the plebiscite. He had his way.

The Council of Four approved the recommendations of the Commission on the Eastern Frontiers of Germany. Lloyd George gave up the British position on the timing of the plebiscite; the period of one or two years was thus adopted. On Lord's suggestion, Headlam-Morley's draft articles defining the powers of the International Commission replaced those recommended by the majority.

Only one task remained: to inform Paderewski. With Dmowski, the Polish Prime Minister heard the final decision of the Council on June 14,[1] Wilson having been chosen for this chore. Solemnly controlling his emotions, Paderewski made the dignified reply: 'The Polish Delegation could only accept the decision (on Upper Silesia) with profound respect but with deep sorrow.' From the ensuing discussion, it appeared clear that the Poles and the Big Three had virtually written off the rural areas of Upper Silesia. It was, in short, a decision to partition Upper Silesia between the two countries without immediately drawing a frontier between them in that disputed area. Dmowski predicted the continued growth of Polish national sentiment in the districts which would go to Germany and asked the members of the Council what they would do if a Polish revolt broke out, fifteen or twenty years later. Hastily and soothingly, Wilson and Lloyd George praised the League of Nations as an instrument of peaceful change. Dmowski's reaction is not recorded.

The British position on the timing of the plebiscite was

[1] *P.P.C.*, VI, pp. 449-52; Mantoux, *Délibérations*, II, pp. 420-3.

supported by Paderewski who advised that the vote be held within three or six months after the treaty had gone into force 'in order to quieten things down'. Not to be denied a little triumph, Lloyd George, after the Poles had departed, self-righteously pointed out to Wilson and Clemenceau that Paderewski's attitude proved he had been right in contending how hard it was to legislate for others especially upon the advice of 'friends of the Poles'. Resignedly, Wilson moved that the plebiscite be held from within six to eighteen months after the treaty was ratified, permitting either an immediate or a delayed plebiscite.

On another issue, Lloyd George met defeat. He wanted the districts of Upper Silesia transferred to Poland (and Danzig) to bear their share of Germany's reparations debt, because 'It is not just to say to Silesia that if she voted out of Germany, she would escape a payment of perhaps 500 million pounds. This was loading the dice against Germany.'[1] What was Lloyd George really seeking in the Upper Silesian negotiations? He had defined several objectives: to induce the Germans to sign the treaty; to get German forces out of the region without fighting; to be fair to both parties; to apply the principle of national self-determination equitably; to give the Germans no just reason for complaint, etc. At the same time, his or his representatives' proposals meant a partition of Upper Silesia, without saying so specifically, to salvage as much for the Germans as possible. In making the 'loading the dice against Germany' charge was Lloyd George simply bearing in mind the burdens of the British Exchequer? He did complain that if the transferred districts bore no share of German reparations, 'this might cost scores of millions of pounds to the British Empire, and hundreds of millions to France, and he had felt bound to make the strongest protest'. But Sonnino pointed out, relief from reparation responsibilities offered a powerful inducement to German landowners and industrialists in Upper Silesia 'to use their influence to the utmost to vote against Germany'. This political consideration may be what most concerned Lloyd George. In any event, Wilson, who indignantly repudiated the accusation of weighing the scales against Germany, and Clemenceau gave no support to Lloyd George's proposal.

[1] *P.P.C.*, VI, pp. 455-6.

IV

Lloyd George, in the British Empire delegation on June 10,[1] optimistically reported on prospects for a satisfactory settlemen of the Rhineland occupation question. According to him, the French were prepared to sign a convention providing for the protection of civilian life against military interference, including no regime of martial law. They were also willing to limit occupation costs to 240,000,000 marks per year, which would support an army of 110,000 men. The question, however, of reducing the occupation forces in proportion to the rate of German land disarmament had not been taken up thus far. Lloyd George doubted that the occupation would last for fifteen years. Balfour agreed that he had made a 'very good bargain from the British point of view'.

Barnes was outspokenly dissatisfied: the fifteen years' occupation was a great mistake. Later, he circulated a paper giving three reasons why he felt the occupation to be unwise: (1) it was contrary to the understanding reached with the French in December 1918; (2) militarily it was unwise, except for the few months during which Germany disarmed; (3) it was dangerous because it would provoke hostile feelings and then actions between France and Germany which would surely involve Great Britain and the United States.[2]

In the Council of Four on June 12,[3] Lloyd George proposed they ask the military authorities whether they preferred a long occupation under weak conditions or a short occupation under hard conditions. Lloyd George expressed a preference for the latter. Clemenceau asked that no change be made in the existing agreement. In an effort to arrange a compromise, Wilson, who feared an Anglo-French rift over this issue, asked Clemenceau if he would agree to reconsider the matter '. . . après une date fixée'. The French Prime Minister was receptive: between themselves, but not with the Germans, he would undertake to return to the question of the length of the occupation, provided the Germans had shown good faith in executing the terms of

[1] B.E.D. 35th Minutes, Foster Papers.

[2] 'Rhineland Occupation. Note by Mr. Barnes, June 10, 1919', *P.P.C.*, VI, pp. 342-3.

[3] *P.P.C.*, VI, pp. 327-9; Mantoux, *Délibérations*, II, pp. 392-4.

peace. Lloyd George picked up the idea: could he announce it in Parliament if he encountered difficulties in getting the Treaty of Guarantee accepted? He explained that his government faced a crisis with the Labour Party: 'M. Barnes, qui répresente l'élément ouvrier dans notre délégation, menace de partir si aucune modification n'est faite. Je vous demande de m'aider.' Clemenceau, who evidently had had in mind a private understanding, hesitantly conceded that a statement might be arranged. Rather ungraciously, Lloyd George went on to comment that the occupation had only a political object: to protect the French ministry against the opposition! In reply, Clemenceau avowed that the occupation rested on neither political nor *military* considerations; its function was to guarantee the execution of the financial clauses of the treaty.

Wilson had pointed the way out of their difficulty, but Lloyd George first had to protect his political flank by satisfying the chief protesters, Bonar Law and Barnes. In an astute and rather amusing move, he brought the two together with Clemenceau, whom he had assured: 'Si vous leur donnez satisfaction, vous n'aurez aucune difficulte à me satisfaire.' In their encounter on June 13,[1] Clemenceau overwhelmed Law and Barnes with his persuasive eloquence. According to him, the heart of the issue was the complexity of the treaty, German bad faith, and the consequent difficulty of enforcing the terms by means short of coercion in the form of a fifteen year occupation. He had originally wanted thirty years, but had accepted the Anglo-American guarantee instead. Pointing out that the treaty provided for reducing the length of the occupation, Clemenceau defined two conditions for this: evidence of German good faith and effective alternative guarantees. He assured Law and Barnes that when these proofs were offered the conversation could be resumed. Law vainly sought to fix a date for the re-examination: three years? Non! Five years? Encore non! Finally they accepted, despite Barnes' grumbling, Lloyd George's formula for re-examination at the undefined time when Germany had proved good faith and offered satisfactory guarantees.

The measure of agreement which the British delegation could obtain was summed up in the tripartite agreement of June 16 on the occupation of the Rhine provinces.[2] If Germany fulfilled

[1] Mantoux, *Délibérations*, pp. 408-12. [2] *P.P.C.*, VI, p. 522.

the agreed conditions, the Allied and Associated Powers were willing to agree on an earlier termination of the occupation. They would also limit the occupation costs to 240,000,000 gold marks as soon as they were convinced that Germany had fulfilled its disarmament obligations. Paris effectively preserved a power of veto over any deviation from the relevant treaty articles and over the cost, and hence the size of the army of occupation. Of course, the degree of Lloyd George's success must also be reckoned in terms of the *Convention Regarding the Military Occupation of the Territories of the Rhine* which provided, *inter alia*, for a civilian Inter-Allied Rhineland High Commission and for the protection of German civilian affairs from undue interference by the military authorities.[1]

By now the Allies had prepared their full reply to the German counter-proposals.[2] They reaffirmed their conviction that their terms constituted 'fundamentally a peace of justice' and fulfilled the pre-armistice agreement. On territorial issues the Allies held to the conditions of May 7, with certain exceptions, maintaining that the 'territorial proposals are in accord both with the agreed basis of peace and are necessary to the future peace of Europe'. Their main concessions were the plebiscite in Upper Silesia, the eastern border adjustments largely in Germany's favour, and the elimination of the third zone in the proposed Schleswig plebiscite. In addition, some conditions involved in the transfer of territory were ameliorated: for example, the new financial and economic clauses covering the German-Polish border settlement, the giving to the League of Nations of authority to supervise the popular consultation in Eupen and Malmedy, and the strengthening of Germany's transit rights across the Polish Corridor. The 'sum of gold' clause was eliminated from the Saar articles. The proposed Rhineland convention offered some protection to the German civil administration. Nowhere did the Big Three make territorial and related concessions to Germany which represented a large sacrifice. The Upper Silesian plebiscite was at the expense of an ally. On the other hand, taking the situation in Paris as it was in May-June 1919,

[1] *Ibid.*, pp. 389-93.

[2] 'Reply of the Allied and Associated Powers to the Observations of the German Delegation on the Conditions of Peace', Paris, June 16, 1919, *P.P.C.*, VI, pp. 926-96.

to have pressed concessions further would have threatened Allied unity. They probably went about as far as they could politically at that time.

In their confidential report to the Berlin government,[1] the German delegates complained of the intensified spirit of condemnation of Germany. They must have recoiled as if stung from the closing retort in the Allied reply, quoting Woodrow Wilson: 'The reason why peace must be guaranteed is that there will be parties to the peace whose promises have proved untrustworthy.' In assessing the modifications in the territorial clauses, the delegation noted their scarcity. The concessions in Posen and Middle Silesia were dismissed as insignificant. The Upper Silesian plebiscite was incorrectly viewed as an attempt to turn 'German Upper Silesia' over to the Poles. As proof, the exemption from reparations and the inter-Allied occupation were cited. The Rhineland convention was criticized on economic grounds and the entire occupation regime interpreted as 'the first step toward permanent political separation of the Rhineland . . .'. In concluding that the entire treaty was unjust, incapable of execution, and dishonouring to Germany, Brockdorff-Rantzau and his colleagues advised the German government not to sign the modified terms of peace.[2] Only after another political convulsion in Berlin could a government and a delegation be found to sign the Treaty of Versailles.

On the territorial and other issues of the peace, the Allied Reply and the German delegation's Report illustrated how far apart, emotionally and physically, the victors and the vanquished were, although to the Germans the unity and malignancy of the Allies looked greater than they were in fact. Negotiation had, in the existing circumstances, accomplished all that was possible to inch the contending sides together by means of discussion, compromise, and agreement. Force or the threat of force alone could bring uneasy and insincere acceptance of a settlement which, however imperfect and unsatisfactory, would at least end the formal state of war and give the world some framework within which men could hope to settle down and begin to work towards a more durable and mutually acceptable international order.

[1] Luckau, *The German Delegation at the Paris Peace Conference*, pp. 483-8.

[2] See map 3 for the final boundary settlement.

GERMANY AFTER 1919
THE FINAL BOUNDARY SETTLEMENT
1919–1923
NORTH SEA
BALTIC SEA
DENMARK
SCHLESWIG
NETHERLANDS
BELGIUM
EUPEN
MALMEDY
LUX.
FRANCE
ALSACE-LORRAINE
SAAR
SWITZERLAND
AUSTRIA
HUNGARY
CZECHOSLOVAKIA
POLAND
LITHUANIA
MEMEL
EAST PRUSSIA
ALLENSTEIN
MARIENWERDER
UPPER SILESIA
GERMANY
Danzig
Königsberg
Warsaw
Vistula River
Budapest
Vienna
Prague
Berlin
Oder River
Leipzig
Hamburg
Elbe River
Bremen
Weser River
Munich
Danube River
Stuttgart
Mainz
Coblenz
Cologne
Rhine River
SCALE OF MILES
0
50
100
BOUNDARY OF 1914
GERMANY AFTER 1919
DEMILITARIZED ZONE
PLEBISCITE AREAS

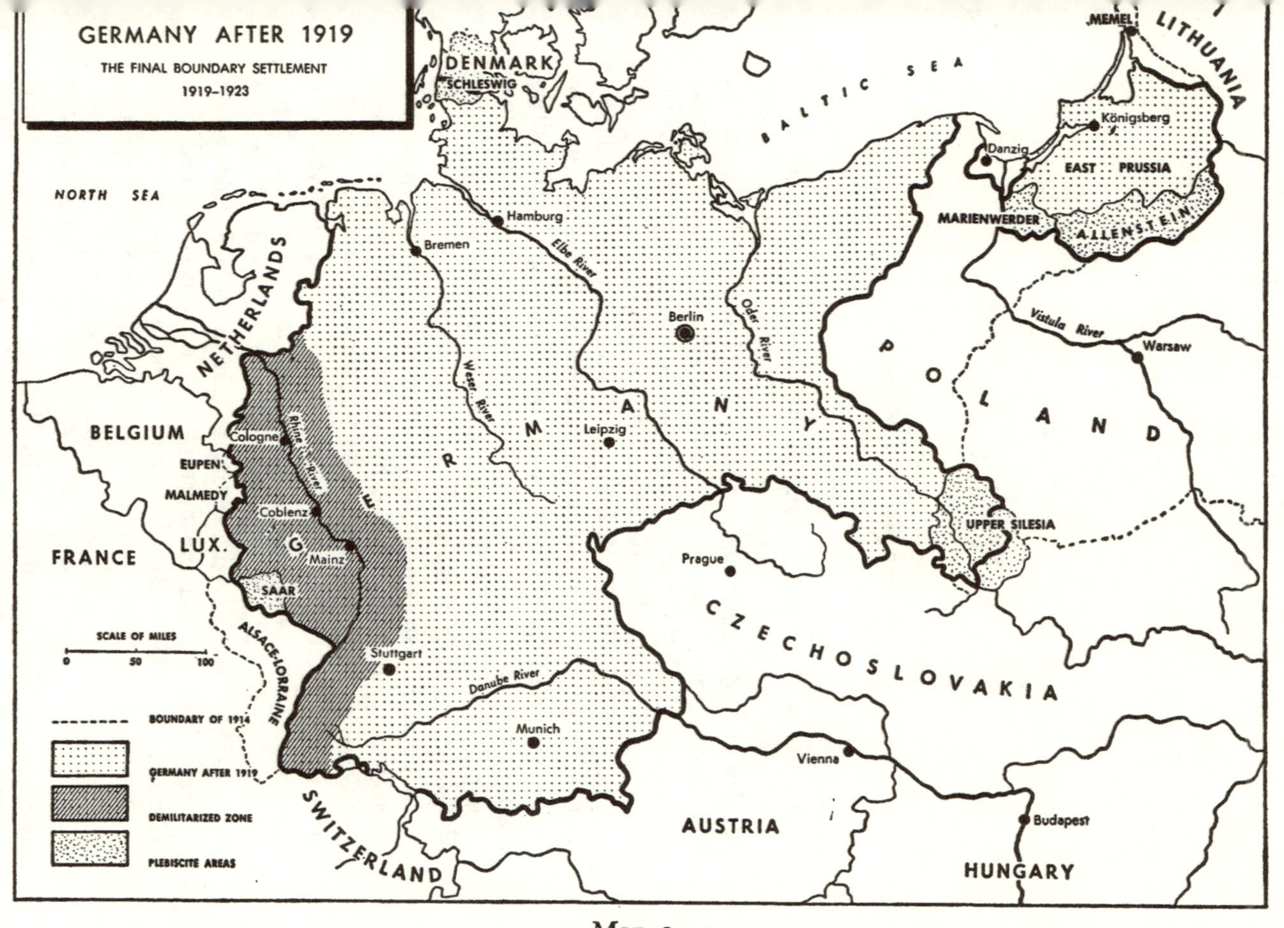

Map 3.

XIV
CONCLUSIONS

THIS study of the making of the German territorial settlement in 1919 has been primarily concerned with official British attitudes and policy, during the First World War and at the Paris Peace Conference, with the international influences affecting British policymakers on this issue, and with the British role, in relation to the policies of France, the United States, and the lesser Allies, in the drafting of the major territorial clauses of the Treaty of Versailles. Entirely apart from the fallibility of the author's judgment, since many private and official British sources of information remain inaccessible, the picture drawn above and the conclusions based upon it are not advanced as a definitive analysis of the subject.

In 1916, British leaders first attempted to define an overall European peace policy. The highly conservative approach of the General Staff, which stressed Britain's traditional interests and policy, envisaged a postwar balance of power system in which the pivot would be a strong Germanic central Europe. An anti-Slav and anti-French bias was revealed. Where the General Staff envisaged a return to Bismarckian Germany and Europe, Balfour and the Foreign Office were convinced that Germany would remain the major menace to European peace and stability. This estimate, combined with the greater emphasis placed on the principle of nationality, led to a different view of territorial revision. Balfour contemplated weakening Germany through the loss of Alsace-Lorraine and eastern lands; so too did the Foreign Office planners. They differed principally over the role of eastern Europe and of

Anglo-French relations in a new equilibrium of power. Balfour, distrusting the viability of the potential new Slav states, preferred to have Germany and Russia balance each other through direct contact and to strengthen western Europe by the transfer of Alsace-Lorraine to France and by the maintenance of the Anglo-French entente. The Foreign Office planners envisaged a radical departure from the prewar system of states by the reconstruction of Europe along nationalist lines. They would keep Germany and Russia from one another's throats by a system of Slavic buffer states, and would restrain Germany in western Europe by a permanent Anglo-French-Belgian alliance.

The authors of the three plans assumed that the American role in world politics would not appreciably alter and that Russia would remain a Great Power. Both assumptions had to be seriously modified as a result of the Russian Revolution and the American entry into the war.

Especially after the October Revolution, several implications of Russian developments for the European settlement caused grave concern in London. They were: (1) the dissolution of Russian power, (2) the danger of the westward expansion of Bolshevism, (3) the grim possibility of a German-Russian combination either under Hohenzollern or under Bolshevik auspices, (4) the strengthening under Bolshevik influence of popular demand in the British Isles and elsewhere for peace without annexations and indemnities, (5) the new environment of the Polish question. The problems posed by the new situation in eastern Europe seemed relatively clear. British policy must seek to prevent a German-Russian alignment, bar a Bolshevik advance and destroy Teutonic *Mittel Europa*. A friendly Russian power should be revived. If this was impossible, some substitute must be found to maintain a European equilibrium in which Germany and Soviet Russia would be held in check. As one means of solving these problems, the buffer state idea seemed more attractive and necessary than before, although the possibility of counterbalancing the Bolshevik menace in eastern Europe by a relatively strong Germany could not be overlooked. The two considerations suggested an effort to strike some balance between German and Slavic interests in eastern Europe which would be reasonably satisfactory to the national aspirations of Germans, Czechs, and Poles. Territorially, such a policy would entail the partial dismemberment of Germany to help create a new Polish state while at the same time appeasing the Germans by refusing to support extreme Polish territorial claims. In spirit this approach was not very different from the prevailing attitude in London on the question of the eastern frontier before the Russian revolutionary storm broke. Now the British government had gradually to give more whole-hearted support for the nationalist aspirations of the east European peoples.

It is doubtful whether the British government or its diplomatic and military advisors believed that the potential buffer states in eastern Europe could assume the role played in the prewar balance by Russia and by Austria-Hungary. Ministers like Curzon, Balfour, Austen Chamberlain, and others doubted whether Poland, for instance, could be a viable, dependable state in the European system. One alternative, of course, was to revive Russian power, as the General Staff advised in 1918; the other was to look to American power to replace Russia in the European balance.

The men in London after April 1917 became increasingly preoccupied with the American factor in British peace policy. As the debate of mid-August 1918, in the Imperial War Cabinet revealed, British and Dominion leaders were concerned not only with the war but with the postwar world and the American role in it. The British government decided well before November 1918 that British and general interests would be best served if the United States pursued an active postwar world policy. To maintain and strengthen Anglo-American co-operation involved working closely with Wilson and the United States on questions of peace policy, with two provisos: first, the British government must honour its obligations to its allies, and second, other vital British interests should not be sacrificed. During the later stages of the war and at the Paris Peace Conference, the British government had constantly to bear in mind that its American policy might fail. The repudiation of Wilson in the November 1918 elections made failure a real possibility. Yet, as long as Wilson was President of the United States, peace negotiations had to be conducted with him even though there was no assurance of continuity in American policy.

Where issues like freedom of the seas, colonies, the Middle

East, and the Italian frontiers had divisive effects upon Anglo-American relations, a wide measure of agreement was possible on German and other European territorial questions. American and British interests in Europe were similar. Conflicts over the European settlement were not primarily between London and Washington but among individuals and groups within each country and government. When, for instance, Lloyd George defined before the Imperial War Cabinet in 1917 his concept of the principles upon which a European settlement should be based—a just, national, democratic, and punitive peace—he was closer in form and spirit to the Wilsonian than to the Balfourian position.

The Wilsonian influence strengthened moderate and liberal tendencies in British policy, disturbed the advocates of European settlement based primarily upon the balance of power, and made difficult open avowals of that element in Britain's continental policy. Yet, that influence was not incompatible with balance of power calculations. As Balfour described the government's general European policy to the Imperial War Cabinet in August 1918, they sought to avoid single-power domination of the continent and to preserve European peace through the establishment of a stable equilibrium of power. To accomplish these ends, some substitute had to be found for Russian power in the European equilibrium. The new 'buffer' states and France alone could not stabilize a continent upon which German power would remain formidable and dangerous. In these circumstances, Great Britain could not expect to revert to the 'splendid isolation' of the nineteenth century. Yet, whether an entente or an alliance relationship was maintained with France, the growing limitations of British manpower and the extensive nature of Britain's imperial commitments narrowed the range of its possible and desirable continental obligations. The problem of establishing a new European equilibrium and of defining Britain's postwar relationship to the continent would largely be solved if American power and influence were thrown into the European balance. America under Wilsonian leadership would be a force making for stability, moderation, and peace in Europe.

Men of narrow vision, like Sir Henry Wilson who indulged in intemperate attacks upon his namesake, did not grasp the advantages which a policy of Anglo-American co-operation could bring, even if the price had to be a bending of British policy—where it had to be bent—to meet the Wilsonian attitude. Balfour and Lloyd George had 'caught the vision'. With the support of Sir Robert Borden, Lord Milner, Austen Chamberlain, and others, they pursued that policy vigorously during the war and at the Paris Peace Conference. It was a policy which rested both upon affinity of thought and action and upon careful calculations of national and imperial interest.

Of course, a perfect identity of views did not prevail between London and Washington on European territorial questions. As their attitudes became more clearly defined from the time of the Balfour Mission onwards, areas of agreement and disagreement emerged. In western Europe, their general position was very close. In eastern Europe, where in 1918 the two governments came to support the dismemberment of the Dual Monarchy, they backed both the Czech and Polish national causes. The British government, however, aimed essentially at the 'Little Poland' solution of the German-Polish borderland question while the Wilson administration was more pliant in its approach to Polish claims. Particular differences of this kind could not overshadow the similarities of outlook on European territorial issues which facilitated co-operation between London and Washington.

During the negotiations leading to the German armistice of November 11, 1918, German territorial issues were involved in several ways. London supported evacuation conditions which signified German surrender of *Mittel Europa*, of western domination, and of Alsace-Lorraine. British leaders divided over the question of inter-Allied occupation of the Rhineland, partly because Haig believed the military situation did not justify this demand, partly because he and Lloyd George, suspicious of French aims in the Rhineland, sought to keep French forces out of the area lest its disposition be prejudiced. Although Woodrow Wilson favoured moderate armistice terms to avoid placing the victors in too strong a position *vis-à-vis* Germany, House failed to support this policy. Lloyd George suffered defeat on the issue. On the other hand, Balfour turned aside the French attempt to prejudge the German-Polish border settlement by requiring German withdrawal to the 1772 frontier.

On the issue of the Fourteen Points, etc., as the basis of the peace negotiations, the moderates in the British and Imperial War Cabinets prevailed. Lloyd George, having secured definite reservations regarding reparations and freedom of the seas, accepted the Fourteen Points, without sacrificing his main aim: to secure the maximum freedom of manœuvre in the peace negotiations on boundary and other questions.

Between the signing of the German armistice and the opening of the peace conference, British and Dominion leaders debated intensively where to strike a balance between the continental and the American governments, more particularly between Wilson and Clemenceau. Although the conclusion must be tentative, the British government probably did not enter into an Anglo-French cabal, although a degree of understanding on territorial issues may have been reached at the inter-Allied conference of early December 1918, which would militate against Wilson's influence in the peacemaking. Fundamentally, the earlier decision was upheld to work closely with Wilson as far as British commitments and interests allowed. In holding to this position, Lloyd George believed that if they bargained hard and took advantage of Wilson's determination to secure a League of Nations, Anglo-American co-operation in the peacemaking would be possible and advantageous. If they could not secure 'the things which mattered most to us' through working with Wilson, 'then the sacrifices of France and Great Britain were such that they were entitled to have a final say, and would say it'.[1]

The second outstanding feature in the post-armistice deliberations on British policy was the advice on territorial matters given to the British and Imperial War Cabinets by the Foreign Office and the other great departments of government. To concentrate here on the 'grand design' of the Foreign Office, the British government was urged to work for a settlement based upon the existence of a League of Nations, to co-operate intimately with the American delegation, but to bear in mind as well the untried character of the proposed League and hence not to neglect traditional safeguards of British security and other interests. In Europe, British aims were formally defined as: peace and order with open facilities for trade, balance of

[1] See p. 140, above.

power, territorial reconstruction based upon the principle of nationality, and the maintenance of British security along the coastline opposite the British Isles. In short, a combination of traditional and liberal-nationalist policies. The dilemma between a policy based upon the balance of power and a policy resting upon the principle of nationality appeared to have been resolved.[1] As the memorandum on the European settlement read, in part:

> ... there is every reason to hope that States based on the conscious existence of a common nationality will be more durable, and afford a firmer support against aggression than the older form of State. ... In this matter our interest entirely coincides with the principle of nationality and the doctrine of self-determination, though there must be very great difficulties in applying it.[2]

In western Europe, the Foreign Office planners saw good prospects for the cessation of territorial disputes if the settlement in that area hewed as closely as possible to national lines. In eastern Europe, they advised the British government to adopt the attitude of an impartial and disinterested observer. They hoped that Britain could win the respect and amity of friend and foe alike in eastern Europe by following this course. The emphasis in this programme on nationality, fair-mindedness, plebiscites, moderation, and the League of Nations sounded a Wilsonian note. On the other hand, the concepts of balance of power and of British interest had been rejected by Wilson as old-fashioned and selfish.

[1] W. M. Jordan in his excellent study *Great Britain, France, and the German Problem, 1918-1939*, writes, p. 2: 'The British ideal for Europe during these years [1918-36] of peace was not the creation of a balance of power—that supposedly traditional concept of British policy was consciously rejected; still less was it the retention of preponderant power by the former victors of the War. The British ideal was a Europe whose ordering should command such general assent that the very justice of its arrangements would provide the true guarantee of their maintenance.' The evidence does not appear to support his statement in the first sentence as far as 1919 was concerned. In part, Mr. Jordan unduly equates the peace aims of British Liberalism with those of the Lloyd George government (pp. 3-5). Of the Liberals he comments, p. 5: 'By their writings and propaganda they set the tone of the declared war aims of Great Britain.' Did they, however, set the substance of actual policy?

[2] See p. 95, above.

At Paris, British representatives faced a French delegation which, although its counsels were divided, generally demanded a draconian peace. In the imbalance of power between France and Germany, the French saw a constant temptation for Germany to commit aggression in the future. Clemenceau and his associates minimized the importance of conciliating German national sentiment because of their profound conviction that the spirit of militarism and conquest was deeply embedded in the German mentality and consequently that Germany posed a long-term threat to the peace and security of Europe. They saw no possibility, at least in the immediate future, of a mutually satisfactory and freely negotiated settlement between victor and vanquished. Therefore, the general French aim was to cripple the Reich's power to make war through the territorial dismemberment and internal weakening of the German state. To underpin this settlement, the French delegation called for precise guarantees of security for the victors, strategic frontiers, and a system of buffer or encircling states to contain Germany.

On the other hand, the British confronted Wilson and his delegation. An interesting recent view of the Americans in Paris has been advanced by Professor W. L. Langer, who concludes, rather sadly, that 'Mr. Wilson and his staff made concessions and compromises which, when put together, contributed to a peace that in many respects violated the pre-Armistice agreements and was certainly harsh if not unjust'. In explaining this outcome, Mr. Langer comments that the American delegation was disorganized and on individual questions lacked a programme. Wilson moreover had initially envisaged the settlement of continental territorial issues by the Europeans themselves. Thus the American approach was 'critical and cautionary rather than constructive'. Further, influenced by wartime passions and accepting the theory of German war guilt, Wilson and his associates were pushed into the agreements which helped to make the Treaty of Versailles so severe and a breach of faith.[1] How far does this interpretation apply to the German territorial negotiations?

This view seems incomplete and misleading in some respects. In part, the identity of outlook among members of the American

[1] William L. Langer, 'Peace and the New World Order', in *Woodrow Wilson and the World of Today*, ed. A. P. Dudden, pp. 88-9.

delegation, especially between Wilson and some of his staff, is exaggerated. We have seen, for instance, the different approaches which Haskins and Wilson took towards the Saar Question. Generally, the American advisors' recommendations with their emphasis on economic, historic, and strategic principles came closer in tone to the French than to the Wilsonian design for peace.

Perhaps the lack of procedure is also overstressed. At least during the Council of Four stage in the negotiations men like Haskins received regular instructions from Wilson who acted as a co-ordinator. Nevertheless, the American procedures compared unfavourably with those of the British. The United States delegation as a whole lacked the relative regularity of procedure and the collectivity of discussion which the British more often realized through their delegational meetings. These sessions dealt with matters of substance where frequently the American commissioners were handling personnel questions. Unity of view and perfect co-ordination of effort were not, of course, accomplished by the British delegation either. Frequently, the activities of Lloyd George and his immediate entourage were as hidden from and criticized by members of the British delegation as Wilson's were within the American delegation.

More importantly, the nature and effect of the concessions and compromises made by Wilson and his associates can be misconstrued as far as the German boundary settlement was concerned. It is true that Wilson was pushed further in the Saar and the Rhineland negotiations than he at first intended. At the same time, some of the concessions and compromises grudgingly made by Wilson and his staff contributed to a peace which was probably less a violation of the pre-armistice agreement and certainly less severe than if the President and his advisors had had their way, for instance, in the Polish-German Question. Moreover, some members of the American delegation actively pressed for certain provisions of Versailles which critics like Harold Nicolson, whom Mr. Langer cites approvingly, have condemned as harsh or violations of the pre-armistice understanding.[1]

This is not the place for a protracted discussion of the role of the enigmatic Wilson. Any final, balanced appraisal of his

[1] Harold Nicolson, *Peacemaking 1919*, p. 43.

approach to the postwar treatment of Germany will have to include the seemingly paradoxical elements in his outlook. It is easy to stereotype and to oversimplify his attitude towards Germany. Undeniably Wilson was an idealist, an apostle of moderation, an advocate of settlements based upon popular consent and free negotiations among equals. It seems true that his judgment at Paris was affected by 'war fever' and by a belief in Germany's guilt for the war. In the latter respect he blamed the catastrophe of 1914-1918 on both the ambitions of the Prussian ruling class and upon the faults of the traditional international system. It is too facile, however, to explain Wilson's apparent deviation from what has been termed the liberal peace programme as the result of inexperience, naïveté, the weakness of his bargaining position, House's 'betrayal', the character of Lloyd George and Clemenceau, and all the other reasons advanced to prove that Wilson was bamboozled, rushed, or otherwise victimized into unwilling acceptance of a harsh, dictated, illiberal peace. In fact, the President's role in the preparation of a hard peace was less a retreat and more positive than has been often supposed.

His concept of justice, his scepticism about a change of heart in Germany, and his political realism certainly influenced his conduct at Paris. In the German territorial negotiations Wilson stood forth as a stern as well as a forgiving judge. While seeking to be impartial towards the contending parties, he was equally resolved to punish the wrongdoers and to compensate the wronged. To him the transgressors were the Teutons who had become infected with the virus of Prussian militarism, authoritarianism, and aggression. The injured were the former subject peoples and the victims of Prussian armed might: the Czechs, the Poles, the French, the Belgians. In spirit and because of long-held convictions, Woodrow Wilson helped to fashion and willingly accepted a peace with punitive aspects. This attitude he clearly revealed in his letter of May 16 to Smuts in which he said: 'I feel the terrible responsibility of this whole business, but inevitably my thought goes back to the very great offense against civilization which the German State committed, and the necessity for making it evident once for all that such things can lead only to the most severe punishment.'

Furthermore, long before the armistice Wilson had postulated a 'soft' and a 'hard' approach to the postwar treatment of Germany, the latter based upon the assumption that the Prussian spirit continued to dominate the German state. In that case, Wilson forecast not peace among equals but a severer settlement. This was not his preferred plan for the treatment of Germany. Yet this was the type of peace which he accepted at Paris, not, I would suggest, simply because it was forced upon him by his Allies but because Wilson himself was unconvinced about the reality of the political change in the Reich. Consequently, as a realist in politics, he recognized, however reluctantly, the need for measures to ensure the containment of Germany after the war, while hoping that time, the League, and the triumph of common sense would utlimately produce genuine reconciliation and stabilization.

As for the British position on Germany boundary issues at Paris, it generally reflected the Foreign Office's approach and recommendations. Generally, too, the British delegation pursued the predetermined policy of co-operating closely with Wilson and the American delegation, a relationship symbolized and formalized by the February agreement between the Anglo-American territorial experts and by the frequent collaboration between Lloyd George and Wilson.

In eastern Europe, the British delegation was clearly divided over the German-Polish boundary at both the technical and the political levels. The British representatives on the Commission for Polish Affairs went further, under American and French influence, towards meeting Polish claims than Balfour and the Foreign Office had advised. Lloyd George successfully led an attack on the original recommendations of the Commission on Polish Affairs. His stand, based upon long-held views of British statesmen and upon the preconference position of the Foreign Office, aimed at a Polish-German settlement which would offer some prospect of durability by being reasonably acceptable to both Germans and Poles. In the case of the German-Czech frontier, the British representatives on the Commission for Czechoslovak Affairs supported a line based upon geographic, strategic, and economic factors, leaving a large German-speaking minority within the new Czech State. They thought highly of the Czechs and saw them as a bulwark against renewed German expansion. In the case of Austria, Lloyd

George had no objection to permanent separation of Germany and Austria if this was indispensable for European security.

In western Europe, the British accepted without question the return of Alsace-Lorraine to France. The other main issues however challenged British diplomatic resourcefulness and threatened to disrupt the unity of the victors.

The initial position on the Rhineland remains obscure. Generally the British government was resistant in its attitude towards the idea of detaching the left bank from Germany. On February 21, its territorial advisors agreed with the Americans that, beyond the return of Alsace-Lorraine to France, further losses of German territory were not necessary for strategic reasons if adequate arrangements were made to give France security along its eastern frontier. Initially, the British representatives advocated the disarmament of Germany, the demilitarization of the left bank, and the support of the League of Nations as the alternative to strategic annexations or to buffer states in the Rhineland. Possibly Balfour, like House, in late February and early March was working towards a temporary separation of the left bank from Germany with its ultimate fate to be decided by plebiscite, thus preserving the right of self-determination while giving France a chance to gain permanent control. If so, whatever Lloyd George's attitude may have been (and he assures us that he opposed any form of separation from the beginning), Woodrow Wilson's categorical refusal to accept the detachment of the Rhineland provinces from Germany under any arrangement barred a solution of this kind. Since Clemencea rejected the Anglo-American formula for French security, an impasse was reached.

The second main position taken by Lloyd George, in close association with Wilson, was to offer Clemenceau an Anglo-American treaty of guarantee against unprovoked German aggression and a short-term occupation of the Rhineland in addition to the three-point formula previously proposed. In winning Wilson's approval of the guarantee, Lloyd George scored a signal success for the British government's policy of securing United States' postwar co-operation in upholding European peace and stability. Clemenceau too recognized the potential value of Wilson's promise, but, like the British leaders, was haunted both by domestic politics and by the prospect of the guarantee not being honoured by Wilson's countrymen. Therefore, while abandoning the demand for separation of the Rhineland from Germany in return for the proposed guarantee, he concentrated upon securing additional physical guarantees of French security along the eastern frontier. In seeking to reduce these demands, Lloyd George and Wilson maintained a common front until early April when the Prime Minister was deserted by the President (probably for good reason) over the question of the length and national character of the proposed Rhineland occupation.

In the British and Imperial War Cabinets, Lloyd George encountered strong criticism of the Rhineland settlement on two main grounds: the occupation would breed friction and hence imperil peace; it was simply a scheme for having the British taxpayers support the French army. Apprehension had also been expressed about the likelihood of the French military authorities oppressing the Rhinelanders and using the occupation regime as a means of detaching the left bank from Germany. Lloyd George, with Wilson's support, did gain Clemenceau's agreement to an occupation regime which minimized military authority and offered protection for the civil rights of the Rhinelanders. On the other hand, he could secure no modification of the length of the occupation.

British conduct in the Saar negotiations seems tortuous and complex. Many aspects remain obscure. In the early phases, the political leaders of the British delegation were advised by the Chief of the Imperial General Staff and by territorial advisors that all or part of the Saar Basin should be ceded to France for economic and strategic reasons, although the latter could not be openly avowed. Did Lloyd George and Balfour accept this advice and covertly work towards its realization in practice? The question is not readily answered, but Lloyd George obviously preferred to sever the Saar from Germany while avoiding formal annexation to France.

As part of the effort to establish a common Anglo-American front in the German territorial negotiations, the meeting of the two delegations' technical experts on February 21 agreed to: French ownership and use of the mines; a special French political and administrative regime with protection for local rights, local self-government, and demilitarization. No agreement could be reached on where sovereignty should reside. Indicative perhaps of the element of confusion in the Paris proceedings, Lloyd George and his Fontainebleau coterie evidently did not have this understanding before them, but later the Prime Minister shifted to the position taken by the Anglo-American experts. It was more favourable to the substance of the French claims than the Fontainebleau proposals and seemed likely to force Wilson's hand. On this issue, Woodrow Wilson took a very different stand from that of his technical advisors. Invoking the Fourteen Points, the President at first would only accept French use of the products of the mines for the period required to reconstruct the devastated areas in France. This was Lloyd George's Fontainebleau position which he had abandoned! In the confused, tense and critical situation which followed Lloyd George pressed Wilson more than Clemenceau until agreement on the special Saar regime was reached. This settlement encountered adverse criticism from members of the British and Imperial War Cabinets but Lloyd George defended it as an essential part of the price for an entente with France.

Whether or not Lloyd George was a 'slippery prestidigitator', as Orlando charged in a moment of frustration, he had to juggle diverse, often purely day-to-day considerations in devising the safest possible course in the Paris negotiations. Lloyd George's conduct at Paris did not, however, rest on expediency and narrow national interest alone. He possessed a keen sense of the general interest. He sought to determine, as Phillip Kerr later Lord Lothian—once suggested, 'the permanent political realities' of the age,[1] as his basis of action. Clearly, Lloyd George regarded the European equilibrium of 1919 as temporary. One of his basic assumptions was that German power inevitably would revive in Europe. Thus his search for a territorial settlement based on this long-term consideration. Hence his concern for strengthening France in western Europe without however permanently antagonizing Germany through the creation of insurmountable barriers to reconciliation between victors and vanquished. Similarly in eastern Europe, Lloyd George fought for a German-Polish settlement which would be mutually

[1] Phillip Kerr to Emil Ludwig, November 26, 1930, Butler, *Lothian*, pp. 77-8.

acceptable to both parties even after Germany had regained its strength. Precise calculations, however, were impossible, and Lloyd George did not always discover the permanent realities for which he was looking.

The British negotiators had to take a stand on the French demands in western Europe for security and reparations. In facing these demands, British leaders knew that German opinion would firmly oppose the territorial dismemberment of Germany in the west, although grudging Teutonic consent had been given to the return of Alsace-Lorraine to France. Where should the balance be struck between France and Germany in western Europe?

As evidenced by British reactions and conduct at Paris, British leaders were sympathetically inclined towards the realization of the general French aims—security and reparations—if only because they coincided with British aspirations and interests in western Europe. More specifically, the first British objective was to strengthen France against Germany so as to establish a more durable equilibrium of economic and military forces between the two countries as a foundation for peace and stability on the continent and to minimize thereby the chances of British involvement in another major European conflict.

Another objective—and here we turn to more universal goals—was to secure a territorial arrangement which would be reasonably acceptable to all the states concerned and so in itself would make for stability and peace. The major difficulty was how to strengthen France and other friends by the transfer of resources from Germany or by drawing strategic frontiers without creating new territorial disputes in western and eastern Europe. The two aims could produce contradictory and self-defeating results. Taken together, pursuit of the two objectives favoured compromise solutions as were realized in the Rhineland, the Saar, and the Polish settlements.

In this respect British recourse to the use of the plebiscitary device was ingenious. To propose a plebiscite was a polite way of saying 'no' to the requests of friends, whether Polish or French. It also served to postpone difficult or embarrassing decisions to a later and perhaps more propitious day. The tendency to temporize was characteristic of British diplomacy at Paris on territorial and other matters.

A third objective of Lloyd George's diplomacy in the European territorial negotiations was to maintain unity among the British, French, and American governments. Lloyd George believed that the future peace of Europe and the world depended upon whether or not the three countries could act in unison in the postwar era. His major difficulty at Paris was to keep the coalition together as each divisive issue arose. His task was not merely to compose the conflicts between Wilson and Clemenceau over the proper treatment of Germany in territorial and other matters. There were contrary tendencies in Anglo-French relations and tensions in Anglo-American relations which had to be controlled. In attempting to reconcile these considerations, the supreme objective for which Lloyd George and his colleagues were striving was the commitment of American power in Europe.[1] This could be the decisive element in a new European equilibrium. Germany would be effectively contained in western Europe. At the same time the German desire for revenge would not be overnourished since France, with the Anglo-American guarantee, would enjoy a sense of security without having had to dismember 'German' Germany in the west.

At no time, however, in the German territorial negotiations, could Lloyd George and his associates forget the possibility that the United States might repudiate Wilson and Wilsonism. They did what they could to avert this danger by co-operating with Wilson and his delegation as far as possible—e.g. on the League, on mandates, on European territorial questions. They could facilitate his getting what mattered most to him, and what he held mattered most to his countrymen, and thus enable him to return home claiming triumph and strengthened in his effort to carry his country along the internationalist course which he had mapped for it. But British statesmen had to hedge against the danger of American reversion to isolationsism. Thus, Lloyd George could not afford to break with Clemenceau during the

[1] Arthur S. Link, *Wilson the Diplomatist*, p. 123. In explaining Wilson's 'failure' at Paris, Link gives as one reason: 'Wilson had no power of coercion over Britain and France, for they were no longer dependent upon American manpower and resources for survival.' Link overlooks the importance to Lloyd George and Clemenceau of an alliance with the United States.

N*

Paris negotiations: in any event, but especially if Wilson failed, a friendly, stable France was essential to British security and for the maintenance of a stable European equilibrium. The British negotiators had also to promote a continental settlement which would protect British interests in case the United States withdrew from participation in European affairs. This meant placing a stress upon strategic factors which frequently had to be obscured. It simultaneously strengthened the search for a 'self-enforcing' settlement based upon the minimizing or elimination of national disputes and rivalries.[1] Britain's hand also had to be kept as free as possible to meet the contingency of American withdrawal. Hence such safeguards as the escape clause in the British guarantee to France which provided that Great Britain was not bound to ratify the treaty if the United States did not.

The final touchstone of British diplomacy in Paris was the domestic political acceptability of any arrangements which the government would place before Parliament and the country. There Lloyd George would run the gamut of the slogan worshippers, the devotees of 'Hang the Kaiser' and of 'No More War'. In the short term, a more drastic German settlement would probably have won majority support, but Lloyd George had an eye on the future. If possible he wanted a settlement which would command the support of the country as a whole. War-whipped passions would abate. Then what would the British public support in the new age of universal suffrage and the popular press? Aloofness from continental entanglements was the national tradition and historic interest, regardless of party. If the habits of decades reasserted themselves, when home and imperial affairs once again absorbed public attention, would

[1] This thought is better put by Professor E. L. Woodward in his explanation of the origins and meaning of the balance of power in European history: 'The proponents of the European settlement at the end of the Thirty Years War had taken the idea of a balance of power . . . as the most practical norm for the maintenance of European peace; they hoped that—given an order in which every state, large and small, had its reasonable claims satisfied—the united action of the community of satisfied states would then be strong enough to prevent such an equilibrium from being overthrown. They would defend it if only for reasons of self-interest. . . .' Sir Llewellyn Woodward, 'A British View of Mr. Wilson's Foreign Policy', in *Wilson's Foreign Policy in Perspective*, ed. Edward H. Buehrig, p. 155.

British obligations, will, and power be in alignment in Europe? That was the consideration advanced in more general terms by Lloyd George when he asked Clemenceau and Wilson whether their countries, five or ten years from then, would be prepared to support Poland against Germany in case the German-speaking minority rebelled in the name of freedom and national rights and appealed for aid from Berlin. Any settlement which might with reasonable expectation be left stranded when the tide of the victors' enthusiasm receded could only be of disservice to the people concerned, damaging to the prestige of its drafters, and a cause of instability. And, in the spring of 1919, there were many signs on both the Cabinet and the popular levels that British opinion was setting definite limits to what it would support on the continent. The Tory elements wanted European obligations kept to a minimum so as to husband manpower resources and to uphold maritime and imperial interests, while liberal and socialist opinion was beginning to attack the German settlement as a violation of the pledges of the victors. Both tendencies moved British policy in the direction of moderate treatment of Germany.

In sum, British policy on the German boundaries aimed at reconciling opposing domestic and international tendencies. This endeavour led to an effort to reconcile balance of power calculations with the forces of nationality. At Paris, the British delegation as a whole pursued a moderate, conciliatory, and pragmatic course in the German territorial negotiations. Although all its flexible aims were not realized, the delegation made a distinctive and generally constructive contribution to the final territorial terms of peace with Germany. Perhaps its approach was overcautious, too subtle, and excessively temporizing, thus helping to shape an indecisive settlement which, while reasonably just and balanced in the circumstances, gave a sense of satisfaction and security to few. Not many aspirations could be satisfied after so violent a conflict and in cases where even legitimate interests overlapped. Territorial disputes were only one root of European insecurity; territorial adjustments alone could not bring peace and stability.

The main condition for peace was maintenance in the postwar era of unity among the United States, France, and Great Britain. In this respect, the primary British defeat at Paris was the failure to realize the objective of the policy of co-operation with Wilson and the American delegation. Could Lloyd George have acted differently in the German boundary negotiations so as to have strengthened Wilson's appeal to the Senate and to his countrymen for American support for the peace settlement? None of the alternatives open to the Prime Minister on German territorial issues would likely have made a particle of difference. He wisely followed the middle road. In the event of American withdrawal from Europe he kept open the door in 1919 to an alternative strategy for the upholding of European peace: Anglo-French collaboration based upon a policy of combined moderation and firmness in the treatment of Germany. A major tragedy of interwar history was the inability of England and France to travel this road together.

BIBLIOGRAPHY

I. Bibliographical Guides

Binkley, Robert C. 'Ten Years of Peace Conference History', *The Journal of Modern History*, 1929, I, pp. 607-29.

Birdsall, Paul. 'The Second Decade of Peace Conference History', *The Journal of Modern History*, 1939, XI, pp. 362-78.

Langer, William L. and Hamilton Fish Armstrong (eds.). *Foreign Affairs Bibliography, 1919-1932*. New York: Harper, 1933.

Woolbert, R. G. (ed.). *Foreign Affairs Bibliography, 1932-1942*. New York: Harper, 1945.

Roberts, H. L. (ed.). *Foreign Affairs Bibliography, 1942-1952*. New York: Harper, 1955.

II. Primary Sources

(a) *Official Archival Records*

The Records of the American Commission to Negotiate Peace, Paris, 1918-19. In the National Archives of the United States, Washington, D.C.

Although much has been published, the 537 bound volumes of the records of the American delegation at Paris contain many unused sources. These include the minutes and other relevant papers of the various territorial commissions and sub-commissions, of the committees for studying the observations of the German delegation, and numerous British, French, Polish, Czech, and other memoranda, in addition to American materials.

The Records of the American Peace Commission. In the Library of Congress, Washington, D.C.

These contain some materials of The Inquiry instituted in 1917 under Colonel House. The data papers throw light on the development of the attitudes of the American negotiators at Paris. They have been used sparingly here, for instance to bring out C. H. Haskins' strongly pro-French views on the Saar Question.

(b) *Documents—Official Publications*

GREAT BRITAIN, FOREIGN OFFICE. *Papers respecting Negotiations for an Anglo-French Pact.* Cmd. 2169. London: H.M.S.O., 1924.

This sheds some light on Anglo-French negotiations respecting the Rhineland and related issues from 1917 on.

GREAT BRITAIN, PARLIAMENT. *Parliamentary Debates, Fifth Series, House of Commons.* London: H.M.S.O.

COMITÉ D'ÉTUDES. *L'Alsace-Lorraine, et la frontière du nord-est.* Paris: Imprimerie nationale, 1918.

COMITÉ D'ÉTUDES. *Le Bassin Houiller de Sarrebruck: Étude economique et politique.* Paris: Imprimerie nationale, 1918.

The French wartime committee for the study of the problems of peacemaking published more than these two works, but here the detailed evolution of French policy has not been analyzed.

UNITED STATES, DEPARTMENT OF STATE. *Papers Relating to the Foreign Relations of the United States. The Lansing Papers, 1914-1920.* 2 vols. Washington: Government Printing Office, 1939-1940.

UNITED STATES, DEPARTMENT OF STATE. *Papers Relating to the Foreign Relations of the United States, 1917.* Supplement 2. 2 vols. Washington, 1932.

UNITED STATES, DEPARTMENT OF STATE. *Papers Relating to the Foreign Relations of the United States, 1918.* Supplement 1. 2 vols. Washington, 1933.

UNITED STATES, DEPARTMENT OF STATE. *Papers Relating to the Foreign Relations of the United States: The Paris Peace Conference, 1919.* 13 vols. Washington, 1942-1947.

The thirteen volumes contain, *inter alia*, the following from the records of the American delegation at Paris. (1) The English language minutes of the Council of Ten prepared by the British secretariat. A brief parallel set was prepared by the U.S. delegation during January 1919. (2) The English language minutes of the Council of Four prepared by Sir Maurice Hankey of the British delegation. This record does not cover all the meetings of the Council. (3) The minutes of meetings of the American Commissioners. (4) The exchange of correspondence with the German delegation. (5) Many reports from such special American missions as Coolidge's and Dresel's in Austria and Germany respectively.

(c) *Documents—Unofficial Publications*

LAPRADELLE, A. G. DE. *La Documentation internationale: la paix de Versailles.* 13 vols. Paris: Les éditions internationale, 1929-1939.

Volume 9, parts 1 and 2, include *inter alia*: (1) the Czechoslovak and Belgian memoranda defining their claims; (2) the report of the Commission on Czechoslovak Affairs, March 12, 1919; (3) the report of the Commission on Belgian Affairs, March 19, 1919. The relevant minutes of the two commissions are not published nor are any of the materials bearing on the German-Polish frontier. Perhaps the publication date, 1939, explains these omissions.

MANTOUX, PAUL. *Les Délibérations du conseil des quatre (24 mars-28 juin 1919): Notes de l'Officier Interprète.* 2 vols. Paris: Editions du Centre National de la Recherche Scientifique, 1955.

These invaluable French language notes on the discussions of the Council of Four made by Professor Mantoux, the official interpreter for the Four, cover meetings not minuted by Hankey and supplement his record of other sessions. Tardieu reproduced some of Mantoux's notes in *La Paix*, but these two volumes contain much new information.

SCOTT, JAMES BROWN (ed.). *Official Statements of War Aims and Peace Proposals, December 1916 to November, 1918.* Washington: Carnegie Endowment, 1921.

(d) *Private Papers—Archival Collections*

(i) The Papers of Sir Robert Borden. In the National Archives, Ottawa, Canada.

Sir Robert was the wartime Prime Minister of Canada and the head of the Canadian delegation to the Paris Peace Conference. Unlike Smuts, Borden was never a member of the British War Cabinet, but he made his influence felt upon British policy through the Imperial War Cabinet and the British Empire Delegation. Significantly, the Borden papers contain no materials on the 1917 discussions on peace policy in the Imperial War Cabinet and the record of the forty-first meeting in 1918 on the inter-Allied conversations is also missing. Tantalizing gaps!

(ii) The Papers of Sir George Foster. In the National Archives, Ottawa, Canada.

Sir George was Minister of Trade in the Borden Cabinet and a Canadian plenipotentiary to the Peace Conference. From this rich source, this study has drawn many new materials.

A major void in both the Borden and Foster Papers is the absence of British War Cabinet minutes (apart from those which coincided with sessions of the Imperial War Cabinet) and of other information on policymaking within the British circle as distinct from the Imperial one. Although Dominion ministers, and some more than others, had an influential voice in the determination of British Empire policy, there remained important areas where a distinction was drawn between the British and the Dominion governments, in the sphere of foreign policy. Of course at Paris, Lloyd George often made policy and conducted negotiations on German territorial issues without consulting British ministers, let alone Dominion ones like Borden.

(iii) The Papers of Sir Austen Chamberlain. In the Library of the University of Birmingham, Birmingham, England.

These are of limited value for this subject.

(iv) The Papers of Woodrow Wilson. In the Library of Congress, Washington, D.C.

While much has been published, the 201 boxes of the Peace Conference series of Wilson's papers still provide grist for the researcher's mill. Hitherto obscure aspects of the Council of Four stage in the negotiations are clarified by fresh evidence. Wilson's papers reveal few secrets about the man himself; marginal notes, for instance, are very scarce.

(v) The Papers of Robert Lansing. In the Library of Congress.
(vi) The Papers of General Tasker H. Bliss. In the Library of Congress.
(vii) The Papers of Ray Stannard Baker. In the Library of Congress.
(viii) The Papers of Vance C. McCormick. In the Library of Congress.
(ix) The Papers of Leland Harrison. In the Library of Congress.

These collections contain much duplicate material. The Harrison Papers in this sense were of little value. Since he was kept so much on the outside at Paris, Lansing's papers, including his desk books and thirteen volumes of diaries, are mainly valuable here for the light thrown on conflicts of personality and views within the American delegation. The same may be said of the Bliss Papers, which would be of more help on military issues at the Conference. Baker, whose emotional adulation of Wilson finally becomes tiring, helps to reveal Wilson's thoughts and to re-create the Parisian atmosphere. Interestingly, Baker's later charges, in *Woodrow Wilson and World Settlement*, are not reflected in his day-to-day journals. McCormick's papers would be of distinct help on the economic side of the Conference; his parties, dancing, and week-end trips recall the social life of the Congress of Vienna.

(x) The Papers of Edward M. House. In the Sterling Library, Yale University, New Haven, Conn., U.S.A.

(xi) The Papers of Sir William Wiseman. Also in the Sterling Library.

The House collection offers much on both British and American policy. The Diary—that impressive monument to the Texan's egoism—has been much quoted but there is no substitute for a first-hand reading to bring out new entries and to check others' use of it. While well used, House's Papers, including the House-Wilson correspondence, are important especially in reconstructing the Council of Four stage in the territorial negotiations. Also in this collection I found the agreement between the American and British territorial experts on February 21, 1919, which lightens a formerly dark corner.

The Wiseman Papers contain information on Anglo-American relations and some striking insights into the activities of the British delegation at Paris. Willert in *The Road to Safety* and Murray in *At Close Quarters* have already dipped into this source.

(xii) Klotz Archives. In the Bibliothèque de Documentation Internationale Contemporaine, Paris, France.

L. L. Klotz was Minister of Finance in Clemenceau's government and a French plenipotentiary at the Paris Peace Conference. These papers contain some new materials on French attitudes towards political and territorial questions.

(e) *Private Papers—Published*

BAKER, R. S. and WILLIAM E. DODD (eds.). *The Public Papers of Woodrow Wilson.* Authorized edition. 6 vols. New York: Harper, 1925-27.

BLAKE, ROBERT (ed.). *The Private Papers of Douglas Haig, 1914-1919.* London: Eyre & Spottiswoode, 1952.

CAMBON, PAUL. *Correspondance, 1879-1925.* 3 vols. Paris: Éditions Bernard Grasset, 1940-46.

MILLER, DAVID HUNTER. *My Diary at the Peace Conference.* 22 vols. New York: privately printed, 1928.

Although largely superseded by such publications as *The Paris Peace Conference, 1919* and by the opening of official and private archives in Washington, Miller's collection of Peace Conference documents still retains a distinct value. His *Diary* aids greatly in reconstructing the negotiations.

III. Memoirs and Biographies

AMERY, L. S. *My Political Life*, 2 vols. London: Hutchinson, 1953.

BAKER, RAY STANNARD. *Woodrow Wilson, Life and Letters.* 8 vols. New York: Doubleday, 1927-29.

BLAKE, ROBERT. *Law, the Unknown Prime Minister: The Life and Times of Andrew Bonar Law, 1858-1923.* London: Eyre & Spottiswoode, 1955.

BONSAL, STEPHEN. *Suitors and Suppliants: The Little Nations at Versailles.* New York: Prentice Hall, 1946.

—— *Unfinished Business.* New York: Doubleday, 1944.

BORDEN, HENRY (ed.). *Robert Laird Borden: His Memoirs.* 2 vols. New York: Macmillan, 1938.

BUTLER, Sir J. R. M. *Lord Lothian (Philip Kerr), 1882-1940.* London: MacMillan, 1960.

CALLWELL, Major-General Sir C. E. *Field-Marshal Sir Henry Wilson, his Life and Letters.* 2 vols. London: Cassell, 1927.

CHURCHILL, WINSTON S. *The Aftermath.* London: Odhams, 1929.

CLEMENCEAU, GEORGES. *The Grandeur and Misery of Victory.* New York: Harcourt, 1930.

DUFF COOPER. *Haig.* 2 vols. London: Faber, 1936.

DUGDALE, BLANCHE E. C. *Arthur James Balfour.* 2 vols. London: Hutchinson, 1936.

ESHER, REGINALD BALIOL BRETT, Viscount. *Journal and Letters.* 4 vols. London: Nicholson, 1934-38.

FOCH, FERDINAND. *Mémoires pour servir à l'histoire de la guerre de 1914-1918.* 2 vols. Paris: Librairie Plon, 1931.

HAMILTON, MARY AGNES. *Arthur Henderson.* London: Heinemann, 1938.

HAMMOND, J. L. *C. P. Scott of the Manchester Guardian.* London: Bell, 1934.

HARDINGE, CHARLES HARDINGE, LORD. *Old Diplomacy: The Reminiscences of Lord Hardinge of Penshurst.* London: Murray, 1947.

HOUSE, EDWARD MANDELL, *see* SEYMOUR.

HOWARD, ESME, LORD HOWARD OF PENRITH. *Theatre of Life: Life Seen from the Stalls.* 2 vols. Boston: Little, Brown, 1936.

HUGHES, W. M. *The Splendid Adventure.* London: Benn, 1929.

JONES, THOMAS. *Lloyd George.* Cambridge: Harvard University Press, 1951.

KEYNES, JOHN MAYNARD. *Essays in Biography*. London: MacMillan, 1933.

LANSING, ROBERT. *The Big Four and Others of the Peace Conference*. Boston: Houghton, Mifflin, 1921.

—— *The Peace Negotiations: A Personal Narrative*. Boston: Houghton, Mifflin, 1921.

LAROCHE, JULES. *Au Quai d'Orsay avec Briand et Poincaré, 1913-1926*. Paris: Hachette, 1957.

LLOYD GEORGE, DAVID. *The Truth about Reparations and War Debts*. New York: Doubleday, 1932.

—— *The Truth about the Treaties*. 2 vols. London: Gollancz, 1938. American edition, *Memoirs of the Peace Conference*. 2 vols. New Haven: Yale University Press, 1939.

—— *The War Memoirs of David Lloyd George*. 6 vols. London: Ivor, Nicholson & Watson, 1933-7.

MARTET, JEAN. *Georges Clemenceau*. London: Longmans, 1930.

MILLIN, S. G. *General Smuts*. 2 vols. Boston: Little, Brown, 1936.

MORDACQ, J. J. H. *Le ministère Clemenceau: journal d'un témoin*. Paris: Plon, 1930.

NEVINS, ALAN. *Henry White: Thirty Years of American Diplomacy*. New York: Harper, 1930.

NEWTON, THOMAS WODEHOUSE LEGH, LORD. *Lord Lansdowne*. London: Macmillan, 1929.

NICOLSON, HAROLD. *Peacemaking 1919*. Boston: Houghton 1933; rev. ed., 1945.

OWEN, FRANK. *Tempestuous Journey: Lloyd George, his Life and Times*. London: Hutchinson, 1954.

OXFORD AND ASQUITH, HERBERT HENRY ASQUITH, EARL OF. *Memories and Reflections, 1852-1927*. 2 vols. Toronto: McClelland & Stewart, 1928.

—— *Speeches*. 2 vols. Toronto: McClelland & Stewart, 1928.

PAUL-BONCOUR, JOSEPH. *Entre Deux Guerres*. 3 vols. Paris: Librairie Plon, 1945.

PERSHING, JOHN JOSEPH. *My Experiences in the World War*. 2 vols. New York: Stokes, 1931.

RIDDELL, GEORGE ALLARDICE, LORD. *Lord Riddell's Intimate Diary of the Peace Conference and After, 1918-1923*. London: Gollancz, 1933.

SEYMOUR, CHARLES (arr.). *The Intimate Papers of Colonel House*. 4 vols. Boston: Houghton, Mifflin, 1926-8.

SHOTWELL, JAMES C. *At the Paris Peace Conference*. New York: Macmillan, 1937.

SUAREZ, GEORGES. *Briand, sa vie—son oeuvre avec son journal et de nombreux documents inédits*. 6 vols. Paris: Librairie Plon, 1938-52.

TARDIEU, ANDRE. *La Paix.* Paris: Payot, 1921. Translated.

—— *The Truth about the Treaty*, Indianapolis: Bobbs, 1921.

THOMSON, MALCOLM. *David Lloyd George.* London: Hutchinson, 1948.

WALWORTH, A. C. *Woodrow Wilson.* 2 vols. New York: Longman's, 1958.

WEMYSS, LADY WESTER. *The Life and Letters of Lord Wester Wemyss.* London: Eyre & Spottiswoode, 1935.

IV. SECONDARY WORKS

BABELON, ERNEST. *La grande question d'occident: le Rhin dans l'histoire.* 2 vols. Paris: Ernest Leroux, 1916-17.

BAILEY, THOMAS A. *Wilson and the Peacemakers.* New York: Macmillan, 1947.

BAKER, RAY STANNARD. *American Chronicle.* New York: Scribner, 1945.

—— *Woodrow Wilson and the World Settlement.* 3 vols. New York: Doubleday, 1922.

BIRDSALL, PAUL. *Versailles, Twenty Years After.* London: Allen & Unwin; New York: Reynal, 1941.

BOWMAN, ISAIAH. *The New World: Problems in Political Geography.* New York: World Book, 1928.

BUEHRIG, EDWARD H. (ed.). *Wilson's Foreign Policy in Perspective.* Bloomington: Indiana University Press, 1957.

—— *Woodrow Wilson and the Balance of Power.* Bloomington: Indiana University Press, 1955.

CHESTER, D. N. (ed.). *The Organization of British Central Government, 1914-1956.* London: Allen & Unwin, 1957.

COBBAN, ALFRED. *National Self-Determination.* London: Oxford, 1945.

COWAN, LAING GRAY. *France and the Saar, 1680-1948.* New York: Columbia, 1950.

DAVIES, JOSEPH. *The Prime Minister's Secretariat, 1916-1920.* Newport: Johns, 1951.

DAWSON, WILLIAM HARBUTT. *Germany under the Treaty.* London: Allen & Unwin, 1933.

DEMANGEON, ALBERT and LUCIEN FEBVRE. *Le Rhin: Problèmes d'histoire et d'économie.* Paris: Librairie Armand Colin, 1935.

DUDDEN, ARTHUR P. (ed.). *Woodrow Wilson and the World of Today.* Philadelphia: University of Pennsylvania Press, 1957.

GERSON, LOUIS L. *Woodrow Wilson and the Rebirth of Poland, 1914-1920.* New Haven: Yale University Press, 1953.

HASKINS, CHARLES HOMER and R. H. LORD. *Some Problems of the Peace Conference.* Cambridge: Harvard University Press, 1920.

HOOVER, HERBERT. *The Ordeal of Woodrow Wilson.* New York: McGraw-Hill, 1958.

HOUSE, EDWARD MANDELL and CHARLES SEYMOUR (eds.). *What Really Happened at Paris.* New York: Scribner, 1921.

JESSOP, THOMAS EDMUND. *The Treaty of Versailles: Was it Just?* London: Nelson, 1942.

JOHNSON, FRANKLYN ARTHUR. *Defence by Committee: The British Committee of Imperial Defence, 1855-1959.* London: Oxford, 1960.

JORDAN, W. M. *Great Britain, France, and the German Problem, 1918-1939.* New York: Oxford, 1943.

KERNER, ROBERT J. 'At the Peace Conference', in OPOCENSKY, JAN. *Edward Beneš: Essays and Reflections presented on the occasion of his Sixtieth Birthday.* London: Allen, 1945.

KING, JERE CLEMENS. *Foch versus Clemenceau: France and German Dismemberment, 1918-1919.* Cambridge, Mass.: Harvard, 1960.

KOMARNICKI, T. *The Rebirth of the Polish Republic, a study in the diplomatic history of Europe, 1914-1920.* London: Cassell, 1957.

LINK, ARTHUR S. *Wilson the Diplomatist: A Look at his Major Foreign Policies.* Baltimore: Johns Hopkins Press, 1957.

LUCKAU, ALMA. *The German Delegation at the Paris Peace Conference.* New York: Columbia University Press, 1941.

MAMATEY, VICTOR S. *The United States and East Central Europe, 1914-1918: a Study in Wilsonian Diplomacy and Propaganda.* Princeton: Princeton University Press, 1957.

MARSTON, F. S. *The Peace Conference of 1919: Organization and Procedure.* London: Oxford, 1944.

MARTEL, RENE. *The Eastern Frontiers of Germany.* London: Williams & Norgate, 1930.

MAURICE, Sir FREDERICK. *The Armistices of 1918.* London: Oxford, 1943.

MAYER, ARNO J. *Political Origins of the New Diplomacy, 1917-1918.* New Haven: Yale, 1959.

McCALLUM, RONALD BUCHANAN. *Public Opinion and the Last Peace.* London: Oxford, 1944.

MERMEIX, *pseud.* (GABRIEL TERRAIL). *Le Combat des Trois.* Paris: Ollendorff, 1922.

—— *Les Négociations secrètes et les quatre armistices, 1914-1919.* Paris: Ollendorff, 1921.

MORDACQ, J. J. H. *L'Armistice du 11 Novembre 1918.* Paris: Tallandier, 1929.

—— *La vérité sur l'armistice.* Paris: Tallandier, 1939.

MOWAT, CHARLES LOCH. *Britain between the Wars, 1918-1940.* London: Methuen, 1955.

MURRAY, ARTHUR CECIL. *At Close Quarters: A Sidelight on Anglo-American Diplomatic Relations*. London: Murray, 1946.

PARES, RICHARD and TAYLOR, A. J. P. (eds.). *Essays Presented to Sir Lewis Namier*. London: Macmillan, 1956.

ROYAL INSTITUTE OF INTERNATIONAL AFFAIRS. *Political and Strategic Interests of the United Kingdom*. London: Oxford, 1939.

RUDIN, HARRY R. *Armistice, 1918*. New Haven: Yale University Press, 1944.

RUSSELL, FRANK MARION. *The Saar: Battleground and Pawn*. Stanford: Stanford University Press, 1951.

SCHIFF, VICTOR. *The Germans at Versailles*. London: Williams & Norgate, 1930.

SMOGORZEWSKI, CASIMIR. *Poland's Access to the Seas*. London: Allen, 1934.

TAYLOR, A. J. P. *The Trouble Makers: Dissent over Foreign Policy, 1792-1939*. Bloomington: Indiana University Press, 1958.

TEMPERLEY, H. W. V. (ed.). *A History of the Peace Conference of Paris*. 6 vols. London: Oxford, 1920-24.

THE TIMES (London). *The History of the Times*. Vol. 4, *The 150th Anniversary and Beyond, 1912-1948*, Part I: Chapters I-XII, 1912-1920. London: The Office of *The Times*, 1952.

TILLMAN, SETH P. *Anglo-American Diplomatic Relations at the Paris Peace Conference of 1919*. Princeton: Princeton University Press, 1961.

WARD, Sir A. W. and GOOCH, G. P. (eds.). *The Cambridge History of British Foreign Policy, 1783-1919*. Vol. III, *1866-1919*. Cambridge: University Press, 1923.

WILLERT, Sir ARTHUR. *The Road to Safety*. London: Verschoyle, 1952.

WRIGHT, PETER E. *Portraits and Criticisms*. London: Nash, 1925.

INDEX

www.ingramcontent.com/pod-product-compliance
Lightning Source LLC
LaVergne TN
LVHW040755070826
844660LV00025B/1155

9781487573676